Allahu Akbar

21.10.2019

Max, with my best wishes

Ranu

Allahu Akbar

Understanding the Great Mughal in Today's India

Manimugdha S. Sharma

BLOOMSBURY
NEW DELHI • LONDON • OXFORD • NEW YORK • SYDNEY

BLOOMSBURY INDIA
Bloomsbury Publishing India Pvt. Ltd
Second Floor, LSC Building No. 4, DDA Complex, Pocket C – 6 & 7,
Vasant Kunj New Delhi 110070

First published in India 2019
This edition published in 2019

ISBN: HB: 978-93-86950-53-6; eBook: 978-93-86950-54-3

2 4 6 8 10 9 7 5 3 1

Typeset in Manipal Digital
Printed and bound in India

To my late grandmother, Maya Devi, who had an amazing sense of history and who would have surely been proud of my effort

Contents

Acknowledgements

It's time to say 'thank you'!

This book wouldn't have been possible without the support of quite a few people.

Firstly, I would like to thank my family. My interest in history was shaped by my family. Both my parents, Surendra Kumar Sharma and Mallika Sharma, are history buffs and would take me to various historical places or buy me such books as a child. As I embarked on this book project, my parents and my brother, Achintyamugdha Sharma, constantly encouraged me, with my mother's sole question on phone being, 'How much have you written?' But it was my wife, Banajyotshna, who was the one who sacrificed more than anyone else as I worked on it. Sunday evenings were always time for us to spend time together. Shopping, movies, eating out, all of it stopped for a full year as I ran a mad race to finish the book in time. And yet, she made no fuss about it and did everything possible not to distract me.

Apart from my family, two other things triggered my interest in history—Sanjay Khan's *The Sword of Tipu Sultan* and the television series *Soldiers* presented by Frederick Forsyth in the 1980s.

Bollywood movies like *Mughal-E-Azam* and television serials like *Bharat Ek Khoj* unknowingly developed my interest in the Mughals, particularly in Emperor Akbar. Even today, the mere mention of the emperor's name throws up the image of Prithviraj Kapoor in my mind.

But this interest would have remained like that without the intellectually stimulating discussions with my teachers in college, who whetted my appetite for history. I opted for history for my bachelor's after reading Professor Irfan Habib's *An Atlas of the Mughal Empire*. If I have remained a lifelong student of the discipline, it is because of the environment that I got in college, which really nurtured my interests, and the books that Professor Habib wrote. I was like Ekalavya, learning indirectly from Dronacharya, but thankfully, I didn't have to sacrifice my thumb as guru *dakshina*.

I would also like to thank Professor Habib for going through my manuscript and sharing his comments. While I was writing the book, I would bother him with my queries. He always answered them patiently.

I also have to thank his colleague, Professor Iqtidar Alam Khan, who is himself a leading authority on Akbar and the Mughals. Iqtidar sahib had asked me to focus on *Muntakhab ut-Tawarikh* by Mulla Abdul Qadir Badaoni besides going through Abu'l Fazl's *Akbarnama*. I benefited immensely from that. Iqtidar sahib was also very generous with his comments on the finished manuscript and has very graciously endorsed my work.

I would like to thank Professor Ali Nadeem Rezavi, Chairman & Coordinator, Centre of Advanced Study, Department of History, Aligarh Muslim University. He was the first one to peer review my work. I felt confident after he read my manuscript and gave it a thumbs up. A constant source of encouragement, Nadeem sahib has supported me even in my journalistic work. There would be times when I would write an article and turn to him for his expert comment. He would always reply and would never give me any last-minute panic attack.

I don't know how to express my gratitude to Professor Jos Gommans of the University of Leiden. Despite being a top academic and having a very busy schedule, he still found the time to go through my manuscript and give it a go-ahead. It is my honour to put his endorsement on the cover of my book.

Professor Harbans Mukhia was the other person I turned to with my queries. Professor Mukhia was always very generous with his guidance. Some snippets of our conversations feature in this book.

Of course, all of this wouldn't have happened hadn't my friend Diya Chowdhury introduced me to Praveen Tiwari of Bloomsbury India. Praveen went through the body of my work online and suggested that I do a book on Emperor Akbar. With so many biographies of him already around, I chose to focus my work on Akbar's modern relevance. Praveen was excited about it and commissioned the book immediately.

After writing the initial few chapters, I subjected Diya to the ordeal of reading through those rough drafts. Despite her doctoral research consuming much of her time, she still found the time to read and offer her valuable comments.

Shreya Chakraborti of Bloomsbury India made my manuscript so much better by putting her team of editors to work on it.

Nitin Valecha of Bloomsbury India was forever patient and fulfilled every tiny request that I made at various points during the production of this book. Hence, I thank him along with the entire team at Bloomsbury India for making this book happen.

I cannot thank my organisation, *The Times of India*, enough for its rich archives that I dipped into, and my supportive colleagues, who encouraged me at every step—particularly my boss Vikas Singh, Associate Executive Editor and Resident Editor of Delhi, whom I told about the book the day I signed the contract with Bloomsbury, and who would from time to time enquire about its progress.

I would also thank my other boss, Rohit Saran, who despite being the Managing Editor still had the time and interest to facilitate my interest in history and heritage by giving me the freedom to choose my assignments.

My boss Subhendu Mukherjee is a hard taskmaster. More than that, he understands what interests whom. He would always make space for my history articles, find me assignments matching my tastes and appreciate what I produce. He gave me the heritage beat to cover considering my interest in it.

My immediate boss, the editor of Sunday Times, Neelam Raaj, lets me explore history like nobody else. For years, she has published my history pieces, whether it was on Emperor Babur's link to Valentine's Day or Emperor Akbar's fall from greatness in the age of Hindutva. In fact, it was one such piece on Akbar that gave Praveen Tiwari the idea that I should write a book on the emperor.

Last but not least, my colleague and photojournalist Anindya Chattopadhyay, who took the trouble one humid afternoon in May to go with me to Shaheed Park and click a photograph for this book at the historic venue where Comrade Bhagat Singh and his revolutionary associates had founded the Hindustan Socialist Republican Association.

I would also like to remember my late colleague Kingshuk Mukherji, who used to tell me often to write a book on history. '*Boi ekta likhe fel* (write a book)' used to be his common refrain whenever we spoke. Alas! He had an untimely death two years ago. He would have surely been proud of me.

I hope lovers of history would favourably consider my humble effort to help understand Emperor Akbar in today's India.

Introduction: Viewing Akbar through a Modern Lens

On 10 October 1941, one Adi K. Munshi of Bombay (now Mumbai) wrote a letter to the editor of *The Times of India*. That was the time of the Second World War, and there was unrest in India. There was a deep chasm between the Indian National Congress and the Muslim League following the Lahore Resolution that had envisaged independent states on the North-west and East of India, where there was a Muslim majority.

The resulting ill feeling had trickled down to the general populace as well. In hindsight, as we understand today, the ground was being prepared for the eventual Partition. But Munshi couldn't have possibly known or had any inkling of what lay ahead in the future. He wished for peace and communal amity, and he longed for a leader whom he thought could unite the Hindus and the Muslims. It was not Mohandas K. Gandhi, Muhammad Ali Jinnah or Jawaharlal Nehru. It was not Subhas Chandra Bose or Vallabhbhai Patel either. It was someone from the glorious past of India. It was Emperor Jalaluddin Muhammad Akbar.

When Munshi wrote that letter, he had the 400th birth anniversary of the emperor in mind, which he thought was on 14 October. However, the newspaper printed it a day later on 15 October, the actual birthday of Akbar. Munshi used phrases for the Mughal emperor that were quite illuminating about his perception among the Indians of that time—like 'great Indian soldier', 'statesman' and 'the greatest Indian nationalist of all time'.

To bolster his point, Munshi invoked the words of a 'great historian' about Akbar—'When we reflect what he did, the age in which he did it, the method he introduced to accomplish it, we are bound to recognise in Akbar one of those illustrious men whom Providence sends, in the hour of a nation's trouble, to reconduct it into those paths of peace and toleration which alone can assure the happiness of millions.' That 'great historian' was Colonel G. B. Malleson, who concluded his book *Akbar and the Rise of the Mughal Empire* (1896) with these profound words.

Munshi ended his short epistle with hope, which read almost like a prayer. 'In these days of domestic discord, communal dissensions and particularly the Hindu–Muslim split, India feels, more than ever, the need of an Akbar—the Apostle of united India.'

Did Munshi have a premonition of the things to come? We don't know. But we know that the image of Akbar as a successful ruler who united multiple warring factions around his throne made him an ideal person to be emulated back then. What made Akbar unique was the fact that he had both physical and moral courage. Anyone who has either kind of courage always wins adulation. But those who are blessed with both not only win admiration but also hearts. Such people make leaders. Great leaders. Even heroes. Akbar was one such man.

In 2017, I was at a talk on the trial of Bhagat Singh by legal eagle A. G. Noorani at the Delhi Legislative Assembly. Noorani, while extolling the virtues of the young revolutionary, had briefly described the relationship between Singh and the then Punjab Congress stalwart, Lala Lajpat Rai. Noorani had said, and I had reported it for *The Times of India*:

> He (Singh) parted ways with Lala Lajpat Rai when he became communal. But when Rai died after being hit by a police baton charge, Singh decided to avenge him, for he was still a man of principles. And he did.[1]

1 Manimugdha S. Sharma, 'If rulers just, courts exemplary; if unjust, quite dangerous', New Delhi, *The Times of India*, 24 March 2017. Available at https://timesofindia.indiatimes.com/city/delhi/If-rulers-just-courts-exemplary-if-unjust-quite-dangerous/articleshow/57800026.cms.

Noorani was referring to the 1928 protest against the Simon Commission during which Rai had sustained fatal blows. Singh and his associates at the Hindustan Socialist Republican Association had responded to it by killing police deputy superintendent C. F. Saunders in Lahore, the city that had once been the capital of the Mughal Empire of Akbar.

The Indian Left often alludes to Rai's communal image, and it is done not without reason. Rai was part of the Lal-Bal-Pal triumvirate (the other two being Bal Gangadhar Tilak and Bipin Chandra Pal) that not only led the Extremist faction of the Indian National Congress but also believed in Hindu nationalism.[2]

In *Indian Nationalism: The Essential Writings* (2017), Syed Irfan Habib wrote about how Rai used his nationalism brush to segregate the medieval Hindus from the Muslims. Habib wrote that while both Daulat Khan Lodhi and Rana Sanga had invited Babur to invade India, to Rai, Lodhi's act was one of opportunism while Sanga's was of patriotism borne out of the wish to liberate his motherland. But for Akbar, Rai had made a rare exception, and he was willing to lock horns with those Englishmen who portrayed a less than flattering picture of Akbar.

In 1918, Rai was in America as the First World War was ending. There, he had reviewed Sir Vincent Smith's biography of Akbar called *Akbar the Great Mogul, 1542–65*, in the *Political Science Quarterly*. Rai's first line in the review was—'Akbar the Great Mogul was by common consent one of the greatest monarchs known to history.'[3]

Rai said, 'Mr. Smith has told the story of Akbar's life and administration with great lucidity, thoroughness and general impartiality, but at places is unduly hard on him, forgetting the times in which he lived and worked.'[4] This was a very important criticism by

2 Sumit Sarkar, *Modern India, 1885–1947* (New Delhi: Palgrave Macmillan, 1989), p. 127. Sarkar quotes from Lala Lajpat Rai's autobiography where, in Rai's own admission, Rai was 'wedded to the idea of Hindu nationality' following the Hindi–Urdu controversy of the 1880s.

3 Lala Lajpat Rai, *Political Science Quarterly* 33, no. 4, 1918, pp. 570–73. Available at JSTOR, www.jstor.org/stable/2141607.

4 Ibid.

Rai, something that holds true even today for everyone but especially for those new detractors of Akbar who bash him up on television studios and in the Twitter world without bothering to check if they are talking about a medieval Indian emperor or some 20th-century tinpot dictator.

Rai's review reveals one thing: even for the orthodox politicians of yore, who may or may not[5] have believed in Hindu nationalism, Akbar was a monarch who was seen as India's own—not some outsider or some oppressor. And any slur on him by anyone was non-negotiable. So, how did things come to such a pass a century later that the official spokesperson of the Hindu nationalist ruling party casually compared Akbar to Hitler[6] and that Members of Parliament (MPs) from the ruling party demanded the change of name of the road in Lutyens'[7] Delhi named after him? This perhaps justifies an old adage: the mob sees no reason. And though popularly elected, and often projected as the strongest Indian government ever, the Bharatiya Janata Party (BJP) government of the present time appears vulnerable and helpless, choosing to be a meek and silent spectator as rampaging mobs pull down the very edifice of the state.

This contrasts with the approach of another man, who was also gifted with physical and moral courage—Jawaharlal Nehru. On more than one occasion, India's first prime minister had recklessly run amok amid rampaging mobs during the Partition riots in Delhi and

---

5 There are scholarly views that counter the view that Lala Lajpat Rai was a communalist. Refer to Sudhir Kumar's 'Nation-in-Narration: Lala Lajpat Rai and the Communal Question' in *Studies in Humanities and Social Sciences* 7, no. 1, 2000, pp. 139–53. Interestingly, this paper was plagiarised by the Rashtriya Swayamsevak Sangh's mouthpiece magazine, *Organiser*, in an article dated 17 November 2018, with the headline 'Marxists labelled Lala Lajpat Rai as a "Communalist"'. It was authored by Shaan Kashyap but didn't give any credit to Sudhir Kumar. Available at https://www.organiser.org/Encyc/2018/11/17/Marxists-labelled-Lala-Lajpat-Rai-as-a-Communalist.html.

6 Manimugdha S. Sharma, 'Akbar was truly great, Pratap only a great warrior', *The Times of India*, New Delhi, 24 May 2016. Available at https://timesofindia.indiatimes.com/blogs/parthian-shot/akbar-was-truly-great-pratap-only-a-great-warrior/.

7 Lutyens' Delhi is used to refer to the new capital city of New Delhi designed by Sir Edwin Lutyens, which today roughly corresponds to the areas under the New Delhi Municipal Council.

engaged in fisticuffs with rioters who had attacked Muslims and their establishments.

Seeing the prime minister in their midst, a rioting mob in Chandni Chowk had lost its nerve, pretty much like the Mirzas near Baroda in Gujarat who had melted away when thousands of them were attacked single-handedly by Akbar after dashing across river Mahi with 50 of his associates following closely behind him, and 150 others further behind. This was the Battle of Sarnal fought in December 1572. Akbar had learnt about Ibrahim Husain Mirza trying to flee Baroda, probably because he had sensed that the imperial army was close. He wasted no time and marched the whole night and the all of the next day without rest with 200 cavalry. By sunset, the Mughals reached the Mahi river and saw the enemy camped on the other side. Akbar was advised by his generals to wait for reinforcements and not to attack before nightfall. Akbar did not pay heed to any advise and recklessly galloped into the river, crossing it through a ford. His generals, Bhagwan Dass and Man Singh, were with him. On the other side of the river, Akbar was surrounded by three enemy horsemen with whom he parried. His life was in serious danger. But the fate of Hindustan, his dynasty and empire was decided by the point of a spear, quite literally. Bhagwan Dass speared one of them to death, and the other two abandoned the fight and fled. Though vastly superior in number, the Mirzas were no match for the crack troops of Akbar who hacked and scythed through them as if they were grass. Ibrahim Husain Mirza fled with the rest of the troops. Akbar not only managed to survive a most serious and utterly avoidable brush with death, but he also turned it into a spectacular feat of arms, and a grand victory won by reckless bravery and bull-headed determination.

Someone in *The Pioneer* described this adventure in beautiful prose with effusive praise a month before Nehru was born. 'Of Wallace Wight, or well-skilled Bruce who ruled the fight,' Akbar's gallantry was described by the English author using Sir Walter Scott's prose to compare him to the Scottish hero, Sir William Wallace. Other accounts, especially of Indologists, described Akbar as a 'prince among men'.

In the late 19th century, it was a prince who had decided to tell Akbar's tale to the German people, introducing his ideas of tolerance and acceptance to a land that was torn apart by war. He was Prince Friedrich August of Schleswig-Holstein-Sonderburg-Augustenberg. A man with an incredible life story himself, Friedrich was also, in his own way, a man ahead of his time. He had consciously given up on the life of an aristocrat and chosen to be a common man. He decided to marry a commoner and gave up his royal title, settling instead for a Prussian peerage of Graf von Noer.

It was Prince Friedrich's second coming to India that took him to Agra, Delhi and Lahore—three cities that were still very richly Mughal, even a decade after the last occupant of the royal throne at Delhi was packed off to Burma. He undertook a sort of a pilgrimage to Akbar's tomb at Sikandra and laid roses on his grave. The majesty of the tomb struck him with awe. He thought it was a befitting tribute to the life of this extraordinary man. Back in Delhi, Friedrich made up his mind to write a book on Akbar. The year was 1868.

Far away in the Netherlands, Akbar was being discussed and held up as an icon by Dutch liberals who were trying to establish a secular state with Akbar's empire as a model. This charge was being led by P. A. S. van Limburg Brouwer, who was, by and large, a man in love with India—her philosophy and her spirit of tolerance. This was the age of orientalism and of Sanskritists like Max Mueller. This was also the age when the Dutch intellectual life was being dominated by debates between the Left and Right-leaning followers of Spinoza, just like the German intellectual arena that had the Left and Right-leaning supporters of Hegel duelling with one another.

For the Spinozists, the East held many solutions to the problems of the West. Hinduism and Buddhism were seen as more than a match for Christianity. Brouwer, who was instrumental in establishing a Sanskrit chair at the University of Leiden, was a Spinozist on the Left side of the spectrum. To him, Akbar was a monarch exemplar. He saw in Akbar a ruler who combined politics and intellectual spirituality to bring different communities together. Just a few months before his death, Brouwer managed to write a book on his favourite monarch and called it *Akbar: An Eastern Romance* (1872). He projected Akbar as an example from whom all rulers of the world could learn. The book became a bestseller as the 20th century dawned, and sold over 50,000 copies between 1900 and 1940.

However, by 1940, a lot had changed in Europe. Friedrich von Noer's book *Kaiser Akbar* (1880) probably had few or no takers in Germany, after a regime of hate and anguish had come to power in that country in the previous decade and had forced another book named *Mein Kampf* as a mandatory buy for all. A book that hadn't sold much previously had become a national bestseller by the time Germany turned aggressor over Czechoslovakia in 1938. The hate-filled propaganda that it contained inspired a generation of youngsters to imbibe it and put it into practice later.

Adolf Hitler, the Nazi dictator, loved the idea of a colony as large as India and lauded the British Empire for its stabilising effect on the world. His ideas about India were not formed by Noer or Brouwer's books but by Hollywood movies like the 1935 Hollywood superhit, *The Lives of a Bengal Lancer*. Hitler, by his own admission before Lord Halifax in 1937, had watched the movie three times. Later, in 1941, before he invaded the Soviet Union, Hitler supposedly had announced that 'The Russian space is our India'.[8]

So, it was quite possible that when Adi K. Munshi wrote that letter, longing for an Akbar in the India of 1941 that was on the verge of being ripped apart by sectarian violence, a reader of Brouwer's work in Holland would have also perhaps longed for someone like him to deliver them from the Nazi yoke.

A year later, though, the Congress launched the Quit India Movement and the entire leadership was packed off to different prisons across the country. Jawaharlal Nehru landed in prison too where he started writing an unofficial history of India. Published in 1946, after he came out of jail, *Discovery of India* reintroduced Akbar to the 20th-century Indian reader. In his book, Nehru described Akbar as 'the great representative of the old Indian ideal of a synthesis of differing elements and their fusion into a common nationality'. Later in the book, he put out a summary of Akbar's character appreciating him in a powerful and evocative sentence:

---

8 Richard J. Evans. *The Third Reich in History and Memory* (New York: Oxford University Press, 2015), p. 361.

> Daring and reckless, an able general, and yet gentle and full of compassion, an idealist and a dreamer, but also a man of action and a leader of men who roused the passionate loyalty of his followers. As a warrior he conquered large parts of India, but his eyes were set on another and more enduring conquest, the conquest of the minds and hearts of the people. Those compelling eyes of his were "vibrant like the sea in sunshine", as Portuguese Jesuits of his court have told us. In him the old dream of a united India again took shape, united not only politically in one state but organically fused into one people.

Yet while founding the new republic of India, it was Ashoka who served as Nehru's guiding light at a conscious level. Ashokan symbols, such as the *Dharma Chakra* and the Lion Capital, became symbols of the new nation state—the first appearing in the national flag and the other becoming the national emblem.

However, at a subconscious level, and in Nehru's own conduct, Akbar was always present. When Congress leader Badruddin Tyabji had told him that Muslims fleeing their homes in the walled city to reach the relative safety of refugee camps, were being attacked at Minto Bridge, Nehru had rushed upstairs and brought out his father's old revolver. He wanted to be at the station in disguise and open fire at the attackers. Tyabji, horrified by the prime minister's recklessness, managed to convince him with great difficulty to abandon that course of action. Even Lord Mountbatten was deeply worried that Nehru would get himself killed and gave him an armed escort[9]—a concern perhaps not dissimilar from what Akbar's generals must have felt at Sarnal.

The viceroy had then asked the governor general's bodyguard to escort Nehru. One could see Akbar in Nehru's daring and reckless spirit. It is tempting to imagine Nehru on horseback, followed by lancers in scarlet tunics. This may have happened even though I have not seen any photographic evidence of it so far. However, at the President's Bodyguard, they still have a framed photograph of Nehru on horseback in the 2IC's office. The regiment, which originated in

---

9 Nisid Hajari, *Midnight's Furies: The Deadly Legacy of India's Partition* (London: Amberley Publishing, 2015).

the 18th century as the Governor General's Troop of the Moghul, has still not forgotten the first Indian prime minister, as it still has not forgotten the old Mughal word for a cavalry unit—*risala*.

As the foundations of the new republic were being laid, Nehru got hold of people of all political hues to lay those first bricks. He engaged even those people who didn't agree with him or his party, people like Dr B. R. Ambedkar and the far-Right leader Dr Shyama Prasad Mookerjee, to set the rules of engagement of the new nation state in the form of the Constitution.

Akbar had in his court Mulla Abdul Qadir Badaoni as a nobleman. Badaoni was a friend of brothers Abu'l Faizi and Abu'l Fazl and their father, Sheikh Mubarak. Later in life, however, Badaoni became their sworn enemy. Being an orthodox Muslim himself, he disliked the religious tolerance and liberal policies of the emperor. Akbar knew that. Yet, when he started the project of translating Hindu epics into Persian, he chose Badaoni to translate the *Mahabharata,* and later the *Ramayana* too, though, of the former, Badaoni only completed two chapters. But the Persian *Ramayana* is one of the two greatest contributions of Badaoni, the other being the *Muntakhab ut-Tawarikh*, a history of Akbar's reign. Akbar had an exceptional ability to recognise and promote merit. He believed Badaoni, despite his bigoted stance towards the Hindus, would still do justice in translating an essentially Hindu work.[10]

The new Indian republic would be made a secular one. But it wouldn't be Nehru but Dr Sarvepalli Radhakrishnan who would give its most accepted definition. 'When India is said to be a secular state, it does not mean that we exalt irreligion. Indian State will not identify itself with or be controlled by any particular religion,' said the man who would be India's second President.

Radhakrishnan, who was once accused of plagiarising from the thesis of a student[11], is today lambasted by Left-wing scholars for the

---

10 See Chapter 7 for details.

11 Idrees Bakhtiyar, 'Subcontinental Plagiarism', *Dawn*, Pakistan, 12 February 2019. Available at https://www.dawn.com/news/742051.

limitations of his version of secularism.[12] They say that the Western concept in its pristine form should have been applied in India too. But consciously or not, Radhakrishnan also articulated Akbar's *Sulh-i-Kul.* Nearly 400 years after Akbar, the new nation state of India, born in severe bloodshed and wounded in body and spirit, banked on this major aspect of Akbar's state system to pull itself together.

In 2002, I was introduced to Emperor Akbar in my final year of graduation, 55 years after the Partition. It would be wrong to say that I wasn't acquainted with him earlier—my study of history had started in school itself. But it was only during my honours class that I was formally introduced to Akbar and the Mughals, courtesy of a paper called 'Medieval India'. The paper had a sad story of its own—a story of exclusion. Medieval India was actually a euphemism for the Mughal Empire since the syllabus covered only the period from 1526 until 1707—from the victory of Babur at Panipat until the death of Aurangzeb. The syllabus didn't include the preceding 500 years, before the Mughal invasion, so the Rajputs and their removal by the Delhi Sultanate were, strangely, not a part of the syllabus.

And yet, nobody pilloried the university for this gross oversight. That's because it was amazingly in sync with the popular understanding of 'medieval India'—that all Muslim dynasties, irrespective of being the Pathans or the Turks, were Mughals. It was this ignorance that led to prejudice.

Nevertheless, my introduction to Akbar gradually turned into a friendship with him over the course of my study. I remember having tried to constantly figure out what the emperor thought, what he felt, and what he understood about the world around him. I still recall the thrill I had experienced when I learnt about his military victories and his open-mindedness—a potent combination that had influenced the very young and impressionable mind of mine. I was not very different from an average 20-year-old who adored men in uniform and fantasised about a life on the border—the memories of the Kargil War

12 Ajaz Ashraf, 'Irfan Habib: The Indian variant of secularism opens the door to majority communalism', *Scroll.in,* 14 August 2015. Available at https://scroll.in/article/748241/irfan-habib-the-indian-variant-of-secularism-opens-the-door-to-majority-communalism.

(1999) were still fresh. Hence, naturally, to read about an Indian king who never lost a battle, but who also won hearts wherever he went, was quite an exhilarating experience for me. To me, he was someone to look up to and emulate—precisely a role model.

It was definitely a coincidence, and rather a rude one, that my initiation to the idea of Akbar happened at a time when horrifying communal riots broke out in Gujarat. And it was then that I was acquainted with another name, which, going by the accounts of the time, was blamed for letting the carnage happen under his watch—the then chief minister of Gujarat, Narendra Modi. Perhaps it was some cruel exercise conjured up by the big guy upstairs to give me a life lesson, to teach me the difference between a man who united hearts and the one who broke them. Of course, I had no idea that Mr Modi would become the Prime Minister of India 15 years later. Therefore, this practical lesson made sense to me only in 2015, when under Mr Modi's watch the vilification of Akbar began.

During my time as a student, however, the history syllabi in many universities in India didn't teach much about Akbar beyond his Rajput and religious policies, particularly the *Sulh-i-Kul*. And while inside the classroom we did try to ask our teacher more to satiate our intellectual hunger, once out of it, and just before the exams, we would mostly focus on writing thousand-word answers to expected and oft-repeated questions by the university. If Jeremy Paxman's 'starter for 10' would intimidate most University Challenge participants on the BBC, these 20-pointers in our university exams rarely surprised us. One of the common questions about Akbar was this—'*Din-i-Illahi* was a monument of Akbar's folly. Explain.' Questions such as this curtailed the scope of informed dialogue, especially because the university had already made up its mind that the *Tauhid-i-Illahi* was nothing beyond a reflection of Akbar's foolhardiness. But sometimes, there would be another question in the paper as an alternative—'Shah Jahan inherited cities in red sandstone and left them in marble. Explain.' We had a set template to deal with this question. First, we would talk about Akbar's 'masculine' architecture and then go on to celebrate Shah Jahan's 'feminine' buildings, many of which were made after rasing buildings raised by Akbar. The rule of Shah Jahan was touted as the

'Golden Age' of India, so Akbar was a less-glamorous figure as compared to the romantic Shah Jahan. And this was lapped up by our generation that mostly saw the Taj Mahal as the crowning glory of Mughal rule and a proud symbol of India, without sparing a thought on how crucial a step it was on the part of Akbar to separate faith from the state—a fact acknowledged even by Dutch liberals in the 19th century, who tried to create a secular state inspired by the 'Great Mughal'.

The lectures on the Mughal Empire would often end with comparisons between the rule of Akbar and Aurangzeb, both ruling for a period of 49 years. We were taught how Akbar united an empire with his tolerance and how Aurangzeb broke it apart with his intolerance—fairly simplistic views with no scope of any nuanced argument. It wasn't the teachers' fault. The course structure was designed in such a way that there was barely any scope for any kind of discussion other than the potential 20 pointers for the exam.

Fifteen years hence, I realise today why there is such a smear campaign on against Akbar and the Mughals—they were never fully studied or talked about even in the universities. And even though Akbar has been omnipresent in folk tales, comic books and even serious academic works, he isn't really that visible to all at a conscious level. And what's not visible or properly understood is often ridiculed, dehumanised and violently rejected.

This explains what's happening in India right now. From the time I started writing this chapter, the anti-Akbar, anti-Mughal campaign has reached its pinnacle of glory. The Mughals have been nearly excised from school textbooks in Rajasthan and Maharashtra, while they have gone completely missing from a book of 'general knowledge' published by the BJP to commemorate the centenary of their tallest ideologue, Deendayal Upadhyaya. In fact, a station bearing the name Mughal in eastern Uttar Pradesh—Mughalsarai—has been renamed after Upadhyaya. In the sphere of pop culture, abusing the Mughal name has become so routine that it has become a part of life. TV serials now portray the Mughals as evil, with one particularly atrocious production on Rana Pratap depicting Akbar as a villainous cartoon. Named 'Bharat Ka Veer Putra Maharana Pratap', this awful TV drama presented Akbar and Rana Pratap as childhood adversaries, with the young Pratap freely mouthing racist abuses like '*us Turk-Mughal ko nahin chhodunga*' (won't spare that Turk-Mughal) in the name of patriotism. While this may appear to be in poor taste for a section of people, it's actually quite in sync with what passes off as patriotism or nationalism in India today. That is, public mouthing of abuses for people you don't agree with, calling any dissenter a traitor and an anti-national, shutting down dialogue and debate by calling the other side you can't defeat with reason as Lefties and communists.

The overarching narrative, though, is this: Muslim rulers were bad for India and Indians (read Hindus). And because of this, Akbar, who was already not quite visible, has been almost buried—not as a just king, though, but as a genocidal monster 'no better than Hitler'. And that's quite a spectacularly unfair fate of the man who in his lifetime and even afterwards was considered to be an avatar of Vishnu by the Hindus, the Jains and the Buddhists. Akbar is the man whom a Bombay resident missed in 1941 as someone who could have kept India united; a man who spoke to a young college lad in 2002 that a nation would stand united if it's welded together by love, tolerance and equality; and a man who has been trying to take us back into his time to show us how in the 21st century we Indians are essentially medieval people who have now started blindly following a saffron *Shahenshah*.

And that's why this book came into existence. I have picked some episodes from Akbar's life story and left out some others. Therefore, my work doesn't pretend to be a definitive biography of Akbar or a chronology of his reign, even though it traces the overall contours of his reign. This isn't going to be the last word on the Mughals either. This is an attempt to understand Akbar in his own time and examine his relevance in our own time. This is an attempt to capture the journey of Akbar from being great to being not-so-great. It's an honest effort to find out why an Adi K. Munshi called Akbar 'the greatest Indian nationalist' ever back in 1941, but the Sangh Parivar called him an anti-national in 2015. It's an attempt to find out why a common man from Bombay in British India, who in no way was 'misguided by Congress-Marxist propaganda history'—as is often alleged by the saffron brotherhood about people in our time who don't have a black and white understanding of history—thought Akbar was the 'Apostle of unity' in 1941 but BJP's national spokesperson, Shaina NC, compared the Mughal emperor to Hitler in 2015.

This is, above all, a journalist and a common man's attempt to understand a great man who was inarguably ahead of his time, straddling a spiritual realm and a violent, mortal world, always delighted and troubled by both. It's an attempt to understand a man who shaped India's destiny with the sword and a tolerant polity at a time when secularism is being understood as a dirty word introduced into the nation's body politic by a self-serving dynasty of politicians.

It's the story of a rare man who was a doting husband, an indolent father, a good boss, a great king and a very good student of life. I hope *Allahu Akbar* will be a small step towards understanding this ruler exemplar of his time in our supercharged times.

Chapter 1

A Star Is Born

> A sleep which tore the veil from before the eyes of the soul
> Cannot be called sleep; it was the heart's waking.[1]

It was a Friday on 10 July 1540, when Emperor Humayun, weary from his conflict with the Afghan challenger Sher Khan or Sher Shah Suri, took a nap in the secured environs of his palace in Lahore.[2] We don't know if it was a siesta or a good night's sleep, but Abu'l Fazl tells us in grandiloquent prose that the emperor had a dream. What did he dream of? Fazl says:

> ...he became aware that God was bestowing on him an illustrious successor whose greatness shone from his forelock, and the lightning of whose splendour was flashing from his temples. From the light of his guidance, the dark regions of thoughts and opinions were illuminated, and the glory of his justice was lighting up the fields of night and day... When his Majesty awoke, he first returned thanks to God for the majestic message and splendid grace and then told the circumstance to the intimates of his harem and the servants of his threshold.

In other words, Humayun had a dream in which he saw his successor—a son. This was before he had married his Shia wife,

1 Divan of Abu'l Faizi as referenced in *The Akbarnama of Abu'l Fazl, Vols. I–III*, tr. H. Beveridge (Calcutta: The Asiatic Society, 1907–39, reprinted in 2010).

2 Abu'l Fazl, *Akbarnama, Vol I*, p. 42.

Hamida Bano Begum. This was apparently the first divine sign of the coming of future greatness.

The second sign was also connected to a dream. But this one was dreamt by Shamsuddin Muhammad Atgah Khan (also spelt as Atka Khan or Ataga Khan) when he was 22 years old. The young nobleman was in Ghazni when he saw the moon come into his arms. When he narrated the dream to his spiritual-minded father, Mir Yar Muhammad Ghaznavi, he interpreted it as a good omen that was to lift the fortunes of the family.

A third sign was from a later time when Hamida Bano was pregnant. Fazl tells us, citing 'right-thinking persons', that there was an almost divine glow on her face that many observed.[3] There were some other signs too, and there are several versions as to the nature of these signs. One of them says that Hamida Bano, during those troubled days when the royal entourage was travelling miles and miles through all kinds of terrain to escape capture, felt like having a pomegranate. That fruit didn't grow in the region they were in, and besides, it was not the season for it.

But cravings don't understand any reason. And the queen would have none of the words of reason given to her. Just then, out of nowhere emerged a caravan of traders. And someone in it had a pomegranate that he gave to the queen. This was later ascribed to the good fortune of the royal one who was in the womb.

But beyond these stories, the real journey was quite perilous and one of enduring hardships and disappointments for the royal family. The emperor's brothers, Mirza Kamran and Mirza Askari, had been conspiring against him. They wanted to capture him and use him as a bargaining chip to strike a deal with Sher Shah Suri. His own followers had been abandoning him one by one to join the service of his brothers. As the number of his followers reduced, so did Humayun's authority.

---

3 Abu'l Fazl says that Hamida Bano was riding a camel during pregnancy (possibly when the royal entourage was escaping capture), when she passed by an orchard and wanted to have mangoes. Her brother Khwaja Mu'azzam brought her some succulent fruits when he saw light emanating from his sister's brows and asked her if she had put on a mirror. On close observation, he realised that there was no mirror and it was some divine light.

One incident that illustrates this quite well is a conversation between Humayun and Tardi Beg, a senior noble who had come along with Babur in 1525 itself. Hamida Bano was feeling uneasy riding in a palanquin and wanted to ride a horse for a while. When Humayun asked Tardi Beg to lend his horse for a while, he flatly refused. So Humayun had no other option but to dismount and let his wife ride his horse while he rode a camel.[4] Never was the House of Timur so perilously poised.

Finally, when Humayun reached the environs of Amarkot[5] (now Umarkot) in Sindh, his camp consisted of less than 50 people, seven of whom were armed horsemen. In today's terms, this could be called a security nightmare. Even for those times, this kind of an escort was barely enough to even ward off organised desert robbers, let alone enemy ambush parties.

The then ruler of Amarkot was a certain Rana Parshad. Strangely enough, there are versions that say his name was Rana Virsal[6]. He received the rather haggard party with warmth and compassion and supplied Humayun with 2,000 horsemen of his own clan and another 5,000 under the command of other chiefs friendly to him. This was quite a remarkable stroke of luck for the dethroned emperor who had been rebuffed by the Marwar king, Raja Maldev Rathore, after inviting him to join forces against Sher Shah Suri. This volte-face was brought about by the Afghan challenger through bullying tactics, though the Jodhpur king's opportunistic nature played its part too. A dethroned emperor steadily losing his adherents to the rival camps as well as the support of the bankers and money

---

4 Different sources narrate this tale differently. Gulbadan Begum, Humayun's sister, narrates the story as I have, and so does T. C. A. Raghavan in *Attendant Lords*. But H. M. Elliot, in *History of India As Told By Its Own Historians*, says that Humayun's horse was killed in a murderous attack on the royal party orchestrated by King Maldev and so he asked Tardi Beg for a horse and was refused.

5 H. Beveridge says it is Amarkot, quoting Gulbadan Begum, Humayun's sister. But Vincent Smith argues in *Akbar the Great Mogul* that Amarkot is incorrect and it should be Umarkot, the fort of Umar of the Sumra clan.

6 J. L. Mehta says in the *Advanced History of Medieval India* that his name was Rana Virsal. The only extant TV biopic on Akbar's life, *Akbar the Great*, by Akbar Khan in the early 1990s also called him Rana Virsal.

lenders wasn't exactly the one anyone could bet his money on. To make things worse, Humayun's troops, forever foraging for food, had slaughtered cattle, either their own draught animals or those owned by locals. This had triggered a backlash, resulting in the locals filling up wells with sand to deny water to the marching imperial contingent in the desert. With a heavily pregnant Hamida to take care of, it must have been a nightmarish experience for the royal entourage.

It is not difficult to guess that the Rajput king, in order to extricate himself from a potential and rather an unnecessary war, milked the cow slaughter incident. Without openly bowing down to the new power bloc in Delhi, he still placated them. At the same time, he found a moral high ground to claim despite violating the unwritten Rajput code of chivalry. No wonder that the Rajput ruling families managed to survive until modern times by bowing to every ascendant star in the political horizon, just like grass blades that weather every storm by bending. The present day *gau raksha* or 'cow protection' politics, which has resulted in several lynchings in Rajasthan, is an ugly manifestation of historical forces that have been at play for centuries in the region.

But Maldev couldn't have possibly known that exactly 20 years later, he would have to cede both territory and fortune to save his throne from the direct gaze of a new star in the horizon, who would be the son of the man he had rebuffed and who was about to be born in the house of another Rajput at Amarkot.

Humayun marched out of Amarkot on a campaign to Thatta, leaving behind his wife, other harem women and followers. But being a man forever mystified by the stars and planets, he left behind his chief astrologer Maulana Chand to record the astral positions at the precise moment of birth of his child and prepare the child's horoscope. Hamida Bano went into labour at a time that Chand considered inauspicious. The worried man apparently wondered if the delivery could be deferred to a later hour that was more propitious and came once in a millennium. Everyone present made light of his worries, saying that man can never influence such things.

But Abu'l Fazl informs that labour pains vanished all of a sudden due to the presence of a local nurse whose 'repulsive appearance' disgusted Hamida Bano so much that she lost her temper, and along with it the urge to deliver. This was much to the relief of Chand, of course, but when his right time approached, a tired Hamida Bano had fallen asleep.

Fazl notes that Chand wanted to wake her up somehow, much against the will of the others in the household, who again insisted that things would happen when god willed it. This, of course, offers a glimpse of the rational-minded high society that the Mughals largely represented in an era when abject superstition dictated life. Humayun was an exception, though, who relied too much on astrology and horoscopes.

Nevertheless, Fazl tells us that the birth happened at that propitious hour. Labour pain woke up Hamida and she delivered a boy early morning on 15 October 1542, or 5 Rajab 949 Hijri, or 6 Kartik 1599 Vikram Samvat.[7] It was a Sunday. Around that time 15 miles away, Humayun had a dream of becoming a father. Master of Hindustan once, he was now the lord of premonition. But the actual news of the birth would reach him only three days later.

Meanwhile, the time came to feed the newborn. The Mughals, like many royal families across the world and in India, depended on a battery of wet nurses to breastfeed the royal babies. The Turkish word for a wet nurse was '*anga*' or '*anaga*', and the Mughal harem had many of them. But before milk, the baby was offered honey—a practice now considered a medical taboo but still followed in many Hindu and Muslim homes (the Muslims call it *tahneek*). Hamida Bano breastfed her baby first, before passing him on to a wet nurse named Daya Bhawal, whom Fazl describes asa 'receptacle of chastity' distinguished for her 'virtue and purity'. Daya Bhawal was a concubine of Humayun's (Fazl calls her *khidmatgar-i-khas*) and

7 Abu'l Fazl gives dates from all calendars known at that time in India. Interestingly, the Hindu calendar date comes immediately after the Hijri calendar date. What is also interesting here is what Abdul Qadir Badaoni says in *Muntakhab ut-Tawarikh*, that on the festival of the eighth of Virgo, or 8 Aban in the Persian calendar, Akbar would wear a *tilak* (talisman) like a Hindu and appear before his subjects publicly even as Brahmin priests tied strings of jewels on his wrists. 8 Aban was Akbar's birthday!

may have been a Hindu.[8] This may have been just an ordinary affair back then. But when I look at it from a 21st-century perspective, I can say with some degree of poetic licence that in that very moment, as this Hindu woman nourished the infant on her bosom, the future Muslim emperor was bound in ties of warmth to his Hindu subjects. His being born in the house of a Hindu Rajput in Sindh had already prepared the ground for him to be called the first Mughal Emperor born on Indian soil. Though Vincent Smith didn't think much of it when he wrote that Akbar 'had not a drop of Indian blood in his veins' and even derided art historian E. B. Havell for saying that Akbar was 'an Indian for Indians'.[9]

Elsewhere at Jun (today in Sindh, Pakistan), Abu'l Fazl says, the emperor threw a feast and gave away gifts and money and *khilats* or royal robes of honour to celebrate the birth. It sounds like a fantastic tale later invented to add respectability to what was otherwise a happy occasion amid abject misery. The emperor had no money to gift nor robes of honour to bestow. So, Jauhar Aftabchi's[10] version is more believable in which he said the emperor asked for 200 *shahrukhis* (silver coins), a silver bracelet and a pod of musk[11], which he cut into several pieces and gave them away to various nobles. Humayun supposedly said that like the perfume filled the tent with its fragrance, his son's name and fame would one day spread to all corners of the world. After that, and in consultation with astrologers, Humayun named his son Jalaluddin Muhammad Akbar. The name Akbar, going by Islamic

8 See point 48 in the 'Errata and Addenda' section at the end of *Akbarnama Vol. I*, p. vi for details. Her father may have been someone named Joga Parihar.

9 E. B. Havell wrote in his 1913 book, *Indian Architecture: Its Psychology, Structure, and History from the First Muhammadan Invasion to the Present Day*, 'Indirectly Akbar's influence upon the architecture of his time was very great; for whereas both his father and grandfather were Persian in their habits and tastes, Akbar was an Indian of the Indians, and disgusted his orthodox Musulman courtiers by the enthusiasm with which he entered into the study of Hindu philosophy and religious teaching.'

10 Jauhar Aftabchi was an ewer bearer of Humayun who remained a loyal follower all his life. Later in his life, he was commanded by Akbar to write an account based on which Abu'l Fazl could write the *Akbarnama*. The result was *Tazkirat ul-Waqiat*.

11 *Kasturi*, which is obtained from the musk deer. It's considered to be sacred in India.

numerology, corresponded to that of *aftab* or the sun (the number is 223). though, Jauhar says the child was named Badruddin Muhammad Akbar as he was born on a full moon night. Jauhar also says that the date of birth was 23 November 1542 or 14 Shaban, AH 949. It's possible that Jauhar went wrong in this, as suggested by the English translator of his work, Major C. Stewart, and also by H. Beveridge who translated the *Akbarnama*[12]; or, the date was adjusted in retrospect to coincide with the date of the conception of Prophet Muhammad, 15 October or 5 Rajab. It is a subject of speculation, but not impossible. But if it indeed happened that way, then Akbar made it a curious paradox later in life by repudiating the Prophet himself, as is alleged by some of his contemporary biographers.

What is also remarkable, if the latter is true, is how this has seen an amazing continuity down to our times, almost becoming a part of Indian tradition. Even today, birth dates of Indian children are often altered in certificates for various reasons—to make them appear younger for future job/career prospects, to coincide with some auspicious date, etc. These often don't become matters of dispute unless it's a prominent Indian. For instance, the chief of army staff in 2012, General V. K. Singh, was embroiled in controversy and had even dragged the Union government to court over a discrepancy over his birthday. He later joined the BJP after retirement and became a minister in the Narendra Modi government. Narendra Modi himself has been in the eye of the storm throughout his term for alleged discrepancies in his date of birth as well. Akbar would have surely been amused to see all this today.

Another aspect to remember as we analyse this is that until a generation ago, it was quite common to remember birthdays with festivals or even celestial events. Somebody could be born on Holi and would celebrate his/her birthday on every Holi thenceforth even though Holi never falls on the same date. Or someone could be born on a solar eclipse and nobody bothers to record the precise date. So,

12 Among his other arguments, Beveridge also says that going by the Hijri era, 14 Shaban 949 would be a Thursday and not a Sunday as almost every court chronicler and even Akbar's aunt Gulbadan Begum says was the day of birth.

if there is a discrepancy about a man or a woman's birth date, it could be also because of ignorance and nothing else. However, birth charts of most Hindus, rich or poor, are prepared quite religiously. Among the Muslims, while there may be families that do prepare birth charts like Hindus, mostly they don't prepare horoscopes as Islam condemns soothsaying and endorses natural sciences. Shias are different in this manner, as their customs and beliefs are closer to those of the Hindus. They have the *Imamia Jantri*, which gives one auspicious days to avoid rituals, like '*poornima*' or full moon night and '*amavasya*' or moonless night. The Hindus do this too. Shias also wear birthstones and many believe in palmistry.[13]

Sufis believe astrology is more than that and is some kind of science. The Mughals from Babur onwards believed in astrology and horoscopes. Humayun, in particular, distinguished himself in astrology, even assigning commands and offices based on the star signs of officers. So, someone with a water sign was put in charge of waterworks, irrigation, riverways etc., while someone with a fire sign was put in charge of artillery. Though absolutely bizarre even by the standards of that time, this act shows the extraordinary existence of the Mughals. Not bound by religious dogma, open to new ideas from other faiths, willing to experiment with and integrate elements of different belief systems into their way of life are pointers to explain why there was no dynasty like theirs before them and ever since.

The baby prince's horoscope was prepared according to the date of 15 October with the help of a Greek astrolabe. A separate

13 Historian Rana Safvi explained this to me in detail. She said that the Shias and the Hanafi Muslims have many similar practices to that of Hindus. Since *Nauroz* itself is an animistic festival that the Shias adopted, Hindu religious practices are not perceived to be alien or heretic by the average Shia. Islam in India, she said, is unlike what it is in the Middle East or anywhere else. But in the 1960s and 1970s, poor Muslims started going to countries in the Persian Gulf—Saudi Arabia, UAE, Kuwait, Iraq etc. There, they were exposed to the more orthodox *Wahhabi* school of Islam. When they came back after making money, they constructed mosques that were very much unlike the traditional Indian mosques, which were a legacy of the Mughals. These resembled the mosque at Medina. Safvi said that it's an alien trend that doesn't fit with the Indian Islam's ethos and is deeply worrying.

chart under the Hindu method was also prepared. The ground for a secular ruler of the future was being prepared. But Humayun was yet to see the child. He would have to wait for another month by when Hamida would join him at Jun. On his 35th day in the world, the infant Jalaluddin Muhammad Akbar was united with his father. The union was happy. But by no means did it imply, as Humayun would have hoped, that this was like some holy talisman to end the troubles of the royal family. In fact, things were about to become more desperate, especially after the Thatta campaign against Sindh ruler Shah Husayn Arghun.

The Arghuns were also Turks like the Mughals and used to earlier rule Kandahar and Kabul, albeit briefly, until they were pushed out by Babur. Thenceforth, they made Sindh their home and base. In Humayun, they saw a second Mughal ruler threatening to push them out from even their second home. It was an existential threat for the Arghuns and surely Shah Husayn was no pushover to take it lying down.

Financially better off than the wandering emperor, Shah Husayn had the will and resources to try every trick to weaken his enemy by buying out his allies. Tarsh Beg was an ally who quietly accepted the blandishments and went over to the rival camp. But Rana Parshad of Amarkot told Humayun about it when he was made a similar offer. Humayun advised the Rana to clothe a dog in the robe of honour sent to him and send it to the camp of the Arghun. The Rana apparently did that. But this strong ally of Humayun left the alliance sometime later after a quarrel with a Mughal noble named Khwaja Ghazi. Jauhar quotes the Rana as having said that 'any attempt to assist the Mughals was a loss of labour and time'.

Just as the Rana left, other local chiefs and zamindars also abandoned Humayun. Sensing vulnerability in Humayun, the Arghuns decided to attack. But owing to Humayun's good fortune (his name literally meant 'good fortune'), Bairam Khan joined the imperial camp a day before the attack. More than a battle, it was a series of skirmishes, which went quite badly for the Mughals. This drove Humayun to make desperate rhetoric, such as asking an attendant to prepare his horse and armour so that he could himself gallop into battle. But then a

Mughal defector told Shah Husayn that Humayun was contemplating leading the imperial army himself. And Shah Husayn lost his nerve.

The Mughals, mostly during Babur's four years in India, had developed a fearsome reputation for themselves. There was no army in India that thought about fighting the Mughals without some trepidation. Sometime before Humayun found himself in that predicament, he had gone in pursuit of the Sultan of Gujarat, Bahadur Shah, who had besieged Chittor. The sultan didn't fight any battle with the Mughals even once; instead, he chose to flee from city to city, province to province, till he landed in the arms of the Portuguese. Humayun hadn't lost to the Afghans at Kannauj and Chausa then, so the Mughal reputation was pretty much intact.

But the Arghun ruler's hesitation to go to battle against the emperor himself, despite knowing the Mughals' weak military situation, shows that the Mughal impact wasn't just military but also psychological. In any case, Shah Husayn sent his emissary to the Mughal camp along with gifts, accepted his 'mistake' in warring against the emperor, and said that his own sense of shame had prevented him from coming in person. This was Humayun's best chance to make amicable peace. Showing great sagacity and still holding the moral high ground, Humayun sent assurance to the Arghun chief that he would leave Sindh. And he did.

After leaving Sindh, the emperor first went to Sehwan and from there marched onwards towards Kandahar and reached Mashtan near Quetta when he learnt that his younger brother, Mirza Askari, was coming with a big force to arrest him. The whole camp couldn't have marched on fast enough to evade the forces of Askari. So Humayun made a big decision to leave his infant son behind along with his retinue in the hope that the boy's uncle would take pity on him and spare his life. He once again asked for a horse from Tardi Beg and was again refused. From this point on, Tardi Beg left his master and joined the rival prince. Many others left Humayun too.

With no options left and no hope of any succour coming, Humayun galloped off towards Sistan with his wife on his steed and 40 trusted followers, including just one other woman. The road ahead was unclear: it could have been a path of promise or a road to perdition. The Mughals could have gone silently into the night or faced a new dawn of hope. Just about anything was possible. Fate hung by a delicate thread. But whatever the outcome would be, Hamida Bano was firm about not leaving her husband's side. She was being as bullheaded in this matter as she was in refusing to marry Humayun a year earlier. And that was itself quite a story.

Hamida was only 14 when Humayun saw her in attendance at the reception held in his honour at the camp of Mirza Hindal, his younger brother, in Paat, Sindh, in 1541. Humayun seems to have been smitten by her. When he enquired about her, Hindal told him that she was the daughter of Shaikh Ali Akbar Jami[14], his preceptor.

Humayun visited Hindal again and told his stepmother Dildar Begum that he wanted to marry Hamida. Hindal objected to it, saying that he considered Hamida as his 'sister and daughter'. 'Your majesty is a king. Heaven forbid there should not be a proper alimony, and that so a cause of annoyance should arise.'[15] This was essentially a snub for Humayun due to his being a man of small means then, and he perceived it well, walking away with a hurt ego. Seeing that her stepson was distraught, Dildar Begum later wrote to Humayun and asked him not to fret. Humayun replied that he would pay whatever *mehr* or alimony Hamida's family expected.

But Hamida was not alright with the alliance. At another time, when Humayun came to Paat and wanted to see her, she refused to come out. Instead, she sent out a message—'If it is to pay my respects, I was exalted by paying my respects the other day. Why should I come again?'[16] This was quite a snub to a 33-year-old emperor by a 14-year-old girl! But Humayun persisted. On another occasion, Humayun's messenger was returned with a message of rejection so profound that it would simply crush the heart and confidence of an average college Romeo. 'To see kings once is lawful; a second time it is forbidden. I shall not come,' Hamida said.[17]

---

14 Gulbadan Begum refers to him as Mir Baba Dost in *Humayun Nama*.

15 Ibid.

16 Ibid.

17 Ibid.

Humayun wouldn't take no for an answer, but he wouldn't take her by force either—quite your principled Bollywood hero who would run after a woman, singing songs like '*Khambhe jaisi khadi hai, ladki hai ya chhadi hai*' (She's stiff like a pole, is this a girl or a stick)[18] of what I call the chasing genre, but also claim that '*aurat agar na kahein toh chhoona nahin, aur haan kahein toh chhodna nahin*' (if a woman says no, don't touch her; if she says yes, don't leave her). In reality, it's a clichéd statement that offends more than it defends a woman's dignity.

On hearing Hamida's rebuff, Humayun said, 'If she is *na mahram*, we will make her *mahram*.'[19] He pestered his stepmother again to convince Hamida. For 40 days, Hamida was advised, even cajoled, and each time, she disagreed. Dildar Begum told her that she would have to marry someone eventually; that someone better be a king. Hamida gave a befitting answer, quite mature for her age. 'Oh yes, I shall marry someone; but he shall be a man whose collar my hand can touch, and not one whose skirt it does not reach.' This was no ordinary girl. She seemed pretty conscious of what she wanted from life. A defeated king without a kingdom and who was twice her age was not her idea of an ideal mate.

Today's Indians, both men and women, would be able to immediately relate to Hamida's thought process. That's how it happens today, doesn't it? But it was quite radical, and revolutionary, for her time. Though we often hear about lecherous professors and middle-aged bosses having a glad eye for younger women, a man turning up as a suitor at the house of a teenaged girl half his age today would actually land up straight in jail under the stringent POCSO (Protection of Children from Sexual Offences) Act.

The Hamida-Humayun episode actually reflects that Mughal women had agency and were fairly independent women going by the standards of those times. No wonder that many ran flourishing business empires with their own fleets of merchantmen, planned and executed massive building projects, organised and led hunts, and even accompanied their husbands on military campaigns. Hamida, in

18 A popular song of the 'chasing genre' from the 1990 Bollywood blockbuster *Dil*. The song featured Aamir Khan and Madhuri Dixit.

19 A consort in this particular sense.

particular, is one of those royal women whose identities have largely remained confined as queen consorts or royal mothers in patriarchal interpretations of historical narratives. Hamida Bano actually exercised tremendous influence on court affairs and her son, who deified her. As we shall examine in the succeeding chapters, her relationship with her son was at variance with the image portrayed by the 2008 movie *Jodhaa Akbar*. In one of the scenes in that movie, Akbar declares that he deferred more towards Maham Anaga than his own mother. That's just a Bollywood fantasy passing off as history.

However, the strong-minded Hamida eventually came around to changing her opinion about Humayun. When she said aye to the marriage, Humayun picked up an astrolabe and fixed an auspicious date and time for it. In the burning, hot desert of Sindh, which perhaps resembled Humayun's condition at that point, his marriage to Hamida was like an oasis of hope.

Two years later, as he rode through the uneven terrain of Helmand, onwards to Sistan, that oasis of hope firmly held on to him from behind. Up ahead lay the gates of Persia and the court of Shah Tahmasp, the Safavid ruler of that empire. And in that court lay the hope for an emperor without an empire.

After arriving at Sistan, and on Bairam Khan's advice, Humayun sent word of his coming to the Safavid empire, to the Shah of Persia ahead. The letter, authored by Bairam Khan, was dipped in over-elaborate courtesy and praise of the Persian monarch. It had the desired effect on Shah Tahmasp who wrote back a courteous letter welcoming Humayun to his empire and inviting him to his court. Shah Tahmasp separately sent word to all his officials posted everywhere on the route to treat Humayun with utmost courtesy as they would treat him. But beyond the veil of courtesy was a sense of superiority and even haughty arrogance that was on display on the part of the Persians. At every step, Humayun was made aware that he was a deposed king and a Sunni seeking refuge at the court of a powerful Shia emperor who presided over a cultural empire too.

Herat in today's Afghanistan used to be the capital of Khorasan in the Persian Empire in Humayun's times. A major trading centre, Herat had been conquered by most of those great conquerors who had also invaded India—Mahmud of Ghazni, the Mongols, Humayun's great ancestor, Amir Timur, in 1380, and Ahmad Shah Abdali.[20] Timur's conquest had led to over 120 years of Timurid rule during which the city attained its pinnacle of glory and prosperity. But just when Babur took Kabul, the Safavids under Shah Ismail took Herat overthrowing the Turks. It's hard to guess if Humayun remembered or felt proud about the historic association of the Timurids with Herat. But when he reached the city, he was greeted by a large crowd. Shah Tahmasp had decreed that everyone aged seven to seventy should come out to greet the Indian emperor.

It's an approach that's very familiar to us in India today. It's been common knowledge that political parties draw crowds by paying money. Indeed, even Bollywood movies allude to it. For instance, there's a scene in the 2001 Hindi movie *Nayak* where the protagonist, who is reluctant to contest elections, is dragged out of his home by a well-meaning bureaucrat and shown a sea of people waiting to see him and support him. The bureaucrat, played by actor Paresh Rawal (now a BJP MP from Gujarat), says that it isn't a crowd that's been gathered by paying money but a spontaneous one.

But often, and increasingly since 2014, diktats are issued to schoolchildren, bureaucrats or factory workers to show up at state or party events. In 2015, for instance, all schools and a crematorium in Chandigarh had been shut and all examinations rescheduled for Prime Minister Narendra Modi's visit.[21] Towards the end of 2017, there

---

20 Abdali's conquest in 1747 made Herat part of the Afghan Empire. The Iranians tried to recapture the city many times after that, the last in 1856, which had triggered the Anglo-Persian War. That war saw the service of Indian troops in the British army and many gallant actions such as the one at Bushehr in which the Indians performed brilliantly. Modern Indian Army regiments like the Rajputana Rifles still have Sovereign's Colours and battle honours from that campaign. The Treaty of Paris in 1857 ended the war in Britain's favour and the Iranians had to give up their claim on Herat for good.

21 Article in *The Indian Express* dated 11 September 2015. Available at http://indianexpress.com/article/cities/chandigarh/city-schools-to-remain-closed-today/.

were allegations of ceramic factories in Morbi[22], Gujarat, being told to shut work for a few hours and send at least 25 workers to attend Modi's election rallies. In early 2018, schools across the country were ordered to ensure that all students attended the live telecast of Modi's address to schoolchildren that also doubled up as the launch of his book, *Exam Warriors.*[23] There was some social media outrage over these recent episodes.

Humayun could have hardly complained about the attention he was getting, even though most people may have come out to greet him out of fear of harm by their own monarch. It was an enjoyable stay, going by Abu'l Fazl and Jauhar Aftabchi's accounts. The king spent a month there before another letter arrived from Shah Tahmasp. This time, the Safavid emperor asked Humayun to come to the holy city of Mashhad, which had the shrine of Imam Reza, the eighth Shia Imam. There the two kings would meet, the letter informed.

At Mashhad, the Mughals spent 40 days with Humayun even visiting the tomb of Imam Reza one night, which must have been a difficult thing to do during the day due to the Shia-Sunni divide of the time, especially under the orthodox gaze of the Safavid dynasty. That also highlights the remarkable nature of the marriage between Sunni Humayun and Shia Hamida. That it happened in India with such relative ease in an age when Shia-Sunni divide was as pronounced as the Catholics and Protestants in Europe can only mean one thing—tolerance as the ethos of the Indian civilisation was more real than imagined, and the Mughals were Muslims of a different nature, unencumbered by diktats foisted by faith. This was the foundation on which the edifice of *Sulh-i-Kul* as envisioned by Akbar would rest.

---

22 Article in *The National Herald* dated 29 November 2017. Available at https://www.nationalheraldindia.com/gujarat-assembly-elections-2017/ceramic-factories-in-morbi-asked-to-shut-down-for-workers-to-attend-modis-rally/.

23 Schools were later told to share photographic and video proof of attendance by students of the event titled 'Pareeksha Pe Charcha' at Talkatora Stadium, New Delhi. Article on that in *The Times of India*, dated 20 February 2018. Available at https://timesofindia.indiatimes.com/india/send-pics-videos-to-prove-students-saw-pm-modis-chat-schools-told/articleshow/62990493.cms.

But there was no meeting as promised by the Shah at Mashhad. Humayun received a fresh word from the Shah that he should march up to Qazvin. This march was long, with breaks at several places lasting for several days. Then as they neared Qazvin, the Shah asked Humayun to send Bairam Khan ahead of him. Bairam, a fellow Shia, was received warmly in court by the Shah, but then he asked him to cut his hair and wear Persian headgear. Bairam refused to do so, saying that he obeys a different master. The Shah got angry and haughtily said that Bairam was free to do as he pleased, but then ordered the execution of some prisoners in Bairam's presence to intimidate him.

Humayun, meanwhile, had also reached Qazvin and was received by the Shah's emissaries. The Shah had sent royal robes for him to wear for the occasion. To test his equestrian skills, an 'unbroken' or untrained horse was sent for him to mount. Jauhar says everyone present was surprised when the emperor mounted the horse and controlled it without much ado. This was actually an insult guised as a test. It wasn't custom in any civilised society to send an untrained horse for a distinguished guest to mount. The expectation seemed to be that Humayun would struggle to mount it, even fall while trying to sit on it and give sufficient reason for mirth to the Persians at his expense.

Humayun, however, was an accomplished horseman and one of the few Mughal emperors who knew stirrup archery of which the Turco-Mongols were masters. The Persians may not have known this. But Jauhar mentions some 'inferior people' coming on horseback and saluting Humayun, which he saw as an assertion that Persians of all ranks, high and low, were still equal to an Indian king. That was an insult of the protocol.

The meeting between the two emperors was by and large cordial, but Shah Tahmasp succeeded with Humayun where he had failed with Bairam Khan—to make him wear the Persian cap or the *Taj-i-Haydari*.[24] Also, it seems Humayun's entourage was not allowed to sit by Shah Tahmasp citing Persian traditions. A reference in Jauhar's account says Humayun asked if the princes could all sit down. I am inferring that he meant his nobles. This moment was captured for

24 It's a conical-shaped turban with twelve parts symbolising twelve Shia imams.

eternity in a fresco painting at the Chehel Sotoun pavilion at Isfahan constructed by Shah Abbas II. This painting shows Humayun and Tahmasp seated at the centre with their attendants on both sides and music and dance underway. The Persian nobles are seated while the Mughal nobles are seen standing. Humayun is also shown as a smaller and a several shades darker man than the Shah, which probably means more than the conventional explanation that they were darker as they came from India. This painting is in stark contrast to two others in the same palace. One depicts the meeting between Shah Abbas II and Nader Muhammad Khan, the king of Turkestan. Everyone is seated in it on both sides. The other depicts a meeting between Shah Abbas I and Vali Muhammad Khan, a claimant to the leadership of the Bukhara Khanate in the early 17th century. He and his supporters are all seated too. So clearly, standing during a reception wasn't a Persian custom; it was a premeditated insult heaped on Humayun with 'tradition' as cover.

There isn't much unique about monarchs or empires insulting each other. The great Abbasid Caliph Haroun al-Rashid, a contemporary of Charlemagne, had felt terribly insulted when Nicephorus I, who had usurped the title of Eastern Roman Emperor by deposing Empress Irene of Byzantium, refused to send tribute to the Caliph, instead demanding it from him in a letter. Al-Rashid wrote back an insulting letter to Nicephorus I that read:

> *Bismillah al Rahman al Rahim* (In the name of God, the compassionate, the merciful)! From *Amir al-Mu'minin* (Commander of the Faithful) Haroun al-Rashid to Nicephorus, dog of the Romans. I have read thy letter, O thou son of an unbelieving mother. Thou shalt not hear, thou shalt behold my reply.[25]

It led to war and the Byzantine Empire had to conclude peace on humiliating terms. There's also the apocryphal insulting letter[26] the Zaporozhian Cossacks supposedly wrote to the Ottoman Sultan Mehmed IV in 1676 as a reply to his territorial demands, which

---

25 Edward Gibbon, *The History of the Decline and Fall of the Roman Empire* (London: T. Cadell, Strand, 1837), p. 939.

26 Victor A. Friedman, 'The Zaporozhian Letter to the Turkish Sultan: Historical Commentary and Linguistic Analysis', *Slavica Hierosolymitana, Vol II,* 1978, p. 25–38.

later became the subject of a famous 19th-century painting.[27] This episode is still considered to be one of the crudest and boldest diplomatic affronts in history. But a monarch rarely invited another only to insult him. So Humayun's case is quite unique.

Today, such excesses are not known but the practice of diplomatic insult or rebuff still exists as a matter of foreign policy. Nations and their leaders do it all the time, whether it is Philippines President, Rodrigo Duterte, who called Obama a 'son of a whore' or US President, Donald Trump, who calls North Korean dictator Kim Jong Un the 'Little Rocket Man'. India also recently delivered what was arguably a diplomatic slight to Canadian Prime Minister, Justin Trudeau, when he visited India in 2018 on a personal invitation of Prime Minister Narendra Modi.

A very junior officer in somewhat informal attire was sent to greet the Canadians even though Modi has, during his tenure, built a reputation for himself by receiving foreign leaders at the airport himself. From Barack Obama to Francois Hollande to Benjamin Netanyahu to King Abdullah of Jordan, Modi has greeted them all. Except for Trudeau.

Trudeau's trip was a disaster in many respects with the press making unkind cuts even for his and his family's sartorial sense or the lack of it. Modi finally met him on the final day of his weeklong trip. All throughout, the Canadian and Indian press reported on this 'insult', with many calling it a 'strong response' by the Indians to the Canadian PM's flirtations with the Sikh separatist ideology. However, Humayun had to endure much more, even the threat of annihilation because of his Sunni faith.

The next morning after the meeting, the Shah passed by Humayun's camp on a procession. Humayun came out of his camp and greeted the Shah, but it was not responded to well by the Shah. Humayun felt deeply insulted, and as Jauhar says in his account, he cursed himself for having come to the Persian court for help.

---

27 It's an oil painting by the Russian artist Ilya Repin variously known as 'Reply of the Zaporozhian Cossacks to Sultan Mehmed IV of the Ottoman Empire' and 'Cossacks of Saporog Are Drafting A Manifesto'. The precise date of the painting is not known, but is believed to have been painted between 1880 and 1891.

But the insults soon gave way to open threats. One day, along with a large quantity of wood sent to Humayun's camp for use by his followers, came a threat from the Shah that said unless they all became Shias, a funeral pyre would be made for them with all that wood. Death by fire is the worst death in Islam as it's a practice associated with animistic religions.

During the 1965 War between India and Pakistan, despite being equipped with the superior US-made Patton tanks, Pakistan's armoured corps personnel would abandon their tanks if hit by the enemy or even without it. The legendary Lieutenant General Harbakhsh Singh, the Western Army commander during the war, wrote in his memoirs later about having encountered a Pakistan Army soldier named Sowar Anwar ul-Haq of 4 Horse, who had come to surrender to the general wearing civilian clothes. When the general asked what put him in his predicament, the trooper replied that after the leading tanks of his unit got hit and caught fire, he abandoned his perfectly all right tank as being a Muslim, he didn't want to burn to death.[28]

Humayun's reply to the Shah was more gallant, though. He said he and his followers wouldn't deviate from their own faith, and their lives were in the hands of God who alone had the power to take them.[29] Humayun also asked the Shah permission to proceed towards Mecca on pilgrimage. To that, the Shah haughtily replied that he would soon draw his forces and annihilate the Sunnis, and since Humayun had come to Persia on his own accord, he must either accept the faith of Persia or be prepared to face the consequences.

Along with this threat, Shah Tahmasp also sent a highly respected man (probably a man of faith) named Kazi Jahan who advised Humayun to be mindful of his situation and accept the Shah's demand. He also told Humayun that to his fate was tied the lives of 700 Sunnis. It was more blackmail than counsel, but eventually, Humayun gave

---

28 Lieutenant General Harbakhsh Singh, *In the Line of Duty: A Soldier Remembers* (New Delhi: Lancer Publishers, 2013).

29 Jauhar quotes Humayun as having written back—'That he and his adherents were all firmly attached to their religion, and would not deviate therefrom; that the Persian monarch might do as he pleased, but that their lives were in the hands of God, without whose permission no injury could reach them, and in his protection they alone trusted.'

in and was even made to sign a document professing his acceptance of the Shia faith. Glad at this surrender, Tahmasp invited Humayun to go out on a hunt with him. And that once again turned out to be an occasion to insult the Mughals.

The Persian hunt was all about an army chasing all game animals to an enclosed space after which the hunters would spear or sabre them riding on horseback. Akbar would do this later in India and such form of hunting would become quite common. The British would adopt the system too and organise *kheddahs* or hunts using elephants.

As the two monarchs hunted down the game, some animals escaped via gaps that were open where the Mughal attendants were standing. The Persian king made Humayun compensate for each game animal lost that way in cash and kind—a horse and a *toman*[30] for each animal.

Decades later, Abu'l Fazl painted a glorious picture of the hunt in *Akbarnama*, where Humayun was shown as a brighter and more important-looking man and the Shah as a somewhat smaller man in dull-looking robes. The Shah is shown with a lance while Humayun hunts with a sabre. The Shah is not shown carrying any other weapon, but Humayun's horse has a composite bow in its typical ornately designed leather carry case and a quiver of arrows. That's an important detail that Fazl gets right and alludes to Humayun's expertise in mounted archery. But what's unmistakable here is the propaganda unleashed by Fazl.

In fact, Fazl's *Akbarnama* also has another miniature that captures the meeting between Humayun and Tahmasp, but it gives an entirely different twist to it. In Fazl's version, Humayun is only slightly darker than the Shah, both are of equal size and there is very little distance between them. Humayun's nobles are also seated while the Shah's nobles are barely visible. This is nothing but a propaganda painting, giving a positive spin to a humiliating event. And it's this spin that makes it so much more topical to examine today.

BJP's election campaigns since 2014 have hinged on almost Goebbelsian propaganda replete with doctored videos, amateurish cut-paste jobs, distortion of facts and morphing of photographs to bump up the public image of Narendra Modi and other tall leaders

30 A Safavid gold coin. This unit is still part of Iranian currency.

of the party. Even the public dissemination of information about the Modi government's achievements has been with the use of propaganda tools like misrepresenting a street in Canada as a Delhi road[31], or the portrayal of the Spain-Morocco border as the India-Pakistan border.[32]

These ridiculous attempts often backfire due to an alert social media, causing dents on Modi and his government's image. The beauty and the consummate nature of Fazl's propaganda lie in the fact that one often appreciates the art of the painting without comprehending the political message that lies underneath.

But Humayun's problems were about to be compounded by the arrival of three Mughal nobles from Mecca—Roshan Beg Koka, Khwaja Ghazi (who had quarrelled with Rana Parshad of Amarkot, resulting in a rupture of his alliance with Humayun) and Sultan Muhammad. Though they were from Humayun's camp, their loyalties lay with Mirza Kamran, Humayun's brother and ruler of Kabul and Punjab. They told the Shah unpleasant things about Humayun—that he had no talent to be a king and that's why his brothers didn't support him; that he had said nasty things about the Shah when he was an emperor in India; and that Babur had treacherously killed a Persian noble, and any help to his descendant might result in more treachery.

What was more damaging was the suggestion that the Shah should imprison Humayun, hand him over to his brothers and get Kandahar in return. The Shah is even learnt to have confronted Humayun about this and had an angry exchange of words with him. Jauhar even says that the Shah contemplated killing Humayun on the counsel of his nobles, but good sense prevailed after his sister Sultana Begum pointed out that it was a sin to kill a man who had sought asylum with him and unwise to make another enemy when the Shah was already surrounded by enemies on all sides.

---

31 Shorbori Purkayastha, 'BJP Municipality Tweet Passes off Canadian Streets as Delhi', *The Quint*, New Delhi, 6 April 2017. Available at https://www.thequint.com/news/india/bjp-municipality-delhi-canada.

32 IANS, 'Oops! It is Spain-Morocco road shown as floodlit Indian border', *Business Standard*, New Delhi, 14 June 2017. Available at http://www.business-standard.com/article/current-affairs/oops-it-is-spain-morocco-road-shown-as-floodlit-indian-border-117061401102_1.html.

Shah Tahmasp then decided to give Humayun a dignified send-off back to India. He first imprisoned the three nobles who had backstabbed Humayun and then prepared to execute them. Roshan Beg, being a milk brother of Humayun, appealed to ties of brotherhood to save his life. Humayun, an unusually lenient and kind man, interceded on behalf of the prisoners on death row. The Shah told Humayun that he would send 12,000 choicest Persian cavalry under the command of his son to assist Humayun in winning back his empire. Humayun, who probably wasn't expecting any kind of assistance from the Persian monarch, was overjoyed. As one final demand, the Shah asked for a feast in Hindustani style with Hindustani food and music. Humayun gladly obliged. The Shah, Jauhar noted, particularly liked a dish called '*dal khuske*' made of rice and peas that was unknown in Persia.[33] Indian food left its imprint on the Persian monarch.

Humayun finally returned to India with actually 14,000 Persian troops towards the end of 1544—yes, he spent only little more than a year in Persia and not fifteen years as many history books tell us. Here was his chance to take back what he had lost. The future was still uncertain because the Persians were not reliable allies and had promised to fight for him only if he gave them Kandahar as compensation. Humayun would need more than good luck to make this arrangement work.

All this while, the infant Akbar was growing up in the care of his uncle, Mirza Askari and his wife Sultana Begum. The Begum was quite fond of the child and treated him like her own son. When the boy first learnt to walk, it was his uncle and aunt who were present to see that moment. Askari even performed a Turkic ritual of tapping on the head of a child learning to walk with a turban, a ritual that a child's father is supposed to perform. But as news broke that Humayun was coming with an army towards Kandahar, Askari panicked. Mirza Kamran asked his younger brother to send Humayun's child to Kabul. The idea seems to have been to hold at least Akbar as a bargaining chip if the occasion arose to parley with Humayun. Askari was confused. He held meetings with his advisors who gave him a

33 I don't know what this dish is. It could be the *kuska*, which is a version of plain biryani made with rice and *toor* dal. Or it could be a *pulav* version.

mixed opinion. One group advised him to send out the children to their father, another said the children should be sent to Kabul. The latter group also said that all bridges between him and Humayun had been burnt and there was no scope for negotiation.

Askari sent out his nephew Akbar and his niece Bakshi Bano to Kabul in what was a perilous journey through the snow. With them went Shamshuddin Ataga Khan, Akbar's chief wet nurse, Jiji Anaga and Maham Anaga. Kamran was less warm to his elder brother's children than Askari. And since he also had a son named Ibrahim Mirza who was a bit older than Akbar, the threat of Kamran killing Humayun's son to keep his own in the race for succession was also quite real. But also present in Kabul was the family matriarch, Khanzada Begum, the elder sister of Babur. She took Humayun's children under her wing and became very fond of Akbar. He resembled, she said, her brother when he was little. Nobody in the entire Mughal harem was as influential as the sister of Babur.

This royal lady wielded as much influence on the family as her maternal grandmother Esan Dawlat Begum once did. Esan Dawlat was the chief consort of Yunus Khan, a direct descendant of Chagatai Khan, Genghis Khan's son. Her daughter was Qutlugh Nigar Khanam, who was married to Umar Shaikh Mirza and was the mother of both Babur and Khanzada Begum. Esan Dawlat secured the succession of Babur when his father died in a freak accident while feeding pigeons at Ferghana. Babur was only 11 then and surrounded by people with doubtful loyalty. She advised Babur in important matters of statecraft as well. A Mughal miniature in an illustrated copy of Baburnama prepared under Akbar's directions shows the young Babur taking advice from Esan Dawlat.

Babur was very close to his sister Khanzada. While being ousted from Samarqand, the Uzbek warlord Shaibani Khan had actually abducted Khanzada and subjected her to cruel treatment. But when Persian king Shah Ismail defeated and killed Shaibani Khan, he liberated her and restored her to her brother along with a drinking cup made from the skull of the slain Uzbek warlord. Babur later made her Padishah (or Badshah) Begum. Though honorific in nature, a Mughal woman with this title became the supreme lady of the harem. And by virtue of that, nothing would move in the harem without her consent. So Khanzada Begum's taking over the custody of Akbar ensured that Kamran wouldn't dare to harm him. Also, Kamran tried to secure the support and consent of the royal ladies led by Khanzada Begum by trying to get the *khutba* read in his name and not in Humayun's. That singular act performed by the Islamic clergy could have sealed Humayun's fate, snatching away his legitimacy as the heir to Babur's throne and empire at a time he was struggling to recapture all that he had lost. But fortunately for Humayun, none of the royal women gave Kamran that permission.

Abu'l Fazl also mentions an interesting incident that happened in Kabul on *Shab-i-Barat* in October 1545. Mirza Kamran brought a decorated kettle drum for his son, Ibrahim, but Akbar liked it so much that he wanted to have it. To settle who should have it, a wrestling bout was organised between the two princes. Akbar supposedly defeated his bigger cousin, much to the chagrin of his uncle. In the years to come, Akbar would develop a strong liking for *kushti* or wrestling and would even play dangerous wrestling matches with elephants, often putting his own life in peril.

A Mughal painting made in the 1590s by Basawan and Chetar as a double page composition for Fazl's *Akbarnama* portrays one such incident in 1561. Akbar tamed and mounted a ferocious war elephant named Hawai, which was in *musth*, and pitted it against another ferocious royal elephant named Ran Bagha (meaning 'tiger of battle'), throwing caution to the wind and ignoring all words of wisdom uttered by people around him. The first frame shows Ran Bagha taking flight and Hawai, goaded on by Akbar, giving chase. The pachyderms run over a bridge of boats on the Yamuna with the boats giving way and people jumping into the river to save their lives. The second page shows a worried Mughal assembly led by Shamsuddin Ataga Khan waiting outside the fort and praying for the safety of the 19-year-old emperor. This was highly irresponsible and reckless behaviour displayed by the young emperor at a time when his hold on the state was weak. But historian Iqtidar Alam Khan argues that this episode also embarrassed Abu'l Fazl later when he wrote his *Akbarnama*. Khan writes in *India's Polity in the Age of Akbar*, 'Fazl quotes a not very bright saying of Akbar from this period, suggesting that he thus risked his life deliberately: if he had displeased God in any manner, "may that elephant finish us, for we cannot support the burden of life under God's displeasure".' But that was in 1561. The painting was made between 1590 and 1595, corresponding to the period of the writing of *Akbarnama*. Akbar was in his 50s then, and while Fazl may have felt the need to visually depict this episode in the emperor's life, it's possible that this also doubled as a medieval facelift for the emperor who was at an advanced age considering the low life expectancy of the time.

One thing that should be remembered here is that the depiction of the incident is quite congruent to the description of the incident in textual sources. However, it's not known how this tale was orally told in the Mughal Empire. It's quite possible for a subject of the emperor, who never saw him, to imagine him as some giant who controlled a rather aggressive tusker.

This is quite possible. The reason why most statues of the Buddha are so huge is because of the understanding that he was a giant who was 20 feet tall and whose begging bowl alone weighed up to 400 kilos. This deduction was probably made due to the erroneous association of an artefact, which was probably a '*dana patra*' or donation box at some Buddhist monastery, with the Buddha far back in time. It is today at the National Museum in Kabul, Afghanistan. This depiction of humans as giants has continued even today. It's a trend in South Indian politics, especially in Tamil Nadu, to put out giant cut-outs of leaders. Though she is no more, it's still possible to find giant cut-outs of 'Amma' Jayalalitha, the former chief minister of Tamil Nadu. Even her mentor, M. G. Ramachandran or MGR, had his giant cut-outs made.

Both MGR and Jayalalitha were huge movie stars who carved out their huge political empires, not by playing kings but Hindu gods on screen. And as actor Arun Govil—who had played Lord Rama in a very popular TV serial in the 1980s named *Ramayan*—had found out, it was difficult to step out of character off-screen due to huge public pressure after playing god once.[34] In the 1980s and 1990s, it was

34 Arun Govil said in a 2014 interview to the English daily *Hindustan Times* that from being a chain smoker, he had to give up smoking as people wouldn't approve of Lord Rama doing something like that. That article is available at https://www.hindustantimes.com/brunch/arun-govil-the-first-ram/story-iKYVwcBwMKdhiw6mfY3o3O.html.

possible to spot large posters of Arun Govil and Deepika Chikhalia as Rama and Sita adorning the prayer rooms at middle-class homes in India.

If an actor playing god can be treated as god, it's not difficult to imagine how Akbar's subjects treated him, since he was called *zill-i-illahi* or shadow of god on earth: a largely pre-Islamic Persian concept of kingship by divine right that was used in India for the first time by Delhi Sultan Ghiyasuddin Balban and subsequently popularised at a grand scale by the Mughals. The *zill-i-illahi* in itself was a title that bumped up the image of a ruler, but kings used various other ways to accentuate that image. The Mughals used the halo, for instance, in their paintings of the emperors—a symbol of divinity. Or the glorification of wars and conquests. This was the propaganda of the time.

Today, images of political leaders are still bumped up in India through the re-telling of tales, both real and apocryphal, with embellishments. There are quite awe-inspiring but rather nebulous tales about Narendra Modi's bravado. Modi had many years ago claimed that he was once attacked by crocodiles, resulting in a few stitches to his foot. In the run-up to the 2014 General Election, which Modi and his party won quite handsomely, this story appeared in a comic book series called *Bal Narendra* with a positive spin to what Modi had originally said. In it, Modi as a little boy jumped into a lake infested with crocodiles to retrieve a ball and caught one such creature and brought it home. In another story, Bal Narendra climbed up a tree to free a bird caught in kite strings. The bird looked at him with gratitude before flying away, the story said.

The previous story became more familiar when US President Barack Obama said at a banquet hosted in New Delhi that he didn't know that Modi had once survived a crocodile attack. The way Obama said it implied that Modi had told him so. Obama used that tale to stress that Modi was 'tough'. A force multiplier in the form of a compliment by a foreign leader created quite an impact among Modi's supporters and adversaries. And a force multiplier in the form of Persian troops in Humayun's army also created a psychological impact on his brothers Mirza Askari and Mirza Kamran.

Kandahar fell after brief resistance and Askari surrendered. The fort was initially taken possession of by the Persians, but Humayun surprised them sometime later and wrested control of it away from them. In a short period, Humayun had raised a new army that must have been powerful enough for the Persians to consider a retreat to their empire. Leaving Hamida Bano at Kandahar, Humayun next marched on Kabul where Kamran abandoned the city and fled towards Hindustan. As Humayun conquered Kabul, he was reunited with his children. Jauhar mentions an interesting incident here.

After entering the fort, a famished Humayun enquired if there was anything in the fort to eat. One of Babur's widows was asked by Humayun's attendants for food and she sent a beef dish for Humayun. As the emperor dipped his spoon into the broth, he realised it was beef. He shrieked in anger and cursed Kamran. He screamed if this is what Kamran ate and if he fed beef to their stepmother. Beef was not fit food for anyone, Humayun exclaimed, and wondered if Kamran couldn't have afforded to keep a few goats for their meat. He also lamented that all the four sons of Babur couldn't keep their stepmother well.

Humayun didn't touch the food, drank a glass of sherbet and decided to sleep hungry. This is a very significant event. Stories abound that Babur had prohibited cow slaughter in 1527 as it was offensive to Hindus. It's quite possible he did so; after all, Babur was a pragmatic king. But a document often cited as evidence for this and called 'sacred testament' or simply Babur's Will, is most probably a 19th-century fake.

There is also a view that Humayun stopped eating beef after that cow slaughter episode in Maldev's kingdom that created so many problems for the Mughals. This particular incident, however, tends to negate such a simplistic explanation. That Humayun himself disapproved of beef is relatively less known. Akbar would also go a step further—he would not only ban cow slaughter and beef in his empire but also have more vegetarian food in court after a point in his reign.

Akbar's successors would issue *firmans* and proclamations banning cow slaughter and beef from time to time right down to the last of the line, Bahadur Shah Zafar. Those dismissive of the Mughals' secular polity often have a fairly straightforward explanation for this, just like that spectator in Stephen Leacock's *The Conjurer's Revenge* who explains away every magic trick of the protagonist as 'he had it up his sleeve', that it was all symbolism driven by political expediency. A man can make symbolic gestures due to political expediency and there can be no doubt about that. But for a hungry, meat-eating man to shun food just because it is beef needs both firm belief and conviction. Perhaps this was the reason why the Mughals were not seen as foreigners like the Delhi Sultans. Hindus could mingle with them far more easily as their food habits were not considered offensive. And the Indian, or let's say Hindu, influence on them was perhaps far more pronounced than we could possibly know.

But the fraternal war didn't end there. As Humayun went about conquering other forts and cities, he was challenged by Kamran. Fortunes changed rather quickly. And Humayun's officers quibbled among themselves. At times, these led to serious differences. One of his most capable commanders, Qaracha Khan, was offended by the haughty behaviour of Khwaja Ghazi, the Diwan. This was the same officer who had broken the alliance between Humayun and the Rana of Amarkot and also said nasty things about the emperor to Shah Tahmasp, but whose life was spared when Humayun had interceded. The issue was over some trifling payment commitment that Humayun had made and the diwan refused to honour. Qaracha Khan was so upset that he went to Humayun, but the latter was too lazy to follow it up with his diwan. Qaracha felt insulted and left Humayun's camp to join Kamran. This hasn't been studied or even analysed in depth but when this nobleman alone was frustrating Humayun at every step, one could imagine how other nobles might have been frustrating his efforts, even cheating him. It's actually quite horrifying to imagine the situation Humayun had found himself in: in a foreign land, leading a foreign army, surrounded by allies of dubious intent and loyalty, and fighting a guilt complex at having to take up arms against his own brothers. Humayun's political task was also a lofty one—he was fighting his brothers without feeling any hate for them. He loved all his brothers and was bent on fulfilling his father's dying wish—that he would love and be kind to his brothers equally, not harm them, and divide his kingdom between them.

Humayun does come across as a misfit for the challenging and cruel environment of his time. Unusually kind, forgiving, tolerating of diverse, even contrarian viewpoints, and often deceived by friends but never taking things to heart, Humayun was a rare monarch. His superstitious and stargazing mind, addiction to opium, and sloth proved to be stumbling blocks on the path to becoming a great monarch. Without these, and if he were not sandwiched between a great father and a great son, and if fate hadn't cut short his life rather abruptly, history would have been perhaps kinder to Humayun in her assessment of his rule. But taints that don't stick on him are fratricide, intrigue and conspiracy against his own family members.

In contrast, Kamran's life had been mostly of intrigue. It was Humayun who had confirmed him as the ruler of Kabul. Yet when he was running away from Sher Shah and wanted to go to Badakhshan to raise a new army, Kamran had objected to it. The route to Badakhshan lay through Kabul, and Kamran, being an insecure man, had feared that Humayun might gobble up his kingdom in the process. All the four brothers together had the capability to repel, even crush Sher Shah. Yet Kamran was the weakest link in such an alliance. It's not that it wasn't experimented with, but Kamran was the first to abandon the resistance. He was like an unreliable and unpredictable ally in modern-day political coalitions, siding with one formulation today, and joining the rival camp tomorrow, citing 'inner voice' or whatever. Like for instance, Bihar's Chief Minister, Nitish Kumar, who resisted the tremendous popularity of Narendra Modi in 2015 and returned to power piggybacking on an alliance with long-time rival Rashtriya Janata Dal and Indian National Congress. This was christened the '*Mahagathbandhan*' or 'grand alliance'. But it didn't last beyond two years, and Kumar walked into the embrace of the BJP in 2017, citing his 'inner voice'. Another leader who jumped ship to join the BJP citing the same 'inner voice' was Naresh Agarwal. He dumped the Samajwadi Party in 2018, with whom he had a long association, after that party gave a Rajya Sabha ticket he had been expecting to film actor-turned-parliamentarian Jaya Bachchan instead.

Kamran was all of it and more. But he was definitely much more treacherous as he even contemplated turning over his brother to the enemy in the hope of keeping his dominions intact and not thinking at all about the bigger empire his father had left behind. Squandering away inheritance? Learn that from Humayun and his brothers!

After a see-saw of fortunes, Kamran was finally defeated and captured. This was after there was a thaw in the relationship between Humayun and him and the former forgiving him for his past conduct. Yet the opportunist in Kamran didn't let gentleman's word come in the way. When he retook Kabul in an almost treacherous manner, Kamran didn't flinch from tying the tiny tot that Akbar was to a rampart of the fort that was being ravaged by Humayun's artillery. It was the sheer good fortune of Akbar that his own father's artillerymen and musketeers didn't hit him. When Kabul was retaken, Humayun still wanted to forgive Kamran. But this time, his well-wishers in the family and nobility forced him to order the blinding of Kamran and his exile to Mecca. Humayun, also with a heavy heart, sent Mirza Askari on a forced pilgrimage to Mecca. Both Kamran and Askari would outlive Humayun and die sometime in 1557, about a year after their eldest brother's passing.

Humayun's youngest brother, Mirza Hindal, was his best brother. Though initially, he was hesitant about supporting the cause of Humayun and saw himself as a claimant to the throne of Hindustan, eventually, he threw in his lot with his eldest brother and fought under his banner. He was the most loved grandson of Khanzada Begum, who actually raised his wife Sultanam Begum. Hindal was formally named Abul Nasir Muhammad. The name Hindal was given by Babur as he was born just as he was on his way to conquer India. Babur considered this birth as a good omen. Hindal in Turkic means 'of Hind' or 'taker of Hind'. He was literally the first Mughal prince whose name tied him to India.

Hindal died when he was only 31 during a battle against the forces of Mirza Kamran. His only child was a daughter named Ruqaiyya Sultan Begum. She became the first wife of Akbar. And even though she didn't have any issue of her own, Akbar made her Padishah Begum. Much later, Akbar took away the young Mirza Khurram from his Rajput mother Jagat Gosain and put him under the direct care and supervision of Ruqaiyya Begum. Khurram later became Emperor Shah Jahan.

With Kabul and Kandahar secured, Humayun set sights on Hindustan. The year was 1554 and an imperial army with Humayun at its head marched out from Kabul towards Jalalabad and onwards to the banks of the Indus. Hindustan was on the other side. It was déjà vu for Humayun, who had in 1525, crossed the feisty river along with his father. That crossing had proved to be a fruitful one as Babur had won one victory after another and managed to carve out an empire in just four years between 1526 and 1530.

Fate had brought him back to the same juncture from where he had once looked expectedly towards the east 30 years earlier. A lot was at stake then; a lot was at stake now. The first foray was to build a fortune in India; this latest was to reclaim all that he had lost. A man so deeply influenced by horoscopes and astrology must have realised the importance of that moment—life had given him a rare second chance. And just like Babur had come with his son, Humayun had also come with his son.

As Humayun crossed the Indus, the new moon was spotted. 'God be praised, may it be propitious!' Humayun said thrice and ended with an '*aameen*'. The whole army entered India without suffering any loss. Akbar was 12 and quite a handful. Jauhar mentions an incident when Humayun asked him to bathe Akbar, make him wear new clothes and bring him before him. When Jauhar went to Akbar, the young prince said he won't appear naked before him and won't let him bathe him. The job was left to the prince's attendant. When he appeared before his father, Humayun made him sit in front of him. Then he recited verses from the Quran and breathed down on Akbar's head at the end of every verse. He was trying to protect his son from evil and harm. He looked very happy and content, Jauhar said, adding, '...it might be said that he had then acquired all the good fortune of this world, and the blessings of the next.'

Nobody could have imagined, not even Humayun, that the next world would beckon him in less than a year. And that the man of God would also die with a prayer on his lips.

Chapter 2

The King Is Dead, Long Live the King

> When death removes a crown by force,
> At once another head is crowned;
> When one old age completes its course,
> A younger rises from the ground.[1]

A lot changes in 15 years. Family, friends, even foes. If you are a professional who has quit or taken a sabbatical for that long, your employability becomes difficult. No one feels this more acutely in India than working women, many of whom quit service in order to raise children but find it difficult to get employed again on the same level and pay after a few years.

For a medieval king out of sight for over a decade, it was a tough proposition to stake claim on the land and people now ruled by someone else. The same happened to Humayun in 1555. The people had seen him lose power back in 1540 when the Sur Afghans under Sher Khan had ousted him. But Sher Khan could enjoy the fruits of his labour for only five years. In 1545, while laying siege to the Chandela Rajput-held fort of Kalinjar, a rocket misfired and fell on

1 Abu'l Fazl, *The Akbarnama of Abu'l Fazl, Vols. I–III*, tr. H. Beveridge (Calcutta: The Asiatic Society, 1907–39, reprinted in 2010).

a gunpowder tumbril resulting in a massive explosion that killed that last flicker of hope for a revival of Afghan power in India.

Sher Khan's successors were average men, without that dash and daring that had distinguished him at a time the Mughals were still powerful and ruling from Delhi. But they more or less held on to their possessions even though internecine warfare kept them busy. Sher Shah's immediate successor was his son Islam Shah. Islam Shah was originally known as Jalal Shah and was chosen by the nobility to be their king and not his elder brother Adil Khan. But the latter had some support among sections of the nobility. An insecure Islam Shah tried to get his brother killed, which failed and led to an abortive bid by Adil to the throne. But the new king didn't remain content with the outcome and carried out an almost Stalinist purge among the nobility. This way, he ensured that the nobility remained subservient to him and not think the king was the 'first among equals' as was the dominant feature of the Pashtun polity. At an earlier time, when Sultan Ibrahim Lodhi had adopted an overbearing attitude towards his nobles, one of them, Daulat Khan Lodhi, had invited Babur to come to Hind and crush his master.

Around the time Humayun finally secured Kabul, Kandahar and Badakshan, Islam Shah died in 1554, leaving his 12-year-old son Feroze Shah to succeed him. But the boy was assassinated by his uncle Mubariz Khan who then became the ruler with a new regnal name of Muhammad Adil Shah. As his vizier, he chose a Hindu whose name was Hemu.

Adil Shah's rule didn't see any spectacular governance, but it saw the de facto division of the empire bequeathed by Sher Khan into four parts. This was especially after his brother-in-law Ibrahim Shah unfurled the banner of revolt and wrested away Agra and Delhi from him. But even Ibrahim Shah was defeated and ousted by another brother-in-law of Adil Shah named Sikander Shah in 1555. In this anarchic plot arrived Humayun to take back what he believed was his.

In early January 1555, Humayun crossed the Indus and advanced towards his destination. One by one, the cities and provinces, starting from Peshawar, began submitting to him without even fighting.[2] The most formidable obstacle that lay in his path was the fort of Rohtas in Punjab[3]. This was then a very recent construction, started in 1541 and completed in 1548. The fort was started by Sher Shah to keep the Gakhar tribals from creating trouble and to block any advance of any invading army from Kabul. Sher Shah's worry was the return of Humayun, which he wanted to prevent. Sher Shah recognised that in the event of his return, the Gakhar tribals, who had refused to accept Sur suzerainty and continued to accept the Mughals as their overlords, could join the Mughals and create more problems for the Afghans.

There was every reason for anyone familiar with India's history to fear the Gakhars. It was the Gakhar tribals who had given Mahmud of Ghazni a lot of headache whenever he had invaded India. There is also a mention of the Gakhar infantry decimating Mahmud's Turkic cavalry in one of the engagements—a very rare instance in history when unorganised infantry got the better of crack cavalry that was also battle-hardened.[4] The Rohtas Fort was supposed to keep such a thing from happening again.

To do the job, Sher Shah appointed a young Hindu officer named Todar Mal Khatri of Laharpur in Avadh, who had first joined him as a clerk and then risen through the ranks quickly.[5] But when he went about looking for labourers to do the job, Todar Mal found that the Gakhars were unwilling to work for him. On his advice, Sher Shah increased the wages to one *rupiya* per stone laid—an inducement that was so irresistible that many of the Gakkhars came forward to work. They worked for their own oppression! But what started off with a *rupiya* per stone was very cleverly reduced bit by bit by Todar Mal

2 Ibid., p. 622.

3 Today, it falls under the Jhelum district of Pakistan's Punjab province.

4 Pradeep P. Barua, *The State at War in South Asia* (Lincoln and London: University of Nebraska Press, 2005), p. 27.

5 Syad Muhammad Khan Bahadur Latif, *Agra: Historical & Descriptive with an Account of Akbar and His Court and of the Modern City of Agra* (Calcutta: Calcutta Central Press Company, 1896), p. 281.

until it came down to 1/40th of a *rupiya.*[6] Indian people have been falling for the '*achhe din*' promise at various periods of history. It's not known if any of the labourers went on strike because of low pay, or even realised that they had been deceived so completely. But the end result was a magnificent fort and a stamp on the fiscal excellence of Todar Mal. His skills would be utilised later by that 12-year-old boy who was travelling with his father on his reconquest of Hindustan.

The Afghan garrison at Rohtas Fort was led by its governor Tatar Khan Khasi. Abu'l Fazl says Tatar Khan had a large force with him[7], but he fled 'merely on hearing of the appearing of the royal standards on the borders of the Indus'. Afghans everywhere started melting away. Upon reaching the Chenab, Humayun sent advance parties under various nobles to Haryana (Harhana, according to Abu'l Fazl) and Jallandhar to see the situation of the Afghans there and report back to him. He himself proceeded towards Lahore, the biggest city in Punjab and entered it amid a warm and rousing welcome on 24 February 1555. A Mughal emperor was back in the city 15 years after he had been ousted.

It was smooth sailing so far. But as February ended, the Afghans made some effort to fight back. At Dipalpur[8], an Afghan commander named Shahbaz Khan made plans to attack the Mughals. To intercept this force, Humayun sent a detachment under Sayyidzada Shah Abu'l Ma'ali. Jauhar says the force of the enemy was 12,000, while the Mughal force was of only had 800 cavalry.[9] Shahbaz Khan made a ferocious charge at the Mughals, which nearly unhorsed Abu'l Ma'ali. Jauhar records this in a matter-of-fact manner but Abu'l Fazl writes derisively about him—'The Sayyidzada Abu'l Ma'ali who was intoxicated with the world and proud of his beauty, got into difficulty but Ali Quli Khan and other heroes performed wonders.'[10]

---

6 Ibid.

7 *Akbarnama, Vol I*, p. 622.

8 In the Punjab province of Pakistan.

9 Jauhar Aftabchi, *Tazkirat ul-Waqiat,* tr. Major Charles Stewart as *The Tezkereh Al Vakiat, or Private Memoirs of the Mogul Emperor Humayun* (London: Oriental Translation Fund for Great Britain and Ireland, 1833), p. 113.

10 *Akbarnama, Vol I*, p. 624.

It would have been game over for this Mughal noble had it not been for an unknown Mughal soldier who, as Jauhar informs, 'placed a small drum on his head instead of a helmet' and dashed towards Shahbaz Khan with the war cry of '*Allahu Akbar*'. This charge was so furious that Shahbaz Khan was thrown off his horse. Seeing their commander fall, the Afghans fled the battlefield. It was the first victory of Humayun in India after his return, though Jauhar does attribute it (rightly) to luck as the force disparity was too big—a force ratio of 15:1 in the favour of the Afghans.

At Haryana, the Afghans under Nasib Khan gave battle to Bairam Khan and were defeated. But following strict orders of Humayun that upon entering India nobody would be made a slave, Bairam Khan sent the families of the defeated Afghans back to Nasib Khan under an armed escort. Earlier at Dipalpur also, the Mughals had released the Afghans captured in battle. Jauhar also shared an interesting incident of his liberating indentured peasants.[11] Humayun had appointed him as the revenue collector of the *pargana*[12] of Haibatpur. 'I found that it had been the custom of the Afghan farmers to give their wives or children in pledge to the Hindu bankers for money advanced on account of the collections,' Jauhar wrote, adding that he sold off grain hidden in dry wells and at other places, paid the Hindu bankers their debts, and liberated the peasant families.

With these acts of kindness, the Mughals won over the local populace. In an age when no quarter used to be given to the enemy, not even to his women and children, this was an enlightened move, though by no means unique. But the defeated who were spared only lived to fight on another day. As Humayun soon found out, the retreating Afghans under Nasib Khan joined up with other units commanded by Afghan commanders like Tatar Khan, Habil (or Haibat) Khan and Mubarak Khan. This now massively inflated army of 30,000 turned towards the Mughals near Sirhind.

Jauhar says at this point, Bairam Khan wrote to Humayun asking for further instructions. Humayun reprimanded him by saying, 'Have

11 Jauhar Aftabchi, *Tazkirat ul-Waqiat*, p. 113.

12 In Sher Shah's administration, the empire was divided into 47 *circars* or *sarkars*, and each *circar* was further divided into several parganas.

you not heard that my young general, Shah Abu'l Ma'ali, with only eight hundred horses, has defeated 12,000 of the enemy, why should you ask for further orders? Do as he did.'

Abu'l Fazl, however, mentions no such letter exchange, though he says that when Humayun learnt about Tatar Khan arriving with 'a large and well-equipped army, at Machhiwara (in today's Ludhiana), he remarked to a number of eager spirits that the place was a great distance off and that whatever the Divine Will intended would take place before they could arrive'. So Humayun chose to pray. The Mughals moved out from Jalandhar and proceeded towards Sirhind. It was May and monsoon wasn't far off. As the army reached the outskirts of the town of Machhiwara, many Mughal officers like Tardi Muhammad Khan advised against crossing the Sutlej as it was raining and the river was flowing angrily. They advised that it was better to camp there, secure all the boats, and cross after the monsoon had passed.

The Afghans stood on the other side of the river, 'puffed up with pride and self-sufficiency'.[13] Yet a similar hesitation seemed to have troubled Mughal ranks too. But Bairam Khan showed firmness of resolve and decisiveness. He overruled all naysayers in his camp and decided to cross the swollen river—a bold and significant move whose usefulness has been displayed multiple times in the annals of military history.

Back in 324 BC, Alexander of Macedon had crossed a swollen Hydaspes River (Ravi in Punjab) with his whole army during heavy rains even as the larger army of Porus stood on the other bank, confident in its belief that the enemy won't ford the river. And over 200 years after Bairam Khan crossed the Sutlej, an Afghan army under Ahmad Shah Abdali crossed the flooded Yamuna, trapping a Maratha army at Panipat in 1760.

His rival Tardi Beg Khan opposed Bairam Khan, but seeing the leader cross with his divisions, he and the rest of the army also followed suit. The Mughal army was then divided under four commands. Bairam Khan controlled the centre, Tardi Beg commanded the

13 Jauhar Aftabchi, *Tazkirat ul-Waqiat.*

left wing, Sikandar Khan Hazara commanded the right wing while his namesake, Sikandar Khan led the vanguard.

The Afghan army rolled forward to crush this comparatively smaller army.[14] It was evening when the two armies finally clashed. The battle raged on even though the darkness of the night set in. Abu'l Fazl talks about the exchange of arrows in complete darkness. But then, either by accident or on purpose[15], the Afghans set fire to a large village near their lines. If this was done by the Afghans to give themselves some strategic edge (wonder what), it proved to be counterproductive. The fire illuminated Afghan ranks and presented clearer target profiles for the Mughal archers who could now aim better.

Something similar had happened to the soldiers of the Red Army's 1st Belorussian Front of Marshal Georgi Zhukov at the battle of Seelow Heights in April 1945. The attack had begun in the predawn hours of 16 April after an hour-long massive Soviet artillery barrage. When the Soviet infantry advanced with their war cry of 'Urra', huge searchlights were turned on by the Soviets to see the enemy better. But because of the cloud of smoke that had still not lifted after the barrage, the light bounced back and blinded the infantry while highlighting their silhouettes for the entrenched 80,000 German infantry to target.[16] Thousands of Red Army soldiers perished at Seelow Heights.

The Afghans also suffered massively at Machhiwara, though we don't know just how many men they lost. Abu'l Fazl says after 'three watches in the night', the Afghans fled. And the Mughals captured immense booty, which was sent to the emperor in Lahore. Incidentally, the battle had happened on the same day that Humayun had got

---

14 We don't know the precise strength of the Mughal army. No record explicitly states it. But Jauhar records Bairam Khan writing to Humayun asking for more troops later when Sikander Shah Sur came with an army of 80,000 (a vastly exaggerated number). In that, Bairam says he only has 700 or 800 troops left and cannot take on such a vastly superior army. So, accounting for the losses at Machhiwara, one could guess that Bairam Khan must have had no more than 1,000 troops when he gave battle to the Afghans.

15 Jauhar says this was deliberately done by the fleeing Afghans to dissuade the Mughals from pursuing them, while Abu'l Fazl merely says it was 'wrought by the exertions of the enemy'.

16 David M. Glantz and Jonathan M. House, *When Titans Clashed: How The Red Army Stopped Hitler* (Kansas: University Press of Kansas, 2015), p. 334.

the news of the overwhelming odds and had gone into prayer, says Abu'l Fazl. This implies that there must have been no time for Bairam Khan to seek the emperor's directions before plunging into battle, as suggested by Jauhar. Bairam Khan, therefore, deserves more credit than he got, at least in the chroniclers' narratives.

This serious reverse resulted in Sikander Shah Sur coming down to Sirhind with a huge army of 80,000 (I suspect this figure is grossly inflated) cavalry. The Mughal chroniclers once again don't tell us the infantry strength of both sides. Even though Mughal armies or *lashkars* were primarily cavalry-based armies, the use of infantry was also fairly wide. Bairam Khan appealed to Humayun for help, for he only had up to 800 cavalry left with him and couldn't have possibly beaten a force ratio of 1:100 against him.

Bairam Khan, waiting for reinforcements, spruced up the defences of Sirhind fort. The Mughals didn't lose their nerve despite the odds stacked against them and waited for help to come from the rear. Humayun sent assurance of help and himself crossed the Sutlej and arrived at Sirhind on 29 May 1555. The total Mughal strength now was 5,000.[17] The force ratio now was 1:16 and still favoured the Afghans. Going by this alone, Humayun faced greater odds than that of his father at Panipat in 1526, who had a force ratio of 3:25 against him. But that was more than compensated for by the clever use of *taulqama*, musketeers protected by *wagon laagers* or *araba*, and the prized and unmatched Mughal heavy cavalry. Besides, Babur had a battle-hardened army as opposed to the Indo-Afghan agglomeration of various fighting groups that Ibrahim Lodhi had brought to the field.

Humayun also had a battle-hardened army with him. This army had brought to Sirhind a reputation of beating the Afghans at Dipalpur and Machhiwara. It had aggressive commanders willing to take risks and had led from the front. Nobody doubted Humayun's personal courage either. But this time, Humayun acted as a strategist and showed realism. He ordered his commanders to ensure that

---

17 Jauhar says in his *Tazkirat* that Sikander Shah Sur commented on the impetuosity of Humayun having come to give battle with just 5,000 troops against an 80,000-strong army.

the Afghan supply lines were severed. In this Humayun recalled his experience fighting against Sultan Bahadur Shah of Gujarat.

Tardi Beg, while engaged in this act of sabotage, had to skirmish with a brother of Sikander Shah. The brother was killed and his royal standards captured. This skirmishing went on for about a month when finally on 22 June 1555, both armies appeared in battle array. The Mughal army was divided into four parts—one led by Humayun and the other three by Bairam Khan, Shah Abu'l Ma'ali and Sikander Khan Uzbek. Abu'l Fazl, however, doesn't mention Sikander Khan and says the fourth part was led by the young Prince Akbar. Akbar may have been given nominal command, but it's unlikely that he wielded any real influence on the battle despite the florid flattery that Abu'l Fazl heaps on the young lad of 12. So, it's possible that Sikander Khan Uzbek was the real commander of this part of the army. The Afghans in full fury attacked Bairam Khan's front. Bairam held out firmly against this onslaught, absorbing the full weight of the attack. While this was on, a massive storm broke with rain. Humayun showed great tactical skill here and ordered Shah Abu'l Ma'ali and Tardi Beg to mount a pincer attack by wheeling around the Afghan rear. This was the standard *taulqama*.

The inclement weather and the flanking attacks by the Mughals demoralised the Afghans so much that they started to flee. Sikander Shah also withdrew seeing this and fled straight to the hills of north Punjab (the Shiwalik foothills of Himachal Pradesh today). The Mughals won another spectacular victory despite almost insurmountable odds. Abu'l Fazl rightly compared it to the victory of Babur at Panipat and said that was nothing like this victory.[18] But then he diluted his analysis by a sycophantic tribute to Prince Akbar and crediting the victory to him.

In fact, Fazl talks about a test that Humayun conducted among his people. 'In order to bring out the jewel of the sincere from the potsherd of service-sellers the question arose, in whose name should the proclamation of victory be recorded? An order was given that everyone should lay in his claim,' Fazl writes.

---

18 Fazl says, '...it wasn't like this present marvel.' *Akbarnama, Vol I*, p. 632.

Shah Abu'l Ma'ali, 'drunk with the wine of negligence', staked his claim. Bairam Khan staked his. Fazl writes:

> The farseeing and wise who knew that the victory was due to the felicity of His Majesty the Shahinshah (Akbar) and nursling of Divine light, opened their eyes and ears in surprised contemplation of the speakers, and the experienced and the just, knowing that this great victory which had shed its rays on the day assigned to the watch of the light of the garden of the *khilafat* was due to the presence of His Majesty the Shahinshah, were astonished at the utterances of those men (Abu'l Ma'ali and Bairam Khan).

Then he says that Humayun finally realised the truth and credited the victory to Akbar. In reality, it was an indolent father giving his son the credit as a gift to gladden his heart and perhaps to encourage him too. Many parents still name important things in their lives, say a new house or a new car, after their children. This was Humayun's way of doing it even though a neutral assessment makes it appear as a partisan act. Just like the boss' son becomes the vice-president of the company without any real experience but nobody from a whole board of directors with decades of fine work and experience gets a shot at it. Or just like Rahul Gandhi, the scion of the Nehru-Gandhi family, became the vice-president of the Indian National Congress (INC), arguably due to his being the son of the party president and a male member of what's often considered as the first family of the party.

But Abu'l Fazl provided an intellectual cover or a justification for this partisan act. These types of justifications still play out, minus the florid language, of course, in the Indian press and elsewhere, for various acts of the Narendra Modi regime and its leader. It's a tradition that has continued. So, when critics question, rightly or wrongly, the partisanship of certain sections of the press, they should perhaps also highlight how this is akin to the sycophancy of a 16th-century chronicler dependent on the benevolence and mercy of a medieval despot.[19]

19 I say in the introduction of this book that Indians are essentially medieval people. This is an elaboration of my argument.

With this victory at Sirhind, Punjab was secure for the Mughals. Humayun moved towards Delhi, leaving behind Shah Abu'l Ma'ali in Punjab to stop Sikander Shah Sur from doing any more mischief. However, instead of staying at Jalandhar and doing the job, Abu'l Ma'ali went to Lahore[20] and dismissed Farhat Khan, the Punjab governor. In his place, he put his own man while acting as the de facto governor himself. He soon started giving himself airs and went about acting independently of the imperial court. Both Jauhar and Abu'l Fazl attest this, though Fazl also adds the charge of misappropriation of imperial wealth.

This bad buzz soon reached Humayun's ears in Delhi. Fazl says the emperor refused to give credence to all that, thinking these were 'inventions of the envious and malignant'. But eventually, the reinstated emperor decided to depute his son, Prince Akbar, as the Punjab governor under the guidance of Bairam Khan, by now the *Khan-i-Khanan* or premier noble of the empire and *ataliq* or guardian to Akbar. The idea was pretty much to clip Shah Abu'l Ma'ali's wings and do something substantial to stop Sikander Shah who was learnt to have come out of the hills with a new army and who could pose a threat to the Mughal rear. But this was done with tactful firmness and shows Humayun's sagacity. Abu'l Ma'ali was a favourite of the emperor and he didn't want to unceremoniously remove him. So Bairam Khan was advised to see if Abu'l Ma'ali could be compensated by giving him the governorship of Hisar whose governor was Akbar.

This was a sensible thing to do without ruffling too many feathers. The king publicly showed that he still hadn't lost faith in his favourite noble; privately, he chose to replace him. At the same time, he gave this most important governorship to his son, thereby asserting imperial authority without any accompanying arrogance as Akbar was still put under the tutelage of Bairam Khan.

When Akbar and Bairam Khan reached Sirhind, a number of generals serving with Shah Abu'l Ma'ali left him and joined the

20 Lahore remained the capital of Punjab until the Partition in 1947. The new Indian state of Punjab had Jalandhar as its capital for a while until a new capital city was built at Chandigarh. Lahore, meanwhile, continues to be the capital of the Pakistani province of Punjab.

prince with their contingents. This seriously weakened Abu'l Ma'ali's position. Bairam Khan also sent him a letter, asking him to proceed to Delhi and meet Emperor Humayun. Sensing that things were going against him, Shah Abu'l Ma'ali wrote to the emperor that his chiefs had betrayed him and poisoned the emperor's ears against him. He submitted that he had severely weakened Sikander Shah's war-making potential and had almost captured him when his commanders deserted him. He wrote a separate letter to Bairam Khan, telling him that the enemy had been weakened and cornered and that the imperial forces under him and Akbar must conduct mopping-up operations.

Akbar and Bairam Khan proceeded towards Kalanaur where they camped. Meanwhile, Abul Ma'ali came there from Lahore and decided to stop for two days to meet the *Khan-i-Khanan* and the prince. That's when they received the bad news from Delhi—the emperor was dead.

Abu'l Fazl wrote that Humayun had been talking about death, about 'departing to the world of holiness' ever since Akbar left for Punjab. Fazl said this was contrary to his nature, as he had a 'laudable habit of regarding such references as unbecoming'.[21] But he would have conversations about his father Babur and say that Babur felt like dying whenever he saw the graves (of holy men) in Ghazni, and that he had the exact same feeling after visiting the various tombs and shrines in Delhi.

Humayun was increasingly becoming superstitious with a fatalistic resignation to fate. Fazl noted another unusual thing—the emperor even reduced his opium intake, something he was so fond of. As I had said in the previous chapter, Humayun was a lord of premonition, he probably was feeling something. One hears such tales even today: an old aunt who remembers her grandma predicting her death, or a family friend who talks about some former colleague who claimed he would die soon and passed away the next morning due to a heart attack. My paternal grandma started saying that she would die soon about two months before her death. So Humayun, a man fond of stargazing, may have just felt that his days were numbered.

21 *Akbarnama, Vol I*, p. 652.

On Friday, 24 January 1556, he asked for his mathematicians for he had heard Venus would rise that night. He wanted to know the precise timing, for he intended to use that 'auspicious occasion' to make some announcements about promotions among his officers. Towards evening, he came down from his study[22] when he heard the muezzin named Miskeen[23] give the call for prayer.[24] Abu'l Fazl says it was a wrong call, but out of deference to the Lord in whose name the call was made, the devout Humayun bent down on the staircase to pray. While doing so, his foot got caught in his robe and he tripped and came crashing down. His right temple was badly hurt and blood started oozing out of his right ear.

The terribly injured emperor breathed his last on the third day of the incident, on Monday, 27 January 1556. He was 48. A messenger was immediately despatched to Kalanaur even as the royal family and its loyalists tried every means to conceal the news of the emperor's death. Regular affairs of the household continued as usual, as did matters of the court. Even alms were given to beggars in the emperor's name to keep up the pretence that he was still pretty much alive and well. This was continued for 17 days even though the dead emperor was quietly buried on the banks of the Yamuna.

This was done for a reason: the hold of the Mughals on their newly recaptured territories was still tenuous. There were still many battles to fight, many rebellions to put down, many heads to crush. Sikander Shah was entrenched in Mankot in Punjab, still posing a threat to the Mughals, while Ibrahim Adil Shah's vizier, Hemu, was fighting his master's rivals for another shot at the throne of Delhi. The loyalty of many a Mughal nobleman was also suspect. So, it was important to hush things up till the time Akbar was proclaimed the

---

22 Historians and archaeologists agree that the building in question is the Sher Mandal pavilion that still survives, largely intact, at the Purana Qila in Delhi. The stacks of niches on the walls of the second-floor chamber suggests these were used to store books, and therefore the chamber must have been a study-cum-office of the emperor.

23 *Miskeen* in Arabic means 'poor'. Either this was the actual name of the muezzin or that's how he was known because he was a poor man.

24 In all likelihood, the mosque was the Qila-i-Kuhna Masjid built by Sher Shah, which still stands not very far from Sher Mandal and within the Purana Qila complex.

successor of Humayun and emperor; and he was on 11 February 1556 in Delhi. The first official *khutba* was read in the name of Jalaluddin Muhammad Akbar. Three days later, on 14 February, at a hurriedly conducted ceremony on a hastily constructed platform at Kalanaur[25], Akbar was seated on a replica of a *masnad* or the royal throne and officially coronated as the emperor of Hindustan. He was just 13. Had she been alive then, Khanzada Begum, who on seeing the baby Akbar for the first time had remarked that his hands and feet were like her brother Babur's when he was a baby, would have surely spotted the similarity of the fate of Akbar and his grandfather. Babur's father, Umar Shaikh Mirza, had died in a freak accident when a rampart of his palace at Ferghana had given way while he was feeding pigeons. Babur was only 11 when he succeeded his father. The little orphaned boy had to wipe away his tears, act like a 'man' and quickly grow up to become a king of his people. The same fate had befallen Akbar, who was anointed on the day Babur was born. And just like Babur's grip on power was weak when he was crowned king, Akbar was in great peril with his father suddenly gone, his mother in Kabul, and he in the middle of a war with only a few close attendants and his guardian, Bairam Khan, around him. But Bairam Khan rose to the occasion, and for that, he hasn't been sufficiently credited by both Mughal chroniclers and history.

Bairam Khan understood the gravity of the situation well. So, he acted with a firm resolve not to allow any opposition to Akbar's succession. One of the first things he did was to send his trusted officer, Pir Muhammad Khan Shirwani, to the Shiwalik region in pursuit of Sikander Shah Sur. But there was another reason for this—it was to stop any news of Humayun's death from getting out.

In court, Bairam Khan showed similar resolve. All the top nobles were bound to show up and pay obeisance to the new emperor. By and large, everyone did but not Shah Abu'l Ma'ali. He gave different excuses for not showing up, like still mourning the dead emperor, not being sure of how the boy emperor would treat him, not being sure where he would sit and how the royal officers would receive

25 It's in Gurdaspur district, Punjab today.

him, etc. These were clearly, as Bairam rightly understood, vague reasons to conceal Abu'l Ma'ali's non-recognition of Akbar's authority.

Badaoni and Abu'l Fazl are on the same page when talking about this nobleman. Badaoni simply states, 'This man was a dullard.' Fazl elaborates on it in his grandiloquent prose, which at times is quite hilarious to read. He writes:

> As the fumes of madness were circulating in the head of that firebrand, and the cap-peak of his understanding had been set awry by the wind of arrogance, the notes of seditious thoughts became visible, and disaffected imaginings came forth from behind their veil.[26]

Yet Bairam kept on requesting him to come to court. On the third day after accession, a grand assembly was called and Abu'l Ma'ali was requested again to come. With an early history of flattery on the part of Bairam Khan[27] to be in the good books of Abu'l Ma'ali, this nobleman from Kashgar perhaps took it as some sort of genuflection on the part of Bairam Khan and the emperor, and acquiesced. He didn't imagine what awaited him at court.

A Mughal painting from the illustrated volumes of *Akbarnama* designed by Basawan and painted by Shankar portrays the court scene upon the arrival of Shah Abu'l Ma'ali. Badaoni tells us that Bairam Khan had plotted to arrest the noble and ordered one particularly

---

26 *Akbarnama, Vol II*, p. 28.

27 While in Kandahar, Abu'l Ma'ali had killed a Shia courtier. Badaoni says in his *Muntakhab ut-Tawarikh* that he was drunk and killed this man in his bigotry. When the family of this noble approached Humayun for justice, Abu'l Ma'ali was summoned. He came dressed in a dead man's robe, carrying the weapon under the robe, and denied his guilt. He was still drunk. Bairam Khan, who was blessed with the ability to create verse on the spot, composed a short verse on Ma'ali's appearance:

His dishevelled locks of hair
To-night debauch confess
Lo! A blazing proof is there
The lamp beneath his dress

Humayun was delighted to hear this and didn't punish the offender, also because the murder was never found out. Badaoni writes, '…but the blood of that innocent one was hidden in the dust, and his murder was never proved.'

strong officer named Tulaq Khan Qurchi[28] to do the job. Badaoni writes that Qurchi 'appeared like a spider's web (ready to catch a fly)'. 'In accordance with a preconcerted plan, (Qurchi) went unseen behind Abu'l Ma'ali and took him prisoner, and asked to be allowed to blot out his name from the tablet of existence,' Badaoni writes.

But Akbar spared his life, saying that it would portend ill for his reign if he started his day of accession by shedding the blood of a possibly innocent man. Abu'l Fazl, writing the *Akbarnama* in the 1590s, gave an elaborate reason for this. He wrote:

> In the institutes of sovereignty, and canons of justice, binding and imprisoning are commended for this reason that a trial should be made of ill-fated and contentious people. For man is a strange talisman, and a riddle hard of interpretation. It is not right to send him to the abode of non-existence for one displeasing act which he may exhibit, for this lofty foundation cannot be rebuilt except by the hand of Gods power. Therefore, wise administrators have not approved of haste in demolishing and annihilating this high palace. (This bit in verse) For the head of the slain cannot be joined on again.

This was amazingly forward-looking and merciful, given the age of wrath that India had been experiencing at the time. But then one must remember that Fazl wrote this in the 1590s when the empire was already secure and most of Akbar's tolerant policies had become the norm. But at that time, Akbar wasn't what he became in the 1590s. He was 13 and someone not very interested in matters of state policy and administration.

Akbar packed Abu'l Ma'ali off to Lahore in chains for imprisonment. The *kotwal*[29] of Lahore was called Pahlwan Gulgaz. The *kotwal* was careless, Fazl says, and his prisoner escaped. Gulgaz was imprisoned,

---

28 Abu'l Fazl calls him Tolaq Khan Qucin and says he was strong and nimble.

29 There is no modern equivalent of this post in the Mughal administration but could be roughly equated with a superintendent of police. In most parts of North India, including Delhi, police stations are still called *kotwali*. And since *kot* in Hindustani means a fort, it is generally understood that a *kotwal* was in charge of security of a walled city. He shouldn't be confused with a *qiladar*, who would be a military officer in charge of a fort's garrison.

and he, fearing disgrace, committed suicide. Abu'l Ma'ali went to Kamal Khan Gakhar, nephew of Adam Gakhar who was loyal to the Mughals even when the Sur Afghans held their sway. They together went off to invade Kashmir where they had a serious reverse.

The two split and Abu'l Ma'ali lived in disguise for a while before being caught and imprisoned again. He was sent off to Mecca from where he would return again to create mischief, or in Abu'l Fazl's words, 'strife and sedition'.

While all this was happening, Hemu was marching towards Delhi, steamrolling every opposition that came his way, to occupy the power vacuum he thought had been created by Humayun's passing and the escape of Sikander Shah Sur to Himachal.[30] And having won 22 battles, his fearsome reputation preceded him. He set out for Delhi with a huge force of 50,000 cavalry, 1,000 elephants, 51 cannon, and 500 *falconets*.[31] This alone suggests that it was a terrifyingly potent force with immense firepower, far greater than Babur had at Panipat in 1526. It had been only 30 years since then and already, Mughals no longer had the monopoly over field artillery.

Mughal garrisons at Bayana, Etawah, Sambhal and Agra capitulated and fled. Sensing the approaching menace, Tardi Beg, who was in charge of Delhi, wrote to the emperor in Jalandhar asking for reinforcements. Bairam Khan, now the Vakil us Sultanate or Prime Minister of the empire, understood Tardi Beg's predicament and immediately despatched his trusted commander, Pir Muhammad Khan Shirwani, with a force to bolster the defences of Delhi. Meanwhile, another trusted Mughal general, Ali Quli Khan, who was fighting in Sambhal, was asked by Tardi Beg to return to Delhi as fast as he could.

---

30 Abu'l Fazl actually uses this word for the Siwalik region in *Akbarnama, Vol II,* p. 31. This suggests the name Himachal must have been in circulation for quite some time and that the state of Himachal Pradesh today didn't get its name for nothing. But what's intriguing is that H. Beveridge, while translating it in 1907, says in a footnote that the name Himachal is no longer used for the region.

31 *Akbarnama, Vol II,* p. 49. A *falconet* was a light field artillery piece that ranged from 1-pounders to 6-pounders. Even though the name 'cannon' is now used commonly, up to the 18th century, it denoted only a particular type of heavy gun that ranged from 42-pounders and above. That Hemu had 51 cannons alone suggests that kind of firepower he had that could blow an opposition to smithereens.

Amid all this, Hemu moved into Delhi and camped at Tughlaqabad on 6 October 1556. The Mughal generals were divided on whether to attack Hemu or wait for Ali Quli Khan to bring up reinforcements. Many didn't quite have the stomach to take on that huge army; others thought it was better to wait out the siege inside the impregnable walls of Dinpanah Fort (today's Purana Qila in Delhi). And yet some who were brimming with bravado but also experiencing a certain kind of fatalism thought it was better to fight and die a glorious death in battle.

Tardi Beg was a clever man. He always found himself on the winning side, even deserting his master Humayun when he needed him the most. He wouldn't risk it at all in fighting unequal contests, as his reticence in the Battle of Machhiwara showed. Yet Tardi Beg decided to give battle to Hemu.

On 7 October 1556, the two armies clashed near Tughlaqabad. The Mughals were fairly outnumbered going by the descriptions given by Abu'l Fazl and Badaoni, yet the Mughal troop strength isn't known. But Sir Jadunath Sarkar says the Mughal army had to battle against tremendous odds.[32]

The Mughal army was drawn up in their traditional manner: a centre, left wing, right wing and a vanguard. Tardi Beg himself stayed at the centre while Haidar Muhammad commanded the right wing and Iskandar Beg the left. The vanguard was led by Abdullah Uzbek. None of the contemporary accounts talk about the role of artillery in this battle. Hemu seems to have had a brute superiority in firepower but how he managed to bear its weight on the battle, if at all, is not known. It's therefore obvious that artillery played no major role in this. But cavalry did. Hemu's elephant corps did. Initially, the Mughal vanguard and left wing[33] overwhelmed Hemu's van and right wing. About 3,000 enemy soldiers were killed, including a prominent

32 Jadunath Sarkar, *Military History of India* (Calcutta: Orient Longmans, 1960), p. 67.

33 Badaoni incorrectly mentions in his *Tawarikh*, p. 6, that Abdullah Uzbek and the Mughal right wing smashed the enemy in front of them and pursued the hostiles as far as Palwal (in Haryana today). I have chosen to go ahead with Abu'l Fazl's version (*Akbarnama, Vol. II*, p. 48), which Sir Jadunath Sarkar also thought right in *Military History of India*, p. 67.

Afghan commander Rai Husain Jalwani, and 400 war elephants were captured by the Mughals. Abu'l Fazl praises this cavalry action in his typical florid language: 'Their deeds and valour were such that the souls of Rustam and Isfandiyar sang their praises, and that the voice of the age and of mankind extolled them a thousand times.'[34] But the battle wasn't over yet. The Mughals, thinking that they had crushed Hemu's forces, started looting the enemy camp even as a big chunk of their troops went in pursuit of the enemy up to Palwal. Tardi Beg was still at the centre, but his guard had thinned. And this was the moment that Hemu seized. With 300 elephants and a select body of troops, Hemu charged at the Mughal centre. This attack took the Mughals by surprise, so much so that many commanders started to flee. Without waiting to see which way the tide turned, Pir Muhammad Khan Shirwani, sent by Bairam Khan to firm up the Delhi forces, bolted. This had a domino effect on everyone else—soon the Mughal ranks melted away and their commander, Tardi Beg, galloped away towards Punjab.

Hemu, incidentally, thought this was some ruse being played by the Mughals so he didn't pursue the fleeing host in front of him. When the Mughal troops who had gone in pursuit of the enemy returned, they saw that their lines no longer existed and the enemy had set up camp there. They didn't continue their pointless resistance and left. Hemu, once again, let them go unmolested. Hemu's conduct was very wise. He had seen the Mughals fight and how his right wing was crushed by the famed Turkic cavalry and didn't want to risk annihilation of his army by sending them out in penny packets to engage the fleeing enemy. Mughal archers, coming from Central Asia, were adept at the Parthian shot.[35] And coupled with their *taulqama* art of fighting, they were a formidable foe even when badly outnumbered.

As Hemu entered Delhi, he abandoned the pretence of acting on behalf of the Afghan king and assumed the title of Hemachandra

34 *Akbarnama, Vol. II*, p. 48.

35 A light cavalry tactic where mounted archers feign retreat, but when chased by enemy cavalry, turn their bodies back and fire arrows. The name owes its origin to archers of the Parthian Empire who destroyed a Roman army commanded by Marcus Linius Crassus at the Battle of Carrhae in 53 BC.

Vikramaditya or Hemaraja Bikramjit. This was, really, the crowning glory for a man of humble origins, who had started off as a grocer and then joined Afghan service as a clerk. One doesn't get too many instances of someone rising through the ranks like this in the early modern period, or even later. Also, given the fact that this was long before 'affirmative action' as a concept was even born, a Hindu *vaishya* becoming a military general and even sitting on the throne was rare.

Hemu rewarded his troops and generals lavishly, even as the news of the Mughal defeat—an 'unnatural occurrence', according to Abu'l Fazl—reached Akbar at Jalandhar. He immediately set out to recover Delhi and issued *firmans* to the defeated commanders, including Tardi Beg, not to lose heart and stand firm. But Bairam Khan wasn't so generous. At Sirhind, where Akbar set up camp, Tardi Beg arrived seeking forgiveness. Bairam Khan, acting on his own, invited the runaway general to his own camp and had him treacherously murdered. Bairam later got it sanctioned by the emperor. While mentioning the rivalry between Bairam Khan and Tardi Beg, Fazl gives religion as the reason for mistrust between the two (Bairam was a Shia and Tardi Beg a Sunni), which, though not improbable, appears unlikely. Bairam's conduct at Shah Tahmasp's court, where he argued for his own Sunni monarch, putting his life in peril, should show this charge to be very superficial.

Earlier in the narrative, Fazl also gives a sort of intellectual justification for the murder of Tardi Beg and hinges it on Tardi Beg's cowardice and past sins of abandoning his master Humayun when he needed him the most. Fazl writes:

> ...it has been proved by a succession of utterances by sages, and is abundantly clear, that a runaway receives more wounds than the brave man who endures the stress of battle, and that lovers of their live and fliers from death are trampled upon by the forces of destruction sooner than those who covet death and are intrepid in fight. If a man will exercise a little moderation, and not show the depression in time of adversity, or intoxication in time of prosperity, he will never see an evil day.

Standards for bravery and loyalty in our popular imagination haven't changed even in modern times.

During the Battle of Stalingrad during the Second World War, the German 6th Army under Friedrich Paulus was not allowed to withdraw and regroup by Adolf Hitler, who was bent on taking that beleaguered fortress of a city. The last hopeless bid to rescue the trapped army was made by a relief force under Generalfeldmarschall Erich von Manstein. But the Red Army closed the ring around the city, making any hope of escape futile. Hitler promoted Paulus to the rank of generalfeldmarschall in the hope that he would shoot himself instead of getting captured. Paulus didn't and surrendered instead. The Nazis declared him a traitor, and long after the war got over, Paulus was still identified as a traitor by the German people, and even von Manstein made it appear in his memoirs later that Paulus hadn't acted on his order to break out of the siege.

Before that, the German general Heinz Guderian was fired by Hitler for withdrawing from outside Moscow in December 1941. And so was General (later Field Marshal) Claude Auchinleck, who was fired by Winston Churchill as he thought Auchinleck (or 'the Auk' to his troops) had withdrawn far too much at El Alamein. That's so much about withdrawal being taboo in all ages. But it often happens that whenever any retreat or humiliating defeat occurs, someone is always made the fall guy. For the Stalingrad debacle, Paulus was made the fall guy by Manstein. Even though Paulus had sought permission to attempt a breakout when Soviet pincers were gradually closing around him, Hitler had expressly forbidden it. Hitler's refusal was backed by the Luftwaffe's assurance that it could supply the 6th Army by air and Manstein being in agreement with Hitler that he could relieve the besieged troops with his new Army Group Don.

As late as mid-November in 1942, Manstein wasn't keen on Paulus withdrawing when it actually made sense for the 6th Army to attempt a breakout. But Manstein later wrote in his *Lost Victories*:

> When General Paulus let the last opportunity slip, when he hesitated and finally decided against the venture, he certainly did so on account

> of the responsibility he felt on his own shoulders. Although the Army Group strove by its order to absolve him of that responsibility, he still felt unable to acquit himself of it, either vis-à-vis Hitler or before his own conscience.[36]

Paulus was made the fall guy. In Tardi Beg's case, too, Bairam Khan made him the fall guy even though the general opinion—even when Abu'l Fazl was writing the *Akbarnama* in the 1590s—was that it was Pir Muhammad Khan Shirwani, his right-hand man, who was actually to be blamed.

Historians are divided on Bairam Khan's motives. Some say it was due to the rivalry between an Irani and a Turani, a Shia and a Sunni, or just between two generals competing for the right to be the closest to the king. Some, like Abu'l Fazl, also try to justify Bairam's act in other ways. They say Bairam Khan wanted to keep the flock together and quell any challenge to the young emperor's authority. So, it was necessary to make an example of Tardi Beg, who was a very senior noble from the time of Emperor Babur.

Whether Bairam Khan had that in mind or something else is now a matter of speculation, but the execution of Tardi Beg had the desired result. The Mughal generals were stunned by the act and fell in line. All of them. At any age, execution of generals or commanders has always had a psychological impact on others. And that impact either led to demoralisation of troops or galvanised them into a more potent force. We can see this in the case of both the Wehrmacht and the Red Army during the Second World War. In Stalin's purges of 1937–39 and again in 1941 in the Red Army resulted in the destruction of the officer corps. Three of the five field marshals, including the very talented Marshal Mikhail Tukhachevsky, were executed and many others at every command level down to the battalion level were purged.

The second round of purges affected the Soviet Navy and the Red Air Force apart from the Red Army. This affected the overall combat

---

36 John F. Richards, *The New Cambridge History of India: The Mughal Empire* (Cambridge: Cambridge University Press, 1993), p. 13.

preparedness of the armed forces, which suffered very heavily when Germany invaded the Soviet Union on 22 June 1941. Outgunned and outmanoeuvred, even outwitted, the relatively inexperienced commanders thrust into leadership positions due to the sudden vacuum created at the top due to the purges performed rather poorly. Courage was never a problem, the experience was. Under pressure from the Stavka as well as political commissars and NKVD units, these Red Army commanders undertook futile retaliatory attacks leading to greater disasters. During the Battle of Moscow alone, 300 Soviet commanders were executed. This led to a joke in the western world that suicide was a sensible career move in the armed forces of the Soviet Union.

However, such summary executions also terrorised other Soviet commanders and troops who fought like possessed men even in hopeless situations. In fact, the Germans knew this and had ordered to summarily execute the commissars whenever they were caught. The Red Army's eventual victory came at a tremendous cost of life.

In the case of the Wehrmacht, this worked the other way. In the First World War, the Imperial German Army or Deutsches Heer had carried out only 11 executions of troops for desertion or cowardice/dereliction of duty. In the Second World War, the Wehrmacht carried out over 30,000 executions of its own troops. This included 88 general officers. This, however, didn't really have the desired effect.

One of the generals who carried out the maximum number of such executions was Field Marshal Ferdinand Schorner, a fanatical Nazi. In the final days of the war in 1945, while ordering thousands of executions for desertions and 'cowardice', Schorner himself fled Czechoslovakia by air and reached Austria where he was arrested by the Americans and later handed over to the Soviets. His troops, even without their commander, kept at their futile resistance against the Red Army.

Tardi Beg's execution had a sobering effect on other Mughal generals whose loyalty was tenuous. This coupled with Bairam Khan's missive to all officers and men made them realise that they really had nowhere to go if they were ousted from India again. They all girded loins to take on the might of Hemu and the entire Mughal camp moved towards Panipat. Time had brought the Mughals to the same juncture where they had arrived 30 years earlier. And the same place.

As Hemu received news of the coming of the Mughals, he sent an advanced guard with his artillery park under the command of his chief officers, Mubarak Khan and Bahadur Khan. He himself followed later.

When the Mughals learnt that Hemu's advanced guard had come to Panipat town, they sent a well-equipped force of battle-hardened warriors to engage the enemy. By using fighting skills as well as ruse[37], the Mughal force managed to stun the Afghans who fled the field without a fight, leaving all their guns behind. This was a major loss for Hemu. A modern army can perhaps not even imagine losing its guns before a fight. But even back in 16th century India, artillery was shaping up as a battle-winning arm.

Twelve years before Babur clashed with Ibrahim Lodhi at Panipat, two of the greatest empires in Asia to the west of India—the Ottoman and Safavid empires—had fought a huge and a rather decisive battle at Chaldiran in modern day West Azerbaijan province of Iran. The Ottomans under Sultan Selim I had something that Shah Ismail of Safavid Persia didn't have—gunpowder weapons. Fought on 23 August 1514, the Ottomans literally blew away the Persians with their cannon and *arquebuses.*[38]

The Ottomans put their Janissary musketeers behind *wagon laagers*, which the Safavid cavalry couldn't overwhelm. The Persians were smashed and Shah Ismail himself was injured and had to be evacuated. The defeat became even more humiliating as the Persian emperor's entire harem, including two wives, were captured by the Turks. This battle stymied the personal fortune of Shah Ismail, but it led to the Persians adopting firearms and developing tactics to go with them. Thirty years later, they had enough firepower to help Humayun

37 '...and the masterful ghazis, who were backed by the Shahinshah's fortune, added feline skill to the deeds of tigers,' Abu'l Fazl writes in the *Akbarnama, Vol. II*, p. 59. Feline skill implies the use of ruse.

38 Jos Gommans and Dirk Kolf, *Warfare and Weaponry in South Asia, 1000–1800* (New Delhi: Oxford University Press, 2001), p. 139.

mount a campaign to recover his empire. But one man who had learnt lessons from Chaldiran was Babur.

Only four years before Chaldiran, in 1510, Shah Ismail had defeated Shaibani Khan Uzbek, Babur's nemesis in his Timurid homeland and to whom he had lost Samarqand in 1501. The Shah had reunited Babur with his sister Khanzada Begum, whom Shaibani Khan had forcibly married, and also gifted him a bejewelled drinking cup made from the skull of the Uzbek chief.

Babur had developed good relations with the Shah and accepted his overlordship too. In fact, the Persians had helped Babur capture Samarqand again in 1513. But Babur once again lost it to the Uzbeks. This time, he had also lost the support of the otherwise sophisticated people of Samarqand who saw him as their legitimate king being a direct descendant of Amir Timur. This was because Babur had overtly patronised the Shiite faith and himself adopted symbols associated with the Safavids like the Qizilbash[39] headgear in a staunchly Sunni realm where the stories of the horrifying persecution of Sunnis by the new Shiite Persian empire were by then reasonably extant.[40]

In 1514, Babur had returned to Kabul a defeated man when he learnt about the disaster at Chaldiran. How could the all-powerful Persians be defeated by the Turks? This question must have bothered everyone East of the Safavid Empire. Even Babur. And why not, for Ismail Safavi, leader of a school of Sufism called the Safaviyya *tariqa* or order, had turned his religio-spiritual lineage into a martial legacy by founding a new dynasty and a new empire at Tabriz in 1501, the year Babur was ousted from Samarqand.

---

39 Central Asian Turks who were followers of the Persian Shah in the *Pir-o-Murshid* tradition.

40 'The news of Shah Ismail's ferocious persecution and killing of Sunni Muslims as he extended his control over the Iranian plateau between 1501 and 1510 must have been generally known in Mawarannahr. More particularly, his murder of Sunni leaders in Harat who refused to accept Shiism in December 1510 or January 1511, had undoubtedly reached Samarqand by this time. The fact that the Iranian Shah attacked the Naqshbandi sufi order with special ferocity must have intensified their revulsion for the intolerant Shia monarch,' writes Stephen F. Dale in his *The Garden of the Eight Paradises: Babur and the Culture of Empire in Central Asia, Afghanistan and India, 1483–1530*, p. 242.

Right up to Chaldiran, Shah Ismail had managed to create an aura of invincibility around him. In fact, in 1501, Shah Ismail had started his empire by defeating the Aq Quyunlu, a Turkmen tribal federation that ruled over what is today eastern Anatolia, Iraq, Iran and Azerbaijan. The Aq Quyunlu were adversaries of the Ottomans. And since the Venetians were enemies of the Ottomans, so Venice had been arming the Aq Quyunlu with firearms since the late 15th century[41] going by the 'enemy's enemy is friend' dictum. Strangely enough, though, the Aq Quyunlu couldn't bring about the weight of their guns to bear on the enemy that didn't have any artillery. The federation folded up after suffering a series of reverses at the hands of Shah Ismail, and its territories became part of the Safavid Empire.

What's even lesser known is the fact that Venetian guns even found their way into the southern coast of India. We know about the Zamorin of Calicut fielding five Venetian artillery pieces on the shore during the Second Siege of Cochin in 1504. The Zamorin had an army of 80,000 infantry[42] and a naval arm comprising 160 vessels of various sizes taking on a tiny Portuguese fleet of five ships armed with cannon. The Zamorin had many other guns, but these were locally made ones notorious for lack of range and accuracy. Against disciplined Portuguese naval gunnery, these were completely useless. But the Portuguese fleet had recognised the threat from the five Venetian cannon, which its gun crews targeted to render out of action. Perhaps an experienced European artillery crew would have serviced the guns better and given a tough time to the Portuguese. But the Zamorin's Indian gun crews didn't show any experience or understanding of the power of their weapons. The Zamorin, despite his brute superiority in men and material, was smashed at Cochin by the Portuguese. And yet nobody seemed to have learnt any lesson from this disaster.

Chaldiran happened 10 years after Cochin. And while Shah Ismail's aura was dented, he and everybody else learnt an important lesson—

41 Stephen F. Dale, *The Garden of the Eight Paradises: Babur and the Culture of Empire in Central Asia, Afghanistan and India, 1483–1530* (Leiden, Boston: Brill, 2004), p. 294.

42 These high figures should always be taken with a bit of salt as exaggeration was the order of the day. William Irvine who wrote *Army of the Moghuls* says it's a problem peculiar to the Orient.

gunpowder artillery was the new god of war. The Persians quickly modernised and so did other small and big players in Central Asia. In India, the Zamorin also learnt his lessons fast. The Italian traveller Ludovico di Varthema, who came to Calicut in 1506, found Portuguese deserters making for the Zamorin various types of artillery guns and also teaching the local gunsmiths the art of making European guns.[43]

Babur was also modernising his army. He managed to reach out to Ottoman artillery officers to make him guns and teach him and his men how to use them. The two Turkish men who would be pivotal in this were Ustad Ali Quli Khan and Mustafa Khan. Ustad Ali Quli may have been a participant at Chaldiran[44], and was much more than an artillery officer. He was the chief gun-caster, chief gunner, chief firearms strategist—all rolled into one. His closest counterpart in the contemporary British military was the Master of Ordnance though the latter would have more responsibilities and a wider field of operation. However, by the time Humayun became emperor, it would be another Ottoman officer, Rumi Khan, who would get greater responsibilities akin to the British chief of ordnance as *Mir-i-Atish* or minister of ordnance.

But at Panipat in 1526, it would be Ustad Ali Quli who would implement the lessons of Chaldiran. Babur says in his memoirs that it was Ali Quli who organised his lines in the Rumi (from Rum or Istanbul, which before the Islamic conquest of 1483 was Constantinople, the capital of the Eastern Roman Empire) fashion. The same strategy would also be adopted a year later at Khanwa in 1527, but for that battle, the *wagon laagers* were prepared and arranged by Mustafa Khan. Babur also writes that Ali Quli was jealous of this Rumi officer, but doesn't really elaborate on it.[45] It could be a healthy professional rivalry that had no bearing on their performance in battle.

43 Iqtidar Alam Khan, *Gunpowder and Firearms: Warfare in Medieval India* (New Delhi: Oxford University Press, 2004), p. 61.

44 Annette S. Beveridge in her translation of the *Baburnama* writes this on page 469 of the second volume: 'These Ottoman (Rumi) defences Ustad 'Ali-quli may have seen at the battle of Chaldiran fought some 40 leagues from Tabriz between SI. Salim Rumi and Shah Isma'il Safawl on Rajab 1st 920 ah. (Aug. 22nd 1514 ad.).'

45 'Mustafa Rumi had the carts made in the Rumi way, excellent carts, very strong and suitable. As Ustad Ali-quli was jealous of him, Mustafa was posted to the right, in front of Humayun.' This is mentioned in *Baburnama,* tr. Beveridge, *Vol II*, p. 550.

However, with all this superb organisation, it seems it was Babur's cavalry that played a decisive role in the first Panipat battle. Particularly his Mongol archers, who deftly executed the *taulqama* tactics. Artillery didn't play much of a role in that battle. Babur mentions three types of gunpowder artillery in his possession while in India: the *kazan, zarb-zan* and *firingi*. The *kazan* was a mortar, the *firingi* a culverin (a medium calibre cannon), and the *zarb-zan* a light artillery piece like a *falconet*. Apart from these, there were the *tufangs*, which were matchlock muskets. At Panipat, Babur used the *firingi* and *zarb-zan* but he only says his *firingilar* (plural, suggesting more than one) fired a few times and his *zarb-zanan* (plural again, suggesting several in use) got a few good shots.[46] Eventually, being hit by artillery, musketry and archery, the Afghans at Panipat had become a confused mass concentrated in the centre.[47] That's when Babur unleashed his heavy cavalry to mop-up the enemy. His grandson 30 years later would also use his mounted archers well in the killing field of Panipat. But despite capturing Hemu's artillery before the battle, the Mughals would, rather strangely, not use them in battle.[48]

The only fireworks that the Mughals indulged in was before the battle when Akbar started from Jalandhar to give battle to Hemu. To lift the morale of the troops, a royal order was given to the *Mir-i-Atish* to prepare a pyrotechnic display. An image of Hemu was prepared and filled with gunpowder. This particular contraption was called *gulzar-i-atish* or 'rose garden of fire'. It was lit much to the enjoyment of everyone present. Abu'l Fazl gives the symbolism behind it—'In appearance it was simply keen amusement, in reality, it was extinguishing a malevolent life.[49] This incident offers a glimpse into the ideological nature of Akbar's empire. An enemy had to be

46 Stephen F. Dale, *The Garden of the Eight Paradises,* p. 329.

47 'Once or twice the enemy tried halfhearted assaults in the direction of our right and left wings, but our men pushed them into their own centre by shooting. The enemy's right and left flanks were so crowded into one spot that they were not able to go forward or to find a way to escape.' This is mentioned in *The Baburnama* translated by Wheeler M. Thackston, p. 326.

48 Jadunath Sarkar, *Military History of India* (Calcutta: Orient Longman, 1960), p. 68.

49 *Akbarnama, Vol. II,* p. 69.

beaten in the mind first. And an enemy that had more numerical strength as opposed to you and was a constant thorn in your side, it was important to dehumanise him, belittle him and direct hate at him before fighting him on the ground.

Stalinist Soviet Union used a similar tactic against anyone it deemed as a counter-revolutionary, and therefore, an enemy of the state. The *Kulaks* or the land-owning peasantry was marked as enemy of the state and packed off to Siberia. This was done to enforce and institutionalise Stalin's concept of collective farming or the *Kolkhoz*. Those who resisted were shot. A similar treatment was meted out to Ukrainians and Kazakhs too. Later, with the rise of Nazi Germany in the 1930s, Stalin carried out purges within the Communist Party of the Soviet Union (to be used as CPSU in subsequent references) as well as the armed forces. The victims were accused of being not just counter-revolutionaries but also fascists or agents of fascists.

The Nazis were doing something similar in Germany in the 1930s. In their race-inspired ideology, Communism was a Jewish plot to the Nazis. They, therefore, called it Judeo-Bolshevism. Socialists, communists and trade unionists were all bracketed in the same group and were subjected to numerous purges. In fact, the notorious concentration camp at Dachau had been set up to incarcerate people of such ideological persuasion.

Also, the Nazis believed the Russians and other Slavic people were sub-humans or *untermensch* while the Germans were Aryans and therefore *ubermensch* or super humans. So when they invaded the Soviet Union, the Germans butchered the people. The Jews, in particular, were referred to as vermin, cockroaches, rats, worms and insects in order to dehumanise them so that their extermination could be justified as 'disinfecting' the earth.

The Soviets came up with similar propaganda against the Germans, though not at all racial. A very popular Russian patriotic song made during the war called *Svyashchennaya Voyna* (Sacred War), is a very ideologically inspired song that calls the 'vast country' to 'arise' to fight the 'dark fascist forces'. It wishes for 'noble wrath' to 'boil over like a wave' and 'shoot the fascist vermin in the head'. This is sacred to the

Russians even today, and they rise whenever it is played, just like their national anthem.

A much milder version of identifying 'enemies of the state' has also been observed in India. When Indira Gandhi declared Emergency in 1975, the argument given was a perceived threat of instability by anti-India forces. Mrs Gandhi, later in a telling TV interview with a British journalist kept, on insisting that she was right and that there was evidence to show that anti-India forces had been plotting to compromise the nation.

More recently, anyone who has observed the election strategy of the BJP under Narendra Modi and the virulent Hindu nationalism that they practise can spot the strong influence of ideology. In the run up to the General Elections of 2014, the BJP, Mr Modi and his acolytes in the press had carried out a relentless propaganda campaign against the rival INC. With lowbrow jibes like 'Italian bar dancer' for Sonia Gandhi by party members to Mr Modi insinuating that the INC has engineered a 'pink revolution' by engaging in cow slaughter and beef trade, the BJP and Modi were largely successful in making the people see the Opposition through the communal lens.

But over the next four years, the Modi regime pummelled the Opposition with jibes and charges to paint it in anti-national colours. Modi himself alleged at an election rally in Gujarat that his predecessor Manmohan Singh, the INC, and Pakistani diplomats were plotting to ensure that the BJP lost the Gujarat election. This was done to make the INC appear traitorous to the nation. Abu'l Fazl, too, referred to Hemu as a 'stock of sedition'. The medieval impulse of the Modi government is all too apparent.

Coming back, on 5 November 1556, 10,000 Mughal cavalry under Ali Quli Khan (later bestowed with the title of *Khan-i-Zaman* for his stellar role at Panipat) faced Hemu's 30,000 Rajput and Afghan cavalry and a huge elephant corps replete with its complement of musketeers and crossbowmen mounted on howdahs.[50] The elephant corps was a formidable one, and Abu'l Fazl says 500 pachyderms were

50 Jadunath Sarkar, *Military History of India*, p. 68.

so fleet-footed that they could outrun the formidable Arab horses that the Mughals had.[51] They were also clad in coats of chain mail with armour plates or *kajim*. Spears and knives were appended to their trunks.[52]

Later, Akbar would improvise it and create entire coats of elephant mail interspersed with steel plates, and forge special heavy daggers that could be attached to the tusks after sawing them off a bit. The trunk of an elephant was always vulnerable to attacks. At Chittorgarh, for instance, some of Akbar's favourite war elephants had their trunks severed by Rajput swordsmen. With daggers attached to their tusks, the contraption used to be more stable and lethal as a horse could be torn apart with one stab, what to say of a man.

Hemu himself rode an elephant named Hawai. The mahouts were also chosen very carefully. To his generals also, he assigned his best elephants. The pachyderm called Ghalib Jang became the mount of Afghan general Hasan Khan Faujdar; Gaj Bhanwar, a 'one in a thousand' elephant was given to Maikal Khan; Jor Banyan, a powerful beast, was given to Ikhtiyar Khan; Fauj Madar was assigned to Sangram Khan; and the elephant Kali Beg, which was Hemu's own mount previously, was given to a mahout named Sapan.

At every age, the elephant as a weapon of war has struck fear in the hearts of armies facing it. Alexander of Macedon had at the Battle of the Hydaspes in 326 BC faced the elephant corps of King Porus. The 2004 film *Alexander* had tried to recreate this battle, though not very convincingly. Yet the psychological impact of the sight of a charging elephant on a Greek hoplite was very well depicted. That particular scene showed the hoplites being led into battle by their gallant commander, but even his exhortations to be steady couldn't wipe off the fear and confusion writ large on their faces.

The Macedonians had faced elephants in battle before. At the Battle of Gaugamela in 331 BC, the Persians had deployed up to 15 elephants. These had little or no impact on the battle, but

---

51 'In might and courage they were exemplars, and the running of those active athletes could not be called running, for though the race-horses of Iraq (Arabia) be swift, they could not outstrip those elephants,' Fazl writes in *Akbarnama, Vol. II*, p. 59.

52 *Akbarnama, Vol. II*, p. 60.

Alexander was impressed by this use of elephants in battle, so much so that he captured these and added them to his army. So, he was familiar with ways to counter war elephants when he came to India. But he didn't expect to face 100-odd elephants in battle, which he did at Hydaspes.

Alexander's successors to his empire, the Diadochi, experimented with elephants too but only Seleucus Nicator, the Satrap of Babylon and master of the eastern empire, had success with them. Seleucus had been worsted by the army of Magadha emperor Chandragupta Maurya, which had a huge elephant corps. Seleucus was forced to make peace with his Indian nemesis and also give his daughter, Helen, to the king's harem. But Seleucus still managed to salvage the situation by convincing the Indian emperor to give him 500 elephants in return.

These elephants were then used by Seleucus decisively in the struggle for supremacy among the Diadochi. At the battles of Ipsus (301 BC) and Corupedium (281 BC), Seleucus used this Indian gift to rout his adversaries who also used elephants, but their numbers paled when pitted against the Seleucid elephant corps.

A year after Corupedium, it was the turn of the new state of Rome to face elephants in battle. Greek king Pyrrhus of Epirus clashed with Rome. The Roman legions met the Greeks at the Battle of Heraclea in 280 BC. At a crucial juncture, King Pyrrhus led his elephants on a maddening charge that scared away the Roman cavalry and which led to the melting away of the Roman infantry lines. The Romans had never encountered elephants in battle, so the shock and awe was too much for them to handle. This battle was also important for another reason—this was the first clash between two different battle systems—the Roman legion versus the Macedonian phalanx.[53]

---

53 A system of infantry fighting developed by King Philip II of Macedon, father of Alexander. It involved using infantrymen armed with 18-foot spears called *sarissa* standing in files 16-man deep and each pointing his spear to the front, resulting in a dense jungle of spears, or a phalanx, that no invading force could penetrate. The Macedonian phalanx eventually got worsted by the Roman legions, but at Heraclea at least, the Romans failed.

A year later, in 279 BC, the Romans returned more prepared to deal with the elephants. At the Battle of Asculum, they managed to wound and kill many elephants, but a final, maddening elephant charge led by Pyrrhus led to the destruction of the Romans once again.

Both Heraclea and Asculum were won by the Greeks amid great slaughter on both sides. This gave rise to the phrase Pyrrhic victory, which is used often even today to explain situations when a victory or success is achieved at great personal cost. The Soviet Union had a Pyrrhic victory against Germany in the Second World War as it lost 27 million of its people. Politically, too, this phrase is used and quite often in India. The Karnataka assembly elections of 2018 could be used as an example of Pyrrhic victory for of the INC, where they lost pole position to the BJP but managed to strike an alliance with the smaller Janata Dal (Secular), offering it the chief ministership of the state to keep BJP out. The 2017 Gujarat assembly election was portrayed as a Pyrrhic victory of the BJP where it managed to maintain pole position with a hair-thin majority and losing many previous gains to the INC.

But Asculum was not the last time Rome would face war elephants; they would face them again at Adyss (255 BC), at Tunis (255 BC) and Panormus (251 BC). Tunis was a repeat of Heraclea but Panormus saw Roman success in deflecting the elephant attack. But that may have been more by fluke than design as the Romans again suffered setback after setback when Carthage's greatest hero, Hannibal, invaded Rome.

Though Hannibal lost most of his elephants during his journey across the Alps, he still had enough to scare and crush the Roman legions at Trebbia in 218 BC. Two years later, at Cannae in 216 BC, Hannibal would have his most famous victory against the Romans. There is some disagreement among historians about the presence of elephants there. Most accounts suggest only the mount of Hannibal himself, an elephant named Surus (from Syria), was alive and at Cannae at the time. However, some writers mention a Roman poet named Silius Italicus writing after the battle that 'the Romans attacked several howdah-bearing elephants with fire and sent them plunging into the nearby river'.[54]

---

54 John M. Kistler, *War Elephants* (United States: Praeger Publishers, 2006), p. 123.

Nevertheless, the Carthagians won the battle due to the tactic called 'double envelopment'. This was used previously by Alexander to defeat Porus whose elephants had terrorised his troops at the Battle of Hydaspes. This is more well-known to the layman as 'pincer movement', a tactic subsequently used by many armies at many battles all over the globe. But 'double envelopment' would have a closer and more efficient successor in the Prussian military doctrine of *bewegungskrieg*[55] or 'manoeuvre warfare' with its ultimate end state of *kesselschlacht* or 'cauldron battle', as theorised by Frederick the Great. The Deutsches Heer would successfully use *kesselschlacht* tactics to surround and destroy an entire Russian field army at the Battle of Tannenburg[56] during the First World War in August 1914. Its successor, the Wehrmacht, would encircle and finish off several Soviet armies in the course of the Second World War at the Eastern Front.

After being at the receiving end of Hannibal's tactics for close to two decades, the Romans, under Scipio Africanus, would have the last laugh at the Battle of Zama in 202 BC. There, Hannibal's famed war elephants would be effectively countered, resulting in the animals fleeing in panic and trampling and crushing their own troops coming in the way.

Hannibal wouldn't raise his head again, and Rome would do to Carthage what the Deccan Sultanates would do to the Vijayanagar Empire after the fateful Battle of Talikota in 1565—annihilate it. But the charm of the war elephant would continue in the east, particularly in India.

When campaigners from Central Asia and Afghanistan started entering India, they were awe-struck by the use of elephants in battle. Mahmud Ghaznavi faced elephants when he fought the army of Hindushahi ruler Jaipal at Peshawar on November 28, 1001 AD. Mahmud had 15,000 cavalry while Jaipal had 12,000 cavalry, 30,000

---

55 For a more detailed understanding of the terms *bewegungskrieg* and *kesselschlacht* and how these were translated into action on the ground, see Robert M. Citino's works, *The German Way of War: From the Thirty Years' War to the Third Reich* and *Death of the Wehrmacht: The German Campaigns of 1942.*

56 For a detailed account of the battle, see Dennis E. Showalter's 2004 book, *Tannenberg: Clash of Empires.*

infantry and 300 war elephants. But the elephants were overwhelmed by Mahmud's use of naphtha balls and arrows or *tir-i-naffatan*.[57]

However, Mahmud still appreciated the value of elephants and used them himself later. In fact, Mahmud had no fewer than 2,500 elephants in his army.[58] The later Delhi Sultans also used war elephants but depended heavily on their cavalry. Sultan Alauddin Khilji, the bad boy of history in the Hindu communalist's view, had an elephant corps in his army, which he used against the Mongols when they invaded India.[59] However, it was always his heavy cavalry that was the ace in his pack.

But whenever Delhi Sultans ignored their cavalry and relied more on their elephants, disaster struck. In December 1398, when Amir Timur was at the gates of Delhi, he faced the army of Sultan Nasiruddin Mahmud Tughlaq that had 10,000 cavalry, 40,000 infantry and 125 armoured elephants, at the Battle of Delhi. Financially and militarily weak, the Sultanate was no longer investing on its match-winning arm, the cavalry. Instead, it relied heavily on its elephant corps, which was prized for its ability to break ranks and disperse cavalry. From Heraclea to Delhi, this perception of the war elephant hadn't changed in a thousand years.

In contrast, Timur had in his command up to 60,000 first-rate cavalry. Timur was a superb general and master tactician who would always personally recce the terrain he was going to fight on. The Delhi Sultan, on the other hand, wasn't much of a warrior though his troops didn't lack courage and fought valiantly.[60] The Sultan led the charge of his elephants on Timur's centre. The elephants carried archers who shot fire arrows on Timur's troops.

---

57 Pradeep P. Barua, *The State at War in South Asia*, p. 27.

58 Ibid.,

59 When fighting the legendary Mongol general Qutlugh Khwaja in 1299, Alauddin lost his best general, Zafar Khan, and many elephants that were part of his contingent.

60 Timur's own words from his biography are quoted by Sarkar on p. 47—'...The soldiers of Sultan Mahmud and Mallu Khan showed no lack of courage, but bore themselves manfully in the fight, still they could not withstand the successive assaults of my soldiers.'

Timur countered this by putting a camel squadron in front and placing stacks of hay on the backs of the animals. His troops then set fire to the stacks and goaded the camels to run forward. With their backs on fire, the camels ran ahead pell-mell. The spectacle of flaming camels coming towards them scared the elephants so much that many of them turned around and fled, trampling the Sultan's men.[61] Many other elephants were felled by the archers and swordsmen of Timur, and his own grandson even managed to cut off the trunk of an elephant.[62] Despite this reversal at the Battle of Delhi, the Delhi Sultanate continued to rely on elephants. So, when Timur's great-great grandson Babur invaded India over 120 years later, the Lodhi Sultan of Delhi marched out to give battle with an elephant corps. It was like Battle of Delhi version 2.0, only this time, the Delhi Sultan had a bigger army than the aggressor. In fact, Babur may have had only around 8,000 troops as opposed to the commonly believed figure of 12,000.[63]

At Panipat on 21 April 1526, Babur's artillery and mounted archers pummelled Sultan Ibrahim Lodhi's war elephants. The boom of the guns, the rattle of musketry, and the devastating injuries sustained from the cannon round shots made the agitated pachyderms panic. And they turned and ran pell-mell, trampling whosoever came in the way. It was Zama 202 BC and Delhi 1398 all over again.

In an ironic and somewhat sad twist, 200 years after Panipat, Babur's descendant, Mughal Emperor Muhammad Shah Rangila, would rely heavily on his elephant corps while facing Persian invader Nadir Shah at Karnal. And ironically, the Persian emperor would put

---

61 Reference in *Philosophers of War: The Evolution of History Greatest Military Thinkers, Vol. I,* by Daniel Coetzee and Lee W. Eysturlid, p. 184, and *War, Culture and Society in Early Modern South Asia, 1740–1849*, by Kaushik Roy, p. 34. Roy gives a slightly different version and says some prefabricated platforms were used and each of these was fixed across the backs of two camels. On these, Timur placed naphtha combustibles.

62 Jadunath Sarkar, *Military History of India*, Sarkar, p. 47.

63 Stephen Frederic Dale, *Babur: Timurid Prince and Mughal Emperor, 1483–1530* (London: Cambridge University Press, 2018), p. 126.

the Mughal elephants to flight by adopting the same 'flaming camel' tactic of Babur's great ancestor, Timur.[64]

But at Panipat on 5 November 1556, Babur's grandson's army faced the terrifying prospect of being trampled by Hemu's war elephants. That's what Abu'l Fazl alluded to in the *Akbarnama*. But Badaoni gives a very interesting counter-factual—'But the Afghans, since they were sick of his (Hemu) usurpation, began to pray for his fall, and in impromptus kept saying things to this effect: "Welcome a vicissitude even against ourselves"....'[65]

Badaoni, later in the text, again states that Hemu's troops were dispirited. But it seems their commander didn't lose his morale upon losing his artillery. Sir Jadunath Sarkar also says that the Mughals fought 'without the help of Babur's profuse firearms'.[66]

By all accounts, the Mughal right-wing was under Sikandar Khan Uzbek, while Abdullah Khan Uzbek commanded the left. At the centre was Ali Quli Khan Shaibani, while the vanguard was under Husain Quli Beg and Shah Quli Mahram with Bairam Khan's own contingent of Turks.

Hemu commanded the centre and assigned the right-wing to Shadi Khan Kakar and the left to Ramya, his nephew (sister's son). It was Hemu who began the attack by sending his elephants charging at the enemy. It was a terrifying charge. Abu'l Fazl writes—'Though the heroes of the victorious army did not fail in steadiness and devotion, yet the onset of the elephants shook the right and left divisions.'[67]

The Mughals suffered heavy losses, but they didn't lose heart. The mounted archers deployed *taulqama* tactics and battered down the enemy with arrows from all sides. The Mughal centre advanced but soon found a deep ravine separating it from the adversary. The Afghans could do nothing about it as it was too steep and unpassable even for the elephants. The Mughal archers in the centre stood at the

64 Kaushik Roy, *Military Transition in Early Modern Asia, 1400–1750: Cavalry, Guns, Government and Ships* (London: Bloomsbury, 2014), p. 34.

65 Abdul Qadir Badaoni, *Muntakhab ut-Tawarikh, Vol. II*, tr. W. H. Lowe (Calcutta: The Asiatic Society, 1884), p. 8.

66 Jadunath Sarkar, *Military History of India*, p. 77.

67 *Akbarnama, Vol II*, p. 63.

edge and showered arrows on the enemy, hitting them with every wave. Hemu's archers, it seems, couldn't return the compliment. This was primarily due to the limited range and power of the Indian bows made of bamboo. The Mughals were armed with the deadly Central Asian composite bow. Essentially a recurve bow, by Babur's time, this choice weapon of the Turks and Mongols had evolved enough to produce 4,000 pounds per square inch of pressure at full draw.[68]

The battle, as Jadunath Sarkar put it, was a 'ding dong' one where fortunes changed frequently. As the Mughals harassed Hemu's army with their Parthian wheeling tactics, they managed to kill two of his frontline commanders, Shadi Khan Kakar and Bhagwan Das. Shadi Khan was commanding Hemu's right. Seeing his commanders killed, Hemu led one elephant charge after another on the Mughals. The Mughals resisted by firing at the pachyderms and their riders. It was during this that Hemu got hit in the eye with an arrow. Both Abu'l Fazl and Badaoni narrate this part rather contemptuously. Fazl writes:

> ...an arrow from the bended bow of Divine wrath reached Hemu's eye, and piercing the socket, came out at the back of his head. Seemingly, the wind of the pride, and the arrogance of that black-fated, inwardly darkened one passed out by that window.

Badaoni narrates it thus—'Suddenly, the arrow of death, which no shield can ward off, struck his squinting eye so that his brain passed clean out from the cup of his head, and he became unconscious.' When both versions are compared, Badaoni, otherwise known for his acidic and at times communal remarks, comes across as the less vile man. The pitfalls of ideology are apparent at every age.

What is also apparent from this episode is the tremendous risk that a commander or a king put himself under when seated on an elephant. Centuries before Hemu, it was Gahadvala Rajput king Jayachandra of Kannauj who had met a similar fate as that of Hemu while fighting on the back of an elephant. Jayachandra

---

68 Reference occurs in 2006 History Channel documentary, *Warrior Empire: The Mughals of India*. An American bowmaker named Lukas Novotny lays the composite bow threadbare.

is also known as Jaichand, whose image was sullied for posterity by Chand Bardai's hit-job on him, *Prithviraja Raso*, as the father-in-law of Prithviraj Chauhan who betrayed him by colluding with Shihabuddin Ghori. The real Jayachandra had faced Ghori at the Battle of Chandawar, which is today known as Chandwal, a place near Etawah in Uttar Pradesh. Accounts of the time suggest Jayachandra was close to victory when a Ghurid arrow hit him in the eye. He fell off his elephant and was trampled by his own mount. Rana Sanga of Mewar, who led the Rajput coalition forged by Hasan Khan Mewati at the Battle of Khanwa against Babur in 1527, was also on an elephant's back when he was hit and fell down from his mount.

Several Mughal princes also met with a similar end while riding elephants. Dara Shukoh had dismounted from his elephant in the thick of the Battle of Samugarh in 1658 to ride a horse. When his troops saw the empty howdah, they presumed that their commander was dead and fled. A year later, Shah Shuja while fighting Aurangzeb's forces at Khajwa in 1659 had dismounted and fled sensing defeat and his army had melted away after that.

Half a century later, Aurangzeb's favourite son Muhammad Azam and Azam's son Bidar Bakht were killed while fighting the forces of the new emperor, Bahadur Shah I, in 1707. Azam Shah had charged on his elephant and was hit by several arrows until a musket ball hit his head and took his life. Both father and son were on two different elephants.

In Assam, a large military expedition was sent by Sultan Nasiruddin Nusrat Shah of Bengal under the command of a general named Tubrak Khan in 1532. The campaign that extended to the short reign of Nusrat Shah's successor, Sultan Alauddin Firuz Shah II, saw spectacular success initially. Eight leading Ahom generals, including the premier noble, Phrasenmung Borgohain, by the Sultan's mounted archers. Many or all of these generals were mounted on war elephants. In fact, when Phrasenmung was killed, his beloved wife Mulagabharu donned warrior's attire, mounted a war elephant, and charged at the enemy to avenge her husband. She went down fighting and became an icon for Assamese men and women for all time to come. But strategically speaking, her bravado couldn't save her from being an easy target for the enemy's mounted archers and her fall probably demoralised the Ahoms even more.[69] With the commanders gone, and the woman warrior who rallied the depleting ranks behind her also gone, the Ahom resistance melted away.

Similarly, when Hemu's troops found their commander missing on the howdah, they panicked and fled. Hemu's elephant was captured and brought to Akbar and Bairam Khan who were camped 20 miles behind the battlefield. Hemu was dragged to the royal presence in a half-conscious state where Bairam Khan, with his sword, 'cleansed the world from the contamination of his existence'.[70] In other words, he was executed.[71]

Abu'l Fazl also says that had the emperor tried or had there been a far-sighted man in the court, Hemu could have been kept alive and persuaded to join imperial service, for he was an 'excellent servant' with a 'lofty spirit'.

But the truth remains that Hemu was not given a dignified treatment even after death. His severed head was sent to Kabul while the trunk was placed on a gibbet outside Dinpanah, today's Purana Qila. This was in stark contrast to the treatment meted out to the body of Ibrahim Lodhi by Babur after Panipat. His body was given a dignified burial and a tomb was constructed by Babur, who also wrote a letter to the dead sultan's mother to tell her about her son's valour.

Hemu was no king like Lodhi, but a general of the runaway king. But it's possible that his being a Hindu had more to do with the undignified treatment he received in death. One can also understand the hatred Akbar had for him. Abu'l Fazl says that before the battle, when Humayun had just moved to Delhi, Akbar had drawn a dismembered corpse. When a courtier asked him who that was, Akbar said it was Hemu. At that time, Fazl says, Hemu's name was unknown. But when Bairam Khan asked Akbar to execute the captured man, he apparently said there was no need for it as he had already slain Hemu in a painting.[72]

---

69 H.K. Barpujari, *The Comprehensive History of Assam, Vol. II* (Guwahati: Publication Board Assam, 2003), pp. 138–39.

70 *Akbarnama, Vol. II,* p. 66.

71 I've elaborated on the execution of Hemu in the final chapter of this book.

72 *Akbarnama, Vol. II,* p. 67.

But in his death, Hemu left behind some tantalising 'what ifs' for future analysts to cogitate on. What if he hadn't been hit by an arrow? Could he have then defeated the Mughals? Could he have then managed to revive a Hindu empire in Delhi that was lost with the death of Prithviraj Chauhan in 1192? This thought is behind a question asked in some quiz contests, including the famous *Kaun Banega Crorepati* hosted by Amitabh Bachchan—who was the last Hindu king of Delhi? The average right-winger might also be tempted to raise this question—could Hemu have thrown out the Mughals completely from India and saved them the trouble of writing them out of the textbooks in the Narendra Modi era?

What ifs are not for the historian to indulge in as s/he can only interpret what happened in the past and not what didn't happen, but one can certainly assume that a defeat at Panipat would have made Akbar's already delicate position even more precarious. And that would have perhaps necessitated Bairam Khan putting his backup plan into effect—withdrawal to Kabul.

But Bairam Khan couldn't have possibly known that four years after this victory, and despite putting his life and faith on the line to serve and save the House of Timur from annihilation, he himself would become an outlaw and face an imperial army as a rebel.

Chapter 3

Out of the Shadows, into the Light

> An invisible angel uttered his chronogram
> Shahid shud Muhammad Bairam.[1]

The end of Hemu neutralised the existential threat for the Mughals but his end had to be announced to the world. The grand statement came in the form of a tower of human heads erected around Panipat.[2] This also served another purpose: to terrorise the masses into submission to the extent that any thought of rebellion could be nipped in the bud. But Akbar certainly was not the first to do it.

The *Shahnameh* by Firdausi talks about the Sassanian king Bahram Chobin erecting a victory tower and studding the heads of his slain enemies on it in sixth-century Persia.[3] This seems to have been adopted

---

1 The last line is in Farsi that says, 'Muhammad Bairam became a martyr.' It occurs in *Akbarnama, Vol. II*, p. 203 and is a lament written on Bairam Khan's assassination.

2 Badaoni, p. 10. Abu'l Fazl and Firishta, surprisingly, don't say anything about this. Abu'l Fazl's predicament is still understandable but why Firishta didn't mention it is not known. But this may be because Firishta right at the beginning of his work pertaining to Akbar mentions that he got all the details from Abu'l Fazl's works and those who were eyewitnesses.

3 Thomas Leisten, 'Mashhad Al-Nasr: Monuments of War and Victory in Medieval Islamic Art', in *Muqarnas Volume XIII: An Annual on the Visual Culture of the Islamic World,* edited by Gülru Necipoglu (Leiden: E.J. Brill, 1996), p. 14.

by the Mongols and Muslims later. Amir Timur did it in Sistan, Ifashan (both in modern day Iran) and Tikrit (Iraq).[4] He is said to have done that at Aleppo (Syria) too. His son Miranshah did it at Herat.[5]

But before these two, Delhi Sultan Alauddin Khilji was also doing something similar to the Mongols who had invaded his kingdom. Tales abound, though without archaeological evidence, that at the foundation of the fort of Siri, Alauddin's new citadel to withstand Mongol raids, were placed severed heads of Mongol invaders.

There is a strange monument in South Delhi's Hauz Khas today, which is locally known as Chor Minar. It has quite a few holes on it—225, going by the legend—from where severed heads of thieves and other criminals were hung.[6] Who knows, it may have also been used to hang Mongol heads. Or, similar arrangements may have been made at other parts of the Sultanate for the Mongols. But what is crystal clear is that such a gruesome building in the heart of Khilji's populated capital city must have been a cause of permanent fear in the hearts of everyone.

Far away in the Americas, Spanish conquistadors led by Hernan Cortez, after conquering the Aztec capital of Tenochtitlan (corresponds to today's Mexico City), had found at the temple of *Huitzilopochtili*, the Aztec sun god, a towering pile of human skulls. The proof of that was found only recently after excavations in Mexico City unearthed those skull racks.[7]

Akbar didn't have to learn from Timur; his own grandfather's example showed him the way. Babur had erected two such skull towers in Kohat (in Pakistan today) after his successful campaign of 1505. About 150-odd Afghans had come out of their pillaged town to shout at Babur's army—a natural reaction of conquered people whose homes have been ravaged. But to set an example, Babur killed them

---

4 Ibid.

5 Ibid.

6 Rana Safvi, *The Forgotten Cities of Delhi*, pp. 20–1.

7 See this *Washington Post* article for more details on the Aztec find. Available at https://www.washingtonpost.com/news/retropolis/wp/2017/07/04/archaeologists-unearth-a-500-year-old-tower-of-skulls-and-another-gruesome-aztec-mystery/?noredirect=on&utm_term=.8fc6d2a5a30d.

and erected a minaret of skulls.[8] A day later, he erected another skull tower of 100-odd Afghans who had fought his troops near Hangu.[9] And a third minaret was also built by his commander Jahangir Mirza at Bannu where the locals had resisted his troops.[10]

Babur didn't do any of this in Mawarannahr or Transoxiana, the Timurid homeland (the land between Amu Darya and Syr Darya), because those were his own people. The Afghans were foreigners. The 'other'. Therefore, to him, it was quite all right to use terror tactics on them.

This tendency of seeing people as the 'other' has continued to this day. Although this was a tad dormant in free India, except for those troubling years immediately after Partition, it has found distinct expression today under the Narendra Modi regime. Today, with majoritarian tendencies almost running riot, more and more people are treating the minorities, and primarily the Muslims, as the 'other'. The only difference between then and now is that unlike Babur, today's Hindutva-influenced Indian sees the 'other' among his own countrymen and not foreigners.

The Ottomans and Safavids also erected skull columns. During the reign of Shah Mohammed Khodabandeh, Khan Ahmad Khan, the ousted king of Gilan (a province of Iran), had invaded Bia-pas. But he was worsted by a Safavid army led by Shirwan Governor Jamshid Khan. As a terror tactic, Jamshid Khan erected a minaret of heads.

The Ottomans erected skull towers until as late as the 19th century. In May 1809, to crush the First Serbian Uprising against the Ottoman Empire, an army led by Hurshid Pasha had destroyed the rebels at the Battle of Cegar and erected a tower with 952 heads of slain rebels in the town of Nis. That grisly statement of victory still stands in Serbia today and is a national monument.

But the same Ottomans had been psychologically worsted by the terror tactics of Vlad III or Dracula, the king of Wallachia, in the 15th century. Under their all-conquering Sultan Mehmed II, who in 1453 had conquered Constantinople, an Ottoman army that had gone on a

8 Stephen F. Dale, *The Garden of the Eight Paradises,* pp. 197–98.

9 Ibid.

10 Ibid.

campaign to deal a heavy blow to the Wallachians in 1461 had to turn back after Vlad created a forest of impaled captured Turks.

Vlad, who got the sombre epithet of 'the Impaler', paid a heavy price for this victory as he had also followed a scorched earth policy and ravaged his own lands and people in order to deny the Ottomans. The Ottoman Sultan, before turning back from Vlad's capital, had installed Vlad's brother, Radu, on the Wallachian throne. Radu then incited the nobles and powerful landlords—the *boyars*—to rebel against Vlad, which resulted in Vlad's capture and imprisonment.

Sultan Mehmed II had also used impaling as a terror tactic before and during the Siege of Constantinople. The Ottomans would have a long history of impaling their enemies and erecting skull minarets even after him. But that they found Vlad's actions revolting speaks volumes for this Romanian king's wanton savagery. And yet, such transgressions on humanity had happened earlier too. But that the Ottomans, who were themselves into impaling their enemies and erecting skull minarets, found Vlad's actions revolting speaks volumes for this Romanian king's wanton savagery. And yet, such transgressions on humanity had happened earlier too.

The great Achaemenid King Darius I, who had started the Persian invasions on Greece, had supposedly impaled 3,000 Babylonians when he crushed a revolt led by Nebuchadnezzar III in 514 BC. Herodotus wrote that Darius did what his predecessor, Cyrus the Great, couldn't do:

> ...first of all he demolished the walls and bore away all the gates; for when Cyrus had taken Babylon before, he did neither of these things; and, secondly, Darius impaled about three thousand of the principal citizens, and allowed the rest of the Babylonians to inhabit the city.[11]

Incidentally, the besieged Babylonians had strangulated their women[12] lest they became a burden on the limited resources available. The Rajputs would also kill their women in later times but for a different reason—honour. Apart from the social strangulation

---

11 Henry Cary, *Herodotus: A New and Literal Version from the Text of Baehr* (New York: Harper & Brothers, Publishers, 1859), p. 236.

12 Ibid.

of womankind that patriarchy has been doing for ages, the Rajput *jauhar* and Babylonian mass murders have been the ugly physical manifestations of the 'patriarchy kills' argument, most recently articulated by CNN columnist Richard Edmond Vargas[13] and for which he was badly trolled.[14]

That apart, killing for 'honour' has been a constant in Indian society ever since, now attaining alarming proportions with the sanctity given by kangaroo courts or '*khap panchayats*', a quasi-judicial institution akin to the Afghan *jirgah*s.

In India, there is literary and architectural evidence to the use of impalement as a form of punishment. There are Tamil texts from the post-classical period, like the 11th-century text by Nampi Antar Nampi, Tirumurai, 12th-century *Periya Puranam* by Cekkilar and Chola court poet Ottakkuttar's war poem *Takkayakapparani* and *Thiruvilayadal Puranam*, that mention the impalement of 8,000 Jain monks by Pandyan king Kunpandyan at Madurai.[15] Even though scholars doubt the historicity of the event, it has found expression in temple motifs too, like a fresco at Meenakshi temple, a mural at Tirupperunturai temple at Avudaiyarkoil, and carvings at Edaganathar temple in Thiruvedagam. The Meenakshi temple actually celebrates this alleged massacre through a special festival.[16]

Impalement exists in folk tales too. In Bengal and Assam, there are stories that talk about two thieves convincing a foolish king and his foolish minister to be impaled on stakes to be the king and minister of heaven. In Assamese, the expression *nososa xool* or 'unsharpened stake' occurs in several stories for children, translated or local. Any offender or anyone speaking against the king would be warned thus: '*Xabodhan, nohole rajai nososa xoolot dibo*! (Beware, the king might impale you on

---

13 See 'Guns alone don't kill people, patriarchy kills people'. Available at https://edition.cnn.com/2018/05/01/opinions/patriarchy-kills-people-opinion-vargas/index.html.

14 See 'CNN columnist faces backlash for 'Patriarchy kills people' op-ed'. Available at https://www.rt.com/usa/426069-cnn-columnist-patriarchy-kills.

15 John E. Cort, *Open Boundaries: Jain Communities and Cultures in Indian History* (New York: State University of New York Press, 1998), pp. 179–83.

16 Oliver Freiberger, *Asceticism and Its Critics: Historical Accounts and Comparative Perspectives* (New York: Oxford University Press, 2006), p. 127.

an unsharpened stake!)' I remember hearing similar bedtime stories as a child and often asking my father what a *nososa xool* is.

Akbar, therefore, wasn't doing anything that hadn't been done before and wouldn't be done again.[17] Yet the shock value of such a step wasn't dented even a bit by the history of violence that India had seen before it. Apart from its strategic location on the busy Agra–Delhi–Lahore route, and the fact that it is still the last important town before Kurukshetra when one comes from Delhi, Panipat would have seen heavy pilgrimage activity. So, more people would have seen the skull tower and carried back home terrifying tales of it. And the fear of the Mughals would have spread that way.

As the tower was being made, Akbar sent his general Sikander Khan Uzbek to Delhi to take control of the city and drive out those from Hemu's army who had fled there. Sikander Khan must have shed more blood there as Abu'l Fazl wrote:

> He acted with rapidity and delivered some of the malignant and useless from the prison of existence, and put the distracted inhabitants of the country in order.[18]

Akbar entered Delhi in pomp. The next one and a half months were spent celebrating his win. It was in Delhi that Akbar's commander Majnun Khan Qaqshal told the emperor about the 'excellent loyalty' of Raja Bharmal (or Bihari Mal) of Amber that he had shown at the siege of Narnaul. A Sur commander named Haji Khan had laid siege to the fort of Narnaul that was held by Qaqshal for the Mughals.

Raja Bharmal had become an ally of the Afghans during the Sur interregnum that had lasted for 15 years. His joining up with Sher Shah Suri had been necessitated by the aggressive manoeuvres of Raja Maldev of Marwar who had gobbled up four districts of Amber, taking advantage of the instability in North India that had prevailed during Humayun's conflict with Sher Shah and his eventual departure from India. It was because of this alliance that Bharmal was with Haji Khan when he invested the fort of Narnaul. But Bharmal, using his

---

17 Akbar would repeat it at a much bigger scale after his victory over Chittor in 1564.

18 Abu'l Fazl, *Akbarnama, Vol. II*, p. 70.

influence and amiability, had secured the peaceful surrender of the fort, giving the Mughal garrison the guarantee of life and liberty, and also helped Qaqshal join up with Akbar in Delhi.[19]

Akbar then asked the Rajput king to come to his durbar in Delhi, which he did with his sons and relatives. He was presented with a *khillat* or robe of honour, and his sons and relatives were also presented with gifts. It was December 1556. After enjoying imperial hospitality for a while, the Rajput king came to seek leave. Akbar was doing something dangerous that day—riding an elephant in *musth*. His reckless physical courage made him do things that often put his life in peril. Akbar almost certainly never knew when to back off, and that always amplified whatever danger he faced. In this case, the elephant, with the emperor on top, was rushing at anyone and anything in every direction. People ran away, but the Rajputs didn't flinch and didn't move. This impressed Akbar so much that he supposedly said, '*Nihaal khwaahim kard*,' or 'We shall plant/rear/cherish you.'[20] Abu'l Fazl implied, as explained by H. Beveridge, the translator of *Akbarnama*, that Akbar was hinting at future alliance via matrimony with the Kachwaha clan.[21]

But while Raja Bharmal got imperial favours for what he did at Narnaul, his boss Haji Khan earned only the wrath of Akbar, who learnt that this Afghan general had established his fief at Alwar. While the Mughals and Afghans were sworn enemies, what seemed to have piqued Akbar was the intel that Hemu's wife and father were living in Haji Khan's territory. Akbar sent Pir Muhammad Khan Shirwani, newly ordained as *Nasir ul-Mulk*, to crush Haji Khan.

Haji Khan fled without giving battle even though he had with him 5,000 cavalry and 150 elephants.[22] The shock of losing at Panipat was still very fresh. But when the Mughal army went to Machari, they faced resistance from Hemu's loyalists still guarding his family.

19 Sir Jadunath Sarkar, *A History of Jaipur: 1503–1938* (New Delhi: Orient Longman Limited, 1984), p 34.

20 Abu'l Fazl, *Akbarnama, Vol. II*, p. 70.

21 Ibid. See footnote 2.

22 *Mirat-i-Sikandari*, as quoted in H. Beveridge's translation of Abu'l Fazl, *Akbarnama, Vol. II*, p. 72, footnote 1.

Eventually, they were overcome and Hemu's 80-year-old father was captured even though his daughter-in-law managed to escape. He was brought before Pir Muhammad in chains. Pir Muhammad told him to convert to Islam. But he replied:

> For eighty years I've worshipped my God, according to this religion. Why should I change it at this time, and why should I, merely from fear of my life, and without understanding it come into your way of worship?[23]

Pir Muhammad executed him. And this became the first recorded instance in Akbar's reign when a non-Muslim, the family of an enemy, was asked to choose apostasy or the sword. We don't know how Akbar would have treated Hemu's old father if he were there, but going by Hemu's fate at Panipat, it may not have been very different. It was his *ataliq*, Bairam Khan, who was pulling all the strings at that time. And it's possible that Pir Muhammad had his mentor's consent. Or he may have acted independently, his stature having been enhanced as *Nasir ul-Mulk*. There are many possibilities here. But the bottom line is this: Hemu's octogenarian father was humiliated and murdered in an expression of sheer hate.

This was in stark contrast to Babur's treatment of Ibrahim Lodhi's family. Babur gave a decent burial to his slain enemy and took care to ensure that his mother, Buwa Begum, and the rest of his family were not harmed. It's a different thing that Ibrahim's mother never forgave Babur and even tried to poison him.[24]

What threat could an 80-year-old man possibly pose to the Mughal hegemony? It wasn't that India didn't have a tradition of old people taking up arms. The *Mahabharata* tells us about the warrior named Bhagadatta, the king of Pragjyotishpur-Kamrup (modern-day Guwahati) and father-in-law of Kaurava prince Duryodhana. Mounted on a fierce war elephant named Supratika, this geriatric father of princess Bhanumati used a bandana to lift his drooping forehead and eyebrows. He was a formidable opponent and very

---

23 Abu'l Fazl, *Akbarnama, Vol. II*, pp. 71–2.

24 Gulbadan Begum, *Humayun Nama*, trans. Annette S. Beveridge as *History of Humayun* (London, Royal Asiatic Society, 1902), pp. 10–1.

skilled with the bow. When Arjuna couldn't defeat him in one-to-one combat, Lord Krishna advised him to somehow aim at Bhagadatta's bandana knot to untie it. When Arjuna did that, Bhagadatta could no longer see, and it became possible for Arjuna to kill him.

While still a story, the *Mahabharata* offers insights into ancient Indian life. And therefore, the Bhagadatta episode suggests that very old men waging war was not unheard of. A real-life example of this comes from the Revolt of 1857. One of the notable Indians to have unfurled the banner of revolt was the 80-year-old *zamindar* of Jagadishpur, Raja Kunwar Singh. He proved to be a formidable opponent for the British, having got the better of the Company troops in several engagements. Eventually, though, he was killed by fever arising from a festering wound sustained while fighting the English.

But Hemu's father was no Kunwar Singh. He was neither a king nor someone with a military background. And after the death of his mighty son, whatever power he had also vanished. Couldn't he have been given the same treatment that Babur had meted out to Ibrahim Lodhi's mother, or Humayun had to the Rajput garrison and their families that held Agra for Ibrahim Lodhi? One can only speculate.

But this illustrates a couple of things. One, Hemu, though derisively mentioned as a 'pretender' to the throne in some accounts, was a much more serious threat to the Mughals than so far imagined; two, the message the Mughals wanted to send across seems to have been this that it was wiser for a non-Muslim to be on their side instead of being an enemy.

Elsewhere, Haji Khan, fleeing from Alwar, reached the environs of Ajmer where Mewar King Rana Udai Singh trapped him with overwhelming force and allegedly made extortionist demands of gold, an elephant, and a woman from his harem.

The *Makhzan-i-Afghani* or *History of Afghanistan* written by Harawi Neamat Ullah for Emperor Jahangir and translated by Bernhard Dorn in 1836 gives a detailed account of this episode in the annotations section. 'On his (Haji Khan) entrance on the territories of Rana Oude-Singh, the governor of Chilore (Chittor), this Rana, from confidence in his troops, and greediness to obtain Haji Khan's baggage and money, intercepted his route near Joudepoor (Jodhpur), with ninety thousand horse,' the account starts.[25]

Ninety thousand cavalry is obviously a much-exaggerated figure. The *Mirat-i-Sikandari* of Sikandar bin Muhammad Manjhu gives a figure of 40,000. But even this figure looks exaggerated, given the fact that when Chittor was besieged by Akbar in 1563, the Rajputs just had 10,000 troops at their disposal. Later in 1576, when Rana Pratap Singh fought Akbar at Haldighati, the former couldn't muster more than 3,000 troops[26] even though Mewar chronicles give a figure of 20,000 for the king's troops.[27]

It is this exaggeration that any reader of medieval Indian texts should be careful about. William Ervine had written this very casually, and even condescendingly, in his 1903 book, *The Army of the Indian Moghuls*, but it makes absolute sense even today: 'That spirit (of exaggeration) runs through everything done in the East, at any rate in the Indian portion of it, as could be easily shown were it worthwhile to labour the point further.'[28] It is this sense of exaggeration that we keep seeing in the Narendra Modi regime's success stories, whether it is the annual growth rate or electrification of villages, even the fight against terrorism in Jammu and Kashmir.

Yet there is little reason to doubt that Rana Udai Singh enjoyed a numerical superiority over the Afghan warlord. When Haji Khan appealed to the Rajput king to let him go unmolested and assist him if possible, the Rana supposedly sent back a rather indecent proposal:

> I demand that Haji Khan shall deliver up to me his favourite lady, Rai Kalapater, who, besides her unparalleled beauty, excels in dancing and singing, and 10 lacs of rupees in specie; and then go wherever he pleases.[29]

---

25 Harawi Neamat Ullah, *History of the Afghans*, trans. Bernhard Dorn (London: Royal Asiatic Society, 1836), Annotations, p. 108.

26 Satish Chandra, *History of Medieval India, 800–1700* (New Delhi: Orient Blackswan, 2007), p. 245.

27 Sir Jadunath Sarkar, *Military History of India* (New Delhi: Orient Longmans, 1960), p. 77.

28 William Ervine, *The Army of the Indian Moghuls: Its Organization and Administration* (London: Luzac & Co, 1903), pp. 6–7.

29 Neamat Ullah, *History of the Afghans*, p. 108.

This was too big an insult for Haji Khan to bear. He summoned his war council and announced that had the Rana demanded gold, elephants and other material things, he would have given it to him.

> But the demand of my favourite lady is not compatible with my honour—this I cannot bear: it would, to the day of Resurrection, be ever in the mouth of the Afghans, Haji Khan has committed such an act, and stained the reputation of the Afghans, and more particularly Sher Shah. Such disgrace I cannot suffer to attach to me: I shall fight him, until the event fall out according to destiny.[30]

In India today, thanks to popular fiction and mass media, such bravado and such statements of honour are mostly associated with the Rajputs. The 2018 movie *Padmaavat*, for instance, had similar dialogues mouthed by the character of Rawal Ratansen when Sultan Alauddin Khilji offered peace in exchange for the king's beautiful wife, Padmavati.

This has also been the template of several other television programmes with historical themes where some Muslim ruler or the other demands or tries to get a Hindu princess by force and is challenged and eventually beaten by a Hindu knight in shining armour, but not before making grand pronouncements about honour and chivalry.

Also, it is nearly impossible to imagine in today's India that a Hindu Rajput king, and no less than the Rana of Mewar/Chittor, could blackmail a fugitive war lord and demand his favourite woman as a price to let him go in peace. And so, one can safely predict that we won't see either a Bollywood producer or a TV serial maker even attempt to show something like that on the big or small screen without risking life and limb.

But in late 1556, Haji Khan dared Udai Singh to battle and announced that he would defend his family alone if his rank and file wished to leave. This speech is perhaps comparable to Babur's pep talk to his outnumbered (and therefore demoralised) troops facing a huge Rajput host before the Battle of Khanwa in 1527. And just like the

30 Neamat Ullah, Annotations, p. 109.

Mughals at Khanwa, the Afghans put up a resolute fight and managed to turn the Rana to flight.[31] And with that, Haji Khan became the master of Ajmer, Nagaur and its nearby areas.

That sounds like a simple and straightforward tale of a man being hunted down being blackmailed by another and redeeming his honour at the end. Just that it is not. There was more to this story than what Neamat Ullah was willing to tell us.

Haji Khan had gone to conquer Ajmer after being pushed out of Alwar. Ajmer then was held by Rao Maldev Rathore of Marwar, the most powerful king of Rajputana then. The king who had given Humayun a cold shoulder and harassed his troops in the desert.[32] Seeing Haji Khan come, other Rajputana states came forward to become his allies to defeat Marwar. Rana Udai Singh of Mewar was the foremost among them, followed by Mertiya Rathore Jaimal Viramdevot of Merta. The Rathores of Merta were the feudatory chiefs under Mewar. The alliance was in place and things were looking to work out when Udai Singh made that supposedly inappropriate demand.

Trapped, Haji Khan sought help from the same Rao Maldev whose territories he was planning to annex. And the Marwar king agreed. The new allies took on the forces of Mewar and others at Harmada in 1557 where the Mewaris were defeated and put to flight. The beneficiary at the end of this was Rao Maldev who got control of the fort of Merta. Jaimal Rathore was thrown out and Jagmal, a confidante of Rao Maldev, was made the master of Merta.

Meanwhile, when Akbar heard of Haji Khan's success, he sent an army to put him down under Muhammad Qasim Khan of Nisapur, Syed Muhammad Barha, Shah Quli Khan Mahram, Tahir Khan and Khurram Sultan. The emperor himself prepared to go eastwards to seize the dominions his father had lost. But while all this was happening, Akbar's rear was once again threatened by Sikandar Shah Sur, who had defeated Mughal commander Khizr Khwaja Khan near Lahore and made him turn back into the city.

31 Ibid., pp. 109–10.

32 See Chapter 1.

But when he learnt about Akbar coming down to put him down, Sikandar Shah retreated to the Siwalik hills and further into the fort of Mankot. Akbar's troops laid siege to the fort, which was well-stocked with provisions that could last many months and sustain the garrison. Sikandar Sur expected Adil Shah, Hemu's boss, to come to his rescue by attacking Delhi.[33] That would have resulted in the Mughals lifting the siege and rushing back to defend their own capital. But things don't always go according to plan. The son of the Bengal sultan, Sadr Khan but who styled himself Jalaluddin, attacked Adil Shah to avenge his father, and killed him in battle.[34] With Adil Shah died Sikandar Shah's last hope of putting up a united Afghan opposition to the Turks.

Logically, it wasn't possible to sustain the resistance for long as all allies of Sikandar Shah, including the hill rajas, gradually submitted to the Mughals. Sikandar then made an offer of parley. The Mughals accepted it. Akbar offered him Kharid (later a Mughal *pargana* in Jaunpur under the *subah* of Allahabad) and Bihar as *jagirs*, and on 24 May 1557, Sikandar Shah surrendered the fort to Akbar and joined Mughal service.

While it has often happened that a smaller state became the client state of a bigger state, and a king became the vassal of another, history doesn't throw up too many instances of a defeated king joining the service of his victor. A more notable instance of that in India's past was when Porus became a satrap of Alexander of Macedon after his defeat at the Battle of Hydaspes in 326 BC. Porus, apart from retaining his own territories, became the master of additional areas on Alexander's orders. And so did Sikandar Shah. Once he controlled Delhi and its surroundings; now he had the whole of Bihar and a part of Jaunpur.

But just as Porus fell out of favour with the Greeks after Alexander's death, and was eventually assassinated by a Macedonian general, Sikandar Shah was also fired from his job by Akbar. He then sought refuge in the Afghan sultanate of Bengal where he died in 1559. The Afghan resistance died with him.

---

33 Abu'l Fazl, *Akbarnama, Vol. II*, p. 89.

34 Ibid., p. 90.

But it was during the Siege of Mankot that seeds of a fresh conflict were sown. And the person found holding the short end of the stick this time was the *Khan-i-Khanan*, Bairam Khan.

Bairam Khan, upon his ascendancy as the *Vakil us-Sultanate*, or prime minister of the empire, had gone about creating an inner circle of nobles whom he praised and promoted. This was essentially a power bloc within the court with Bairam Khan at the helm to pacify other nobles who were potential threats to the *Khan-i-Khanan*'s authority.

Those who could threaten his authority in any way were either removed by force, like Shah Abu'l Ma'ali and Tardi Beg, or sent to the borderlands of the fledgling empire where they could not exercise any influence on court matters. Just like Narendra Modi packed BJP's veteran leaders—the old guard—into a toothless panel called *margdarshak mandal* while raising loyalists, however inexperienced, to powerful ministries like defence and human resource development.

As regent, Bairam Khan's personal authority was immense. But he went about appropriating other powers of the state in his office of *vakil* by dismissing officers and merging their offices into his own. This was rare in Timurid polity.

In India today, this sounds very familiar as, since 2014, there has been an amazing concentration of state's power in the Prime Minister's Office or PMO. We have been given to understand that nothing moves without the PMO's nod. As proof of it, we have seen how foreign relations are maintained through the PMO while the External Affairs Minister mostly tweets about issuing visas on compassionate grounds to foreign nationals, mostly Pakistanis needing medical treatment, or passports to beleaguered Indians abroad.

Or, look at the erstwhile Planning Commission of India. It was an arm of the central government with real fiscal powers. It gave a direction to India's economy with its five-year plans. The Modi regime disbanded it and created a new think tank in its place called NITI Aayog, a body devoid of fiscal powers that can only advise but not implement anything. The government no longer consults the think tank on policy matters, which are almost exclusively decided by the PMO. This was just how Bairam Khan had taken over the *diwani* (revenue department).[35] This was just how he had taken away the powers of *wazir* Khwaja Sultan Ali. The PMO today has seen a very Bairam Khan-like way of centralising authority.

Powerful nobles like Munim Khan, who could be potential challengers to Bairam Khan's authority, were kept as far away from the court as possible. Munim Khan, in particular, was not allowed to come out of Kabul. An unprovoked attack by Mirza Suleiman of Badakshan on Kabul gave Bairam Khan the perfect excuse to send those he deemed a threat to Kabul. Bapus Beg, the *faujdar* of Lahore, was transferred to Kabul to help Munim Khan. Later, Shamsuddin Ataga Khan, Muhammad Quli Khan Barlas, Mirza Khizr Khan Hazara and Khwaja Jalaluddin Mahmud[36] were also sent thither to bring the royal ladies home.

Amid this power game, the royal ladies arrived at Mankot in April 1557. The leading Mughal woman of the harem was Hamida Bano Begum, now called Maryam Makani, being the mother of the emperor. And the power equation suddenly changed.

One of the first things that Hamida Bano did was to betroth Akbar to the daughter of Mirza Abdullah Mughal and then quickly organise the wedding, much to the chagrin of Bairam Khan. Abu'l Fazl says the *Khan-i-Khanan* didn't approve of the alliance because Abdullah Mughal's sister was married to Mirza Kamran, and so Bairam Khan understood him as an*az Kamrani,* a Kamran loyalist.[37] Bairam Khan continued to oppose the alliance until Pir Muhammad Khan Shirwani counselled him to abandon his opposition.

That he did, albeit reluctantly. But he must have understood that it was a political move by his rivals to loosen his grip on power. Professor Iqtidar Alam credits Hamida Bano for this.[38]

The air of opposition in the camp must have been palpable to Bairam Khan. And since he himself was given to intrigue, the *Khan-i-Khanan* must have been paranoid about things, both imaginary

---

35 Iqtidar Alam, *Age of Akbar*, p. 98.

36 Ibid., p. 99.

37 Abu'l Fazl, *Akbarnama, Vol. II*, p. 88.

38 Iqtidar Alam, *Age of Akbar,* p. 108.

and real. Abu'l Fazl tells us[39] that towards the end of the siege, Bairam Khan took ill with boils (on his posterior?) that made it difficult for him to mount a horse.

Akbar, being very fond of elephant fights, organised one between two pachyderms named Fateha and Lagna. During the course of it, both animals came dangerously close to Bairam Khan's tent. Bairam Khan understood this as a deliberate ploy to get him out of the way and suspected it was ordered by Akbar.

He protested to Maham Anaga through a trusted servant and said he hadn't done anything disloyal or traitorous to have incurred royal wrath. Maham Anaga tried to alleviate his suspicions with 'soothing expressions'. It may have worked to defuse the situation, but the seeds of mistrust were sown in Bairam's mind.

The seeds were watered by 'strife mongers' close to the *Khan-i-Khanan*. That's what Abu'l Fazl says, but the way things unfolded from there, an impartial reader will surely spot the contours of an elaborate design to remove Bairam from his position of influence.

Bairam Khan wasn't just imagining things, as Abu'l Fazl writes dismissively of him. There was already a clique of nobles in court that disliked, even hated him. These were all Chagatai nobles who were all Sunni. Apart from religious hate that they felt for Bairam being a Shia, it was Bairam's stranglehold on affairs of the state and his inclusion of Shias and Hindus into the civil and military bureaucracy that these nobles detested the most. For instance, it was Bairam Khan who had recruited Todar Mal from Afghan service. These Chagatai nobles particularly detested Shaikh Gadai Kambu, a Shia but whose ancestors were Hindus. Their charge was Bairam was promoting Shias to higher ranks at the cost of Sunnis.

After Mankot, when the imperial camp returned to Lahore, Bairam Khan still felt slighted and vulnerable. And he thought Shamsuddin Ataga Khan was poisoning Akbar's mind against him. Abu'l Fazl quotes him:

> Although the countenance of my loyalty and devotion to the sublime family be free from the stain of deceit or dissimulation and know that

39 Abu'l Fazl, *Akbarnama, Vol. II*, p. 91.

> His Majesty's glance of grace and kindness to myself is without flaw and so I have no fear of any breach in the pillar thereof, yet as His Majesty occasionally treats me with disfavour I believe this must come from your contrivances and calumnies. What have I done that you should gird up the loins of hostility against me and that in thirsting for my blood you should turn the sacred mind against me? And should even go as far as to attempt my life?[40]

This was a serious accusation. And it would be wrong to assume that a man who was running the affairs of the empire almost single-handedly was only imagining a threat to his life.

Ataga Khan went to Bairam Khan with all his family to beseech him not to suspect his intentions. And fences were mended, at least temporarily. But the court intrigues continued, as did the Mughal state's wars for territorial expansion. And the first ethnic group that the new, revived Mughal state came in conflict with was the Baloch.[41]

Abu'l Fazl tells us that Mughal general Bahadur Khan was sent to Multan as its new *jagirdar* with express orders to 'give a lesson' to the Baloch who had 'raised the head of refractoriness'.[42] Fazl hints at this being quite a struggle as he says the Balochis 'displayed great obstinacy' and the fighting lasted for a month, at the end of which the Mughals won.

Yet the Baloch people still gave trouble to the Mughals as their state expanded westwards. The Mughal governor of Multan exercised control over the Baloch through his proxies in Makran, and yet he would have to send out punitive expeditions once in a while to chastise the Baloch. When Bairam Khan's son, Mirza Abdur Rahim Khan, the *Khan-i-Khanan,* became the governor of Multan later, he sent out

40 Abu'l Fazl, *Akbarnama, Vol. II*, p. 94.

41 The Mughals had fought the Baloch earlier. Babur had sent a commander named Chin Timur Sultan in 1529 with an army stocked with provisions to last six months to punish the Baloch for ravaging several places in the south of Punjab. When Humayun went into exile, a Baloch tribal union under Fateh Khan Dodai occupied Multan. When Humayun re-entered India, he regained control of Multan by pushing the Baloch out. I am talking specifically of the new, revived Mughal state under Akbar.

42 Abu'l Fazl, Akbarnama, Vol. II, p. 94..

many such expeditions.[43] But by and large, the Baloch wouldn't cause any large-scale trouble to the Mughals until the reign of Akbar's great-grandson, Aurangzeb. It would be during Aurangzeb's reign when the Baloch would find their own state called the Khanate of Kalat while nominally acknowledging Mughal suzerainty first, then briefly Iranian and eventually Afghan overlordship.

The British in the 19th century entered the scene and established their primacy. But the Kalat Khanate lingered on in some form with relative freedom until 1955 when it was fully merged into Pakistan. The British chief commissioner's province of Balochistan had joined Pakistan in 1948, much against the will of the people. This was followed by a long period of insurgency that resulted in several military operations carried out by the Pakistan armed forces.

Even today, a section of Balochis have carried forth their banner of revolt by demanding an independent state of Balochistan. In 2016, they received some moral support from India when Narendra Modi declared it in his Independence Day speech at the Red Fort.

This didn't mean much on a strategic level as India didn't really have the wherewithal to aid the Baloch struggle physically, with there being no geographical contiguity between Balochistan and India. But surely this was perceived as a sign of India willing to extend its support to the demand for an independent Balochistan officially. This gladdened many Baloch hearts, and the Indian PM soon heard from a galaxy of Baloch leaders and sympathisers of the Baloch movement. One of them was a young female voice from Balochistan, Karima Baloch. The chairperson of an organisation called Baloch Students Organisation, Karima, sent Modi a special Rakshabandhan or Rakhi message, asking him to be a voice of the Baloch struggle.

One feels tempted to compare it to the story of Chittor Queen Karnavati sending a rakhi to Emperor Humayun. Colonel James Tod, the East India Company's resident at the Mewar court in the 19th century who wrote *Annals and Antiquities of Rajasthan*, narrated this tale in the first volume of his work. In 1535, the Chittor queen regent,

43 For a more detailed reading, please see Naseer Dashti's *The Baloch and Balochistan: A Historical Account from the Beginning to the Fall of the Baloch State* (USA: Trafford Publishing, 2012).

facing an invasion by Gujarat Sultan Bahadur Shah, sent a *rakhi* to Humayun and sought his intervention to save her state and honour, both.

Tod said a *rakhi* was sent 'only in times of necessity or danger'. This made the recipient a '*rakhi-band bhai*'. 'He may hazard his life in her cause, and yet never receive a smile in reward, for he cannot even see the fair object who, as brother of her adoption, has constituted him her defender.'[44]

The custom, according to Tod, was to send a *rakhi*, like the queen did, in times of danger, and if the recipient accepted it, he had to do so by sending a *kachhli* or corset. Tod writes:

> The monarch of India (Humayun) was so pleased with this courteous delicacy in the customs of Rajasthan, on receiving the bracelet of the princess Karnavati, which invested him with the title of her brother, and uncle and protector to her infant Udai Singh, that he pledged himself to her service, 'even if the demand were the castle of Ranthambhor'.

He adds:

> Humayun proved himself a true knight, and even abandoned his conquests in Bengal when called on to redeem his pledge to succour Chittor, and the widows and minor sons of Sanga Rana.[45]

Later historians have taken this story with a pinch of salt and argued that this story is of later vintage. The late Satish Chandra held that this story may not be true at all.[46] The indecisive Humayun was late in coming to her assistance, and Chittor fell to the sultan. Karnavati and other Rajput women committed *jauhar* or self-immolation while the men committed *saka*, a suicidal all-out battle by Rajputs when defeat is certain and the object is to take down as many of the enemy before going down fighting. In this, it's similar to the Japanese *kamikaze* pilots of the Second World War, who would

---

44 J. Tod, *Annals and Antiquities of Rajasthan: Or the Central and Western Rajput States of India* (Delhi: Low Price Publications, 2000).

45 Ibid.

46 Satish Chandra, *Medieval India*, p. 213.

crash their aircraft on Allied ships to take them down. Tod says over 32,000 Rajputs died fighting.

Tod, who toed the Mewar line in his work, having served at that court for long, paints a positive picture of Humayun:

> He (Humayun) fulfilled his pledge, expelled the foe from Chittor, took Mandu by assault, and, as some revenge for her king's aiding the king of Gujarat, he sent for the Rana Bikramjit, whom, following their own notions of investiture, he girt with a sword in the captured citadel of the foe.

Humayun did eventually push out Bahadur Shah from Chittor and reinstated Karnavati's son, Vikramaditya, to the throne of Mewar. Going by Tod's account, one could deduce that the Mewar royals believed in this story, at least until the time Tod wrote his account in the first half of the 19th century. In the aftermath of the Revolt of 1857, however, most of the Rajputana states, former allies of the Mughals, would make efforts to whitewash their association with the Mughals. They would do so by commissioning literature, which would later give rise to dubious and bizarre tales totally derisive of the Mughals. These would find expression in even later paintings. Like the tale of Kiran Devi, a princess of Mewar married to the king of Bikaner. It says Akbar abducted Kiran Devi from a *Nauroz mela* he organised in Delhi, but the Rajput queen overpowered him, put a dagger on his chest, and let him go after extracting a promise that he wouldn't hold the *mela* again and never cast a glad eye on Hindu women. A painting illustrating this exists at the Bikaner fort. In more recent times, versions of this painting as well as the story are popular in the Hindutva ecosystem, which obviously comes with a certain kind of political messaging.

The story of Rani Karnavati and Humayun also comes with a certain kind of political messaging—a more secular one. But what's fascinating in the story is that a Hindu Rajput queen appealed to a Muslim king to save her honour by invoking a Hindu religious symbol. In 2016, 481 years after this supposed episode, a woman leading a struggle for survival once again sought the intervention of the ruler of Delhi by sending him *rakhi* greetings. A modern Muslim woman appealed to an avowedly Hindu Indian prime minister to defend the honour of the wholly Muslim Baloch people by invoking a Hindu religious symbol! Things have changed so much and yet remained the same in so many ways. It's a different matter that the Indian PM hasn't been able to help the Baloch struggle beyond offering mere platitudes and lip service.

Yet despite the Mughal success against the Baloch, Akbar had reasons to loathe the overbearing manner in which Bairam Khan was acting. The next action of Bairam Khan was more revolting. Takht Mal, the zamindar of Mau (today's Pathankot), was an ally of Sikandar Shah. When the Mankot affair went badly for the Afghan challenger, Takht Mal submitted before Akbar and was accepted into his service. It was the lay of the land and there was nothing unusual about it. Petty chiefs would go with the flow and support whomsoever had his star in the ascendant. Todar Mal was also a Sur servant but Bairam Khan himself recruited him into Mughal service.

But Bairam Khan got Takht Mal executed for no apparent reason other than suspecting him of being disloyal in future. In his place, he installed Bakht Mal. All this was done without informing Akbar. The young monarch detested this unnecessary shedding of blood, and that too of someone who had submitted willingly and was accepted willingly. It was a direct challenge to the emperor's own authority by the regent.

Akbar didn't like it, but again, he didn't show it in the open. In fact, this was responded to with largesse. Humayun had in his lifetime betrothed Bairam Khan to Salima Sultan Begum, his niece and daughter of his half-sister, Gulrukh Begum. The marriage was solemnised in Lahore, after the victory at Mankot. It's interesting to note that this even occurred in the midst of a period of serious intrigue and increasing bad blood between Bairam Khan and the rival camp. Therefore, it looks like a deliberate attempt to placate Bairam by ceding to him some ground. Salima was a Timurid princess. And marriage with a Timurid princess was a matter of honour as that catapulted Bairam Khan into the biggest league—the imperial family. This was perhaps a way thought up by the royal women led by Hamida Bano and Maham Anaga to keep Bairam Khan in good humour as, though slighted, Bairam Khan was still very powerful and capable of hitting back.

And he did. But the victims this time were people of his own clique who, according to him, had turned rogue. The first was someone named Musahib Beg. He had been appointed to high office by Bairam Khan. But he caused some affront to the *Khan-i-Khanan*, which led to his execution. The emperor's permission wasn't sought before exercising this extreme measure. And this caused anguish to the royal household and the rivals of Bairam Khan. It was important to clip the *Khan-i-Khanan*'s wings. But how?

The details are not known, but an effort must have been made to wean away Pir Muhammad Khan Shirwani from Bairam Khan's influence. Conferring the title of *Nasir ul Mulk* on him, which only the emperor could do, suggests that this was a resolute step in that direction.

Badaoni makes it clear that Pir Muhammad was getting royal favours when he writes that he was 'the closer and opener of every important affair of state, and finance' and that 'all the pillars of the state used to go to his house'.[47]

A sharp man like Bairam couldn't have possibly missed the signs of his apprentice growing too big for his shoes or tolerated a potential rival. So, he started looking for an occasion, an excuse, to cut his protégé down to size. He didn't have to wait too long.

In October 1558, Akbar shifted his capital to Agra. There, Pir Muhammad fell ill and couldn't attend court for a few days. Bairam Khan went to see him one day. A Turkish slave who said he would have to ask his master's permission to let him enter blocked his entry. Bairam Khan got offended by this and supposedly said, 'For a wilful fool there is no cure!'[48] This was a direct pun on Pir Muhammad's illness and an insinuation of a dangerous fate.

Pir Muhammad, conscious of the fate that might befall him if he incurred his mentor's wrath, promptly came out to apologise for the

47 Badaoni, *Tawarikh*, p. 19.
48 Ibid., p. 20.

affront caused to him. 'Forgive me, for my porter didn't know you,' he said. 'Nor you either!' Bairam retorted and left.[49]

Two or three days later, Bairam Khan sent a missive to Pir Muhammad. It was an angry and sentimental note in which a boss had remonstrated with his apprentice. Pir Muhammad was a 'poor scholar' when he had come to the service of Bairam Khan when he held Kandahar for the Mughals when Humayun ruled from Kabul. Bairam Khan stressed on his humble origins to thrust the knife of insult deep into Pir Muhammad's heart.

Badaoni quotes Bairam Khan[50]:

> You will remember that you came to Kandahar in the position of an unfortunate student, and that when we found that you possessed ability and the quality of fidelity, and when also some worth services had been performed by you, we raised you, a mere student and beggar, from the lowest step among the degraded, to the highest grade among the exalted in Sultanship and Khanship, and to the post of an Amir of Amirs: but, since the carrying of a high position is not in your capacity, nothing but suspicious rebelliousness and baseness remains in you. So we will take away from you for a time the insignia of your pride, that your base disposition and inflated brain may come to their senses. Now it is right that you should surrender the standard, and kettle drum, and paraphernalia of pomp.

As Pir Muhammad surrendered his official insignia and credentials, he was arrested and packed off to Bayana where he was imprisoned at the fort there. He was then ordered to push off for Mecca under escort. Some punishment for a perceived slight! Haji Muhammad Khan Sistani was elevated as *vakil* to take the place of Pir Muhammad while Shaikh Gadai was promoted as *sadr*.

But as Pir Muhammad was about to move out, he received letters from Mirza Sharfuddin Husain and Adham Khan, Maham Anaga's son, to stay put and not leave the country. And soon, Pir Muhammad made good his escape and took shelter in Jhain (believed to be Chhan

49 Ibid.

50 Ibid., pp. 20–1.

near Ranthambore in Sawai Madhopur district of Rajasthan today). But Bairam Khan pushed him out of there too towards Gujarat.

For the young emperor, this arbitrary killing of Musahib Beg and the banishment of someone he raised to the status of Amir without his consent must have been a real affront to his authority. But Bairam Khan managed to divert Akbar's attention from it by proposing an invasion of Gwalior.[51] Shortly after that, Bairam Khan didn't extend courtesy to Sufi saint Sheikh Muhammad Ghaus as ordered by Akbar, which resulted in the saint going back to Gwalior from Agra feeling slighted: something that angered Akbar. Even if we don't study anything about Akbar's relationship with Ghaus, we can understand its importance from two things: Akbar constructed a magnificent tomb for him in what is today the older part of Gwalior city (this author has been there), and Akbar's chief musician Tansen is buried under the shade of Ghaus' tomb. Akbar's anger, therefore, was natural. But Bairam Khan once again deployed a diversionary tactic, this time proposing a campaign against Malwa.[52]

There have been similar allegations against the Modi government today: that it diverted attention from core issues like healthcare, education, employment, economy, etc. by ramping up petty issues like nationalism, respect for the military, standing up for the national anthem in cinemas, singing of *Vande Mataram* and so on. Critics also argue that the political use of cross-border military operations, demonetisation of high-value currency notes, putting the blame squarely on past prime ministers for failures during the Modi regime are attempts to divert attention from a flailing political narrative.

But every strategy has a use-by date and cannot be perennially used. The same happened with Bairam Khan.

One of Akbar's elephants in a state of *musth* attacked one of Bairam Khan's elephants one day. The attack was so severe that the entrails of Bairam Khan's elephant came out.[53] Bairam got the mahout of the royal elephant executed without informing the emperor. It was

51 Raghavan, *Attendant Lords*, pp. 53–5.

52 Ibid.

53 Abu'l Fazl, *Akbarnama, Vol. II*, p. 139.

one of Akbar's personal elephants, so Akbar didn't take it very kindly, though he didn't make a public fuss of it.

But then there was a repeat of the situation, well almost. During a boat ride on the Yamuna one evening, a royal elephant went out of control and charged at the boat. Its mahout somehow brought the animal under control before it could hurt Bairam Khan.

When Akbar learnt about it, he got the mahout arrested and sent to Bairam Khan to calm him down, despite knowing that the mahout was innocent.[54] But instead of appreciating the gesture of Akbar, Bairam Khan got that mahout executed as well. This was someone who was in the personal employ of Akbar. This transgression was not taken kindly at all. He resolved to axe Bairam Khan from his regency, and confided in Maham Anaga, Mirza Sharfuddin Husain and Adham Khan.[55]

On 19 March 1560, Akbar went to Coel (Aligarh) for a hunt and proceeded to Delhi from there. It seems Maham Anaga had arranged for it. Akbar's mother was in Delhi then. So, it's quite obvious that the young emperor, now 18, was coming to his mother to plan something together. This gives a fairly strong clue as to the pivotal role played by Hamida Bano in securing her son's monarchy.

From Delhi, Akbar issued orders to those loyal noblemen who had been sent away to distant corners of the empire. He summoned Shamsuddin Ataga Khan from Punjab and Munim Khan from Kabul. Pir Muhammad Khan was also asked to come back to court. And soon, people who were formerly loyal to Bairam Khan also started to leave Agra and come to Delhi. The *Khan-i-Khanan* realised what was happening. So, he wrote to Akbar multiple letters professing his loyalty and allegiance. Akbar, though, would have none of it.

Bairam Khan then sent his trusted aides—people like Haji Muhammad Khan Sistani whom he had appointed vakil after firing Pir Muhammad Khan Shirwani—to argue his case before the emperor in Delhi. But it didn't work. Abu'l Fazl writes that these men were not allowed to leave the court. That's a euphemism for their arrest. Akbar

54 Ibid.

55 Ibid., p. 141.

wanted to isolate Bairam Khan and dismantle his support system—the nobles loyal to him.

Bairam Khan then proposed to come personally to Delhi to pay obeisance to the emperor and convince him of his loyalty. Akbar asked him to stand down instead and not make a move as he suspected that Bairam Khan might mount an attack on Delhi in the guise of paying homage. And if that happened, a decisive general like Bairam Khan could have swayed the outcome in his favour.

After contemplating several courses of action, Bairam Khan decided to move out of Agra towards Alwar in April 1560. From there, he went to Bayana and freed Muhammad Amin Diwana and Shah Abu'l Ma'ali—two nobles who had been imprisoned by Bairam Khan himself for suspected disloyalty towards the emperor. Abu'l Fazl reads Bairam Khan's motive well, for he writes:

> Though he professed to tell them to resort to the sublime court, yet his object in releasing such experienced troublers was nothing but to give them the opportunity for sedition.[56]

This releasing of prisoners with ulterior motives has been a constant in history. During the Revolt of 1857, when rebel *sowars* from Meerut had arrived in Delhi on 11 May, they had released all prisoners from jails. That had led to tremendous looting and overall chaos in Delhi that made the people of the city detest the rebels. Similarly, when the Empire of Japan had captured the Andaman Islands during the Second World War in 1942, the Japanese had released all prisoners of the Cellular Jail. They soon had to shoot down some of them as they went about looting the villages and troubling the locals.

Bairam Khan moved towards Punjab, and Akbar decided to pursue him. Just then, Shah Abu'l Ma'ali came to Akbar's presence and offered his services. Abu'l Fazl is so full of scorn for him that his description of him is hilarious at times. He narrated Abu'l Ma'ali's coming to the royal presence thus—'...Shah Abu'l Ma'ali, who was a repository of strife and sedition, arrived with his evil ideas at the sublime court...'

56 Ibid.,

Abu'l Ma'ali very haughtily rode up to Akbar and tried to embrace him while being mounted. That infuriated Akbar and he ordered his arrest and banishment to Mecca. Clearly, Humayun's son wasn't going to tolerate an arrogant nobleman whom Humayun had indulged.

But Akbar wasn't going to indulge Bairam Khan either. So, he issued a *firman* (a royal order or decree) to the *Khan-i-Khanan* in which he listed out all instances of overreach. A part of the order was a royal rant against Shaikh Gadai. And this bit is worth quoting here:

> …in these five years some improper acts of his (Bairam Khan's) came to light which disgusted everyone, such as his patronage of Shaikh Gadai so that made him Sadr, and in spite of the office's requiring consummate ability and knowledge, he, on account of his own private companionship and intimacy, chose him from among all the men who were fit for it by capacity and lineage. And in addition to making him Sadr and allowing him to endorse decrees with his seal he exempted him from the ceremony of homage, and in spite of his utter ignorance and want of capacity, he gave him precedence in the paradisaical assemblies over all the Syeds of noble rank and all the distinguished ulema, to whom we paid reverence on account of their rank and qualities.[57]

It's quite clear that Shaikh Gadai's Hindu ancestry and his being a Shia were being held up against him. The collective, pent-up emotions of all those nobles who had to swallow their pride in the face of the power of the regent, including the emperor, had just burst forth like a dam in this *firman*. The Syeds, being members of the Prophet's family, still consider themselves as the most blue-blooded Muslims. Back in the 16th century, though, they definitely were the *crème de la crème* of the Muslim society. And the appointment of the descendant of a Hindu convert over their heads must have come to them as an unpardonable affront. The same Akbar, who would later try to place himself over the *ulema* (clergy) as the supreme interpreter of Islamic law, pointed out his own reverence for them in order to make a case against Bairam Khan. And Akbar, who would later promote meritocracy himself, held Bairam Khan's promotion of it against him.

---

57 Ibid.,

The *firman* also had Akbar's threat of killing Bairam Khan if he didn't surrender. But Bairam Khan still paid no heed. So, Akbar sent an army under Ataga Khan to challenge him. The two armies engaged each other in the town of Phillaur[58] (in today's Jalandhar district, Punjab), and Bairam Khan was beaten back. The *Khan-i-Khanan*, like Sikandar Shah Sur, went to the Siwalik and sought refuge with the *zamindar* of Talwara (in Hoshiarpur district of Punjab today bordering Himachal Pradesh) named Raja Ganesh.

Akbar now moved towards Lahore and sent his armies in pursuit. Many Hindu kings and *zamindars* opposed them and were slaughtered. With the dragnet tightening around him, Bairam Khan offered to surrender. And it was accepted by Akbar. Abu'l Fazl writes that Bairam Khan prostrated himself before the emperor and wept, but Akbar lifted him up, wiped away his tears and embraced him. He then made him sit next to him like before, pardoned him completely, and accepted his wish of going to Mecca.

As Bairam Khan left, Munim Khan was made *Khan-i-Khanan* and Bairam Khan's house in Agra was also given to him. Bairam Khan, meanwhile, reached Patan in Gujarat in January 1561. His family was with him. There, he was spotted by an Afghan named Mubarak Khan Lohani, who supposedly nursed a grudge against Bairam Khan for having killed his father at the Battle of Machhiwara.[59] On 31 January 1560, when Bairam Khan visited *Sahasralinga Talav* (tank), a famed tourist spot of the time, this man came forward to meet him along with 40-odd other Afghans. On the pretext of offering his respects by way of an embrace, Mubarak Khan stabbed Bairam Khan in the back, quite literally. His other associates then joined in the stabbing and killed that veteran of many battles and the sturdiest pillar that held up the once tottering throne of the House of Timur. He had his revenge, though Bairam Khan became a martyr going by the tenets of Islam.

The *Akbarnama* makes no mention of the presence of Haji Khan, who had been pushed out of Alwar and then Ajmer by the Mughals, in Patan at that time. But Badaoni does. And he tells us that Patan governor Musa Khan Fuladi (Lodhi, according to Firishta) and Haji

---

58 Badaoni, *Tawarikh*, p. 35.

59 See Chapter 2 for details of this battle.

Khan had received Bairam Khan well and extended to him good hospitality.

But it seems they did next to nothing to save his family from harassment at the hands of Afghans, who went about looting and plundering Bairam Khan's camp and retinue. With great difficulty, Bairam Khan's son and wife were taken to Ahmedabad with Afghans still pursuing them. From Ahmedabad, they were sent to Delhi where the emperor took them under his wing.

At some point later, a story circulated that Haji Khan had got Bairam Khan killed to avenge his master Hemu. Abu'l Fazl, Badaoni, Nizamuddin Ahmed and Firishta don't mention any such thing. And yet, it is still a popular story that's mentioned as fact on Wikipedia and elsewhere. This author hasn't been able to independently verify the source of this, but it's a remarkable tale nevertheless where a Muslim general avenges his slain Hindu overlord by killing another Muslim. People also talk about a mausoleum to Bairam Khan existing in Patan[60] even though the *Akbarnama* says Bairam Khan's mortal remains were sent to Mashhad (in modern-day Iran) for burial.

Today, Bairam Khan has been nearly forgotten in India, but he is the national hero of Turkmenistan.[61] A former Soviet republic, Turkmenistan had to begin with a clean slate in the 1990s after the dissolution of the Soviet Union. And it shook off its Soviet and Tsarist legacies in search of an ethnic one. In the course of it, it rediscovered Bairam Khan.[62]

With Bairam Khan ended a chapter of Mughal rule in India. An assertive Akbar had shaken off the regency, but he wasn't entirely free of influence. There were Maham Anaga, her son Adham Khan and nobles who had been plotting with her against Bairam Khan but who could also turn against Akbar. The young emperor must have recognised the task at hand. But he would find an opportunity to clip

---

60 Pramod Panwar, 'Bairam Khan's mausoleum in Patan lies in shambles', *The Times of India*, Palanpur, 23 November 2013. Available at https://timesofindia.indiatimes.com/city/rajkot/Bairam-Khans-mausoleum-in-Patan-lies-in-shambles/articleshow/26278708.cms.

61 He belonged to the Baharlu clan of Qara Qoyunlu, a Turkmen tribal federation.

62 See T. C. A. Raghavan's *Attendant Lords* for a comprehensive picture of the life and times of Bairam Khan and his legacy in Turkmenistan today.

the wings of the woman who was called *Bega* in Mughal records and her son during the campaign of Malwa.

Malwa was a rich sultanate ruled by Sultan Baz Bahadur, also known as Malik Bayazid. He ascended the throne a year before Akbar ascended his, but he was less of an administrator and more devoted to the arts. In fact, Abu'l Fazl paints a picture of a man given to worldly pleasures, drinking and debauchery—wine and women, if you will. But music was a key aspect of his life. It was music that tied him to his wives and concubines.

So, Abu'l Fazl remarks:

> Music and melody which the wise and farsighted have employed at times of lassitude and depression...as a means of lightening the mind and of cheerfulness, were regarded by this scoundrel as a serious business, and he spent upon them all his precious hours—for which no exchange is possible. In the arrogance of infatuation he wrought works of inauspiciousness, and regarded not what has been said.[63]

Malwa was the gateway to the Deccan, while the route to Gujarat and its rich ports also lay through the southern part of Malwa called *Khandesh*. This wasn't some new reality for the Mughals to confront; it was always so since ancient times. The two major trade and military routes in ancient India were the *Uttarapatha* and *Dakshinapatha*. These roughly translate into 'northern path' and 'southern path'. The Mauryan Empire was the first to subjugate almost the entire Indian subcontinent, so they were the first to control both *Uttarapatha* and *Dakshinapatha*. Goods, as well as Mauryan armies, crisscrossed the subcontinent through these highway systems.

By the time the Imperial Guptas came over 600 years later, Ujjain in Malwa had become a key city that controlled the approaches to the ports of Gujarat like Bharuch. The Gupta Emperor Samudragupta after his military campaigns or *digvijaya* became *Uttarapathapati* and *Dakshinapathapati* (master of the northern and southern paths).

---

63 Abu'l Fazl, *Akbarnama, Vol. II*, p. 211.

Though Akbar came over 1,800 years after Chandragupta Maurya's empire-building campaigns, he also had to stick to these traditional Indian highway systems as India's geographical realities were still pretty much the same then. Bairam Khan had earlier convinced Akbar to turn towards Malwa. Now, after his downfall, Akbar put together a campaign to snatch Malwa from the man who would prove to be the last independent sultan of the region.

After the fall of Bairam, Adham Khan's fortunes had risen, more because his mother now wielded even greater influence in the court and harem. Adham had already given a good account of himself at the Siege of Mankot. So, Akbar put him at the head of the Malwa campaign. To aid and assist him, Akbar also sent a smattering of competent generals, including Pir Muhammad Khan Shirwani. Writing over 30 years after the campaign, Abu'l Fazl gave an intellectual backing to this aggrandising event by invoking the good of the people. He said the army was ordered 'to proceed southwards and display justice and liberality and to be balm for the wounds of the oppressed ones of Malwa'.

Now, one doesn't really hear of Baz Bahadur carrying out atrocities on his people. But Fazl quickly gave out the real intention behind the campaign—that of subjugation of the province and making it a vassal state. 'If the ruler of that country should awake from his negligent slumbers and be prepared to amend his ways, he was to be made hopeful of the royal clemency and to be exalted by kissing the lofty threshold, so that he might be treated in accordance with his behaviour,' Fazl wrote.

The Mughal army advanced to Sarangpur, which Fazl called 'the fool's paradise of this drunkard', and engaged Baz Bahadur's army. The battle lasted a few days after which Baz Bahadur was defeated. He made good his escape to Khandesh, but his harem wasn't so lucky. In fact, Abu'l Fazl informs that Baz Bahadur had, before going for battle, ordered his harem guards to kill his wives and concubines if he lost so that they may not fall into the hands of the Mughals. Fazl calls it the 'Indian custom', which looks like a euphemism for *jauhar* practised by the Rajputs. Despite the florid prose of Fazl, the gory nature of what followed is difficult to miss.

Fazl wrote:

> When the form of Baz Bahadur's defeat appeared in the mirror of results those devil-born ones acted according to the arrangement and with the water of the sword wiped out some of the fairy-framed puppets from the page of life. With the knife of injustice they erased from the world's folio the life records of those innocents. Some were wounded and yet retained a breath of life, and for many the turn of slaughter had not come, when the victorious troops hastily marched into the city.[64]

As the text suggests, not all women could be killed due to paucity of time. Some were not touched and some were wounded or left for dead. Scenes like these had repeated in Rajputana in the past and would repeat again in the future. In fact, a very similar scene was witnessed by an East India Company army led by Major General Arthur Wellesley upon the fall of the fort of Gawilgarh (Gawilghur in British records) during the Second Anglo-Maratha War in 1803.

Gawilgarh was an imposing fort belonging to the Bhonsle of Berar to which Maratha armies (Arabs, Rajputs and Purbiyas) had retreated after their defeat at Argaon during the Deccan campaign of the future Duke of Wellington. When the pursuing Anglo-Indian army laid siege to the fort, the garrison refused to hold parleys or ask for surrender terms. The reason being this was a Rajput-dominated garrison inspired by the martial spirit of Rajputana. A dogged resistance was guaranteed. But the bane of the Rajput way of war—a fatalistic resignation to fate—also plagued the garrison of 3,000. So, when the British managed to breach the walls of the force on 15 December 1803, the garrison committed *saka*.

The defenders carried out sally after sally and engaged the British infantry in close quarters combat using musket butts and bayonets. They died by their hundreds. Finally, when the British went inside the fort, they were faced with a horrifying scene—that of women dead and dying. Their throats had been slit by the men to ensure that they didn't fall into British hands. This was *jauhar*. And the

64 Ibid.,

description matched with that of Abu'l Fazl. Anyone who lauds *jauhar* as a glorious act today needs to be confronted with these bare details. There was no honour, no glory in killing or forcing women to embrace death when faced with military defeat. The women were treated as property that had to be destroyed to deny the victors spoils of war. It was a scorched earth policy involving humans. Abu'l Fazl also rightly called out this system for its barbarity.

At Sarangpur, among the wounded was Rupmati, Baz Bahadur's great love and muse. Fazl wrote:

> The villains had not time to lay hands on these innocent women. The chief of them was Rupmati, renowned throughout the world for her beauty and charm. Baz Bahadur was deeply attached to her and used to pour out his heart in Hindi poems descriptive of his love. A monster who had been left in charge of her uplifted the sword of wrong and inflicted several severe wounds on her. Just then the army of fortune (the Mughal army) arrived and brought out that half-slaughtered lovely one.

Adham Khan's primary intent was to seize all of Baz Bahadur's wealth, his singers (Baz Bahadur had 400 musicians in his employ) and dancers and concubines whose 'beauty and melody' and 'heart ravishing charms' were known far and wide. Then he sent people to look for Rupmati. But when Rupmati learnt about Adham Khan wanting to have her too, she committed suicide by consuming poison as she couldn't bear the thought of becoming another's man's keep when she loved Baz Bahadur. History would remember Baz Bahadur and Rupmati as great lovers, in the same league as Laila and Majnu, Heer and Ranjha, Soni and Mahiwal, Khusro and Shirin.

The story would be immortalised by Bollywood in 1957 in a movie named *Rani Rupmati* starring Nirupa Roy as Rupmati and Bharat Bhushan as Baz Bahadur. More than anything else, it's the film's music that became legendary, with a particular romantic number called '*Aa ab laut ke aaja*', in which an anxious Rupmati called out to her lover to come back to her, becoming a chartbuster of the time. The popularity of the song can be gauged from the fact that it still pops up at various FM channels in the major metros of India once in a while.

But it wasn't love that the Mughals gave to Baz Bahadur's subjects, it was sheer hate. Those on Baz Bahadur's side who were captured were put to death in a wanton display of bloodlust. Badaoni blamed Pir Muhammad Khan Shirwani for it. Badaoni wrote: 'On the day of the victory, the two captains (Adham Khan and Pir Muhammad) remained on the spot, and had the captives brought before them, and troop after troop of them put to death, so that their blood flowed river upon river…'[65]

Badaoni said that he was present at the spot when all this happened. He wrote, 'When I, without any prejudice against either side, came to that army and saw the terror, like that of the Judgement Day, I said to my friend Mihr Ali Khan Beg Sildoz, "Though the rebels have met with their deserts yet it is not at all in accordance with the Sacred Law to kill and imprison their wives and children".'

Badaoni also wrote that he took up the matter with Pir Muhammad to no avail. The *Nasir ul Mulk* was uncompromising, whether it was a Hindu or Muslim captive.

> And the same night these plundering marauders, having stowed away their Muhammadan captives, consisting of the wives of Shaikhs, and Sayyids, and learned men, and nobles, in their boxes and saddle bags, brought them to Ujjain and other districts. And the Sayyids and Shaikhs of that place came out to meet him with their Qurans in their hands, but Pir Muhammad Khan put them all to death, and burnt them.

Adham Khan sent news of his victory to Akbar at Agra through Sadik Khan and also some elephants as war spoils. But he kept most of the booty for himself and also Baz Bahadur's harem. Adham Khan also parcelled out the kingdom among his generals, keeping Sarangpur and other parganas for himself and giving out the rest to others. Pir Muhammad was given Mandu and Ujjain. The strategic importance of Ujjain has been mentioned earlier.

When the news of the Malwa affair reached Akbar through Sadik Khan, he got worried. It's not known whether the bloodletting troubled him. But Akbar worried about Adham Khan acting too independently.

65 Badaoni, *Tawarikh*, p. 42.

Indeed, retaining the war spoils and dividing up a conquered kingdom without informing the emperor would have appeared to anyone in that age as steps towards founding an independent kingdom. Abu'l Fazl wrote that Adham Khan was becoming 'seditious'.

Akbar decided to take matters in his own hands. He dashed off towards Malwa with a small band of followers on 27 April 1561. Through forced marches, Akbar reached his destination in 16 days. Maham Anaga had sent her messengers to warn Adham Khan about the emperor coming, but Akbar reached Sarangpur before them. Adham Khan couldn't believe his eyes when he saw Akbar, but quickly put up a fake show of goodwill and submission.

Without Akbar's asking, he offered an explanation for not sending the war booty, saying that he wanted to keep it safe until Akbar could see it himself. Baz Bahadur's women were also sent to him. Akbar didn't admonish Adham, though he knew that Adham was pulling a fast one. Instead, he played along, expressed satisfaction with Adham Khan's hospitality and gesture. He decided to bury the hatchet quietly.

But Adham Khan once again tested Akbar's patience when he, in league with some servants of Maham Anaga, abducted two of Baz Bahadur's women from Akbar's seraglio. Abu'l Fazl says they were in the emperor's enclosure, so it's obvious that Akbar had developed a liking for them and kept them close to him. When Akbar learnt about the two going missing, he sent out his men to look for them. He wasn't willing to part with them. They were found and were being brought to Akbar when Maham Anaga, realising that her personal reputation could be wrecked if the two women testified before the emperor that her servants and son were involved, got both of them killed on the way. Akbar was disturbed to know it, but he didn't say much out of deference to his foster mother. Abu'l Fazl says Akbar 'overlooked this gross outrage, as the veil was not yet removed from his world-illuminating countenance'.[66]

That either means Akbar was too innocent to suspect anything wrong, or he lacked the power to do it because Maham Anaga was still a powerful presence in his life. It's unlikely that Akbar didn't

66 Abu'l Fazl, *Akbarnama, Vol. II*, p. 221.

know what had happened. He anyway suspected the intentions of Adham Khan. What's more likely, despite Abu'l Fazl saying so, is that it may have strengthened Akbar's resolve to break free from any kind of influence.

Akbar spent only four days at Sarangpur before returning to Agra. The return journey took him 17 days, and the entire trip, Abu'l Fazl says, took a month and seven days. But once he was back in his capital, Akbar recalled Adham Khan and gave Pir Muhammad full command over Malwa. Adham Khan's first independent command was a disaster for him and his ambitious mother. And this must have frustrated the mother-son duo quite a bit. Akbar's logic may have also been to keep a closer eye on him, and that was possible only when he was in Agra.

But Pir Muhammad's ruthlessness only won him spurs. And he must have read his elevation as an official sanction for cruelty. Feeling emboldened, he led an army to Burhanpur where he won the fort of Bijagarh and carried out a general slaughter. Thereafter, he turned his attention towards Khandesh where Baz Bahadur had withdrawn. There, too, the Mughal army left behind a trail of death and destruction. Badaoni writes:

> Pir Muhammad was not content with himself unless he practised to the utmost, the Code of Changiz Khan, massacring, or making prisoners of all the inhabitants of Burhanpur and Asir, and then crossing the Narbadah he raised the conflict to the very heavens, and utterly destroyed many towns and villages of the district, and swept everything clean and clear.[67]

Even back then, the name of Chingiz Khan was used to describe mass slaughter. One must also mention here that in almost all Persian chronicles in India right from the time of the Delhi Sultanate down to the time of the Mughals, the Mongols were portrayed as uncouth and boorish. Barbarians and savages. The term used for them was Mughal, Persian for Mongol. In the Indian imagination, the term Mughal represented carnage. It represented a brute military force made of savages that didn't even leave a blade of grass standing wherever it went.

---

67 Badaoni, *Tawarikh*, p. 46.

But the term was also applied later to other Central Asian Turks. Amir Timur, while being referred to by his lofty title of Sahib-i-Qiran in Mughal records, in Sultanate records, he was called the Mughal. Of course, Timur was not a Chingizid or Genghisid prince, and he himself shared the general contempt for the Mongols. But for legitimacy in Mawarannahar, he married into the family of Genghis and became a *guregen* or 'royal son-in-law'. Guregen was Persianised to Gurgan or Gurkan. His royal signature after his marriage bore the name 'Amir Timur Gurgan'.[68]

The Mughals, being descendants of Timur, also took pride in the fact that their great ancestor was a son-in-law of Genghis Khan. In fact, Babur's grandmother, Esan Daulat Begum, was also a Chingizid princess. But at the same time, they shared their great ancestor's contempt for the Mongols. Jauhar Aftabchi wrote in his *Tazkirat ul Waqiat* how Humayun, while bestowing an honour on him, said something nasty about the 'Mughals' to give him an example. The Mughals referred to themselves as Gurkaniyya or Gurkanids, that is royal sons-in-law of Genghis Khan, and *nasl-i-Timur* or Timurids. It is, therefore, ironic that they eventually came to be known as the Mughals.

As it often happens, something that is feared and despised also becomes a subject of ridicule. Over time, as the memory of fear lapses, that of ridicule stays on. And when that happens, only the jokes remain. By the time the Mughals arrived on the scene, the Mongols were already a spent force. A part of history. So, funny tales and jokes about them were all that remained in the public mind. So, Humayun cracking jokes on the Mongols appears to be the order of the day.

If we analyse humour in India and Pakistan, we find that the two communities that have the most number of jokes about them are the Sikhs (India) and Pathans (Pakistan). One of the oldest popular expressions used to mock the Sikhs is, '*Sardaron ke baarah baj gaye*' or 'It's 12 o clock for the Sikhs.' When used today, it means 'These Sikhs are crazy'. It's believed to have originated from the night raids

68 Walter J. Fischel, *Ibn Khaldun and Tamerlane: Their Historic Meeting in Damascus, 1401 A.D. (803 A.H)* (Los Angeles: University of California Press, 1952), endnote 167, p. 102.

that insurgent Sikhs used to conduct on Mughal troops during the time the Sikhs under Banda Singh Bahadur were resisting the Mughal Empire. This undoubtedly was an expression of fear at the time. But later, either during the climacteric of the Mughal Empire or in the colonial period, it became something to joke about.

The Pathan jokes in Pakistan are similar in nature. The Pathans or Pashtun people were the other group of people who gave immense trouble to the Mughals, perhaps even more than the Sikhs. Their great emperor Ahmad Shah Abdali even captured the Mughal capital of Delhi. In later times, they proved to be formidable foes for the British just like the Sikhs. And yet, the British, while subjugating the Sikh Empire, also meddled in Afghanistan as part of the 'Great Game'. They recruited both Sikhs and Pathans into the Indian Army, who eventually became the mainstay of it, especially after the British came up with their 'martial races theory'—a dubious race theory pooh-poohed by all historians worth their salt today, but which identified some Indians as more war-like than others and therefore worthy of bearing arms. As both these independent groups became part of the British military system, over time, their independent resistance to both Mughals and British receded from public memory. What remained were the jokes and insults.

The Mughals may have despised the Mongols, but Pir Muhammad Khan Shirwani didn't seem to have any qualms about carrying out Mongol-like depredations. But he didn't go unchallenged for long. Baz Bahadur had recruited fresh troops in Khandesh. With support from some local zamindars, he shocked Pir Muhammad in a brief encounter. The Mughals were forced to turn back towards Mandu. But they had to cross the Narmada for that. Ignoring wise counsel, Pir Muhammad decided to cross the river on horseback. As he was doing so, a mule train[69] was also crossing the river. One of the mules kicked Pir Muhammad's horse on the side, unsettling both the animal and its rider. Pir Muhammad fell into the river and drowned.

Abu'l Fazl lamented his death. There was no question of Badaoni doing so, for he gave enough reasons to dislike Pir Muhammad for

69 Abu'l Fazl says it was a pack of mules, but Badaoni says it was a herd of camels.

his wanton violence. But Fazl, who was silent about the *Nasir ul Mulk* war crimes earlier, and had even written disapprovingly of Adham Khan for not paying heed to what Pir Muhammad had said during the Malwa campaign, blamed it on karma. Pir Muhammad's karma. He wrote:

> He was drowned and went to the ocean of annihilation, either as a retribution of the oppression which he had committed in this expedition, or for his conduct Tardi Beg Khan's battle (at Tughlaqabad against Hemu in which Pir Muhammad had fled first, abandoning the senior general, and for which Bairam Khan had punished Tardi Beg with death).... By heaven's decree so loyal, able, and gallant a man underwent such a fate.[70]

One can only guess that Abu'l Fazl glossed over Pir Muhammad's dark exploits as he perceived these to be blemishes in Akbar's illustrious rule. That begs the question: was violence and bloodshed really the norm of pre-modern and early-modern India, as is often argued? Did people back then really have different standards for judging violence as we do today? It is hard to answer any of these questions convincingly. But the way Abu'l Fazl tries to bring in karma while analysing Pir Muhammad's death, it's quite clear that mass killing was not acceptable then as it is now.

What is also interesting to note here is that covering up dark truths to save the leader from blemish is still done today, in India and elsewhere. For the 1984 anti-Sikh riots, enough noise has been made over the years to ensure that the buck doesn't stop at Rajiv Gandhi who was the Prime Minister of India when the violence—some would say genocide—had happened in the aftermath of the assassination of Indira Gandhi. It's been the same for the 2002 Gujarat riots too where all kinds of reasoning and whataboutery has ensured that Narendra Modi appears as an innocent victim of propaganda by vested interests and never questioned why so many lives were lost under his watch as chief minister.

At times, these cover-ups are extended to entire communities. For most part of free India's history, the violence perpetrated by Hindus

---

70 Abu'l Fazl, *Akbarnama, Vol. II*, p. 259.

on Muslims during Partition has almost never been talked about, but what the Muslims did to Hindus has always been amplified. This did three things: firstly, it made the Muslims appear in poor light; secondly, it helped in furthering the myth that Hindus are the only peaceful community; and lastly, it created a sense of hurt and victimhood among Hindus that often finds expression in phrases like '*Hindu khatre mein hai*' or 'the Hindu is at risk of annihilation'.

In Pakistan, the dominant national narrative since 1947 has been of Muslim liberation from Hindu oppression after a hard fight. A sense of hurt and victimhood took root right at the birth of that nation among the Muslims there, and which then resulted in a prejudiced view of the religious minorities in Pakistan: a view that continues till today and results in the persecution of the minorities.

After Pir Muhammad's death, the expedition returned to Agra in disgrace and Baz Bahadur recaptured Malwa. The commanders were punished, Abu'l Fazl says, though we don't know what punishment they got. Akbar put together another expedition to Malwa, this time under Abdullah Khan Uzbek, an officer who possessed 'excellent sense as well as abundant courage, and perfect energy together with judicial calm'. He was given 'the power of life and death' and also a capable aide in Khwaja Muinuddin Ahmad Farankhudi who was raised to the status of Khan and whose job was to regulate the province and the fiefs. Fazl says that Akbar's orders to both officers were very clear: Abdullah Khan should rule the province and Muin Khan should 'hearten the peasantry, the farmers and other inhabitants'. In other words, Muin Khan's job was to reach out to the farmers and other common people, hear their grievances and redress them in order to make the Mughals endearing to them. This was also very necessary after the bloody campaign of Pir Muhammad, which was surely a public relations disaster. It was clear that Akbar wanted to rule the hearts of the people. And why not, after all, no ruler could rule if he was at conflict with his own people or didn't enjoy their support.

Baz Bahadur once again became a fugitive, and after wandering around listlessly, he eventually sought refuge with Rana Udai Singh of Mewar in 1562. It was around the same time that Akbar went for a pilgrimage to Ajmer. For Akbar as well as the Mughal Empire, this proved to be a momentous visit.

Akbar decided to go to Ajmer for hunting in early 1562. Abu'l Fazl says he was looking for 'spiritual game' there, an allusion to a holy pilgrimage to the tomb of Sufi saint Shaikh Muinuddin Chishti. Akbar was warned not to go there as it was a remote place and there could be people who could harm him there. But Akbar paid no heed to the warnings and set off on January 14, 1562, with a small hunting party. Clearly, more than a spiritual purpose, this expedition had a political and military objective.

Until the Mughals controlled Khandesh, the road to Gujarat and its rich ports opened through Ajmer. And since it sat in the heart of Rajputana, it could also act as a launchpad for campaigns to different parts of Rajputana. With Agra and Lahore as the other two points, Ajmer formed a strategic triangle for the Mughals to establish control over large parts of the subcontinent. A campaign to the eastern parts of the country, like Bihar and Bengal, could be sent out from Agra while Lahore was key to controlling Kabul.

The overland trade routes to Iran and the rest of West Asia passed through Rajputana and Gujarat while Gujarat was also on the maritime trade route. It was imperative for the Mughals to control these trade routes to get a healthy supply of their primary weapon of offence, the horse. Cavalry was the match-winning arm of the Mughal army and the most prized among the horses was the Iraqi horse or the Arab horse.

Akbar's later spiritual trips to Ajmer, which became an annual affair until about 1580, for the urs of the Chishti saint coincided with the arrival of the camel caravans from Surat and Ahmedabad.[71] But this first trip to Ajmer was eventful for other reasons.

A nobleman named Chagatai Khan interceded with the emperor on behalf of Raja Bharmal, who was at the receiving end of hostile behaviour by Mirza Sharfuddin Husain who had been made the subedar of Ajmer, Nagor and Mewat in 1559. Bharmal's nephew, Sujamal, had joined up with the Mirza and sought his support to

71 Jos Gommans, *Mughal Warfare: Indian Frontiers and High Roads to Empire, 1500–1700* (London: Routledge, 2002), p. 26.

remove Bharmal and become king in his place.[72] Sujamal's father, Puranmal, was a Mughal ally who had died fighting for Humayun. Bharmal complained to Akbar that Sharfuddin Husain had held some of his family members as hostage.

Akbar, who had a high opinion about Bharmal, intervened on his behalf and firmly ordered Sharfuddin to release the hostages. This was actually a remarkable, non-partisan move by Akbar. Sharfuddin was Akbar's brother-in-law, having married his elder sister Bakshi Bano Begum. So, going against his own family member and that too so publicly must have been a tough thing to do for Akbar. But this wasn't an order that got caught in bureaucratic red tape; Akbar kept pushing the Mirza until he handed over the hostages. A grateful Bharmal then offered his daughter's hand in marriage to the emperor. And Akbar agreed.

After this, Akbar proceeded to Ajmer to do pilgrimage. Ajmer had been snatched by the Mughals from Rao Maldev of Marwar in 1559, who had captured it in 1557 together with Haji Khan by defeating Rana Udai Singh of Mewar and Jaimal Rathore of Merta. At Ajmer, Jaimal approached Akbar for help through Mirza Sharfuddin. Akbar agreed to help him and sent an army under the Mirza to Merta. Jaimal accompanied the Mirza and so did Sujamal.

The garrison at Merta was loyal to Rao Maldev of Marwar and put up a stubborn resistance. Then the Mughal sappers managed to successfully mine a fort wall, which resulted in a breach. The Mughal troops then stormed the fort but were fiercely resisted by the Rajputs. Individual soldiers came out of the fort to seek asylum, but Mirza Sharfuddin refused. Eventually, the garrison made an offer for parley, and the Mughals accepted it. The Mughals agreed to let the garrison leave the fort unharmed if it left behind all property. Garrison commander Jagmal agreed. He came out, and so did some others. But then, Jagmal's deputy Deo Das, ignoring the terms agreed upon, set fire to all property inside and rode out with four or five hundred horsemen in a final, fatalistic charge. Jagmal, who had come out to surrender, also eventually joined his comrades, choosing to die

---

72 For more details, see the final chapter.

in battle than escape to safety.[73] Even though Abu'l Fazl doesn't say it explicitly, but looks like these Rajputs changed their minds and decided to commit *saka*.

Jaimal Rathore and Lonkaran then advised Mirza Sharfuddin not to give any quarter to the garrison as they had violated their agreement. Sharfuddin accepted their point and measured swords with the Rajputs.[74] The Mughal right was commanded by Jaimal, Sujamal, Lonkaran and other Rajputs. They went after Deo Das, who then led a murderous charge at the Mughal centre commanded by the Mirza himself. He was unhorsed and cut up even as the other Rajputs 'escaped half-dead from the battlefield'.

Fazl says that there was talk later that Deo Das survived the battle and reappeared after over a decade dressed as a hermit. Some believed he was Deo Das, some didn't. This reappearance was just like that of 'Gumnami Baba', an ascetic who was believed by some to be Subhas Chandra Bose in disguise. The Bose legend never really faded because of this fantastic tale, the authenticity of which was never proved. One can therefore assume that resurrecting dead heroes as ascetics who give up worldly pleasures has been part of Indian society since time immemorial.

Merta was returned to Jaimal Rathore by the Mughals and he was reinstated on the throne. Just as Akbar had promised. Only five years later, Jaimal and Akbar would find themselves in opposite camps at Chittor. And the same Jaimal who egged the Mughals to finish off the Merta garrison would become, along with Patta Sisodia, one of the two legendary defenders of Chittor who went down fighting the Mughals.

As Akbar returned to Agra, he had a Hindu wife, her father Bhagwan Das, and her nephew Man Singh with him. The Kachwahas became the first Rajput clan to have a matrimonial relationship with the Mughals, and in the days to come, this single factor was going to bring them immense power, pelf and prestige. In fact, they would rise above others in the nobility to occupy topmost *mansabs* and court positions. Man Singh would be the first Mughal noble to rise to the

---

73 See Abu'l Fazl, *Akbarnama, Vol. II*, pp. 248–50 for the whole account of the battle.

74 Abu'l Fazl, *Akbarnama, Vol. II*, p. 249.

rank of a saat hazari mansabdar or an 'officer of the rank' of 7,000. This was the highest rank anyone in the court could obtain and was just below that of the princes. That a Hindu could rise so high in the hierarchy, higher than the noblest of nobles, was a testament to the meritocracy that the Mughal state promoted. In fact, Man Singh was recognised as *farzand* or son of the emperor. And the Kachwahas gave to the Mughals their fierce loyalty.

But while this new beginning was being made, another relationship of Akbar's was about to come to an abrupt end. Adham Khan, who returned in disgrace from Malwa, found himself in another power struggle, this time involving his mother and *Khan-i-Khanan* Munim Khan on one side and Khan-i-Kalan Shamsuddin Ataga Khan on the other. Abu'l Fazl hints at Munim Khan having incited Adham Khan to 'strife and intrigue'. But Adham Khan, without bothering to play with diplomacy, decided to settle the matter once and for all with the sword.

On 16 May 1562, Adham Khan barged into the court where Ataga Khan and other nobles were still conducting official business and got Ataga Khan murdered.[75] With an open sword, Adham then went to the imperial quarters where Akbar was enjoying an afternoon nap. As Adham entered the palace, there was commotion and noise, which woke up Akbar. When he enquired about the root of the noise, he was shown the body of Ataga Khan lying out in the open. Akbar lost his temper seeing the body of one of his most favourite people in life, his foster father.

Wearing just a lungi, he came out of his quarters and was given a sword by an attendant. Once outside, he saw Adham Khan waiting. Akbar screamed expletives at Adham, who became fearful immediately and tried to explain away the murder. Adham tried to stop Akbar's hand from drawing his sword, but Akbar punched him hard on the face which knocked him down. Then he ordered his guards to seize him and defenestrate him from the ramparts. Stunned though as they were, the guards tried to be a bit lenient even as Adham's protestations failed to move Akbar. He was thrown down headlong, but because it

---

75 See final chapter for a detailed description of the assassination, the intrigues and its impact.

wasn't done properly, he was half dead.[76] When he didn't die, Akbar had him dragged up through the stairs and by his hair and hauled over again. This time, the fall was fatal. Things happened in such a flash that nobody, including Akbar, must have been prepared for it.

Seeing Akbar's wrath, both Munim Khan and Shihabuddin Ahmad Khan, who were present in court at the time of the assassination but did nothing to intervene, fled. One gets the impression that even they didn't think Akbar would execute his foster brother. Ataga Khan's family too didn't believe it when they heard that Adham Khan had been executed at the spot. His eldest son, Yusuf Muhammad Khan, when he first heard the news of his father's assassination, assembled his clan or the *khail* and looked around for both Adham Khan and Maham Anaga to exact revenge.

But then the news came that Adham Khan had been killed. The Ataga clan refused to believe it— this just shows the perceived improbability of Akbar's act among all and sundry. They asked for visual proof of the act, and this was represented to the Emperor by some other courtiers. The Emperor acquiesced. So, one Shaikh Muhammad Ghaznavi was sent as a representative of the Ataga clan to see the body of Adham Khan. It was only then that the clan stood down.

Meanwhile, Maham Anaga, who was ill at the time and resting in her own house, heard the news of Adham Khan's crime. But the news of her son's execution hadn't reached her; she had heard that Akbar had imprisoned him. She came out of her house and went to Akbar's palace to plead with him for her son's release. Akbar told her: 'Adham Khan killed our Ataga, we have inflicted retaliation upon him.' Maham Anaga calmly said, 'You did well.' And yet she, Abu'l Fazl says, didn't believe that Akbar had executed him.

Then someone named Bibi Najiba Begum came from Adham Khan's house and confirmed to her that Adham Khan was indeed dead. When Maham asked how he was killed, she said, 'There is the mark of the blow of a mace on the face: I don't know anything more.' Fazl says that mark was from the blow of Akbar that had knocked

76 Abu'l Fazl, *Akbarnama, Vol. II*, p. 272.

Adham down. Now convinced, Maham still kept her calm but was 'inwardly wounded by a thousand fatal blows'. She wanted to see her son's body. Akbar comforted her with words of consolation but refused to let her see the body 'in such a condition'.

Fazl doesn't tell us if she was allowed to see the body later. He only says that the bodies of Ataga Khan and Adham Khan were sent to Delhi that very day, and Maham Anaga was permitted to go to Adham Khan's house the next day. It seems very cruel of Akbar not to allow a grieving mother see her dead son's face for one last time, and that too a woman who had served him and his family loyally; a woman who had always kept his best interests in mind even if that had meant putting her own life in peril; and a woman who didn't protest or accuse him of injustice even though he had snatched her son away from her.

The next day, Maham Anaga went to Adham Khan's house to grieve him. When she returned to her own house, she lamented and wept. Her son's violent end wrecked her. The morose woman never recovered from her grief and wilted away. She died 40 days later.

The body was sent to Delhi to be entombed along with Adham Khan's. Akbar decided not to separate the mother from her son in their eternal sleep. All of Bairam Khan's principal rivals—Pir Muhammad Khan Shirwani, Shamsuddin Ataga Khan, Adham Khan and Maham Anaga—were dead within a year of his fall from grace and subsequent murder.

For Akbar, this meant that there was now no one who could pose as a parallel authority to him. He was finally that sovereign king he always wanted to be: that master and commander of his own life and that of the empire.

Chapter 4

High Thinking, High Ambition

Arre tantri ne khoob kiya, sentry ne khoob kiya
Mantri ne khoob kiya Raj, aayi ab Munni ki baari.[1]

In 2017, American FMCG (Fast-Moving Consumer Goods) major Procter & Gamble, which owns the over-the-counter medication brand Vicks, came out with a new advertising campaign called 'Touch of Care'. It had a little girl narrating her life story of how she was orphaned and how she found a new mother who pulled her out of a life of misery and gave her all the warmth in the world that a mother could give. Simply put, she gave the child a new life. Towards the end of the ad, it was revealed that this foster mother was a eunuch or *hijra*, as such people are often referred to in the subcontinent.

The advertisement was globally appreciated for its powerful social message: that eunuchs who are abandoned and ostracised by society are people capable of doing great things in life; that beyond the wall of taboo lay real emotions like loving, longing, caring and sharing.

---

1 Song from the 2008 Hindi comedy film *Welcome To Sajjanpur* sung by the character Munni Bai (played by Ravi Jhankal) as her election campaign song. Though the film was a comedy, this character was tragic and was assassinated for daring to challenge the socio-political hierarchy.

This centuries-old taboo about eunuchs has been nurtured even by the mass media where the portrayal of a *hijra* is often intended to provide comic relief. Over time, the word *hijra* became a pejorative expression to signify cowardice. Though originally, it may have only meant departure from the normal as the root of it is the Arabic word *hijr*, which means to 'leave one's tribe' or just 'separation'—remember the line '*hijr ki oonchi deewar banayi*' in the 1980s super hit song *Lambi Judai* as a reference to the protagonist's prison sentence? In the Indian case, at least, eunuchs became so by choice and got separated from their families, and even the society at large. That was their *hijr*. In both India and Pakistan today, the Hindustani term *khwajasara* is used for such people as a politically correct alternative.

The term *khwajasara* has its origin in the Mughal Empire. Mughal records from the time of Akbar onwards use *khwaja* as a prefix for a eunuch courtier or officer and/or *nazir*.[2] In Akbar's time, eunuchs were mostly harem guards. In fact, those harem guards who had killed and maimed Baz Bahadur's women upon his defeat at Sarangpur may have also been eunuchs. But at an even earlier time, eunuchs had been military commanders too. Sultan Alauddin Khilji's most famous general and confidant, Malik Kafur, was also a eunuch.

Akbar was conscious of the tall legacy of the Delhi Sultan who preceded him by over 200 years. He wanted to surpass him.[3] Whether or not that may have been the motivation we don't know, but one of the first things that Akbar did after becoming free from any external control was to appoint a eunuch named I'timad Khan to enforce fiscal discipline in the administration.

His real name was Khwaja Phul Malik[4] and was previously in the service of Afghan king Islam Shah Sur, son of Sher Shah. He was known for his integrity and had been conferred with the name of Muhammad Khan. Akbar, having a natural eye for talent, hired him just like he recruited Todar Mal. Akbar was soon impressed with

2 Shadab Bano, 'Eunuchs in Mughal Household and Court', proceedings of the Indian History Congress 69 (2008): 417–27. Available at http://www.jstor.org/stable/44147205.

3 See Cynthia Talbot.

4 Abu'l Fazl, *Ain-i-Akbari, Vol. I*, p. 13.

his intellect and fiscal prudence. So he raised him to the full status of a *mansabdar* and also conferred on him the name I'timad Khan. He eventually became a *seh-hazari mansabdar* or an officer holding a *mansab* of 3,000—a fairly high rank in the bureaucracy.

But I'timad Khan wasn't an isolated example; there were other *khwajasaras* too who were given either high *mansabs* or positions of importance in the court. And whenever that happened, the emperor also bestowed a lofty name or title on the individual. There was one named Ambar who was made an imperial officer and governor of Delhi and given the lofty name of I'tibar (or Aitbar) Khan. There was a Khwaja Khas Malik who was given a *mansab* of 1,000 and given the name Ikhlas Khan. Then there was Khwaja Daulat who was made a courtier with the new name Daulat Khan and eventually made the boss of all eunuchs with the title of Nazir-ud-Daulah.[5]

After I'timad Khan, it was another *khwajasara* named Firoz Khan who rose to prominence in the court of Shah Jahan. Like I'timad Khan, he too rose to become a *seh-hazari mansabdar* and was made *Diwan-i-Kul* by Shah Jahan. All these prominent *khwajasaras* lived opulent lives amid grandeur and made grand building projects. Nobody objected to their amassing of wealth because without any children to inherit their fortune, all their wealth became state property upon their death. So their building projects were the only way to leave behind a lasting legacy. And it's because of their buildings that their names are still known today. The town of Etmadpur in Agra district of Uttar Pradesh is named after I'timad Khan. His grand water pavilion and adjacent tomb is a designated tourist destination advertised by the Agra Circle of Archaeological Survey of India as *Burhia Ka Tal* group of monuments. Firoz Khan has an exceptionally beautiful and very uniquely designed tomb to himself that not only reflects Mughal architectural glory but also the refined tastes of the builder—Firoz Khan himself.

It is remarkable that so many eunuchs rose to prominence in the Mughal period even though during the time of Babur and Humayun,

---

5 Shadab Bano, 'Eunuchs in Mughal Household and Court', proceedings of the Indian History Congress 69 (2008): 417–27. Available at http://www.jstor.org/stable/44147205.

no eunuch got any favourable mention anywhere, let alone earn respectable positions in society. Babur didn't mention a single eunuch in his memoirs even though Ambar or I'tibar Khan was in his seraglio.[6] It can, therefore, be concluded that the rise of the *khwajasaras* was all due to one man, Emperor Akbar.

But it doesn't mean that the societal attitudes towards eunuchs changed in any great way because Akbar promoted them. Those outside the court were still treated with contempt, and even those who held high *mansabs* experienced ill-treatment by fellow nobles or others in positions of power.

In India today, eunuchs continue to be ostracised by society but there is absolutely no member of that community occupying a high position in government or administration. Actually, something like that in today's India is very difficult to imagine. Former MLA (Member of Legislative Assembly) Shabnam Mausi, who was the first eunuch to become a legislator in India, had in July 2018 alleged that the Indian National Congress was not giving her membership just because she was a eunuch. As a result, she cursed the party to stay out of power for 15 more years.[7]

Another eunuch named Kali Hijra, who was a leader of eunuchs in Bihar, had also contested Lok Sabha and Bihar assembly elections but was unsuccessful in both attempts. She and her group had demanded that eunuchs be given the role they had in society and administration of the Mughals.[8] Akbar's visionary step should be analysed in this backdrop: that even today, Indian politicos and the society at large have not been able to do better than Akbar.

By mid-1562, of the clique of nobles that had plotted the downfall of Bairam Khan, only Mirza Sharfuddin Husain was alive. But in

---

6 Ibid.

7 Suchandana Gupta, 'Former eunuch MLA curses Congress to stay out of power for another 15 years', *The Times of India*, 21 July 2018. Available at https://timesofindia.indiatimes.com/india/former-eunuch-mla-curses-congress-to-stay-out-of-power-for-another-15-yrs/articleshow/65085430.cms.

8 Press Trust of India, *'Eunuchs want Mughal-era role back'*, *The Times of India*, 27 April 2008. Available at https://timesofindia.indiatimes.com/city/patna/Eunuchs-want-Mughal-era-role-back/articleshow/2987565.cms.

October that year, weeks before Akbar's 20th birthday, the Mirza fled from Agra and withdrew to his fief of Nagore. That was an act of rebellion. Akbar sent his two officers, Sadiq Muhammad Khan and Husain Quli Khan, to subdue the Mirza. With imperial officers in his rear, the Mirza went to Ajmer, put a trusted aide in charge of the fort, and went off towards Jalaur. This aide turned against his master in no time and welcomed the imperial force.

At Jalaur, Sharfuddin met an unexpected person returning from Mecca. It was Shah Abu'l Ma'ali, returning after being almost banished to the Arab land. Why he was back nobody knew, but the Mirza decided to utilise the opportunity to shake off his pursuers from his tail. He asked him to create a diversion for imperial troops by attacking the fort of Hajipur where Husain Quli Khan had left his family, and then go to Kabul and bring Mirza Muhammad Hakim, Akbar's half-brother, to Hindustan. The idea, as it clearly appears, was to organise a revolt by propping up Mirza Hakim as a rival claimant to the throne of Hindustan.

Abu'l Ma'ali, though, failed in the bid when he learnt about imperial troops coming towards Hajipur. He fled to Narnaul instead. Mirza Sharfuddin, on the other hand, fled from the empire's limit when he realised that the imperial troops were more than a match for him. Just why he rebelled, though, is not known. But it's possible that he feared loss of stature after the fall of Adham Khan and Maham Anaga.

With the Mirza fleeing, his proteges and friends lost imperial favours too. One of the first to feel the heat was Jaimal Rathore of Merta. Husain Quli Khan removed Jaimal and handed over the fort back to Jagmal.[9] And Jaimal went into the arms of Rana Udai Singh of Mewar.

The court of Mewar had become the prime refuge of those in conflict with the ever-burgeoning Mughal Empire and running away from it. Earlier, it had sheltered Baz Bahadur, now it had taken Jaimal under its wing. It was just a matter of time before the Mughals arrived at Mewar's doorstep. But more immediately, time was running out for Marwar as Husain Quli Khan next set his eyes upon Jodhpur.

9 Abu'l Fazl, *Akbarnama, Vol. II,* p. 305.

Rao Maldev died in 1562 and was succeeded by his third son, Chandrasen Rathore. When Husain Quli Khan arrived, the elder son of Maldev, Ram Rai, came over to the Mughals and was given a *mansab*. Earlier, Chandrasen had ousted him and another brother Udai Singh from the kingdom after a war of succession. And he would have his revenge.

The fort was taken after a siege that lasted for over a year. But the Marwar Rathores didn't give up and relocated their capital to Siwana. Chandrasen continued to resist the Mughals intermittently until his death in 1581 after which Marwar firmly became a Mughal client state with Udai Singh Rathore as king.

But when the Merta affair was on, Akbar had gone hunting towards Mathura. These hunts have a story of their own. For most part, these were routinely undertaken from the time of Akbar to test and improve military efficiency. A modern comparison would be a battle simulation or war-gaming. The emperor didn't go alone for most hunts; either his entire court went with him or those courtiers who commanded his armies. Their presence was very important as speed and manoeuvre were key aspects of Mughal warfare and also necessary ones as smaller Mughal armies were taking on much larger enemy hosts. Mughal mounted archers were the trump card of the army and enemy armies either lacked it or their archers weren't as effective as those from the Mongol homelands and Mawarannahar. The wheeling tactics of Mughal archers were unmatched. These were tested in hunts.

Akbar, in his lightning trip to Malwa, had still managed to go for a short hunt while returning and sabred a tiger himself.[10] Mughal paintings of the time show how a tiger or a group of them were surrounded by his retinue who gradually closed the gap, forcing the predator to come closer to the hunter, often mounted on an elephant with a musket in hand. The tiger was a 'royal' animal and a symbol of power. None other than Babur was named after the tiger. So, it was clearly ingrained in the Mughal mind that to conquer the tiger was a statement of power.

---

10 Abu'l Fazl, *Akbarnama, Vol. II.*

A few hundred years later, the English ruling elite in India and the Indian maharajas would also hunt tigers in the exact same fashion but without the need to keep their armies in good nick. There was also no need for any strategic mobility by then, but for the British as well as the Indian princes during the British Raj, hunting involved a lot of strategic thinking. The 19th-century Briton understood the emblematic significance of the tiger in the Indian imagination. They had first-hand experience of it while fighting Tipu Sultan of Mysore, who banked heavily on tiger imagery to strike terror in the heart of his enemies. When the British finally humbled Tipu, they awarded their troops the 'Seringapatam Medal', which had a lion humbling a tiger. Lion symbolised the British, being part of the coat of arms of Great Britain. The tiger symbolised Tipu.

For the British, a hunt was a way of showing who the boss was and also a way of making the point that they and they alone were the true successors of the Mughals.[11] J. Sranek explained perfectly what the British were up to, particularly with the tiger hunts:

> On the one hand, they consciously sought to emulate the Mughals and other Indian rulers by killing tigers. On the other hand, in the course of destroying these animals, they were also symbolically staging the defeat of Tipu Sultan and other Indian rulers who dared to get in the way of Britain's imperial conquest of India.[12]

For the Indians, a hunt was a way of finding some semblance of parity with the lord of the land by showing him that the maharaja also had the same appetite and tastes. It wasn't very different from what Akbar's Indian nobility was doing back in the 16th century: accompanying the emperor on his hunts, playing their part in the kills, and later claiming their shares of the kills.

The hunts during Company Raj and British Raj saw amazing bloodlust by both Indians and the British. Viceroy Lord Linlithgow felled 120 tigers in 10 weeks alone in 1938. But an all-time worst

---

11 Joseph Sramek, '"Face Him like a Briton": Tiger Hunting, Imperialism, and British Masculinity in Colonial India, 1800-1875.' *Victorian Studies* 48, no. 4, 2006, pp. 659–80. Available at http://www.jstor.org/stable/4618910.

12 Ibid.

record in tiger killing rests with the late prince of Surguja state, Maharaja Ramanuj Saran Singh Deo, who killed 1,710 tigers during his lifetime.[13] Contrast this with Jahangir's 86 tiger (and lion) kills over a 36-year period from 1580 to 1616[14] and one can see how brutal British rule was to India's rich wildlife.

The hunting expeditions also helped the Mughals in another way: these were also talent hunts. By moving from one place to another, the Mughals could tap into the South Asian military labour market spread over the regions where they hunted. Even though many people seeking to make a fortune often came to the Mughal court from what were the original recruiting bases in Central Asia, this trickle couldn't have sustained the vast ambitions of the Mughal state that needed a flood of manpower to oil its military machine. With Mawarannahar now in the distance, this manpower had to come locally. The Mughal Empire didn't struggle in attracting talent being an equal opportunities employer. It also served another purpose: it helped the Mughals appear more Indian.

This Mathura hunt, too, was for the tiger. In just one day, Akbar hunted seven predators. Abu'l Fazl writes[15]:

> Five were levelled with the dust by arrow and bullet, and one that repository of courage (Akbar) caught alive and so was the subject of a thousand wonderings. The other was caught by the united efforts of a number of *bahadurs*.

But this hunt was also very significant for another reason: something that defines Akbar even today—his religious tolerance—found a strong expression for the first time in an incident during the hunt. Fazl writes[16]:

---

13 William Mitchell, 'Tiger Hunting in India 1924', *National Geographic Magazine*, originally published in 1924 but re-released on 2 August 2014. Available at https://news.nationalgeographic.com/news/2014/08/140803-tiger-hunt-1924-india-maharaja-safari.

14 The original reference occurs in Salim A. Ali, 'The Moghul Emperors of India as Naturalists and Sportsmen', *Journal of The Bombay Natural History Society* 31 (1927), p. 841.

15 Abu'l Fazl, *Akbarnama, Vol. II,* p. 294.

16 Ibid., pp. 294–95.

> It was brought to his (Akbar) notice that for a long time it was the custom in India for the rulers to take sums from the people who came to sacred spots to worship, proportionate to their rank and wealth. This (worship) was called *karma*.

This is what the historians today refer to as the pilgrimage tax. Ever since the establishment of state systems in India with Islam as the central faith in the 12th century, it was levied on non-Muslims visiting their holy places of worship. Even today, Mathura is a place of pilgrimage for Hindus due to the belief that it's the birthplace of Lord Krishna. This was also the case back then, with people coming from far and wide to pay homage to the god.

Akbar decided to abolish the tax. Fazl writes[17]:

> The *Shahinshah* in his wisdom and tolerance remitted all these taxes, which amounted to crores. He looked upon such grasping of property as blameable and issued orders forbidding the levy thereof throughout his dominions. In former times, from the unworthiness of some, and from cupidity and bigotry, men showed such an evil desire towards the worshippers of God. His Majesty often said that although the folly of a sect might be clear, yet as they had no conviction that they were on the wrong path, to demand money from them, and to put a stumbling block in the way of what they had made a means of approach to the sublime threshold of Unity and considered as the worship of the creator, was disapproved by the discriminating intellect and was a mark of not doing the will of God.

In simpler words, Akbar meant that he may not believe in a particular religion, but he wouldn't stop anybody else from believing in it. And the state wouldn't come in between an individual and his faith. It was a profound step: one that had not been taken by an Islamic sultanate in India before; a step that would shape Mughal polity in the years to come, making it a unique blend of syncretism and inclusion. That the young emperor supervising a relatively young state with its finances still not secure could sacrifice 'crores' of money

17 Ibid., p. 295.

in taxes in order to give his subjects the freedom to choose their faiths is indeed remarkable.

Apart from the financial aspect of it, it was an amazingly forward-looking step for its time if one considers what was happening in contemporary India and the world. The Inquisition had become the scourge of Europe back then with the Spaniards and the Portuguese both having their own versions of it. Only three years before Akbar's Mathura hunt, the Portuguese colonial administration of Goa had instituted the Goa Inquisition in 1560 that would torture and kill thousands of people until its closure in the 19th century.

It was during this hunt that Akbar learnt about the coming of Shah Abu'l Ma'ali and his resumption of hostility against imperial troops. He immediately returned to Agra and from there he went to Delhi. He sent backup for Husain Quli Khan. The imperial troops chased out Abu'l Ma'ali from Narnaul, who had, by then, plundered all the imperial treasures of the fort and distributed them among his men. From there, he went to Jhanjun (Jaipur), but fled towards Hisar Firuza (Hisar in Haryana today) when he couldn't take the fort. All this while, imperial troops were on his tail.

From Hisar Firuza, Abu'l Ma'ali fled to Kabul. He didn't have much of an option. His ally (more an instigator) Mirza Sharfuddin was no longer there to watch his back. But the idea of going to Kabul and instigating a rebellion against Akbar with Mirza Muhammad Hakim as a rival was too tempting for him. And off he went.

Once he was within striking distance of Kabul, Shah Abu'l Ma'ali wrote to Mah Chuchak Begum, a widow of Humayun and mother of Mirza Hakim and the de-facto ruler of Kabul. Through a series of intrigues, she had managed to overthrow the powerful imperial officer Ghani Khan, who had been left behind in control of Kabul when Munim Khan had got imperial summons to come over in 1561 when the plot against Bairam Khan was on. The Begum loathed the control of Ghani Khan. One day, when he had gone out of the fort, she got its gates closed behind on him. Unable to make any headway in getting it back, he left Kabul and came to Hindustan.

When Akbar learnt about it, he reappointed Munim Khan to Kabul when the latter had fled the court in the aftermath of the assassination of Shamsuddin Ataga Khan and the execution of Adham Khan. The coming of Munim Khan was perceived as bad news by the Kabul court. It was seen, and perhaps rightly so, as an attempt by Akbar to put a leash on his half-brother. Besides, Munim Khan wasn't expected to take it kindly that his own brother was ousted. Mah Chuchak Begum wouldn't allow any control from Agra. She decided to stop Munim Khan in his tracks and before he could reach Kabul.

Munim Khan was at Jalalabad when the Kabul army came. The two sides clashed and Munim Khan's forces were worsted. This was particularly so because the Kabul army's artillery proved to be very effective. Abu'l Fazl writes that a *topchi* or gunner by the name of Abu'l Maali, who was probably an Ottoman officer as the Kabulis called him Rumi Khan (Rum being the Persian for Istanbul), created havoc on Munim Khan's lines and killed a top commander by throwing grenades.[18] Munim Khan lost the battle and managed to flee, as the Kabul army got busy in plundering his camp. They looted goods and cash to the tune of 30 lakhs of rupees, but the biggest thing that they looted was Munim Khan's pride. The architect of all this was Mah Chuchak Begum.

Shah Abu'l Ma'ali wrote the most flattering letter to her, professing his unflinching loyalty. He wrote a couplet in that which read—'We are not come to this door, for the sake of pomp and grandeur; We are come here as a refuge from the evil of circumstances.'[19]

The Begum replied—'Show kindness and alight, for the house is thy house.'[20]

The Begum's calculation seems to have been to make an enemy of Akbar her ally. This was a risky proposition considering the troubled history of Shah Abu'l Ma'ali. But the Begum went ahead and offered this Tirmizi Sayyid sanctuary. Perhaps because of his high birth, the Begum even got her daughter married to Abu'l Ma'ali. But things spiralled into a crisis fast.

Abu'l Ma'ali loathed the controlling nature of his mother-in-law. And he soon found out that he wasn't alone in hating her. With the

---

18 Ibid., *Vol. II*, p. 292.

19 Badaoni, *Muntakhab*, p. 56.

20 Ibid.

help of some of the Begum's disaffected courtiers, Abu'l Ma'ali staged a coup and got the Begum and her vizier executed. He would have perhaps even got rid of Mirza Muhammad Hakim, but the young lad managed to seek help from his cousin, Mirza Sulaiman of Badakshan. The messenger was Muhammad Qasim Kohbar, the younger brother of the vizier killed by Abu'l Ma'ali.

Mirza Sulaiman, furious at the actions of this usurper, marched towards Kabul with a big force.

Abu'l Ma'ali took Mirza Hakim along with him and both sides faced each other on either side of the river Ghorband. At an opportune moment, when Shah Abu'l Ma'ali tried to reorganise his right flank disorganised by the attack of Mirza Sulaiman's left flank, Mirza Hakim crossed the river with his troops and went over to Mirza Sulaiman. Seeing his situation was utterly hopeless, Abu'l Ma'ali once again showed his back to the enemy. Kabul was taken by the Badakshis and Mirza Hakim restored. But Mirza Sulaiman sent people in pursuit of the fugitive Tirmizi Sayyid, who managed to catch him.

Abu'l Ma'ali was brought back to Kabul where Mirza Sulaiman handed him over to Mirza Hakim who ordered his execution by strangulation.[21] The chroniclers haven't left behind the details of how it was done, but in the Ottoman Empire, this was also the preferred method of execution of people of high rank. It was usually done with a silk cord. This was how the Ottoman Grand Vizier Kara Mustafa Pasha was executed for his disastrous defeat at Vienna in 1683. This was how Sehzade Bayezid and his five sons were executed on orders of Sultan Sulaiman the Magnificent. Bayezid had taken refuge with Shah Tahmasp, just like Humayun had at an earlier date. But while Tahmasp helped Humayun with money and an army, he handed over Bayezid in exchange for money.

With both Mirza Sharfuddin and Shah Abu'l Ma'ali out of Akbar's way, the general mood was of safety. Abu'l Fazl writes that 'sedition which had awoke with bleared eyes went into a profound slumber'. Akbar had entered Delhi on January 8 1564. Three days later, on

21 Abu'l Fazl, *Akbarnama, Vol. II*, p. 321.

11 January, he went to the shrine of Nizamuddin Auliya. On his way back from there, when he arrived at a *chaharsu* or crossways (modern Hindi equivalent is *chauraha*) near the madrassa of Maham Anaga, an assassin struck at him.

Maham Anaga's madrassa is identified today as Khairul Manazil. It straddles both Subramanium Bharti Marg and Sher Shah Road and is located right at the T-junction where both these roads meet Mathura Road. The two traffic signals here are among the busiest in the capital. The building is right opposite the Purana Qila, which is where Akbar would have lived. A bowman named Qatlaq Faulad was standing on the terrace of the madrassa. When Akbar crossed him, he fired an arrow that hit the emperor on the right shoulder.

Akbar later told Abu'l Fazl that at first he thought someone had thrown a stone at him unwittingly. But moments later he realised that an arrow had hit him. The wound wasn't very deep, Fazl tells us, and the emperor continued to ride his horse. The description of the wound may not have been very accurate. And there was a valid reason for that. For someone who was understood as *zill-i-Illahi*, god's image on earth, a major physical injury caused by an assassin's arrow could have dented the aura of invincibility about Akbar. Even though young in age, Akbar was expected to know these tenets of kingship and power show, especially at a time when there were still people who could challenge his rule.

The 2008 movie *Jodhaa Akbar* showed this incident with a modern twist. Akbar was shown to be hit by a poison-tipped arrow, the impact of which dislodged him from his mount. The assassin was caught by Akbar's guards, but he popped a cyanide-like pill that instantly killed him!

In reality, the assassin was immediately caught and put to death on Akbar's orders. Some of his nobles wanted to interrogate the man to know who all were involved in the plot, but Akbar insisted that he be put to death 'lest a number of loyalists should fall under suspicion'. Faulad was a slave of Mirza Sharfuddin Husain and had been sent from Jalore by his master to join Shah Abu'l Ma'ali. When Abu'l Ma'ali left for Kabul, the Mirza sent Faulad to Delhi instead to take a shot at the emperor's life.[22] Akbar assumed that the Mirza was the architect of the plot and got Faulad executed without any questioning.

Akbar rode back to his palace where the arrow was dislodged and his wound treated. Abu'l Fazl gives an interesting medical detail here when he writes that 'skilful leeches who possessed Jesus' breath attended to the plastering and curing of it'. 'Leech therapy' is one of the most ancient forms of treating wounds that the ancient Egyptians, Babylonians and Indians were familiar with. It also forms part of modern surgical medicine where leeches are used in post-skin grafting, reattachment of body parts or organ-replacement surgeries. Apart from their blood-sucking skills that help prevent engorging, leech saliva mimics histamine that encourages local bleeding, acts as a local anaesthetic, contains *hirudin* that acts as an anticoagulant, and also has antibiotic properties.[23] Akbar was cured in a week's time.

Abu'l Fazl also talks about an interesting incident involving a pet dog of the emperor named Mahuwa in Agra. The day Akbar was attacked in Delhi, Mahuwa showed signs of disquiet and refused to eat or drink. This apparently lasted for a week until news reached Agra that the emperor was all right. What's often missed is that the Mughals gave Hindu-sounding names to their favourite animals. If elephants were named Rann-madar and Sudhakar, dogs and deer were given names like Mahuwa and Manas Raj.

Akbar began his return journey to Agra on 21 January through slow marches. He rode a litter or a palanquin for most of the journey as holding the reins of a horse was becoming difficult. He reached Agra over 10 days later. This suggests the wound wasn't just a scratch that Abu'l Fazl had described it as.

But what didn't happen because of this murderous attack was a weakening of Akbar's resolve to reform. Upon returning to Agra, Akbar carried out his most radical reform yet: something that would earn him more enemies and detractors among the orthodox Muslims but would make him more endearing to his Hindu courtiers and

22 Ibid., p. 314.

23 Richard L. Pullen Jr. EdD, RN, 'Using leeches to treat wounds', *Nursing 2010* 40, no. 3, 2010, p. 62.

subjects. Akbar abolished Jizya, the tax levied on some non-Muslims[24] by a Muslim state to receive its protection.

The abolition of the pilgrimage tax less than a year ago had been the prelude to this even more revolutionary step. The impact of this on the state exchequer would have been tremendous at a time the revenue rich regions of Bengal and Gujarat were not part of Akbar's domains. Abu'l Fazl gave a tremendous intellectual backing to this move, which was uncharacteristic of a state based on the tenets of Islam or which professed Islam as a state religion. Indeed, it would have been heresy on the part of an Islamic sultanate to end this fundamental distinction it made between its Muslim and non-Muslims subjects or the *dhimmis.*[25]

Abu'l Fazl's words must be repeated here ad verbatim:

> As the far-seeing glance of the Shahinshah looked to the administration of the world, he paid great attention to the issuing of this edict, which might be regarded as the foundation of the arrangement of mankind. In spite of the disapproval of statesmen, and of the great revenue, and of much chatter on the part of the ignorant, this sublime decree was issued.[26]

Fazl then explained why other Muslim rulers in India levied the tax in the past:

> When this tax was imposed in former times by those who held outward sway, the reason for it was that they on account of heart-rooted enmity were girded up for the contempt and destruction of opposite factions, but for political purposes and for their own advantage, they fixed a sum

24 Historically, women, children, the elderly, disabled, sick, intellectually challenged, monks, hermits, slaves and the indigent were exempted from paying *jizya*. Also, in India, those non-Muslims who served in the armies of a Muslim state and Brahmins didn't have to pay the tax as well.

25 Pronounced as *zimmis*, it's an Islamic term to describe non-Muslims who are protected by an Islamic state against payment of *jizya*. Originally applied to the *ahl al-Kitab* or 'people of the book'—Jews and Christians—it was later applied on Zoroastrians and Hindus too, as Muslim conquering armies took Islam outside Al Hijaz, into Persia and India.

26 Abu'l Fazl, *Akbarnama*, *Vol. II*, p. 316.

> of money as an equivalent therefore, and gave it the name of *jizya*. Thus they both gained their object and also derived a profit.[27]

Jizya was passe, Fazl argued, and should be done away with. Fazl wrote[28]:

> At the present day, when owing to the blessing of the abundant goodwill and graciousness of the lord of the age (Akbar), those who belong to other religions have, like those of one mind and one religion (read Muslims), bound up the waist of devotion and service, and exert themselves for the advancement of dominions. How should these dissenters, whose separation is founded merely on habit and imitation, and whose zeal and devotion are the real things, be classed with that old faction which cherished mortal enmity and be the subjects of contempt and slaughter? Moreover, the prime cause of levying the tax in old times was the neediness of the rulers and their assistants.

The official biographer then tried to answer Akbar's critics for abolishing *jizya*. Fazl wrote[29]:

> At this day, when there are thousands of treasures in the store-chambers of the worldwide administration, and when every one of the servants of the threshold, and when every one of the servants of the threshold of fortune is rich and prosperous, why should a just and discriminating mind apply itself to collecting this tax? And why should it from imaginary advantage advance on the path of definite dissension?

In Abu'l Fazl's articulation we see the influence of his present. He was no more than a lad of 13 when Akbar abolished *jizya*. But he was writing the *Akbarnama* in the 1590s, when he was in his 40s. Akbar's empire in the 1590s had 'thousands of treasures in the store-chambers', but this wasn't so in the early 1560s when resources were fewer and Akbar still had most of India to win. Turning the tap off on a steady source of revenue, therefore, was brave and quite significant a move. When viewed from a modern prism, it appears

---

27 Ibid., p. 317.

28 Ibid.

29 Ibid.

as populism of its time. But Abu'l Fazl, despite heaping high praise on his master for doing this, still failed to underline the significance of this move early in Akbar's reign.

Not his fault. Writing history during Abu'l Fazl's time was essentially chronicling of events. Today, it's much more than that. A historian's craft is supposed to offer insights and contexts. And yet, it often happens that a historian's present clouds his/her judgement of the past[30], even if the past were to be of a more recent vintage. Any historian worth his or her salt would say that this is the bane of history writing even today. Good, professional historians overcome this by letting their sources speak to them; amateur historians often succumb to the temptation of putting out their own prejudiced views of the past through selective citing of sources, or without allowing a full conversation with their sources.

But, to his credit, Abu'l Fazl also manages to offer us glimpses into the politics and society of the time. Consciously or not, he even offers a sneak-peek into the social prejudices of the time and the apathetic treatment of tribal people by the state and society at large. And when it is not someone like Hemu or Shah Abu'l Ma'ali, Fazl also appreciates the bravery of adversaries of the Mughal state, even if the challenger is a woman.

All this is visible in Fazl's description of the Mughal conquest of Central India, or Gondwara as Fazl calls it. Today, the unofficial collective name Gondwana is used to describe these places that are spread over several Indian states. The term Gondwanaland was coined in the 19th century to refer to a supercontinent that existed between the Neoproterozoic and Carboniferous geological epochs, which lasted between 550 and 320 million years ago.

Abu'l Fazl says the Gonds were a numerous tribe and mostly lived in the forests and were mostly into eating and drinking. He describes them as a 'low-caste tribe' whom the 'people of India despise' and 'regard them as outside their pale of realm and religion'.

---

30 In an interview with me in August 2018, US historian Dr Audrey Truschke told me that while writing about Aurangzeb, she had to deal with her own inherited 21st-century biases. Scholarly biases exist in most historiographies.

In this land of the Gonds was the territory of Gadha Katanga. Fazl gives the geographical coordinates too: the eastern part of the region joined Ratanpur in Jharkhand[31] while the west of it was contiguous to Raisin in Malwa. The length of it was estimated to be 150 *kos* and width 80 *kos*. To the north of it was Panna while to the south, Deccan. There were 70,000 inhabited villages, Fazl estimates.

Ruling Gadha Katanga was a dowager queen named Durgavati. She had about 23,000 villages in her possession, 2,000 cavalry, 1,000 elephants and an unknown number of infantry. Fazl says the forces of Islam never conquered this territory.[32] So, when Mughal commander Asaf Khan conquered Panna, he turned his attention towards Gadha Katanga.

Rani Durgavati, Fazl says, was a crack shot with both bow and arrow and musket. She often went hunting and shot animals with a gun. Fazl also says that whenever she learnt about a tiger sighting, she wouldn't drink water until she had killed the beast with a gun. She threw lavish feasts and was well-known in Hindustan for her prowess and largesse. But she had one fault: she was an independent-minded woman. Fazl says her flaw was her becoming proud of her successes due to flattery and being arrogant in her own might due to which she didn't bow down before Akbar. The reality, as should appear to any modern reader of the text, was this that she was a proud sovereign who wouldn't accept suzerainty of Akbar.

Fazl says the Rani wasn't apprehensive of Asaf Khan winning Panna as she was 'infatuated with the strength of her army, her courage and abilities'. The Khan, a Tajik with no soldierly background, was rising in the estimation of the emperor through his martial prowess. But he didn't rush into Durgavati's kingdom. He sent in his spies and 'experienced traders' into her territory to find out more about her earnings and expenditure. It was quite clearly a recce mission. And this seems to have been standard practice of the Mughal state to send traders to areas where Mughal embassies of friendship were not welcome. The first Ahom-Mughal conflict had broken out during

31 Yes, Abu'l Fazl uses this term. This suggests the term was historically in existence.

32 Abu'l Fazl, *Akbarnama, Vol. II*, p. 327.

Emperor Jahangir's time in 1617 when Mughal traders were arrested by the Ahom authorities for illegal trade and trespass.

Rani Durgavati didn't arrest or stop anyone, but when Asaf Khan got the reports of the Rani having abundant treasures, 'the desire of lordship of the country entered his mind and he longed to embrace the bride of the territories'. He made friendly gestures to the queen initially, but when these weren't responded to, he started attacking and plundering villages on the border of the Rani's domains. Eventually, he got imperial sanction to put together a force of 10,000 cavalry and an unknown number of infantry for his conquest of the Rani's kingdom.

The Rani was negligent, Fazl says, in the defence of her country. She didn't seem to have any prior intelligence of a likely invasion. She learnt about it too late, when the Mughal force had already approached the city of Damoh.[33] Shocked and unprepared, her soldiers dispersed to defend their own families. Only about 500 troops remained with their benefactress. With this small force, Rani Durgavati chose to give battle.

Her minister named Adhar advised her against it and asked her to retreat and regroup. The Rani blamed him for the desertion of her troops and said she won't suffer the ignominy of flight from battle. Interestingly, Fazl quoted her having said that had Akbar come in person, she would have submitted to him but Asaf Khan was a man lower in rank to whom she couldn't submit to and so she would die in battle.

The queen managed to rally 2,000 men around her to give battle, but she was eventually persuaded by some of her generals to retreat to another, more naturally well-protected place and bide her time. This place was Narrai, surrounded by mountains on all sides and the river Gaur (a tributary of the Narmada) in front of it. It was about 12 miles from Jabalpur (in today's Madhya Pradesh).

When Asaf Khan learnt about it, he went after the queen to her hideout. By now, the queen's ranks had swollen to 5,000. The Rani ambushed an advance party under Nazir Muhammad and

---

33 It's in the Sagar division of Madhya Pradesh today.

Aq Muhammad in the ravines and 300 Mughals were slain. Abu'l Fazl suggests the attack had been plotted by the Rani herself and showed great strategic thinking on her part. The rest of the Mughal force retreated, handing over mastery of the field to Durgavati. The queen, chuffed by the victory, suggested that a night attack be carried upon Asaf Khan's camp or else he would personally come the next morning, take the pass and fortify it with artillery. This was great strategic thinking too, but due to her bad luck, her commanders weren't blessed with that kind of battlefield genius and strategic foresight. They didn't cooperate, so the attack didn't happen.

But the next morning, Asaf Khan did what the Rani had predicted he would. The Mughals placed guns in the ravines and their troops entered the pass. The Rani didn't relent and gave battle. Her son, the nominal king Raja Bir Narayan, fought bravely as did her Muslim commanders, Shams Khan Miana and Mubarak Khan Baloch. But the boy king was wounded and the Rain ordered him to be removed to safety. As the young king was being taken away, many of the Rani's troops abandoned the battlefield until just 300 people remained around her. And still, the Rani didn't back down and continued to fight from the back of an elephant named Sarman.

At length, she was struck on the right temple by an arrow. She broke the arrow and threw it away even though the point still remained lodged. Then another arrow hit her in the neck. This too she extricated herself, but it was very painful and she lost a lot of blood, which made her weak. Realising that defeat was now certain, she asked her Diwan, Adhar, to put an end to her life so that she isn't captured alive and disgraced. Perhaps the fate of Hemu was all too well known by then and she didn't want to suffer the way he did. Adhar said he couldn't kill his own queen and said her elephant was fast enough to take her away to safety. The queen supposedly got very angry at this and stabbed herself with her dagger.

The queen's 14-year-rule thus ended, but tales of her valour are still sung today. She was larger-than-life in her lifetime; today, she's even bigger than that. Another queen of similar mettle would rise to prominence in the region several centuries later to fight a superior power to retain her sovereignty. She would gain immortal fame as

Lakshmibai, the Rani of Jhansi. In effect, she followed the path that Durgavati had walked earlier, but Lakshmibai would become a much bigger heroine in death as she fought a foreign enemy—the British—in league with the direct descendant of Emperor Akbar. She too, like Durgavati, wasn't captured alive, which added to her mystique and elevated her to the pantheon of the greatest Indians of all time.

Fazl called Durgavati a brilliant ruler and a 'noble lady'. There are no sexist or patronising remarks about her in the text—a remarkable thing for the age in which Fazl existed. Contrast this with modern times when leaders, writers and commentators routinely pass sexist comments on women and one would understand the importance of Fazl's writing. Even while heaping praise upon praise on Bangladesh Prime Minister Sheikh Hasina Wajid in 2015, Prime Minister Narendra Modi had said she had waged a successful war on terror 'despite the fact that she is a woman.'[34]

After Durgavati, Raja Bir Narayan took over the banner of resistance. He had withdrawn to the Chauragarh fort in today's Jabalpur and stayed put. Asaf Khan, meanwhile, went about subduing the Miyana Afghans. This kept him engaged for about two months, after which he turned towards Chauragarh. The king fought gallantly and stubbornly, like his mother, but didn't last long in battle. He had communicated his death wish to two of his trusted lieutenants named Bhoj Kaith and Miyan Bhikari Rumi: that they would organise and supervise *jauhar* for the palace women. Fazl described what *jauhar* is:

> ...it is the custom of Indian rajahs under such circumstances to collect wood, cotton, grass, ghee and such like into one place, and to bring the women and burn them, willing or unwilling.[35]

Anybody who didn't want to sacrifice her life that way was killed by the two men. Fazl doesn't describe the gory scenes that must

34 Times News Network, '#DespiteBeingAWoman PM Modi faces flak for sexist comment', *The Times of India*, 8 June 2015. Available at https://timesofindia.indiatimes.com/india/despitebeingawoman-pm-modi-faces-flak-for-sexist-comment/articleshow/47583088.cms.

35 Abu'l Fazl, *Akbarnama*, *Vol. II*, p. 331.

have unfolded there, but he says a 'wonderful thing' happened four days after the *jauhar*. Two women were found to be alive when the Mughal forces opened the door. One was Kamalavati, Rani Durgavati's sister; the other was the daughter of Raja Puragadha who had been brought to Chauragarh to be married off to Raja Bir Narayan. Both women were sent off to Agra to be part of Akbar's harem.

Jauhar would easily qualify as one of the worst crimes against women and humanity today along with rape. But even back in the 16th century, *jauhar* and the more frequent Sati were not seen as virtuous acts by non-Hindus. The reaction to the monstrous crime of Sati by the previous Muslim sultanates was one of condescension, but none of them took any steps to stop these. Akbar tried to be different in this and banned involuntary Sati. To enforce this ban, he posted officers at various places. Abu'l Fazl wrote:

> From the time that this ever-vernal country has been kept verdant and fresh by the justice of the world's lord, vigilant and truthful men have been appointed in every city and district in order that the two classes of cases (voluntary and involuntary Sati) may be continually kept distinct, and that forcible burning may not be permitted.[36]

Akbar didn't ban voluntary Sati, but a century later, foreign travellers like Tavernier and Bernier noted that even voluntary burning of widows was becoming difficult as for that permission had to be taken and the Mughal state didn't readily give it.

Francois Bernier wrote in his *Travels in the Mogul Empire*:

> What has been said so many travellers will confirm concerning women burning themselves that I suppose people will cease to be sceptical upon this melancholy fact. The accounts given of it have been certainly exaggerated, and the number of victims is less now than formerly; the *Mahometans*, by whom the country is governed, doing all in their power to suppress the barbarous custom. They do not, indeed, forbid it by a positive law, because it is a part of their policy to leave the idolatrous

36 Abu'l Fazl, *Akbarnama, Vol. III*, p. 595.

population, which is so much more numerous than their own, in the free exercise of its religion; but the practice is checked by indirect means.[37]

He then went on to add:

No woman can sacrifice herself without permission from the governor of the province in which she resides, and he never grants it until he shall have ascertained that she is not to be turned aside from her purpose: to accomplish this desirable end the governor reasons with the widow and makes her enticing promises; after which, if these methods fail, he sometimes sends her among his women, that the effect of their remonstrances may be tried. Notwithstanding these obstacles, the number of self-immolations is still very considerable, particularly in the territories of the Rajas, where no Mahometan governors are appointed.[38]

Tavernier echoed Bernier. He wrote in his *Travels in India*:

But it should be remarked that a woman cannot burn herself with the body of her husband without having received permission from the Governor of the place where she dwells, and those Governors who are Musalmans, hold this dreadful custom of self-destruction in horror and do not readily give permission.[39]

But the state policy could always be altered or influenced by greasing palms of those executing it. Tavernier wrote:

The Governor, seeing that all the remonstrances with women, who are urged to burn themselves even by their relatives and by the Brahmans, fail to turn them from the damnable resolution which they have taken to die in so cruel a fashion, when his secretary indicates by a sign that he has

37 François, Archibald Constable and Vincent Arthur Smith, *Travels in the Mogul Empire, A.D. 1656–1668,* Translated on the basis of Irving Brocks version and annotated by Archibald Constable (1891). II ed. (London: H. Milford, Oxford University Press, 1914), p. 306.

38 Ibid.

39 Jean-Baptiste Tavernier, Valentine Ball, and William Crooke, *Travels in India, II ed., Vol. II* (London: Oxford University Press, 1925), p. 163.

> received a bribe, at length allows them to do what they wish, and in a rage tells all idolaters who accompany them that they may 'go to the devil'.[40]

People still have their way in India by greasing palms. This kind of everyday corruption is still pretty much rampant in the society at large. But what Bernier said about the Muslim state failing to stop Sati in the dominions of the Hindu kings is correct and revealed two things: firstly, the Mughals didn't interfere in religious matters of the Hindus and allowed everyone the liberty to follow their faiths; lastly, they could not enforce penal action against their Hindu nobility for practising Sati and killing of the girlchild.

Abu'l Fazl, though, recorded one particular incident[41] in which Akbar personally intervened and stopped forcible Sati of Rao Maldev of Marwar's granddaughter. She was married to Jaimal, son of Rupsi who was the nephew of Raja Bharmal. Jaimal died near Chausa while on his way to Bengal on an imperial mission. His widow was the daughter of Raja Udai Singh, also known as Mota Raja. She wasn't willing to immolate herself on her husband's pyre, but her son along with a few other 'bold and foolish persons set themselves to work the injustice (to make her burn)', Fazl wrote.

Akbar learnt about it early morning when he was at his *zenana* or women's quarters. 'The just sovereign fearing that if he sent others there would be delay, mounted a swift horse and went off to the spot,' Fazl wrote. Akbar managed to stop the crime from happening and saved the life of the widow. Her tormentors' lives were spared because they regretted their act, but they were imprisoned.[42]

While this was a commendable action by Akbar, it cannot be held that this was the general template that was followed. Many Hindu nobles had committed infanticide or condoned it and the Mughal state could do nothing against them. Just like it is today, in India, rulers have always found it tough to act against the powerful and support the plebeian, and the Mughals were no exception.

---

40 Ibid., p. 164.

41 Abu'l Fazl, *Akbarnama, Vol. III*, pp. 594–96.

42 Ibid.

But in matters of sexual crimes like rape, the Mughals, now considered the bad boys of Indian history, often acted decisively even if it was not always to a woman's advantage. Punishments used to range from maiming to execution. Though in most democratic countries today such medieval forms of punishment are unheard of, whenever a rape happens in India, many people demand such kinds of punishment for the perpetrators.

In 2018, India's conscience was shaken by the gang rape and murder of an eight-year-old Muslim girl in Kathua, Jammu, and the rape of another girl in Uttar Pradesh's Unnao. Both these cases triggered massive outrage not just due to the horrific nature of the crimes but also the ruling BJP's reluctance to keep its members from supporting the accused.

It often happens in rape cases today that the police cast aspersions on the survivor, hinting that it may have been a deal for paid sex gone wrong. In the Unnao case, the accused was a BJP MLA who resorted to victim shaming when his name emerged as the perpetrator. The attitude wasn't different in Mughal India when a woman's testimony wasn't enough to nail a rapist. Rape or any sexual transgression was called *zina* and carried a severe punishment. Therefore, it required four witnesses to attest the victim's version.[43]

Abu'l Fazl wrote in the first volume of *Ain-i-Akbari* that when Mughal commander Muhibb Ali Khan attacked Bhakkar, its ruler Sultan Mahmud's vizier, Mubarak Khan, defected to him. Later, the Mughal commander learnt that the defector's son, Beg Oghlu, had 'criminal intercourse' (rape) with a concubine of Sultan Mahmud. Muhibb said Oghlu would be given the death penalty. Mubarak Khan tried to flee to save his son but was captured and killed.[44]

Akbar's other chronicler, Nizamuddin Ahmad, wrote in his *Tabakat-i-Akbari* about a Brahmin man who made a mistress of his daughter and had children with her. Both were arrested and tried.

---

43 Satya Prakash Sangar, *Crime and Punishment in Mughal India* (Delhi: Sterling Publishers, 1967), p. 181.

44 Abu'l Fazl, *Ain-i-Akbari, II ed. Vol. I,* Trans. H. Blochman (Calcutta: Royal Asiatic Society of Bengal, 1927), p. 464.

When the father confessed, Akbar gave him the death penalty and spared the daughter.

Father Monserrate, the Jesuit priest at Akbar's court, gave another account of Akbar's punishment for rape. In his *Commentary*, Monserrate wrote:

> The King has such a hatred of debauchery and adultery that neither influence nor entreaties nor the great ransom which was offered would induce him to pardon his chief trade commissioner (a man named Jalal), who although he was already married had violently debauched a well-born Brahman girl. The wretch was by the King's order remorselessly strangled.[45]

In Emperor Jahangir's time, his childhood friend and physician Muqarrab Khan was accused of rape. Khan was the son of Shaikh Bhina, the personal physician of Akbar. 'When Jahangir became king, he elevated Muqarrab Khan to the *mansab* of 5,000, and made him governor of Gujarat, a position usually reserved for people of royal blood. Later, he was made the *subedar* of Bihar. Jahangir would visit his house and Khan would send the emperor gifts,' historian Professor Ali Nadeem Rezavi told this author in a private conversation in April 2018.

When he was Gujarat governor in 1610, Muqarrab Khan was accused of raping a Hindu woman. 'Jahangir suspended him and launched an inquiry, which found him guilty. His governorship was taken away, his *mansab* was reduced, and he was in the wilderness despite his relationship with the emperor,' said Professor Rezavi, who heads the Centre of Advanced Study, Department of History, Aligarh Muslim University.

The Kathua girl was raped in a temple for several days. This has a parallel in Greek mythology that offers some lessons about the treatment of rape victims in a deeply patriarchal society.

Medusa was an exceptionally beautiful priestess at the temple of Pallas Athena, the Greek goddess of war and industry. Poseidon,

---

45 Antonio Monserrate, John S. Hoyland and S. N. Banerjee, *The Commentary of Father Monserrate, S. J., on His Journey to the Court of Akbar* (London: H. Milford, Oxford University Press, 1922), p. 210.

the god of the sea, lusted after her. One day, he raped her inside the temple. Athena was enraged that her temple had been desecrated by this crime. But it was Medusa who faced the wrath of the goddess. Athena condemned Medusa to a hideous form of a Gorgon. That was not all—her lustrous hair turned into venomous snakes, and she was cursed that whosoever would look into her eyes directly would be turned into stone. What's more: she was banished to an isolated island where one could go only by bribing Charon, the ferryman of Hades. That was quite a punishment for a victim of rape! But that's what patriarchy does.

Modern analysts of this tale see in Medusa's horrifying transformation her rape, brutalisation and death. It's a commentary on the deep-rooted patriarchy of the time because of which even Athena, one of the handful of women among the 12 Olympians—a big boys' club of the gods—sides with her fellow Olympian and blames and punishes the victim.

The moot point here is this: power isn't always enough to hold the powerful accountable, it takes will to do that. However, it would be wrong to claim that Akbar didn't have the will. The episode of the *Mota* (fat) Raja's daughter gave proof of both his will and intent. But in the absence of more numerous examples, one is forced to conclude that Akbar faced the same dilemma that political leaders of today face—support of the people.

Akbar and his successors couldn't penalise the Hindu *mansabdars* enough as their withdrawal of support would have made things difficult for the Mughal Empire. They had to be welcomed with all their customs, traditions, biases and prejudices intact. These *mansabdars*, to give a more modern analogy, held premium stakes in the rich enterprise called the Mughal Empire. They both added to the riches of the empire and were enriched by it. They upheld the Mughal state and added to its military strength. The state had to be indulgent towards them.

Similarly, the prejudices of the Muslim *mansabdars* had to be tolerated too. Raja Todarmal, who succeeded I'timad Khan in managing the finances of the empire, was despised by a section of the Muslim nobility, Iranis and Turanis alike. When Akbar also made Khwaja Muzaffar Ali Khan Turbati a finance minister, he started to have run-ins with the Hindu minister. There was professional rivalry here, but it was also a competition of an unhealthy kind. Khan couldn't countenance the fact that a Hindu could be rated higher than him by the emperor, a fellow Muslim.

Turbati and others would often ridicule and insult Todarmal. One of the ways Turbati did it was by twisting a pejorative couplet that was used to insult Hindus by way of insulting their oldest and holiest city—Kashi or Banaras (Varanasi today). It said—'A dog of a Kashi is better than an *Isfahani*, although a dog is a hundred times better than a Kashi.'[46]

Turbati played on it and made it thus—'A dog of a Raja is better than Muzaffar Khan, although a dog is a hundred times better than a Raja.'[47]

That faction of nobles also complained to the emperor about Todarmal and asked him to fire him from his job. Akbar countered them with the following reply, as quoted by Badaoni—'Every one of you has a Hindu to manage his private affairs. Suppose we too have a Hindu, why should harm come of it?'[48]

The answer not only quietened them down, it also prompted the yes-men to look for ways to please the emperor and his favourite minister. So the opposition to the Hindu officer and his criticism were replaced with showers of praise. An inspired sycophant came up with a couplet to praise Todarmal—'He who of Indian affairs made a mull, Was the Raja of Rajas Todarmal.'[49]

In India's political firmament today, one would find a very strong parallel of such contempt as well as sycophancy. INC president Rahul Gandhi comes across as a left-leaning leader with a liberal impulse. Secularism has been his and his party's calling card for long. And yet, for over a year now, the Congress president has gone about calling himself a 'Shiv *bhakt*' or devotee of Lord Shiva and the party has been trying to discard the label of a 'party of Muslims' that it has earned, courtesy the BJP. Suddenly, all those followers who had been harping on the secular credentials of the party have started asserting the Hindu

46 Badaoni, *Tawarikh*, p. 64.

47 Ibid.

48 Ibid., p. 65.

49 Ibid.

identity of their leader while vehemently denying the charge that it's a party of Muslims.

An even stronger parallel can be seen in Congress' rival BJP. The party members and their minions outside—pejoratively referred to as *bhakts* (devotees of Narendra Modi) or Modi toadies—have totally switched off logic and reasoning in order to parrot the line set down by their leader. So, while rationalising the lynching of Muslims and Dalits by *gau rakshaks* or cow-protection vigilantes with whataboutery, abuses, obscenities and absurd logic, the backers of Modi, both online and offline, changed tack immediately, the moment Modi himself denounced these vigilantes as cow protectors by the day, criminals by the night.[50] Suddenly, the 'defenders of Hindu pride' became 'criminals sullying the Hindu faith'.

The Mughal Emperor had to do a balancing act with his nobility. But that didn't mean that every transgression was allowed, as the incidents involving the Mota Raja's daughter or Muqarrab Khan suggest. Yet, by and large, the Rajput *mansabdars* from Rajputana were one of the most pampered lots among Mughal nobles.

But not all in Rajputana were willing allies in those early years of Akbar's monarchy. If Amber had become an ally, Mewar wasn't willing to even have a dialogue on this. And even though defeated by the Mughals in a few engagements, even Marwar wasn't willing to come to terms with Mughal suzerainty. For the Mughal military to retain its edge in combat, it was crucial to control the overland trade routes through which war horses were imported from Central Asia and the Middle East. And these routes went via Malwa and Rajputana.[51]

Malwa was earlier conquered by Akbar. The next logical destination for conquest was Rajputana. Standing up somewhat obstinately in the Mughal path of conquest was the state of Mewar, with its imposing citadel of Chittor.

---

50 Rituparna Chatterjee, *'I Get Angry At Criminals Posing As "Gau Rakshaks", Says Prime Minister Narendra Modi'*, *Huffington Post*, 6 August 2016. Available at https://www.huffingtonpost.in/2016/08/06/i-get-angry-at-criminals-posing-as-gau-rakshaks-says-prime-mi_a_21446243/.

51 Jos Gommans, *Mughal Warfare*, p. 115.

Chapter 5

Master and Commander

> Wherever the eye looked, there was sign of victory.
> Wherever the ear applied itself, there was news of conquest.[1]

The paths of Mewar and the Mughal Empire had crossed a few times in the first few years of Akbar's reign, but these were not happy intercourses but inimical ones. A big clash was due for many years but the opportune moment for the Mughals to strike had not presented itself.

Rana Udai Singh giving refuge to Baz Bahadur was a serious provocation that Akbar ignored at the time as Malwa wasn't secured. But in 1567, Akbar finally got the opportunity to strike at Mewar. A series of events actually aided his cause.

Ali Quli Khan, whom Akbar had given the title of *Khan-i-Zaman* as a reward for his stellar role in the victory at Panipat against Hemu, had rebelled against Akbar in 1565. He was the governor of Jaunpur then, and his act of insubordination came close on the heels of that of Abdullah Khan Uzbek in Malwa. Both Khan Zaman and Abdullah Khan were Turani nobles (Uzbeks) who detested Akbar's perceived

---

1 Abu'l Fazl, *Akbarnama, Vol. II,* p. 496.

closeness to Persian nobles and the centralised nature of his monarchy.[2] In this, they resembled the *Bandagan-i-Chahalgani* (also variously referred to as *Turkan-i-Chahalgani* or *Amir-i-Chahalgani*) or the group of 40 nobles of the Delhi Sultanate when the Mamluk dynasty held sway. The *chahalgani* were Turks who played kingmakers. Though not as fiercely independent as the Afghan warlords of the time of the Lodhi Dynasty, who treated the sultan only as the first among equals, the *chahalgani* could and did depose sultans.

In a similar fashion, Khan Zaman, his brother and uncle were planning to depose Akbar and prop up his cousin Abu'l Qasim Mirza, son of Akbar's uncle Mirza Kamran, on the throne of Hindustan. Akbar got wind of this affair, and when the royal troops were beaten back by the rebels, he quietly got his cousin executed so as to neutralise the possibility of the rebels actually doing what they had been contemplating. Less than a year earlier, Mirza Sharfuddin Husain and Shah Abu'l Ma'ali had contemplated bringing Akbar's half-brother Mirza Muhammad Hakim, the ruler of Kabul, over to Hindustan to place him on the throne. So, the threat of a coup was real. It was the time for Akbar to take stern action. And he did.

Akbar led an army himself and forced Khan Zaman to retrace his steps. Raja Todarmal was initially sent to the rebel camp for parley but it didn't work out well as the Raja was not in favour of pardoning the rebels. It was then left to *Khan-i-Khanan* Munim Khan to meet Khan Zaman and negotiate. The Uzbek noble agreed to stand down and the rebellion was over. But it was only a temporary truce and Akbar knew it. Abu'l Fazl quotes him as having said, 'We pardon him, but it will be surprising if he remained constant in his obedience.'[3]

Akbar had figured out his senior general's intentions quite well. No sooner did he turn his back on the Khan Zaman affair and moved towards Benares, Khan Zaman resumed hostilities. Akbar was furious! He harangued Munim Khan for having interceded on Khan Zaman's behalf. Munim Khan hung his head in shame. Akbar turned back and gave hot chase to the Uzbek.

2 Stephen M. Edwardes and Herbert Leonard Offley Garret, *Mughal Rule in India* (New Delhi: Atlantic Publishers and Distributors, 1995), p. 32.

3 Abu'l Fazl, *Akbarnama, Vol. II,* p. 394.

Ali Quli Khan avoided conflict as far as possible and kept on running from one place to another. He narrowly escaped capture on one occasion when Munim Khan tipped him off and stopped the imperial troops from going out on campaign one night. But his position was becoming utterly hopeless and he realised that. So, he once again asked the *Khan-i-Khanan* and other senior nobles trusted by Akbar to intercede on his behalf for one last time. Munim Khan refused but others did speak to the emperor and appealed for his mercy.

Akbar once again gave in to their demands. But by now he was convinced that Ali Quli Khan would give him trouble again in the future. And he did, just a few months later.

In November 1566, Akbar got news that Muhammad Hakim had come out of Kabul and invaded Punjab, reached the gates of Lahore and invested the fort. Clearly, Akbar's half-brother was hooked to the Uzbek rebellion in Hindustan and tried to tap into it and take his shot at the throne of Hindustan. Akbar was livid! He decided to march on Lahore and teach his half-brother a lesson.

Akbar left behind Munim Khan to manage Agra and himself led the army. Abu'l Fazl says that he enjoyed the pleasures of hunting on the way and took 10 days to reach Delhi. It might appear strange to a lay reader that a man in a hurry to repulse an invasion of the most important city in Punjab should march at such a leisurely pace and enjoying the pleasures of a hunt as if nothing was amiss. Perhaps an incomplete idea of this and other Mughal military practices led some western historians like Philip Mason to write disparagingly of the Mughal military, calling it unwieldy, incompetent and ineffective.

But Mughal hunts, as pointed out earlier, were essentially war games involving complex cavalry manoeuvres and mounted archery that were key elements of Mughal warfare. This hunt too seems to have been a way to train his army and officers on the march to prepare them for the impending conflict.

Elsewhere, when Khan Zaman heard of Muhammad Hakim's siege of Lahore, he and his comrades declared their support for the

Mirza, even reciting the *khutba* in his name and accepting him as their emperor.[4] This was open sedition.

Around the same time, Akbar's relatives named Ulugh Mirza, Shah Mirza, Ibrahim Husain Mirza and Muhammad Husain Mirza rebelled against him at Sambal (in today's Uttar Pradesh). They are collectively referred to as the Mirzas in history books and their revolt is called the Mirza Revolt. They went to ally with Ali Quli Khan but were spurned as Khan Zaman wanted to be a sovereign ruler himself. They tried attacking Agra, but the city's defences were made more robust by Munim Khan. The Mirzas decided on going to Malwa as it was pretty much open territory.

Malwa's previous commander, Abdullah Khan Uzbek, had been earlier forced to leave Malwa and go to Gujarat in disgrace by Akbar. But around the time the Mirzas entered Malwa, Abdullah Khan also re-entered his former fief after being pushed back from Gujarat.

So, this was that moment in history when the most serious challenge to Akbar's monarchy was mounted by his extended family in league with a section of his disaffected nobles. But when push came to shove, none could show cohesion or courage to face Akbar in combat.

Muhammad Hakim withdrew from Lahore when he heard that Akbar was coming at the head of an army. Akbar entered Lahore and sent a portion of his army to secure the frontiers. With imperial troops coming after him, Mirza Hakim returned to Kabul.

To celebrate this, Akbar organised a mega hunt. For a month, game was collected and about 50,000 beaters assembled to drive the game towards the hunting ground that was 10 miles in circumference.[5] Abu'l Fazl tells us that the tactic of *qamargha* was used to close the dragnet around the game.

Jos Gommans describes what the *qamargha* was:

> From an area that could be as large as about 100 km in circumference, all the wild game was driven together into a small, enclosed circle where the king started the actual hunt. Since the rounding up of wild animals involved similar manoeuvres to those on the battlefield, i.e. skirmishers

---

4 Ibid., p. 420.

5 Ibid., p. 417.

> in front of the centre with two flanks wheeling around the enemy, it was a most useful training camp.[6]

In March 1567, Akbar turned back towards Agra from Lahore. As the royal entourage came near Thaneshwar, the ancient capital city of King Harshavardhana of the Pushyabhuti-Maukhari dynasty, Akbar was petitioned by two groups of *sanyasi*s or ascetics known as the Kurs and Puris. Abu'l Fazl writes:[7]

> Near that town there is a tank which might be called a miniature sea. Formerly, there was a wide plain there known as Kurkhet (Kurukshetra of *The Mahabharata*) which the ascetics of India have reverenced from ancient times. Hindus from various parts of India visit it at stated times and distribute alms, and there is a great concourse.

These two sanyasi sects vied for a bigger share of alms. The Kurs thought the Puris occupied an area that gave them greater access to pilgrims and therefore higher chances of getting more alms. Abu'l Fazl very correctly spots the irony when he writes:

> The asceticism of most of these men arises from the world's having turned its back on them, and not from their becoming cold-hearted to the world. Consequently, they are continually distressed and are overcome of lust and wrath, and covetousness.[8]

This paradox exists even today in India with religious cults and spiritual gurus wielding immense material and political power in India. The serving chief minister of the state of Uttar Pradesh, Yogi Adityanath, is a Hindu monk and leader of the Natha Yogi sect and chief priest of the Gorakhnath Temple in Gorakhpur.

Three other so-called ascetics but very renowned and popular spiritual gurus—Sri Sri Ravi Shankar, Jaggi Vasudev or Sadhguru, and Baba Ramdev (more a yoga guru than a spiritual master) either manage or own business empires. Ramdev is the most well-known face of his retail giant, Patanjali Ayurveda Limited, while his yoga institute,

---

6 Jos Gommans, *Mughal Warfare*, pp. 110–11.

7 Abu'l Fazl, *Akbarnama, Vol. II,* pp. 422–23.

8 Ibid.

Patanjali Yog Peeth, even managed to get a tax-exempt status. They may have renounced the world, but renunciation of worldly matters is tough even today as it was in Akbar's time.

The leader of the Puris complained to Akbar that they had been pushed out by the Kurs, and even though they didn't have sufficient strength to resist them, the Puris wouldn't go into the night without a fight.

When Akbar asked the Kurs, they said the place was theirs by inheritance and they wouldn't give it up as long as they were living. Abu'l Fazl says Akbar tried to reason with both parties and asked them to patch up. But 'it was like casting pearls on the ground, and their absurdity and error only increased'.

'Their desperation and disposition to kill themselves augmented and they entreated with fervent supplications that there might be a fight and slaughter,' Fazl writes. Akbar finally gave his nod to a clash of arms between both parties to decide the dispute. Both sides used swords, bows and arrows, but the outnumbered[9] and outgunned Puris started stone pelting.

Akbar signalled to people in his army to bump up the ranks of the Puris and aid them in fighting with stones. The scales tipped in favour of the Puris immediately and the Kurs ran away with heavy losses.

This is how Abu'l Fazl describes the incident. Badaoni gives a more bigoted account of the event and of the Kurukshetra War while heaping curses on the Hindus.[10] But he also gives more interesting details like Akbar's troops smearing ash on their bodies and wearing dresses like that of the Puris to mix with them so that the Kurs couldn't make out that the emperor had unfairly intervened in favour of their enemy.

The Indian epic *The Ramayana* that tells the story of Lord Rama narrates a similar incident when Rama unfairly intervenes in a duel between Kishkindhya King Sugreeva and his mightier elder brother Bali. It was Bali who was the Kishkindhya King, but while fighting a demon named Mayavi, Sugreeva thought Bali was

---

9 The Puris were only 300 in number as opposed to 500 Kurs.

10 Badaoni, *Tawarikh, Vol. II,* p. 94.

dead and proclaimed himself king, only to realise later that Bali was alive.

Bali didn't take this kindly and accused his brother of treachery. Sugreeva accepted his brother's challenge of a duel but not before securing an assurance from Rama to intervene on his behalf. Bali was much more powerful than Sugreeva and the latter knew that. Eventually, when the two brothers clashed, Rama took Bali down in a sniper-like action, and justified his killing of Bali, saying that he had only hunted a monkey.

For whatever reason, Akbar did something similar at Thaneshwar. Either he genuinely wanted to help the weaker side like Barbarik, Bhima's grandson in *The Mahabharata*, or he just wanted to have some sinister fun. Or maybe he saw in the Puris an underdog who had to be supported. All of this is conjecture, and all of it may have been true or none of it. But even today, stories of weak sides trumping stronger ones, like David beating Goliath, or challengers toppling champions, like Rocky Balboa beating Apollo Creed (in Hollywood film *Rocky*), are celebrated by the masses. And underdogs often become darlings of the masses. Like the Aam Aadmi Party, which challenged the Congress in Delhi and removed it from power as the people cheered its every move, every slogan, every comment on TV, even its sweeping statements not founded on reason or fact.

But this historic episode, like most others involving the Mughals and other Muslim rulers, is today misrepresented by many social media commentators of the Hindu right. They give a communal colour to the entire incident and spread falsehoods about it, attributing things to Akbar that he never said. One such mis-attribution is a line in Persian that says, 'Whichever side may be slain, Islam is the gainer.' Akbar never said that. No primary source indicates that, not even Badaoni who is otherwise quite unreserved in his bigoted words.

Akbar returned to Agra soon after and didn't waste time to get ready for his next campaign: to deal with the rebellion of Khan Zaman for the third time. On 6 May 1567, Akbar himself led the Army out of Agra leaving behind *Khan-i-Khanan* Munim Khan to manage the capital. The emperor had already sent out an advanced force towards

Kannauj to relieve the garrison there besieged by Khan Zaman Ali Quli Khan.

In a repeat of the old saga, Khan Zaman withdrew from Kannauj hearing Akbar's coming. When the emperor reached Raebareli, he learnt that the rebels were planning an attack on Gwalior and would cross the Ganges soon. Through forced marches, where many of his followers could barely keep up with him, Akbar covered the distance in no time and also crossed the flooded Ganges on an elephant, much to the horror of his followers who must of have been taken aback by this utterly reckless crossing of the river when there was no urgency. Abu'l Fazl gives a positive spin to it, but it isn't hard to imagine what the reality must have been.

Fazl wrote[11]:

> As it was the beginning of the rainy season, and the river was in flood, a strange agitation and outcry arose from the people when His Majesty drove his elephant into the water. For the crossing of such a destructive river was an impossibility and it was only by the miraculous power of the Shahinshah that this swelling ocean gave a passage to that mine of holiness.

When Akbar set up camp that evening, the distance between him and the rebels was 1 kos (up to 3 km). But despite being warned, Khan Zaman refused to believe that Akbar had crossed the swollen river with his whole army—an incredulity expressed by the Maratha army at Panipat over 200 years later when informed about Ahmad Shah Abdali crossing the flooded Yamuna and setting up camp behind them.

The following morning, Akbar put on his chain mail armour and rode a war elephant named Bal Sundar to give battle to Ali Quli Khan at Sakrawal near Allahabad. But Khan Zaman once again started to withdraw when he saw the Mughals close in on him. This time, though, Akbar wasn't willing to let him get away. He dismounted from his lumbering mount and rode a horse and very soon the imperial cavalry was carrying through shock charges on Khan Zaman's ranks.

---

11 Abu'l Fazl, *Akbarnama, Vol. II,* p. 428.

Khan Zaman had to give battle and it turned out to be a fierce one. Akbar's *taulqama* tactics proved to be more than a match for the rebels who were pushed back in disarray, their wings collapsing into the centre and the centre becoming a muddle of man and beast. Two of Akbar's elephants, Chitranand and Gaj Bhanwar, oblivious to the ongoing fierce battle around them, broke into a fratricidal conflict. Chitranand was in *musth* and charged at Gaj Bhanwar. Luckily, for Akbar, Gaj Bhanwar and Chitranand ran ahead instead of turning around and crushed many rebel troops.

Midway, another elephant named Udiya showed up and Chitranand abandoned the pursuit of Gaj Bhanwar and charged at Udiya, wounding him fatally. All this troubled the rebels even more. Sensing trouble, Khan Zaman pushed his brother Bahadur Khan ahead with a troop of mounted archers. Bahadur Khan fought gallantly, but then an arrow shot his horse and Bahadur Khan was flung away. As he landed on the ground, he was overwhelmed by imperial troops and captured. When he was taken before Akbar, he didn't ask for mercy. Akbar still wanted to spare his life but was opposed by other nobles. At length, he ordered his two officers, Shahbaz Khan and Bansi Das Kambu, to execute Bahadur Khan.

But Ali Quli Khan was nowhere to be found. Someone said he ran away, some said he died in battle. Without any means to retrieve bodies from the battlefield and identifying them, Akbar devised a way to do the job without much fuss. He ordered that whoever brought him the severed head of a Mughal rebel would be given a gold mohur, while the head of a Hindustani would fetch a rupee (silver).

The crowd got excited and started bringing in severed heads and collecting prizes. Eventually, one head came that was identified by a Hindu man named Arzani as that of his master, Ali Quli Khan. Arzani was a powerful officer of the Khan Zaman and there was no ground not to trust him. Eventually, based on eyewitness testimonies, it was found that an arrow hit the Khan Zaman and unhorsed him. As he lay injured, an elephant driver named Somnath guided his elephant Nain Sukh towards him and trampled him. The Uzbek challenge was thus crushed, quite literally.

Akbar now turned towards Malwa to crush the Mirzas. But he understood the political significance of the move—these were Timurid princes themselves, and Akbar didn't want to accord them any legitimacy that he thought they would get if he moved against them personally. So, he appointed imperial officers to do the job while he himself contemplated on moving against Mewar.

But this had to be done with caution, lest the enemy got wind of it and further fortified the defences of Chittor—the grand prize. So, Akbar went to Bari pargana for a hunt on 30 August 1567. Today, it is a city within the Dholpur district of Rajasthan. But back in Akbar's time, it was a *pargana* separate from Dholpur and a big source of red sandstone that Akbar mined to build his grand fort at Agra and would mine to build his grand city of Fatehpur Sikri.

The hunt then proceeded to Dholpur where Akbar next set up camp. Here, Abu'l Fazl tells us that Sakat Singh, a son of Rana Udai Singh, came to attend on the emperor.[12] What happened next isn't clear, but it seems Akbar expressed his displeasure that Sakat Singh's father hadn't yet submitted to him and that he intended to march against him. Fazl tries to give a weak argument that Akbar said that either in jest, which Singh misunderstood, or to give a false impression to the Mirzas that Akbar was focused on Chittor and not them.

But it seems Sakat Singh read the emperor's mind pretty well as Akbar asked him in what way he would help the Mughals in fighting his father. He gave 'hypocritical' assurances and made good his escape from court back to his father. Abu'l Fazl describes it in indignation:

> At last that crooked-minded one, from want of understanding and from taking a jest seriously, ran away. In his folly, he ran away from apparent dishonour, and fell into real disgrace. For the ignorant fellow imagined that His Majesty was meditating the punishment of Rana under the pretence of hunting, and that he himself would get a bad name to the effect that he had gone and brought His Majesty against his father. He did not know that it was all a joke, and that there was no reason why this powerful and God-restrained one should personally proceed against such a class of landholders. Nor did he perceive that, on the supposition that

12 Ibid., p. 442.

> his notion was correct, his running away from such a good fortune was to throw himself into the lowest hell of destruction and to hurry from disrepute to misconduct.[13]

Fazl next tries to make his readers believe that it was because of this act by Sakat Singh that Akbar got angry and actually decided to attack Chittor:

> When the news of his flight reached the royal hearing, the Shahinshah's wrath was stirred up, and jest became earnest. And in truth this was proper, for, from the time of the accession, most of the leading men of India who had cocked the hat of pride and had not lowered the head of obedience before any of the Sultans, had bowed down and kissed the ground, except Rana Udai Singh, than whom there was in this country no one more foolish and arrogant. This audacious and immoderate one, in whom the turbulence of ancestors was added to his own haughtiness, was proud of his steep mountains and strong castles and turned away the head of obedience from the sublime court. His brain was heated by the consciousness of his possessing abundant land and wealth, and numbers of devoted Rajputs, and so he left the path of auspiciousness. His Majesty's world-conquering genius decided to chastise him.[14]

Fazl's account gives one a fair idea of how governments always find the flimsiest of grounds to base their actions on or use the weakest of explanations to justify their conduct. Fazl here is going beyond being an apologist of Akbar: he is making it appear as if it is Akbar who is to be pitied for his aggressive move against Mewar.

Nevertheless, the Mewar campaign began on 19 September 1567. We do see the 25-year-old Akbar as a strategist and master tactician in this. He didn't make a dash at Chittor; he started taking one fort after another and posting Mughal garrisons there so that his rear was never threatened in his quest for Chittor.

He first moved to Hindwara, where the army encamped near a fort that Fazl calls Sivi Supar. This fort was under the control of Rao Surjan Hada of Ranthambore, but the garrison abandoned it

13 Ibid., p. 443.

14 Ibid.

when it heard Akbar was coming. The fort was secured, and a new garrison posted under Nazr Bahadur. Akbar then went to Kota, which was easily taken and another garrison posted under the command of Shah Muhammad Qandahari. Then Akbar conquered the imposing Gagron Fort (a UNESCO World Heritage Site today).[15]

From Gagron, Akbar despatched an army under his generals Shihabuddin Ahmad Khan, Shah Budagh Khan, Murad Khan and Haji Muhammad Khan Sistani to Malwa to chastise the Mirzas. When this imperial force arrived in Ujjain, the Mirzas first fled to Mandu where the eldest of them, Ulugh Mirza, died. The other two brothers, Ibrahim Husain Mirza and Muhammad Husain Mirza, then fled to Gujarat where they joined ranks with Chingiz Khan, a former slave of Sultan Mahmud of Gujarat who had seized the forts of Champaner, Bharuch and Surat upon the death of his master.[16] Though the rebellion wasn't completely over, yet for the time being, Malwa was clean and Akbar could focus wholly on Chittor.

Akbar's commanders, Asaf Khan and Wazir Khan, next took the powerful fort of Mandalgarh, which was held for Mewar by Rawat Balvi Solanki. Fazl gives no details of the fight, but hints at it being a tough one as it was conquered 'by the prestige of the *Shahinshah*'.

At this point, Fazl says, the emperor's army wasn't big. But Akbar decided to push ahead in the hope that Rana Udai Singh would be tempted to come out of his defences to attack a numerically inferior enemy. However, this didn't have the desired effect. On the contrary, when the Rana learnt that Akbar didn't have a siege train (heavy artillery, including mortars and howitzers, meant for sieges) with him, he assumed that Akbar wouldn't be foolhardy enough to attack Chittor. To be doubly sure, he strengthened the fort, posted a garrison of 5,000 Rajputs, stocked up supplies that could sustain the people inside for years, and laid the areas around the fort waste so that the approaching Mughals couldn't live off the land. Not even a blade of grass was left standing, it is said. This was the scorched earth policy that Imperial Russia would successfully employ against the Grande

15 Ibid., p. 444.

16 Ibid., pp. 462–63.

Armee of Napoleon on 1812, and the Soviet Union would repeat when invaded by Nazi Germany.

The Rana withdrew further deep into the hills while leaving the Chittor garrison to face the Mughal might. Jaimal Rathore of Merta, the former Mughal ally who once led Mughal armies against fellow Rajputs, commanded the garrison. His task now was to defend the crowning glory of Mewar even with his life, if need be.

Akbar wisely avoided following the Rana into the hills. Instead, he chose to lay siege to the fort. On 20 October 1567, the Mughal army camped around the fort in what must have been an intimidating sight for the garrison. The terrain outside the fort even today is flat. From the imposing heights, the garrison must have spotted the imperial army approaching when it was miles away.

As Akbar set up camp, a storm broke accompanied by thunder and lightning. In that open country, the intensity of a storm must have been more acutely felt than in the Mughal walled capitals. The 'earth was shaken', Fazl writes. Going by the superstitious society of the time, it could have been perceived as a bad omen, we don't know. But Akbar was of sterner mind. In any case, the storm lifted in an hour and made it possible for the imperial camp to plan a siege.

The following morning, Akbar rode out towards the fort that was atop a hill and went around it. It was a recce. The Mughals figured out that the circumference of the fort was over 2 *kos* (6 km) and was about 5 *kos* at the part used by the people. Today, we know that the circumference of the existing fort is 13 km—a huge, formidable fort even today. Akbar must have realised by now that he had an uphill task at hand, literally. So, at the end of the recce, he ordered the artillery to be brought ahead and asked his engineers and artillery officers to select spots to erect the batteries. Additional artillery was also called for. And even though Napoleon was still several centuries in the future to tell the world that 'God fights on the side with the best artillery', it must have been apparent to Akbar that the fort will have to be taken by the might of his guns. It took Akbar a whole month to set up his artillery.[17]

17 Ibid., p. 465.

Akbar's zealous generals, in a bid to rise in the emperor's favour, subjected reason to over-enthusiasm and risked life and limb in making intrepid yet fruitless charges at the fort. Akbar reprimanded them for being rash and lectured them on the true meaning of courage. Good commanders are also the ones who don't unnecessarily put the lives of their men at risk. This is what distinguishes the Earl of Cardigan, who sacrificed his Light Brigade at Balaclava while foolishly charging at Russian guns[18], from the Duke of Wellington who made an orderly retreat at Quatre Bras while facing a superior force under Marshal Ney[19]; or Field Marshal Sir Douglas Haig under whose flawed leadership the British suffered a disaster at the Battle of Somme during the First World War in 1916,[20] from Marshal Alexander Suvorov who withdrew with his Russian army from Switzerland fighting brilliant rear-guard actions against a nearly four-times bigger French army, thereby earning for himself the sobriquet of 'the Russian Hannibal.'[21]

---

18 Battle of Balaclava was fought during the Crimean War (1853–56). The tragedy of Cardigan's cavalry inspired Alfred Lord Tennyson's *Charge of the Light Brigade* with that famous refrain, 'into the valley of death, rode the six hundred'.

19 The Battle of Quatre Bras (16 June 1815) and its sister Battle of Ligny (same day as Quatre Bras) were two battles fought two days before the Battle of Waterloo (18 June 1815). In the first, Napoleon sent his deputy, Marshal Michel Ney, to engage the British-led coalition force at Quatre Bras while he himself fought the Prussian Army under Marshal Blucher at Ligny. Ney's forces stopped Wellington from going to the relief of Blucher but had to concede defeat allowing the British to withdraw to Waterloo and set up position at an advantageous location. The British and French suffered almost equal number of casualties but the British walked away with the strategic advantage.

20 The British lost nearly 60,000 men on the first day of the battle and eventually suffered half a million casualties as the battle ended, in large parts due to Haig's failure to appreciate the devastation a machine gun could cause on the battlefield, and sticking to the human wave tactic despite machine guns cutting down wave after wave of infantry charges.

21 This was during the end of 1799 after another Russian army lost the Second Battle of Zurich. Suvorov's army of about 23,000 faced a Republican French army of nearly 90,000 under Andre Massena. Suvorov's army retreated via the Swiss Alps, fighting off the pursuing enemy. The army more or less stayed intact despite some losses and reached the safety of the Rhine valley.

Akbar's counsel, though, had limited effect on these spirited troops who carried out mindless sallies at the fort but were felled by its defenders. Abu'l Fazl says the bullets and arrows fired by the Mughals couldn't go past the fort walls but the hail of bullets and arrows showered by the garrison claimed many Mughal lives. This prompted Akbar to change position and also order the placing of mines under the fort walls to breach them. To offer protection from enemy fire, Akbar ordered the construction of a *sabat* or approach trench.

There are no intact specimens of a Mughal *sabat* today, but it appears the Mughals, whenever faced with the necessity to lay siege to a fort, extensively used these. We can also surmise how it must have looked if we look at the concept of *al-fina*[22] and *sabat* as they appear in Islamic architecture. A *sabat*, even today, is an arched and roofed pathway or a street in countries of the Mediterranean and Middle East that funnels in air to offer shelter from heat and the sun. Usually these are attached to or extensions of buildings. An example of a grand *sabat* is the Chhatta Bazaar at Red Fort, Delhi, which is the first building upon entry from the Lahori Gate. It was a covered market place for the palace and even today is dotted with shops, many of whose owners claim descent from Shah Jahan's shopkeepers.

Akbar's sappers started making a robust *sabat* that was wide enough to let 10 men pass through walking side-by-side and tall enough for a mounted elephant to pass.[23] The construction work was carried out under heavy fire from the fort, which resulted in 200 workmen getting killed daily.[24] This must have been terribly demoralising for the Mughal army and its workforce, but the workers were paid in gold and silver coins to risk their lives repeatedly.[25] And by sacrificing their blood and sweat, life and limb, the workers managed to build robust

22 For more details on al-fina see, Hoshiar Nooraddin, '"Al-fina", in between spaces as an urban design concept: making public and private spaces along streets in Islamic cities of the Middle East', in *URBAN DESIGN International* (United Kingdom: Palgrave Macmillan, 1998), pp. 65–77.

23 Vincent Smith, *Akbar the Great Mogul*, p. 87.

24 Abu'l Fazl, *Akbarnama, Vol. II*, p. 467.

25 Ibid., pp. 467–68.

mud walls on either side of the *sabat* that could absorb the impact of cannonball hits.

This seems to be the reality of the Indian proletariat even today. It's quite a regular phenomenon to have factory supervisors or municipal contractors to offer a few hundred rupees more to work a faulty but hazardous machine or get inside a clogged manhole, at times even to ordinary workers who don't have the skill for that kind of work. The employers save money on engaging a more skilled worker in this way, but sometimes this leads to fatal experiments. A recent example of this comes from Delhi where five housekeeping staff of a condominium called DLF Capital Greens died of asphyxiation when made to clean a sewer by the firm that had the maintenance contract, allegedly to save money on hiring trained cleaners who also had the right kind of gear for the work.[26]

The work of the *sabat* was done under the supervision of Raja Todar Mal and Qasim Khan Mir Barr-u-Bahr. Todar Mal's credentials as a builder of defensive works had been burnished during Sher Shah Suri's time when he had been tasked to build the Rohtas Fort.[27] Qasim Khan, on the other hand, had built the Agra Fort for Akbar. It is no surprise, therefore, that these two men were chosen for such a challenging task of building the *sabat* while facing tremendous enemy fire.

As the *sabat* kept on moving forward, the fort's defenders realised that it was just a matter of time before Mughal artillery would be in a position of delivering devastating blows on the fort walls. Akbar was casting a massive siege gun on site, and the garrison must have managed to put two and two together: that the gun would be brought forward through the *sabat*. If that happened, the fort would fall. So, the garrison commander, Jaimal Rathore, decided to parley with the Mughals.

He first sent one Sanda Silahdar to negotiate terms of surrender. The talks failed and Silahdar returned empty-handed. Then another

---

26 For more details, see this article by *The Wire*, 'They Were Hired for Housekeeping and Then Forced to Enter the Sewer', 2 October 2018. Available at https://thewire.in/labour/delhi-manual-scavenging-sewer-deaths.

27 Please see Chapter 2 for more details.

commander named Sahib Khan Rathore was sent to resume dialogue. Abu'l Fazl writes that the Chittor officers resorted to 'entreaties and lamentations' to make the Mughals accept their surrender. They also offered to recognise Akbar's suzerainty and also send an annual tribute. Akbar's officers found the terms agreeable and beseeched their emperor to accept the surrender of the garrison. Akbar refused. He imposed the condition that Rana Udai Singh would have to come himself and surrender.

Any self-respecting king would not accept such a demand. Besides, it appears to this author that Akbar had made it personal—he had to personally slight the Mewar king who had been a constant thorn in his side and who would regularly offer refuge to his enemies or those rebelling against his authority, Baz Bahadur of Malwa and Jaimal Rathore being two notable examples. Otherwise, there was no reason why he would ignore such a generous and desperate offer of surrender when he had and would continue to be very lenient with other Hindu and Muslim chieftains when they parleyed with him.

This shows that the Chittor garrison was actually a pragmatic lot and not a bunch of rash and excitable soldiers who were set on a suicidal course of action right from the beginning, as is often suggested by proud but less-informed right-wing commentators, weekend historians[28] in the media and on social media, and poorly researched TV programmes. It wasn't their fault that they had to eventually choose to fall with the fort. Akbar was being uncharacteristic of himself and any other Indian king of his time who would prefer to buy out or secure the surrender of enemy armies instead of annihilating them.

With their surrender terms rejected, the Chittor garrison had no other option but to fight on till the last man. And they defended the fort with all their might and ferocity. The artillery fire and musketry from the fort really wreaked havoc on Mughal lines with Akbar himself escaping injury and even death by a whisker several times.

---

28 An informal term used by historian Professor D. N. Jha to describe amateur commentators without any grounding or training in history who make sweeping, often infantile statements on historical matters, ignoring academic rigour and reducing history to black and white narratives. This crop of amateurs is often found putting out invective-loaded commentaries on social media.

The musketeers were Muslims from the eastern part of the country or the *Purbias*. Their fire was accurate and devastating, and Akbar was particularly angry with them. Their leader was a man named Ismail, who was reportedly a crack shot himself. One day, while Akbar was watching the battle progress from the safety of a defensive position, Ismail managed to hit Jalal Khan, a trusted servant of Akbar who was standing near him. Akbar was so enraged by this that he vowed to avenge Jalal Khan if the musketeer showed up. Akbar kept his promise and Ismail was felled by a shot fired by the emperor himself.[29]

But that didn't solve the problems of the Mughals. Taking out members of the garrison by ones and twos wasn't helping, and whatever damage the Mughal guns were making to the fort's walls were being repaired by the garrison overnight. The walls or a wall would have to be taken down in one forceful strike. So, the sappers and miners came forward and started placing mines. On 17 December 1567, the miners placed two mines under a fort bastion. The first one exploded, bringing down the bastion and killing the defenders on it. Seeing this, a Mughal contingent dashed forward to enter through the breach without waiting for the second mine to explode. When it did, moments later, it killed 200 Mughals on the spot, half of whom were worthies personally known to the emperor. 40 other imperial troops who were waiting for their opportunity nearby were crushed under the falling debris. The garrison lost 40 men too.

Another mine elsewhere near the fort also prematurely exploded on the same day, this time killing 40 men of the garrison and nobody among the Mughal ranks. But the fallen bastion couldn't be taken advantage of as by the time confusion among the Mughal ranks ended, the garrison had repaired it. The mining operation backfired and quite badly. It put Akbar on the backfoot even though he didn't let his or his troops' morale down. He focused on completing the *sabat*. Abu'l Fazl writes that 'excellent quarters were constructed on the top of the *sabat*' where the emperor spent two nights and a day and personally supervised the completion of this covered trench.

29 Abu'l Fazl, *Akbarnama, Vol. II*, p. 470.

When the *sabat* was completed, it helped the Mughal troops to attack the fort from a closer distance. Akbar would himself take position at the *sabat* and shoot his matchlock. On 22 February 1568, the Mughals unleashed an artillery barrage on the fort from all sides, which created several breaches. Right in front of the *sabat*, the wall was destroyed, which resulted in the defenders closing the gap with their own bodies and placing flammable materials at the breach to set fire to when the Mughals attempted to break in.

Directing his men from the ramparts was an officer whose special chain mail armour topped with a cuirass called the *hazaar mikhi* (thousand nails) gave out his special status as a man of eminence. It wasn't known immediately who he was, but Akbar, figuring out that he was a key person in the defence, picked up his favourite musket called Sangram (struggle in Hindi) and shot at the man. At that time, Akbar's commanders Shujaat Khan and Raja Bhagwan Dass were with him. The man disappeared from the ramparts, suggesting that he had been hit.

In an hour's time after that, one Jabbar Quli Diwana told the emperor that the fort's defenders had disappeared. At the same time, fires erupted all over the fort, confusing the Mughals even more. Then Raja Bhagwan Dass pointed out that it was *jauhar* that was happening, and that means the Rajputs are getting ready for *saka* or their final battle.

By morning, it became clear that the man Akbar shot was Jaimal Rathore and he was dead. Jauhar fires raged in the houses of Patta Sisodia, Sahib Khan Rathore and Aissar Das Chauhan. In these were killed 300 women of these chiefs. It's important to note that Sahib Khan was now the leader of the Rathore clan in the fort and his women, too, committed *jauhar* while he got ready for *saka*. This suggests that Muslim Rajputs also shared the martial practices of the Hindu Rajputs and that way were joined at the hip with the Hindus. And yet no modern depiction of Rajput glory at Chittor mentions Sahib Khan or Ismail or the Muslim musketeers and artillery men.

Mughal troops entered the fort as the Rajputs fought to death. Akbar brought forward his war elephants some of which were named Girdbaz Dhokar, Madhukar, Jangia, Sabdiliya and Kadira. About 300 elephants wreaked havoc on the garrison. The elephants trampled men or tore them asunder with huge daggers attached to their trunks. But some of them had their trunks cut off by the Rajputs too and dying eventually of the wounds. Jangia and Madhukar shared a similar fate.

But the war elephants killed many prominent Rajputs too. Akbar, who himself entered the fort on an elephant, was shown a Rajput warrior who had been trampled by an elephant near the Govind Shyam Temple. The man was still alive but died shortly after. He was Patta Sisodia. It was total carnage going on, yet Abu'l Fazl notes there were chivalrous exchanges too. He says Akbar was impressed to see a duel between a Rajput soldier and one of his own when the former challenged him. Another Mughal soldier who came to assist was asked not to intervene by this Mughal soldier as it went against the code of chivalry. This one-on-one fight ended with the death of the Rajput.

The fort had 8,000 soldiers and over 40,000 peasants. As the battle ended, Abu'l Fazl informs that nearly 30,000 were killed. But later on in the text, he contradicts himself by saying that 'a large number were made prisoners'.[30] Why this discrepancy? It may have been due to a desire to appear greater than Alauddin Khilji.

Fazl explains that when Khilji had taken the fort on 16 August 1303, after a siege of six months and seven days, he had spared the lives of the peasants as they weren't involved in the fighting. But during the Mughal siege, the peasantry allegedly collaborated with the garrison and showed great zeal in fighting off the Mughals. In giving out the time taken by the Delhi Sultan to conquer the fort, Fazl also subtly hinted at Akbar achieving a greater feat by conquering the fort after a siege of five months and four days.

But amid this glory were glaring lapses on the part of Akbar's troops in capturing those alive in the garrison. Akbar was enraged by the musketeers and had personally ordered that all of them be captured and executed, and a skull tower be made with their severed heads. But the musketeers mounted a ruse to get away from the fort with their families: they bound their wives and children and marched them off, appearing as Mughal troops capturing the enemy's women and children.

30 Ibid., p. 475.

Akbar spent three days in Chittor and then marched off to Ajmer to pay obeisance at the tomb of Moinuddin Chishti. At Ajmer, on March 9 1568, was issued a victory proclamation or *fatehnama-i-Chittor* in his name.[31] Professor Ali Nadeem Rezavi told this author that these victory proclamations had a set language. This language appears abominable when read from a 21st-century perspective. But one needs to understand that these victory proclamations were religious rhetorical invocations that talked about *mujahids* (holy warriors) defeating *kaffirs* (infidels).

The Chittor victory stunned the whole of Rajputana. Anybody who had any doubt about the permanence of the Mughal rule or in their ability to impose their writ on the country was by now convinced that Akbar meant business. And by denying the Chittor garrison the chance to surrender, he also made it clear that it would be a bad idea for anyone to rub the Mughals on their wrong side or defy their authority. But Akbar wasn't done conquering Rajputana. Chittor was a magnificent victory, but there was still the fortress of Ranthambore that Alauddin Khilji had famously conquered by defeating the Chauhan King Raja Hammiradeva, and which was now the stronghold of the Hada Rajputs under Rao Surjan Hada. The Hadas were a Chauhan branch ruling Bundi and governing Ranthambore as deputies of the Mewar king.

On 21 December 1568, Akbar once again marched out of Agra. This time to conquer Ranthambore. The siege of Chittor was a good learning experience for him, so he went to Ranthambore more prepared, carrying more siege guns. He went via Delhi where he paid obeisance at his father's tomb and shrines of other holy men and also organised a *qamargha* hunt near Palam village; a place that is known today for the Indira Gandhi International Airport. The hunt was, as usual, war-gaming before the actual battle for Ranthambore.

Akbar reached Ranthambore on 10 February 1569, a year after conquering Chittor. And just like at Chittor, he went about surveying the fort to place batteries. This time, the Mughals didn't make any rash charges and Akbar ordered the construction of a *sabat* under the leadership of Qasim Khan Mir Barr-u-Bahr and Raja Todar Mal.

---

31 For the translated text, see Ishtiaq Ahmed Zilli, 'Fathnama—I Chitor, March 1568 an Annotated Translation' in Proceedings of the Indian History Congress 33 (1971): pp. 350–61. Available at http://www.jstor.org/stable/44145352.

Akbar then brought up his siege artillery. These were huge culverins (a type of cannon with a long barrel) that needed 200 pairs of oxen just to drag one of them on level ground, according to Abu'l Fazl. This sounds like an exaggeration, but it surely must have taken a lot of pack animals to drag such a heavy piece of ordnance. Each of these was dragged up the mountain, requiring additional support from strong porters and *kahars* (palanquin-bearers). This must have been considered an impossibility back then. But Akbar did it. And because he did it, he won a psychological victory over his Rajput opponent.

The Mughal guns blazed away to glory, the sound of every discharge echoing through the defiles. The heavier cannonballs broke away the walls with every hit. The Hada chief knew he wouldn't last longer. So, when Akbar gave him an ultimatum on 19 March 1569, to surrender or perish, he chose life. Akbar's treatment of the Ranthambore garrison was in stark contrast to what he did to the Chittor defenders.

Rao Surjan Hada sent his two sons, Duda and Bhoj, to negotiate the terms of surrender. They secured an imperial audience and parleyed on behalf of their father. They accepted Mughal suzerainty by performing the *sijdah* or prostration before the emperor and were rewarded with robes of honour and other gifts by Akbar. He even ignored a murderous attack on a servant of Raja Bhagwan Dass and a Mughal nobleman named Bahauddin Majzub of Badaon by a bodyguard of the Hada princes who assumed that Akbar would kill the boys.

The princes returned to their father with good news. The Hada chief then requested Akbar to send a noble who was also a confidante of the emperor so that he may meet him, get to know him and in turn introduce him to Akbar. The emperor agreed again and sent Husain Quli Khan. The meeting went well, and Husain Quli led him to Akbar on 22 March 1569. Rao Surjan Hada prostrated before Akbar and handed over the keys of the fort that were made of gold and silver. He asked for three days' time to pack up and leave with his family and followers. It was granted. And the Hadas evacuated the fort that they held for the king of Mewar.

Rao Surjan Hada and his sons joined imperial service, and the Bundi chief remained a loyal officer until his death in 1585. In fact, when his elder son Duda rebelled, Rao Surjan Hada sent his younger son Bhoj to put down the rebellion. And since he went against his own son, Akbar raised the Bundi chief to a mansab of 2,000, which was offered to some of the emperor's confidantes like Raja Birbal. Mughal service actually lifted this subordinate chief of Mewar to royalty, as Cynthia Talbot argues in her paper.[32]

For the Mughals, Ranthambore was a more spectacular victory than Chittor as the siege didn't drag on for months and the enemy capitulated in just a month. From the standpoint of propaganda, this one afforded Akbar a greater opportunity to project himself as a greater conqueror than Alauddin Khilji. Abu'l Fazl does this PR job very well for his master when he writes:

> The conquest of such a lofty fort, which great rulers had not been able to accomplish after long sieges, and which Sultan Alauddin had taken with great difficulty after a year, was effected by His Majesty the Shahinshah in the space of one month.[33]

This constant competition with Khilji would be a hallmark of Akbar's reign. And he wouldn't be the only one to do so as Khilji himself thought of himself as a conqueror as great or even greater than Alexander of Macedon. Khilji christened himself as *Sikandar-i-Sani* or Alexander II.

We see this trait even in Narendra Modi today when he tries to outdo Jawaharlal Nehru, India's first Prime Minister. From rebranding the Nehru Jacket as Modi Jacket, to borrowing Nehru's humble phrase calling himself '*Pratham Sevak*' or 'First Servant' and declaring that he is the '*Pradhan Sevak*' or 'Prime Servant'; from renaming Nehru's Planning Commission as NITI Aayog to trying to deliver a Nehru-like, 'The Light Has Gone Out Of Our Lives' kind of speech on Atal Bihari Vajpayee's passing, Mr Modi has either tried to replicate, or belittle and erode Nehru's legacy. He and his party members have this constant jousting with Nehru's legacy in

32 Cynthia Talbot, *'Justifying Defeat: A Rajput Perspective on the Age of Akbar'*, *Journal of the Economic and Social History of the Orient* 55, no. 2/3, 2012, pp. 329–68.

33 Abu'l Fazl, *Akbarnama, Vol. II*, p. 495.

their bid to outdo India's first PM or surpass his legacy. And whenever Mr Modi belittles Nehru through snide remarks or unkind cuts, his sycophantic supporters cheer it with chants of 'Modi! Modi!' In fact, his party and its supporters even coined a slogan loaded with Hindu religious symbolism. Through '*Har Har* Modi', Mr Modi was raised to the stature of a god. It suited the political imaging of Mr. Modi where he was portrayed as the 'Hindu *Hriday Samrat*' (Emperor of Hindu Hearts) and who would lead the culture war for the Hindus with the war cry of '*Har Har* Mahadev!'

When Akbar entered the Ranthambore fort after Rao Surjan Hada left with his entourage, 'cries of "God is great" (*Allahu Akbar*) resounded in that heaven-like mountain, and songs of exultation rose high from holy celestials'. *Allahu Akbar*! This is what Akbar's followers shouted to hail the emperor and thank god. Akbar loved the ambiguity of it. And he never discouraged any of his followers from using it. In fact, it became a customary salutation for the followers of his *Din-i-Illahi* later. Akbar would hear this cry till the very end of his life, basking in the divine aura it brought him, and making it easier for him to enforce his will on the people as god's writ. Akbar used this to bring his people together and unite them under his banner. He didn't use it to wage a culture war on behalf of the Muslims against Hindus and other non-Muslims. This brought him into conflict with the Islamic clergy and other hardliners who declared him a heretic and announced that rebelling against Akbar was akin to fighting a holy war.

The twin victories of Chittor and Ranthambore, and the wresting of Kalinjar fort from Raja Ram Chand of Panna in August 1569[34], brought joy to Akbar. It was enhanced by another news later that month: that he was now a father to a boy. The boy was named Sultan Salim after Sheikh Salim Chishti, the Sufi saint who had his *khanqah* at Sikri.

Akbar's victories brought Rajputana to its knees. One by one, the remaining kingdoms sought imperial favour by either submitting or by seeking alliances. The only state that didn't submit was Mewar.

---

34 For a detailed account of the battle, see Ibid., pp. 498–99.

And this prepared the ground for a future conflict between Akbar and Rana Udai Singh's son who would succeed his father on his death four years later. His name was Pratap Singh. And history would know him as Maharana Pratap.

Chapter 6

Expanding to the East, Consolidating the West

> For in war the result is from the stars
> Not from wealth and a large army.[1]

The Sultanate of Gujarat was, to use a modern phrase, an '*achhe din*'[2] state. It was vast and prosperous, had flourishing commercial relations with countries in the Middle East and the Mediterranean, and was a military power that rivalled the Sultanate of Malwa, the Deccani sultanates and even the Delhi Sultanate. In fact, it was an offshoot of the Delhi Sultanate when the Tughlaqs were losing their grip on power, especially after the invasion of Amir Timur in the late 14th century.

The story of the Delhi Sultanate in its climacteric was like that of other empires in Indian history—the Mauryas, Guptas and Cholas before them, and the Mughals after them. As central authority weakened, provincial governors became independent and found their own kingdoms, resulting in the collapse of the empire.

1 Abu'l Fazl, *Akbarnama, Vol. III*, p. 21.

2 An election phrase coined by the Hindu nationalist BJP as a promise to Indians that if they are voted to power and Narendra Modi is made the Prime Minister, '*achhe din*' or 'good times' will would come.

In 1411, Zafar Khan, the *wazir* (governor in this case and not minister as is usually understood) appointed by the Delhi Sultan to run Gujarat, proclaimed his sovereignty and christened himself Sultan Muzaffar Shah. Only a century earlier, the Delhi Sultanate had taken Gujarat from the Rajput Vaghela dynasty when Sultan Alauddin Khilji defeated Raja Karan Dev II or Rai Karan as Muslim sources call him. The Delhi Sultans ruled their vast empire through deputies or viceroys, pretty much like the Mughals would do after them. These viceroys were called *iqtadars* and their provinces *iqtas*. Originally a Muslim practice from the land of the crescent, the *iqta* system was all about collecting taxes.

The system in the Delhi Sultanate also began similarly, though with time, it became more than revenue farming. An *iqta* became an elaborate system of administration during the early sultans, with *iqtadars* being appointed from Delhi and given a full but smaller version of the state apparatus to run. These were not permanent appointments with *iqtadars* being transferred around from one province to another. Also, *iqtas* were not hereditary positions. An *iqtadar*'s family could not inherit the appointment. That changed during Sultan Feroze Shah Tughlaq's time when these were made hereditary possessions.

With their positions becoming permanent, the *iqtadars* could develop pretences of royalty, imitating the Delhi court. Over time, these viceroys became provincial magnets who attracted talent from all over. And gradually, *iqtadar* became synonymous with power and authority. That is probably why the Urdu word *iqtidar* has stayed with us and means power, authority or control.

In the late Mughal period, the *subahdars* or viceroys would act like the *iqtadars* and set up their own power blocs. Culturally and materially, in the mid-18th and early 19th centuries, the courts of Lucknow, Murshidabad and Hyderabad outshone the Delhi durbar. The Delhi durbar itself retained symbolic power and pre-eminence, but when it came to actual power, it wielded even less of it than smaller Mughal provinces like Sira[3] and Arcot.[4]

The Sultanate *iqtadars* had a battery of state officials under them right down to the village administration level. The bureaucracy was multi-layered and well-oiled. So, when Zafar Khan broke free of Delhi's control, he already had a proper set up in place. Though he didn't live very long after that, his successors took the new sultanate to greater heights of glory.

Sixteen more sultans succeeded Muzaffar Shah, and the sultanate stayed independent for over 160 years, with Sultan Mahmud Begarha being the most successful ruler. The Gujarat Sultanate had a navy of its own with the port of Cambay (Khambat today) as its lynchpin. They fought European powers like the Portuguese and also allied themselves with other European powers, like the Ottomans and the Venetians. The sultanate had thriving international commerce, making the Gujarat sultans quite well-known in the Western world. This is evidenced by the fact that a decade after Akbar conquered Gujarat, Queen Elizabeth I of England wrote to him and addressed him as 'The Most Invincible And Mightie Prince Lord Zelabdim Echebar, the King of Cambaya'[5] or the king of Gujarat. Such was the importance of Gujarat, which would flourish even more under the Mughals, becoming the province with the second highest number of urban centres (13) in the empire after Agra[6], with Ahmedabad accounting for the 'second largest amount of urban tax'.[7]

Gujarat also produced a Mughal emperor—Aurangzeb Alamgir who was born in Dahod in 1618. Four hundred years later, when

---

3 Sira is a taluk in Tumkur district of Karnataka today, which includes the town of Sira. The Mughal province of Sira had seven parganas, which included what is today Kolar and Hoskote. Hyder Ali crowned himself Nawab of Sira, which made him the lord of Mysore as Mysore was a vassal state of this Mughal province.

4 Arcot is a town in Vellore district of Tamil Nadu today. It was among the last provinces created by the Mughal Empire and one of the first Indian allies of the British East India Company in the latter's contest against the French power in India.

5 Vincent Smith, *Akbar the Great Moghul*, p. 229.

6 Shireen Moosvi, *The Economy of the Mughal Empire c. 1595: A Statistical Study* (New Delhi: Oxford University Press, 2015), p. 316.

7 Ibid.

Gujarat gave India a prime minister in Narendra Modi, his ardent followers declared that 800 years after Prithviraj Chauhan lost the throne of Delhi, another 'proud Hindu' was going to be its occupant.[8] Modi himself declared soon after his elevation to the nation's top office that Indian 'slave mentality' was a problem and 1,200 years of slavery were to be blamed.[9] The messianic figure of Modi was bumped up by the epithet 'Hindu *Hriday Samrat*' or 'emperor of Hindu hearts'. It was as if time in the Hindutva universe had stopped in 1192 and resumed in 2014, with the return of another king. The medieval impulse behind all this was too strong to escape notice.

The world would court Mr Modi as the Prime Minister of India. At home, though, and because of his seemingly partisan attitude towards Gujarat, he would be mocked and derided as the prime minister of Gujarat by his detractors. It was an Akbar-like fate for Mr Modi but in a twisted sense: Akbar's was an international recognition for Gujarat; what Modi has got is a taunt and an unflattering remark for Gujarat.

But Akbar got the chance to meddle in Gujarat when its last sultan, Muzaffar Shah III, faced a series of rebellions from some of his powerful nobles who joined ranks with the Mirzas of Sambhal who had escaped to Gujarat from Malwa after rebelling against Akbar. The immediate opportunity was provided by the regent of the sultanate, Itimad Khan, who petitioned Akbar for help several times when a rival Pathan noble besieged him in Ahmedabad.[10]

Itimad Khan was the slave and vizier[11] of Sultan Mahmud Shah III. The sultan wouldn't let his wives get pregnant without his will and forced them to abort if they did.[12] This was a rather strange practice done to ensure there were not too many claimants to the throne.

---

8 Kumar Vikram, 'Delhi ruled by Hindus after 800 years, says VHP chief Ashok Singhal', New Delhi, *India Today*, 22 November 2014. Available at https://www.indiatoday.in/india/story/vhp-ashok-shinghal-hindu-ruling-delhi-after-800-years-228175-2014-11-22.

9 Debobrat Ghose, '1,200 years of servitude: PM Modi offers food for thought', New Delhi, *First Post*, 13 June 2014. Available at https://www.firstpost.com/politics/1200-years-of-servitude-pm-modi-offers-food-for-thought-1567805.html.

10 Abu'l Fazl, *Akbarnama, Vol. III*, p. 8.

11 Badaoni, *Tawarikh*, p. 145.

12 Abu'l Fazl, *Ain-i-Akbari*, *Vol. II*, footnote, p. 272.

But when the sultan was assassinated by a slave in 1554—who held a grudge against the Sultan for humiliating him for a homosexual act[13]— he had no son to succeed him. It was left to Itimad Khan to find a successor, and he did. The new sultan was a relative of the murdered Sultan[14] and was christened Ahmed Shah III. Itimad Khan was chosen by other nobles to act as regent as the new sultan was underage.

But seven years later, in 1561, Itimad Khan had the sultan assassinated.[15] To retain power, Itimad Khan propped up a young boy named Nathu[16] and called him the son of Mahmud Shah III and even swore on the Quran[17] that he was telling the truth. He literally pulled a rabbit out of an empty hat and the other nobles didn't oppose it.[18] Nathu assumed the regnal name of Muzaffar Shah III.

The young sultan was firmly in the grip of Itimad Khan who kept him in the palace at Ahmedabad.[19] But Itimad Khan wouldn't have all that power alone, other nobles would vie for it too. The Fauladis of Patan were among the principal challengers. They were Pathans and their leader Sher Khan decided to bring the challenge to Itimad Khan's doorstep itself. He laid siege to Ahmedabad that lasted for six months.

During the siege, the sultan somehow joined the camp of Sher Khan Fauladi. Besieged, with the sultan teaming up with the Pathans, Itimad Khan's situation became desperate. He frantically sent messages to Akbar to come and help him. He also repudiated the claim of Muzaffar Shah III to the throne and said he wasn't the son of Sultan Mahmud Shah III. This man had sworn on the Quran! But when was

---

13 E. C. Bayley, *The History of India As Told By Its Own Historians: The Local Muhammadan Dynasties. Gujarat,* based on a translation of *Mirat-i-Sikandari* of Sikandar ibn Muhammad Manjhu (London: W. H. Allen And Co, 1886), p. 448.

14 Ibid., p. 454; Ali Muhammad Khan, *Mirat-i-Ahmadi,* trans. M. F. Lokhandwala (Baroda: Oriental Institute, 1965), p. 73.

15 Ali Muhammad Khan, *Mirat*-i-Ahmadi, pp. 77–8.

16 Ibid., p. 80.

17 Abu'l Fazl, *Akbarnama, Vol. III,* footnote 3, p. 12.

18 Abu'l Fazl, *Ain-i-Akbari, Vol. II,* footnote p. 272.

19 Badaoni, *Tawarikh,* p. 145.

political opportunism and reneging on one's pledge or promise the sole preserve of the present?

As news reached Gujarat that Akbar was coming and had reached Deesa[20], there was consternation among the nobles and Sultan Muzaffar Shah III. Alliances were made and unmade. As Akbar moved towards Ahmedabad in mid-November 1572, Sher Khan Fauladi lifted the siege and fled, leaving behind the sultan.

The sources vary here. Abu'l Fazl says that when Akbar learnt about it, he sent his generals Mir Khan Yesawal, Farid Qarawal, Abu'l Qasim Namakin[21] and Karm Ali. Abu'l Fazl doesn't refer to Muzaffar Shah by his proper name or as sultan; he refers to him as 'Muzaffar Gujarati'.[22] The sultan, on the run from the Mughal force, hid in a corn field and was arrested from there. He was brought before Akbar who took pity on him and spared his life.

But Badaoni[23] and Nizamuddin Ahmed[24] say the sultan turned himself in after seeking an appointment with Akbar. He was packed off to Agra to live on a pension of ₹ 30 per month.[25] Nevertheless, there were celebrations in the imperial camp after this great victory. But at Hajipur, someone spread a rumour in the imperial camp that an order to loot and plunder the locals had been given by the emperor. There was large-scale looting by people from the Mughal camp. When the news reached the emperor, he immediately went about restoring law and order. The rioters were arrested and trampled to death under the feet of elephants.[26] The looted items were also returned to the people. Thus, order was not only restored, but the trust of the locals was also earned.

---

20 A town in the Banaskantha district of modern Gujarat.

21 He would compile the *Munshaat-i-Namakin*, a collection of imperial letters and documents of Akbar. The sole copy of the *Fathnama-i-Chittor* or the Chittor victory proclamation occurs here.

22 Abu'l Fazl, *Akbarnama, Vol. III*, p. 10.

23 Badaoni, *Tawarikh*, p. 145.

24 Nizamuddin Ahmed, *Tabakat-i-Akbari*, trans. H. M. Elliot, *The History of India as Told by Its Own Historians*, Vol 5, p. 342.

25 Badaoni, *Tawarikh*, p 145.

26 Abu'l Fazl, *Akbarnama, Vol. III*, p. 11; Ali Muhammad Khan, *Mirat-i-Ahmadi*, p. 95.

If we look at it from the modern perspective, then a contrast is clearly visible. Today, in India at least, nobody gets punished for fomenting riots, sectarian or otherwise. Of course, a modern, democratic country cannot be expected to, and must not ever, hand down instantaneous justice as a medieval despot could afford to: there's a constitutionally-established modern legal process in place. But the lack of political will to bring rioters to the book makes the legal process drag on for years without any positive outcome. People accused in the 1984 anti-Sikh riots—a fit case to be declared a genocide—either escaped the famed long arm of the law or started coming into its grip only in 2018.[27] Those accused in the Hashimpura massacre of 1987 were convicted only in 2018.[28] And outcomes of some of the trials in some of the cases pertaining to the Gujarat riots of 2002 that had happened under Narendra Modi's watch as chief minister have not had satisfactory outcomes for the survivors. Some cases are also in the trial stage even now.[29]

But Akbar's instant justice at Hajipur alone weren't enough, as future events showed. Akbar announced that Itimad Khan would be put in charge of governing Gujarat as a Mughal viceroy[30] and the state officials and nobles absorbed into the Mughal administration subject to guarantees of loyalty. A more modern example of this kind of an arrangement could be corporate mergers where a company either merges with or is taken over by another and the staff are either retained or reassigned.

By and large, everyone guaranteed for everyone else except for the Abyssinian corps or the *Habshi* contingents of the Sultan's army for

---

27 Times News Network, '1984 anti-Sikh riots case: Delhi HC convicts Sajjan Kumar, sentenced to life imprisonment', *The Times of India*, New Delhi, 17 December 2018. Available at https://timesofindia.indiatimes.com/india/1984-anti-sikh-riots-case-delhi-hc-convicts-sajjan-kumar-sentenced-to-life-imprisonment/articleshow/67123074.cms.

28 Express Web Desk, 'Hashimpura case: 16 PAC men sentenced to life imprisonment for murder of 38 Muslims', *The Indian Express*, New Delhi, 1 November 2018. Available at https://indianexpress.com/article/india/hashimpura-case-delhi-high-court-verdict-16-life-imprisonment-5426836/.

29 Sruthi Radhakrishnan, 'The 2002 Gujarat riots cases and their statuses so far', *The Hindu*, 20 April 2018. Available at https://www.thehindu.com/news/national/the-2002-gujarat-riots-cases-and-their-statuses-so-far/article23617950.ece.

30 Ali Muhammad Khan, *Mirat-i-Ahmadi*, p. 95.

whom nobody was willing to act as guarantor. Akbar intervened and said that they would now serve the Mughals directly with the same terms of service as under the sultan. They were assigned to Mughal nobles and not Gujarati ones.[31]

The racial undertones of this episode illustrate the condition of blacks in pre-modern India: that despite their military prowess, combat performance and loyalty, blacks were seen with suspicion even in an age when many of them as slaves rose through the ranks and became powerful generals and kingmakers in the India of that time. In modern India, unfortunately, and particularly in the northern part of the country, black Africans only inspire xenophobic reactions. The word *Habshi* has become a form of insult heaped on blacks, and the age-old suspicions have now manifested in violent attacks on people from African countries in India.[32]

The Gujarat Sultan's captivity would only last for a decade. In 1583, he would flee from Agra and return to Gujarat to briefly revive his independent rule in Ahmedabad with the help of former allies and Jam Sataji of Nawanagar (today's Jamnagar in Gujarat). The Jam refused to hand over the Sultan to the Mughals and was forced to wage an unsuccessful military campaign against the Mughals too. But eventually, he had to back down in the face of Mughal might and the Sultan fled to Dwarka in the territory of the Raja of Kutch, Rao Biharimal (referred to as Bihari Jareja by Abu'l Fazl, which probably indicates that he was a Jadeja Rajput, just like the Jam of Nawanagar).

The Kutch King extracted favourable terms from the Mughal commander giving chase to the Gujarat Sultan, Mirza Aziz Koka, on the condition of handing over Muzaffar Shah to the Mughals. He then sent word to the Sultan that he was coming to see him as his servant. The Sultan, assuming that this was a genuine show of fealty, came out to greet Rao Biharimal. But he was captured, and the Rajput

---

31 Ibid.

32 For a more detailed understanding of this, please see the article 'From medieval Delhi to Noida: Hate for 'habshi' is still on', *The Times of India,* New Delhi, 29 March 2017. Available at https://timesofindia.indiatimes.com/city/delhi/from-medieval-delhi-to-noida-how-hate-for-habshi-is-still-on/articleshow/57881297.cms.

chief went about fulfilling his side of the deal with the Mughals. But Muzaffar Shah committed suicide before the Mughals could lay their hands on him again, preferring death over dishonour.[33]

It's important to note here that any kind of regional sentiment was missing among these Gujarati princes when faced with an aggressor from the north. While the Hindu Rajput ruler of Nawanagar supported the Sultan and even lost one of his sons fighting the Mughals in 1591, his clanmate, the Raja of Kutch, suffered no guilt pangs in traitoring the Sultan to the Mughals for material gains. This flexibility of approach ensured that both Nawanagar and Kutch states continued till the 20th century when they were merged with the Indian Union. By then, the practice of looking at the past through a communal lens—where medieval Muslim kings are traitors and Hindus patriots—had also started.

Akbar, though, didn't take the rebellion by the Mirzas very kindly. While he was in Ahmedabad in 1572, he rebuffed a peace overture by Ibrahim Husain Mirza that was couched in a tribute to the emperor on his victory in Gujarat.[34] He was determined to put it down by force of arms than by diplomacy. But in his pursuit of this action, we see Akbar play like a crafty old fox. Even though he had announced his intention to leave the affairs of Gujarat to the charge of Itimad Khan, he actually put Mirza Aziz Koka in charge of Ahmedabad and other conquered territories. The territories that were either under the control of the Mirzas or saw their activity—territories like Baroda (under Ibrahim Husain Mirza), Champaner (under Muhammad Husain Mirza) and Surat (under Shah Mirza)—were placed under the Gujarat officers who had switched their loyalty to Akbar, including Itimad Khan.[35]

Akbar then decided to march onwards to the port of Cambay where he took a ship ride into the sea. For him, it was the first glimpse of the Arabian Sea and a chance to meet merchants from foreign shores, who probably utilised the opportunity to flatter the Indian monarch and

33 For the entire episode, see *Akbarnama, Vol. III,* pp. 962–64.

34 Abu'l Fazl, *Akbarnama, Vol. III*, p. 12.

35 Ibid., p. 13.

extract trade privileges. We don't know the details of those meetings but it's possible to infer that from Abu'l Fazl's description.[36]

As Akbar enjoyed the sea breeze, a storm gathered behind him. The Gujarati officers plotted to throw off Mughal suzerainty. Akbar took pre-emptive measures and reassigned those officers to some of his trusted nobles. They became their prisoners though not formally. Akbar then turned back from Cambay towards Baroda to deal with the Mirzas.

Once in Baroda, Akbar learnt that the Mirzas were in Champaner. He divided his army and sent a large part of it thither. Then he learnt that Ibrahim Husain Mirza was passing by just 8 *kos* (roughly 25 kilometres) away. It was past midnight when Akbar received this news and his army was also away. Yet Akbar decided to seize the opportunity and lead a small band of followers in pursuit of the Mirza. He left his camp to the care of a few trusted officers and took off, ignoring counsel, with a very small force.[37] However, he did send word ahead to his army to turn back and join him near the Mirza's camp.

On the face of it, it appears a reckless move. But Akbar's reasoning makes sense:

> His Majesty did not judge it proper that more than two or three servants (*mardum*) of his companions should go with them lest Ibrahim Husain should decamp on account of the crowd of victorious warriors.[38]

A bigger army on the march could alert the enemy from far away, as in the quiet of the night, noise travels far, and hundreds of horses on the gallop would certainly be akin to, to give a modern example, police vehicles going to raid a den of criminals by blaring sirens from afar.

---

36 Ibid. Fazl writes: 'The merchants of Rum (Ottoman Turkey), Syria, Persia and Turan (Central Asia) regarded the advent of the Shahinshah as a great boon and paid their respects.'

37 The precise number isn't given anywhere, but while describing the action at Sarnal, Abu'l Fazl indicates that when Akbar forms his line on the banks of the River Mahi, he only has 40 men with him even as he waits for his army turning back from Champaner to join him.

38 Ibid., p. 14.

But Akbar's party lost its way and lost a lot of time in the process. Eventually, when they set their course right, the day was coming to an end. That's when they learnt from a Brahmin that Ibrahim Husain Mirza had crossed the River Mahi and set up camp in the town of Sarnal. His generals once again advised him to wait till the rest of the army arrived, and attack only at nightfall.[39] But Akbar disagreed. He deemed it a 'deception and fraud' to attack an enemy at night and insisted on attacking while there was still some daylight left. He also gave his troops a pep talk, which was logic couched in rhetoric:

> Courage is a helper, and many cowards become brave men out of shame. It is far better not to put off the work of the day till the night, and to fight with the smartness and alacrity that we are marching with.[40]

Akbar's pep talk reveals his sharpness. He wanted to engage the enemy during the day so that his troopers couldn't sneak away from battle using the night as cover[41]—a king abandoned by his troops in battle is as good as dead. The part about alacrity also makes sense as fatigue would have overtaken them if they had halted, resulting in a longer halt, which would have given time to the Mirza to prepare for a stand at Sarnal or escape further away. And the part about procrastination is an all-weather template used even today by taskmasters—parents, teachers or office bosses.

In the meantime, about 150-odd troopers from Akbar's army arrived to join him in the attack on the Mirza's army, bumping up the numbers to about 200. Among the commanders were Raja Bhagwan

---

39 Ibid., p. 19. Abu'l Fazl quotes an officer named Jalal Khan: 'Our troops have not come up yet, and the enemy is in force. When we are so few in number it is not advisable to engage in daylight with so many. The proper thing is to halt a while and make a night-attack.'

40 Ibid., pp. 18–9.

41 Ibid., footnote 1, p. 19. My interpretation is based on this footnote in which Beveridge makes sense of Abu'l Fazl's complicated prose.

Dass, his brother Bhupat[42] and son Kunwar Man Singh. The young Man Singh begged Akbar that he be placed at the front of the army as it would be his honour to serve together with the emperor in such a small band that had no separate divisions. 'It is the privilege of devotion to go a few steps in front and to show life-sacrifice.'[43] Akbar heeded his request.

Even though the former royalty of Rajputana like to dissociate themselves from the Mughals today, the fact is that they were willing to put their lives on the line in the service of the emperor as a show of valour and uncompromising loyalty. They would also show this loyalty later to the British. The imperial war service of Maharaja Sir Ganga Singh of Bikaner is a case in point. When the First World War broke out in August 1914, the Bikaner king, saw in it an opportunity to lead his troops into battle. Ancestral pride was associated with it, for 17 of the 21 Bika Rathores had led their armies into battle.[44] The Maharaja sent a cable to the British monarch, King George V. In that he begged the King Emperor to be sent into combat at the head of his troops just like Man Singh had beseeched his emperor. Panikkar says:

> I beg leave most dutifully, should Great Britain also have resort to arms, to place my own sword and services at Your Imperial Majesty's command, either as Member of Your Imperial Majesty's staff, or at the head of my troops and Rajputs, all of whom are equally eager to fight for Your Imperial Majesty in Europe, India or elsewhere, for the safety, honour and welfare of Your Imperial Majesty and your Dominions...I implore Your Imperial Majesty most earnestly, if the Empire is involved, to give me an opportunity for that personal military service which is the highest ambition of a Rathore Rajput Chief and to be graciously pleased to command me to at once proceed to the Front in Europe. I should esteem it the highest honour possible to serve during the War on Your

---

42 Beveridge calls Bhupat son of Raja Bhagwan Dass even though Abu'l Fazl himself calls him the brother of Bhagwan Dass (*Akbarnama, Vol. III,* p. 84). Vincent Smith calls him the brother of Bhagwan Dass (*Akbar the Great Mogul,* p. 120) as does Rajiva Nain Prasad in his biography of Man Singh (Raja Man Singh of Amber, p. 28.)

43 Abu'l Fazl, *Akbarnama, Vol. III,* p. 19.

44 K. N. Panikkar, *His Highness the Maharaja Of Bikaner: A Biography* (London: Oxford University Press, 1937), p. 150.

> Imperial Majesty's Staff but am ready to go anywhere in any capacity for the privilege of serving my Emperor in war as I have endeavoured to serve him in peace during the last twelve years. As the opportunity is one of a life-time I humbly beseech Your Imperial Majesty not to leave me here inactive if the Forces of the Empire are engaged, for the duty of a Rathore Chief calls me to fighting service...[45]

Ganga Singh's offer and request were accepted, and he was sent to the Western Front while his camel corps, the Ganga Risala, was sent to Egypt.[46] Eventually, in February 1915, Ganga Singh also fulfilled his wish to lead his own troops into battle when a small detachment of his troops he commanded came face to face with the Ottoman army at Katib el Khel. Ganga Singh led a camelry charge at the enemy, firing his cavalry carbine 19 times before the enemy broke up and fled.[47]

At Sarnal, the Rajputs covered themselves with glory. Man Singh led the van with the Mughal emperor beside him and the river was forded. All the horsemen crossed without any casualty. Akbar climbed the steep bank to reach the Water Gate of Sarnal where he was surrounded by three of Mirza's soldiers. As he parried with them, Raja Bhagwan Dass drove his spear through one of the attackers. The other two then showed Akbar their backs. But while Bhagwan Dass saved the emperor, he couldn't save his own brother Bhupat who got caught in thorny bushes, was surrounded and cut down.

The daring raid by the Mughals demoralised the Mirza's troops so much that they began to flee. Many of them were pursued by the

---

45 Ibid., pp. 150–51.

46 The camel corps needed a desert terrain to operate so it was sent to Egypt to face the Turks while the Maharaja himself was sent to France attached to the 7th Meerut Division. In France, he was appointed to the staff of Field Marshal Sir John French, the Commander-in-Chief of the British Expeditionary Force. But being on the staff, he saw no action and no opportunity to repeat the feat of his ancestors. But then news came that his daughter was seriously ill, and he was forced to return. The return voyage was via Egypt where he was reunited with his risala and also got the chance to exchange fire with the enemy.

47 K. N. Panikkar, His Highness, p. 159.

Mughal troopers and cut down. But most of them managed to escape along with the Mirza using darkness as cover.

For his gallantry, Raja Bhagwan Dass was presented a banner and a kettledrum by Akbar—the first time a Hindu was honoured in this way.[48] The other leading Hindu, Todar Mal, was sent to Surat to observe the sea-side fort there and prepare a military report on it, just like he did at Chittor and Ranthambore.[49] Surat was the last stronghold of the Mirzas. And it was resolutely defended.

Akbar laid siege to it in mid-January 1563. There was a tremendous exchange of artillery fire, and shots fired from the fort landed all around Akbar's own tent, forcing him to change location to a grove near a lake. His own artillery also wreaked havoc on the fort. The lessons learnt at Chittor and Ranthambore were improvised at Surat where Akbar's sappers and miners made *sabat*s and raised mounds of earth to place siege guns on to give them greater elevation, and therefore greater reach inside the fort. The besieged garrison had even called for Portuguese help, resulting in a flotilla coming there. Apparently, the garrison wanted to hand over the fort to the Portuguese in exchange for safe passage to Portuguese dominion. This was déjà vu for the Portuguese as during Akbar's father's reign, Sultan Bahadur Shah had similarly called for Portuguese help when pushed to the wall by Emperor Humayun in 1534. In exchange for that, the Sultan had to cede control of Bassein (Vasai), Daman and Diu. When he tried to recapture these territories from the Portuguese, the Sultan was treacherously killed by the Portuguese and his body thrown into the sea. Bassein was captured by the Marathas under Chimaji Appa in 1739, while Daman and Diu were wrested from the Portuguese by the Indian Army in 1961. Today, Daman and Diu is one administrative unit, a Union Territory where tourists and other Gujaratis flock to, often to escape the prohibition laws of Gujarat.

Abu'l Fazl says that the Portuguese abandoned the thought of fighting the Mughals, seeing Akbar's superior numbers and firepower, and decided to send an embassy to the emperor instead.[50] However,

48 Vincent Smith, *Akbar the Great Mogul,* p. 112.

49 See previous chapter for details.

50 Abu'l Fazl, *Akbarnama, Vol. III,* p. 37.

Vincent Smith concludes, and rather abruptly, that the 'truth' was that Akbar feared an attack by a Portuguese naval squadron and decided to court the Portuguese himself by sending an embassy to them. It seems Smith's assertion is based on an account by the Portuguese historian Diego do Couto in which he talked about Akbar sending an embassy to the Portuguese viceroy, Dom Antonio de Noronha. It is important to see Beveridge's footnote on this in the *Akbarnama* (Volume III) in which he doubts Couto's chronology and narration of events while not dismissing them thoroughly. In fact, Beveridge says that Akbar may have wanted to keep the Portuguese in good humour because of members of his immediate family going for Haj by sea.

Nevertheless, two *firmans* by him are important to understand this. The first was issued on 13 December 1572—before the Siege of Surat—to Aires Telles, the Captain of Diu. In it, Akbar professed his friendship to the Portuguese and said he had heard great things about Telles through other Portuguese (this probably means that Couto's assertion that many Portuguese men of influence met Akbar at Cambay, and he allowed them to kiss his hand, was true) he knew. He then demanded that his name be 'spoken among the Moors' and his coinage be circulated in all Portuguese-held territories.[51]

The second *firman* was dated 18 December 1573, in which Akbar told all his officials not to attack or seize the Portuguese territory of Daman or assist the Malabar pirates. In fact, he asked his officers to protect the Portuguese. In this one, Akbar referred to the embassy of Antonio Cabral and said it's the Portuguese viceroy who sought his friendship.[52]

So, while Akbar may not have feared a Portuguese naval attack on Surat—he certainly had the firepower to deal with them—he most certainly wanted to be friends with them because of their hegemony over the high seas, oceanic trade and pilgrimage routes. What is also certain is that seeing the Portuguese make peace overtures, the morale

51 Hermann Kulke and Dietmar Rothermund, *A History of India* (Kiel and Heidelberg: Routledge, 2009), excerpts available on the book's website under the 'Resources' tab, extract number 45 titled 'Akbar and the Portuguese (1572–1601)', excerpt 1.

52 Ibid., excerpt 2.

of the Surat garrison was broken. They surrendered the fort after withstanding the siege for a month and 17 days.[53]

Among the items seized from the fort by the Mughals were some Turkish cannon used in the Siege of Diu (1538) by the Ottoman fleet of Sultan Suleiman I, often referred to as Suleiman the Magnificent in the West and as Qanuni Sultan Suleiman in the erstwhile Ottoman Empire. These guns had to be left behind by the Turks after their unsuccessful mission. Akbar ordered that these guns be transported to Agra.[54] But there is some lack of clarity about the carrying out of this order.[55] Two of the guns are today known as Neelam and Manek and are parked right outside the main entrance to Uparkot Fort in Junagarh[56], though it isn't clear how these found their way there.

After the victory, the Mughal nobles went on a drinking binge with their emperor. And just like many Indian men today who talk too much when drunk, often exaggerating things, these nobles also indulged in tall and boastful talk. These were about Indian bravado. The nobles bragged about Indian braves not caring about their lives. They gave the example of two Rajput rivals who would run towards a two-headed spear held by other Rajputs until the spear had gone through their bodies and come out of their backs so that they could indulge in close combat.[57]

The story appears outright rubbish—one of those many tavern tales that we often hear even today. Who would first get speared and then engage in close combat? But clearly a dead-drunk Akbar was no longer able to exercise his logic and reasoning. Being utterly reckless, he was anyway not the man to shy away from any opportunity to show physical prowess. He took out his sword and fastened it to a wall so that the tip pointed towards his chest. Then he announced that if

53 Abu'l Fazl, *Akbarnama*, *Vol. III*, p. 28.

54 Ibid., pp. 40–1.

55 Ibid., footnote 1, p. 41. Beveridge cites the translation of *Mirat-i-Ahmadi* by James Bird (page 322) and says the guns were not removed to Agra. I didn't find a copy of Bird's translation of the Mirat, but the translation by M. F. Lokhandwala that I have consulted mentions no such thing on page 100, which is about the capture of the Surat fort. It says what Abu'l Fazl says—that the guns were ordered to be moved to Agra.

56 This author saw them in 2009.

57 Ali Muhammad Khan, *Mirat-i-Ahmadi*, pp. 100–1.

the Rajputs were brave enough to run against a spear, he would run against his own sword and be like the Rajputs. It's quite apparent that he wanted to show that he wasn't any less a hero than a Rajput. It's not difficult to see in him a yearning to be seen and accepted as an Indian.

Everyone was dumb-founded by this senseless action. But eventually Man Singh had the good sense to blow the sword off with his hand as Akbar made a dash at it. The falling sword cut Akbar between his thumb and index finger. Denied a shot at Rajput-like bravery, Akbar was mad with rage. He flung Man Singh to the ground and squeezed his neck. The grip was so strong that Man Singh could have been killed had someone not intervened. But another nobleman named Sayyid Muzaffar reacted in time and twisted Akbar's injured finger to free Man Singh from the emperor's grasp.[58]

But despite his victory in Gujarat, the Mirzas stayed out of Akbar's grip. Ibrahim Husain Mirza had escaped to Punjab after his defeat at Sarnal. At Multan, he was taken prisoner by the Baloch after a fight. He was captured by Akbar's men but died before they could bring him to Agra.[59]

Muhammad Husain Mirza, who had escaped to the Deccan during the Siege of Surat, returned to Gujarat when he learnt about Akbar's return to Agra. He went about retaking some of the lost territories, including Bharuch and Cambay,[60] before laying siege to Ahmedabad. Akbar then returned to Ahmedabad, and through forced marches, arrived there in just nine days[61] when ordinarily it took about a month to reach Ahmedabad from Agra. This had completely stunned Muhammad Husain Mirza whose scouts had reported to him a fortnight earlier that Akbar was staying put at Fatehpur Sikri, his new capital.[62]

---

58 Ibid.; Abu'l Fazl, *Akbarnama, Vol. III,* pp. 43–4.

59 Abu'l Fazl, *Akbarnama, Vol. III*, pp. 53–4.

60 Ibid., p. 59.

61 Ibid., p.74.

62 For a scholarly, in-depth history of this capital city built by Akbar, please read *Fathpur Sikri Revisited* by Syed Ali Nadeem Rezavi.

Akbar once again charged at the Mirzas at the head of his army with the battle cries of *Allahu Akbar* and *Ya Moin.*[63] This was a desperate battle where at one time, Akbar was left with just two troopers guarding him as he got surrounded by the enemy. His charger was wounded and there was even a rumour that Akbar had been killed, which triggered panic in the ranks. But once his troops realised that their emperor was still alive and soldiering on, they fought with renewed vigour.

Muhammad Husain Mirza was defeated and captured. Akbar reluctantly agreed to his execution, which was demanded by his nobles Raja Bhagwan Dass and Raja Rai Singh on the ground of necessity.[64] However, there was no reluctance on his part while slaying Shah Madad, the *koka* or milk brother of Muhammad Husain Mirza. Shah Madad had killed Bhupat, brother of Raja Bhagwan Dass, at Sarnal, so Akbar speared him to death to avenge the brave Rajput.[65] About 1,700 of the enemy[66] were killed against about a hundred of Akbar's own troops. Akbar ordered the erection of a tower studded with the heads of the enemy troops to strike terror in the hearts of the locals to prevent another insurrection in the future.[67] Clearly, this terror tactic wasn't just reserved for the Hindus, as is often claimed by 'weekend historians' and Twitter professors. The Mirzas were Akbar's own family members and the troops fighting for Muhammad Husain Mirza were the same Turks from Mawarannahar. And among those who fell fighting for Akbar was a Hindu general named after Lord Rama, Raghu Das.[68]

Shah Mirza was the only rebellious Mirza who stayed out of reach of Akbar. He didn't pose much of a threat to Akbar again as he seems to have wandered away into oblivion.[69]

---

63 An obvious reference to Moinuddin Chishti of Ajmer.

64 Abu'l Fazl, *Akbarnama, Vol. III*, p. 86.

65 Ibid., p. 84.

66 Ibid., p. 87. Abu'l Fazl says that the enemy dead on the battlefield was counted at 1,200, and 500 more who were wounded were found dead near the battlefield.

67 Ibid., p. 88.

68 Abu'l Fazl, *Akbarnama, Vol. III*, p. 87.

69 Ibid. The reference reads: 'Shah Mirza threw the dust of disgrace on his head and became a desert-wandering vagabond.'

With the conquest of Gujarat and Rajputana, Akbar consolidated western India. The overland and oceanic trade routes with the western world now passed through Mughal territories. This provided the launchpad for further expansion of the Mughal Empire. Akbar's successes would be built on by his successors. To commemorate his victory, Akbar built the Buland Darwaza at Fatehpur Sikri, his newest capital. The imposing majesty of the gateway even today inspires awe in an onlooker. That's how symbolic the victory over Gujarat was.

And though the present is a different country, yet Gujarat has continued to hold significance in the politics of India. The Freedom Struggle, in its most decisive phase (1919–42)[70], was led by a Gujarati named Mohandas Karamchand Gandhi. When freedom came riding on a monster called Partition, it was left to another Gujarati named Vallabhbhai Patel to play a stellar role in pulling together the remnants of the British Indian Empire to make the new nation state of India in 1947. And when the nation sought a new leader in 2014, he came from Gujarat.

With the west firmly in his grip, Akbar turned towards the east. The rich regions of Bengal, Bihar and Odisha, were beckoning him. It made absolute sense to establish control over the region between Agra and Bengal as it 'was the richest and most settled agrarian area of Hindustan'.[71]

Bengal was a materially and culturally rich region ruled by successive Muslim dynasties ever since Bakhtiyar Khilji overthrew King Lakshmana Sena of the Sena dynasty from Gauda or Lakhnauti (ancient name was Lakshmanavati) in the early 13th century. In Khilji's time, it was referred to as *Dayar-i-Lakhnauti*[72] by the Muslims. A century later, it became one of the three administrative regions of

70 Expert opinion may vary on this timeline; but in my opinion, the period after the Jallianwala Bagh Massacre in April 1919 and up to the Quit India Movement of 1942 was the most agitational and decisive phase of the Freedom Movement.

71 Jos Gommans, *Mughal Warfare*, p. 26.

72 Ghulam Husain Salim, *Riyaz-us-Salatin: A History of Bengal,* trans. Maulavi Abdus Salam (Calcutta, The Asiatic Society, 1902) footnote 1, p. 9.

Bengal comprising northern and central parts after Bengal was divided into three parts during Delhi Sultan Ghiyasuddin Tughlaq's time.[73]

But for much of the ancient period, Bengal was referred to as Vanga[74] or Gauda or synonymously.[75] Since the 11th century, however, another name started occurring in epigraphic and literary records—Vangala-desa.[76] And it was really this third name that gave rise to the Mughal name for the region, Bangal (Bengal). And this is the name that's still used by North Indians to refer to the modern state of West Bengal.

Ancient Bengal either accepted vassalage of bigger empires like the Mauryas and Guptas or had independent kings and dynasties who made their own destinies. The foremost among them was King Sasanka in the 7th century who was the first independent Bengal ruler to have expanded territorially beyond the accepted frontiers of the region, becoming the master of not just Gauda but Magadha, Utkala (Odisha today) and Kongoda.[77] Sasanka's expansionist policies had set the stage for conflict with the Pushyabhutis of Thaneswar and Maukharis of Kannauj, two of the most dominant powers in North India.

These two power centres united when the Maukhari King Grahavarman married Rajyashri, the daughter of Pushyabhuti King Prabhakaravardhana. When this happened, Sasanka joined hands with Devagupta of Malwa who fought and killed Grahavarman and captured Rajyashri when King Prabhakaravardhana passed away. To avenge him, the new king of Thaneswar, Rajyavardhana, went to war with Devagupta but was killed when Sasanka turned up with reinforcements.

The new Pushyabhuti King Harshavardhana then went to war with the two and received an alliance offer from King Bhaskaravarman

73 Ibid., p. 10, see footnote.

74 India's National Anthem *Jana Gana Mana* uses Vanga to refer to Bengal.

75 R. C. Majumdar, *A History of Bengal: Volume I, Hindu Period* (Dacca: The University of Dacca, 1943), p. 14.

76 Ibid., p. 18.

77 Ibid., p. 66.

of Kamarupa.[78] Devagupta and Sasanka were defeated and pushed out of Kannauj and Harsha managed to rescue his sister. Sasanka, however, managed to keep his kingdom safe until his death when Harsha and Bhaskaravarman divided it among themselves.

Sasanka was also an iconoclast of his time who persecuted the Buddhists and defiled their places of worship. He had expelled monks from a *vihara* in Kusinagar, thrown into the Ganges a stone having the footprints of the Buddha in Pataliputra, removed an idol of Buddha and replaced it with that of Lord Shiva, and cut down the sacred Bodhi tree at Gaya.[79]

Just like the Hindu rulers of Bengal before them, the Bengal sultans also acted either as vassals of the most dominant sultanates in the North or as independent rulers with their own imperial ambitions, often expanding their kingdoms to include Bihar, Avadh and Odisha, just like Sasanka. And the ethnicity of these sultans was much varied—there were Turks, Afghans and even Abyssinians who sat on the *masnad* of Bengal. In fact, Bengal was the only place in India that had four black African sultans, or *Habshis* as they were called then, rule in quick succession between 1487 and 1494.

Among the independent sultans of Bengal, the most notable were Alauddin Husain Shah (1493–1519) and his son Nusrat Shah (1519–32). Husain Shah had come to the throne after murdering his master, the last *Habshi* sultan, Shamsuddin Muzaffar Shah. His reign and that of his son saw an amazing confluence of Hindu and Muslim cultures that found expression in art, architecture, literature and culture. This was largely because these sultans, while not fully abandoning Persian etiquette, wholly embraced the Bengali culture and language. In fact, they promoted Bengali over Persian as a language of literature and communication in court.[80] They also promoted Hindus to high offices and were openly generous to them.

78 R. C. Majumdar also calls the kingdom of Kamarupa a dominant North Indian power, perhaps based on this alliance.

79 R. C. Majumdar, *A History of Bengal*, footnote 3, p. 67.

80 Pika Ghosh, *Temple to Love: Architecture and Devotion in Seventeenth-Century Bengal* (Bloomington: Indiana University Press, 2005), pp. 84–5.

Militarily, too, these sultans had adapted to the conditions typical of the region. Their predecessors who came to Bengal from North India with their cavalry-dominated armies had to unlearn a lot of things due to the changed terrain. With so many rivers and riverine channels, and swamps and marshes, any military here had to use war boats and more infantry. The humid climate was also unsuitable for horses that largely came from drier climates of the Middle East, Central Asia and even western India.

But because of the swampy terrain, which is suitable for snakes, the veneration of the snake goddess Manasa was very popular in Bengal.[81] And the Hussain Shahi sultans promoted and patronised the Manasa cult. It's not surprising then that several works of literature devoted to Manasa, like *Manasa-Mangala* by Vijaya Gupta and *Manasa-Vijaya* by Vipradas, presented the sultans in glowing terms.[82] Indeed, the Hindu subjects treated the sultan as one of their own, referring to him as *raja* and *ishvara* (god).[83]

Alauddin Husain Shah was also equated with other Hindu gods such as Yama, the god of death (used to imply that he brings death to his enemies), and Kama (god of love) for his beauty.[84] In the first Bangla translation of the *Mahabharata* prepared by Vaishnava poet Kabindra Parameshwar, Husain Shah was referred to as 'Nripati Husain Shah', who was also *mahamati* (magnificent), *Gauda ishvar* and 'Krishna avatar' in the *kali yuga*.[85] That is why their reign is often referred to as the 'golden age' of Bengal.[86]

When the Mughals were added to this curious mix, they didn't radically alter the fabric but only added more colour to it. Less than 50 years after Akbar's conquest of Bengal, poets and authors were

81 Ibid.

82 Ibid.

83 Richard M. Eaton, *The Rise of Islam and the Bengal Frontier, 1204–1760* (Berkley: California University Press, 1993).

84 Ibid. The comparisons are made in the opening verse of a 1494 work glorifying goddess Manasa authored by Vijaya Gupta.

85 Nitish K. Sengupta, *Land of Two Rivers: A History of Bengal from the Mahabharata to Mujib* (New Delhi: Penguin Books, 2011).

86 Richard M. Eaton, *The Rise of Islam and the Bengal Frontier, 1204*–1760 (Berkeley: University of California Press, 1993).

putting out intellectual efforts that reinterpreted Islam from a local perspective. In *Nabi-Bangsha* (also spelt as *Nabi-Bamsa*), a work on the prophets of Islam from Adam right down to Muhammad authored by Saiyid Sultan of Chittagong, the Islamic notion of prophethood was compared to that of avatars in Hinduism. The god that Muslims worship was referred to as *Prabhu* and *Niranjan* while Muhammad was portrayed as His avatar.[87]

This was a very bold and unique experiment when seen from a modern viewpoint. In its own time, while being quite radical and bold, it actually borrowed from and expanded on a much older tradition started in a small way by Sultan Mahmud of Ghazni. Mahmud had minted a coin in 1018 that had on its obverse an inscription in Sanskrit that read, '*Avyaktam ekam Muhammadah avatarah nripati Mahmudah.*' It really meant that Muhammad is the avatar of the Infinite One (god) while Mahmud is the king.[88] That these early Muslim conquerors tried to make the Hindus understand their religious dogmas through totems of their own faith, or tried to reinterpret their faith from the perspective of Hindus, is remarkable enough anyway; but the author of *Nabi-Bangsha* really pushed the envelope further. And that he did that in the first quarter of the 17th century, after the Mughals had conquered Bengal and replaced dynastic rulers with centrally-appointed *subahdars*, really speaks volumes for a culture of tolerance that continued to grow under the new masters of the region.

But when Akbar set his sights on Bengal, the province had already seen its cultural high phase. Its Pathan ruler Sultan Sulaiman Kararani, in the earlier period of Akbar's reign, had neutralised the possibility of conflict by offering tribute to the Mughal emperor and reading the *khutba* in his name.[89] But when he died in 1572, his successor was appointed without the customary permission from the Mughal emperor. Daud Khan Kararani, the new sultan, also didn't

---

87 Ibid.

88 Carl W. Ernst, *Eternal Garden: Mysticism, History, and Politics at a South Asian Sufi Center* (New York: The State University of New York Press, 1992), p. 52.

89 Abu'l Fazl, *Akbarnama, Vol. III*, p. 96.

make those outwardly gestures of submission that Akbar expected him to make.[90]

Akbar sent an army under his Mir Bakshi, Lashkar Khan, and a fleet under Parmanand, a relative of Todar Mal. Eventually, Todar Mal himself was sent by the emperor to operate this military machine as he could keep it well-oiled, given his organising skills. The overall command was placed in the hands of Munim Khan, the *Khan-i-Khanan*. The attack on the Bengal sultan's territories started from Bihar where Munim Khan laid siege to the city of Patna and got stuck. The rainy season was on, so the *Khan-i-Khanan* requested Akbar to come there personally. And he did, in a specially constructed fleet of houseboats, along with his sons and wives.

But since the journey was during the rainy season, the fleet couldn't always take on the choppy waters very well. Several of the boats capsized, resulting in loss of life and material at several places. In one such incident, two of Akbar's favourite hunting cheetahs, Daulat Khan and Dilrang, were lost.[91] As the presence of the cheetahs suggests, Akbar engaged in hunting whenever he touched land during his river journey. And the reason should be pretty obvious to the reader of this book by now—he was practising for war. But Akbar was also learning to adapt to this new terrain and the new style of warfare that it necessitated.

Akbar asked for the surrender of Patna. This was rejected by Daud Khan. Then Akbar offered him three alternatives: a duel with him to settle the winner, or a duel between two men from either camp, or a duel between two elephants.[92] Daud Khan ignored it.

Akbar then decided to take the fort of Hajipur in order to isolate the fort of Patna. A land force was sent to attack the fort while a flotilla of boats was also sent to assist. The Patna garrison saw that and probably realised what the Mughals were up to. So, they sent a few war boats to challenge the Mughal flotilla. The Afghans were routed both on land and in water, and Hajipur fell to the Mughals.

---

90 Ibid.

91 Ibid., p. 132.

92 Ibid., p. 137.

Daud Khan panicked and fled from Patna by water to Bengal even as Akbar marched into the city. Many of the Afghan troops were drowned while trying to cross the river. The Mughals got a large war booty, which included 265 elephants. Abu'l Fazl's comment on the impact of this defeat on the Afghan sultan stands out among comments he makes on other kings defeated by Akbar. He mocks Daud Khan Kararani and says, 'Their secular and spiritual reputation was destroyed.'[93] This is perhaps an allusion to the acceptability of the Afghan sultans even among their non-Muslim subjects, given the glorious reign of the Husain Shahi sultans before them, as discussed earlier in this chapter.

Akbar wanted to pursue Daud Khan all the way to Bengal, and that seems to have been his plan all along. But he had a change of heart and decided to let the *Khan-i-Khanan* and Todar Mal take over. Todar Mal was also presented with a standard and a drum[94]—the second Hindu to be honoured that way after Raja Bhagwan Dass.

Akbar turned towards the fort at Rohtas[95] instead. This was another stronghold of the Afghans in Bihar, but once again, he was counselled to depute another army to take control of it. This he did and moved away towards Jaunpur to coordinate both his armies. The army in Bengal started pushing out Daud Khan from one stronghold to another. Surajgarh was taken first, followed by Monghyr (or Munger today), Bhagalpur and Kahalgaon (where the famous ancient university of Vikramashila was located). Local Hindu *zamindar*s swore fealty to the Mughals too. Finally, the Mughals reached Tanda, the capital of Daud Khan, forcing him to flee Bengal and go to Odisha.

Mughal general Muhammad Quli Khan Barlas wanted the imperial army to campaign in Odisha against Daud Khan. Many others, however, were against it. Todar Mal supported Barlas and swayed the opinion of others in his favour. But just then, Barlas was poisoned by someone of the rival faction, and that changed the power equation all of a sudden. Barlas' removal emboldened the rival camp who rallied

93 Ibid., p. 143.

94 Ibid., p. 144.

95 Not to be confused with the Rohtas Fort in Jhelum district of Pakistan. A short history of that fort has been given in Chapter 2 of this book.

behind Qiya Khan who was a rival of the *Khan-i-Khanan*. Todar Mal, after failing to resolve the crisis at his level, advised the *Khan-i-Khanan* to bribe his rivals to gain their support. That he did and also came down himself to lead the army at Todar Mal's suggestion. This way, Todar Mal and Munim Khan managed to defeat this opposition.[96]

But this sort of internal revolt in the Mughal camp encouraged Daud Khan to make a move against them. He had the support of his Odisha governor, Khan Jahan Lodhi. With a large force, he decided to crush the Mughal army. Both sides met at Tukaroi on 3 March 1575. It was a tremendous clash of arms that dragged on for three days. The Afghans deployed their elephant corps under Gujar Khan, which made such a ferocious charge that the Mughal vanguard and the *altamash*[97] broke. That resulted in the centre reeling under pressure. Many Mughal commanders went down fighting, and even the *Khan-i-Khanan* sustained several wounds.

With the Mughals in such discomfort, the Afghans reached the Mughal camp and started plundering it.[98] But the Mughals had only been stunned, not shocked out of action. The Mughal line reformed as the military provost started to pull back troops fleeing and turning them back into battle.[99] Successful generals do it in terms of crisis. Ahmad Shah Abdali did just that when his troops started fleeing the battlefield at Panipat in 1761 while facing the superior Maratha artillery and musketeers. Soviet generals did that too during the Second World War.

At this crucial juncture, something happened to Gujar Khan that had happened to Hemu at Panipat 20 years earlier: a stray arrow hit him. As soon as Gujar Khan died, his troops melted away. When Daud Khan heard this and also about the reverses suffered by the

---

96 Abu'l Fazl, *Akbarnama, Vol. III*, pp. 172–3.

97 A special contingent placed between the vanguard and centre. If the vanguard lost its link to the centre, the *altamash* contingent came to the aid of the centre. For this reference please see Kaushik Roy's *Military Transition in Early Modern Asia, 1400–1750: Cavalry, Guns, Government and Ships* (London: Bloomsbury, 2014), p. 67.

98 Abu'l Fazl, *Akbarnama, Vol. III*, p. 177.

99 Ibid.

Mughals, he disbelieved the news about the Mughals and suspected it to be a ruse.

So, despite the odds being against them, the Mughals won at Tukaroi. But this was a hard-fought battle, which also showed the fierceness and resolve of the enemy—the Pathans were always fiercely independent. The Mughals repeated their terror tactics to dissuade any further rebellion or resistance—they slaughtered the prisoners of war and built eight minarets with their heads 'as a warning to spectators'.[100] Even at Chittor the Mughals didn't erect so many skull towers after defeating a primarily Hindu enemy as they did in Bengal fighting a Muslim enemy.

All this forced Daud Khan to seek truce. At Cuttack on 12 April 1575, he submitted to Munim Khan and the Mughals and was given Odisha as *jagir*. But this would prove to be a fragile peace. When Munim Khan died shortly afterwards, Daud Khan tried to retake Bengal from the Mughals, which resulted in another imperial army fighting him at Rajmahal (Abu'l Fazl calls it Ak Mahal. The place got its name Rajmahal because Raja Man Singh chose to reside in this city[101]) in 1576. The battle fought on July 12 resulted in the defeat, capture and execution of Daud Khan.[102]

Abu'l Fazl says that the end of Daud Khan finally turned Bengal into an 'abode of peace' from being a *bulghak-khana* or a 'house of contention' (strife or sedition could be alternative words for it).[103] Bengal to the Mughal world view was a 'house of sedition'. And it would produce challenges to the Mughal rule in the future too.

Strangely enough, from the latter part of the 19th century, the British would increasingly view Bengalis as seditious people and Bengal as a place of sedition. The British 'martial races' theory that would evolve in the aftermath of 1857 would pit communities more

100 Ibid., p. 180.

101 Ibid., footnote 2, p. 230.

102 Ibid., p. 255.

103 Ibid., p. 256.

loyal to the British Raj against those that engaged in nationalist[104] activities. The English-educated Bengali middle class came to represent this class of people who were perceived to be troublemakers and sedition-mongers[105] for being part of revolutionary movements or the INC.

Even today, the term 'Bengali babu', a colonial pejorative, is often used as a racist term to mock the supposed non-martial spirit of Bengalis. It's for a sociologist to dig deep into this, but it is interesting to note how colonial narratives still dictate terms of engagement among Indians. Indians today largely look at one another the way the British used to look at them. So, the colonial cultural tropes like 'manly Sikh', 'war-like Jat', 'effeminate Bengali' or 'unruly tribal' are still used by Indians.

This author also thinks that the colonial propaganda about Bengal and Bengalis is similar to the modern Hindu nationalist propaganda about the region and its people. In the last few years, with the coming of Hindutva forces to power, the state of West Bengal is being increasingly portrayed by saffron groups and commentators as some sort of a place of sedition where Muslims are appeased, and the Hindus persecuted. West Bengal chief minister Mamata Banerjee is often portrayed as a scheming Muslim woman wearing a hijab in Hindutva propaganda, and called Mumtaz Begum[106] who is often in cahoots with anti-Hindu, and therefore anti-India, forces.[107] Ironically, it was

---

104 Heather Streets, *Martial Races: The Military, Race and Masculinity in British Imperial Culture, 1857–1914* (Manchester: Manchester University Press, 2010), p. 162.

105 Mrinalini Sinha, *Colonial Masculinity: The 'Manly Englishman' and the 'Effeminate Bengali' in the Late Nineteenth Century* (Manchester: Manchester University Press, 1995), p. 42.

106 HT Correspondent, 'There is a hate campaign against me: Mamata Banerjee takes a dig at BJP', *Hindustan Times*, Kolkata, 19 April 2017. Available at https://www.hindustantimes.com/india-news/there-is-a-hate-campaign-against-me-mamata-banerjee-writes-on-facebook/story-sUgRitc9LIkhPBmcBRUwEK.html.

107 PTI, 'UP BJP MLA calls Mamata Banerjee surpanakha', *The Times of India*, Ballia, 25 April 2018. Available at https://timesofindia.indiatimes.com/india/up-bjp-mla-calls-mamata-banerjee-surpanakha/articleshow/63912371.cms.

West Bengal under Mamata Banerjee that arrested the greatest number of people for sedition in the country in 2016.[108]

The conquest of Bengal was made possible by the Mughal ability to adapt to different styles of warfare. Where they struggled at the start of the campaign to navigate the waters properly, as evidenced by the sinking of many boats of Akbar's own flotilla, towards the end they managed to hold their own in riverine combat. The use of a fleet in the river equipped with artillery, musketeers and archers to support a traditional land army with its own park of artillery helped them mount very effective offensives and sieges. That the Mughals couldn't often use their trump card—cavalry—was no longer a limiting factor in the East. And this was quite significant, for the Mughal war psychology was tied to the stirrup.

A Mughal army going to war without its cavalry was akin to the Indian cricket team in the 1990s taking the field without its star batsman Sachin Tendulkar, to give a modern analogy. But the ability of the army to deploy infantry and a fleet, and to utilise cavalry troopers in a dismounted role was the one that kept the Mughal military machine well-oiled. Again, to give a cricketing analogy, it was like the Indian cricket team of the noughties where Virender Sehwag and Saurav Ganguly would smash the opening bowling attack while Tendulkar, Rahul Dravid and the rest of the middle order would consolidate the innings.

The conquest of Bengal also expanded the Mughal Empire's borders to the gates of Assam where the first Mughal army would campaign during the reign of Emperor Jahangir. But even without going there, the Mughals began to influence, albeit indirectly, political affairs in Assam that was largely divided between the Koch and Ahom kingdoms, with a smattering of smaller kingdoms thrown in between.

For a while, the Koches were the supreme power in north-eastern India while the Ahoms vied with them for primacy in the region. The high tide of success came the Koches' way during the reign of King Nara Narayan. Like Akbar, King Nara Narayan also ruled for close to

---

108 Saibal Gupta, 'Bengal tops in sedition arrest', *The Times of India*, 18 September 2016. Available at https://timesofindia.indiatimes.com/city/kolkata/Bengal-tops-in-sedition-arrests/articleshow/54386342.cms.

half a century (1540–87) and left behind a tall military and cultural legacy. But while he lived, he sparred with various kingdoms in the Northeast like the Ahoms, Jaintias, Kacharis and Manipuris and even had territorial designs on the Sultanate of Bengal. Together with his younger brother Chilarai (Sukladhwaj being his formal name), Nara Narayan struck terror in the hearts of his adversaries.

His conflict with the Ahom kingdom was something he inherited from his father, Visva Simha. In 1546, when Ahom King Suklenmung attacked and pushed back a Koch garrison to Nagaon, three Koch princes were sent with an army of 3,000. In the ensuing engagement with the Ahoms, the Koches killed a senior Ahom officer and forced the Ahoms to retreat amid heavy losses. To teach the Ahoms a lesson, Nara Narayan's troops erected a *daul* (the word is deceptively similar to doul, which is used for a temple in Assam) or a skull tower with 100 heads of the enemy.[109] While it's very interesting to note that the Koches used a Timurid terror tactic against the Ahoms, the act also underscores something more significant: that a Hindu kingdom did to another Hindu kingdom what a Muslim kingdom (Mughals) did to another Muslim kingdom (Afghans in Bengal). Hindutva propagandists now largely attribute such terror tactics to medieval Muslims, but as always, a careful study of history shows nothing is ever black and white, there are always shades of grey.

The Ahoms eventually pushed back the Koches three years later and recovered the territories lost earlier. Nara Narayan tried to tread on the path of diplomacy, but the embassy he sent was insulted and sent back. This infuriated him and his brother and they went to war again. The Ahoms were soundly defeated and the king was forced to flee to the Naga hills. Eventually, the Koches withdrew when the Ahom king accepted the Koch king's vassalage.

But even this didn't last long as the Ahom king reformed his army after the Koch withdrawal and went about employing terror tactics against his own people who submitted to Koch authority and the troops Koches left behind to guard the newly acquired possessions. They were executed, and their severed heads were put up on display

109 H. K. Barpujari, *The Comprehensive History of Assam Vol. II*, p. 75.

on stakes[110] at Mathadang (in Sibsagar district of Assam today), just like Alauddin Khilji had done with Mongol heads, or the Rohillas had done with the head of Maratha general Dattaji Scindia at Burarighat in 1760, or the Marathas had done with the head of Qutub Khan (who had beheaded Dattaji Scindia) at Kunjpura in 1761.

This winning and losing of territory continued between the Koches and Ahoms. But Chilarai defeated every kingdom that lay in his path of conquest: the Kacharis, the Jaintias, the Tripura kingdom and so on. Many others submitted to Koch authority without fighting, like the Khasis and Manipuris. These kingdoms accepted Koch vassalage and even put the Koch king's name in their coins. Chilarai became an icon in Assamese popular culture, earning the epithet 'Bir' or 'brave'. A huge equestrian statue of Chilarai has forever welcomed visitors to Guwahati.

But the Koch good luck ended when they tried to expand westwards to Bengal. Sultan Sulaiman Kararani defeated King Nara Narayan sometime in 1568. The sultan's general Kalapahar defeated the brilliant Chilarai and took him captive. But more than his military prowess, Kalapahar is remembered in eastern India today for his iconoclasm. He supposedly sacked the Konark Temple in Odisha and the Kamakhya Temple[111] in Guwahati, Assam, which was then part of the Koch kingdom. The temple was rebuilt by Nara Narayan and Chilarai later, but according to a legend, both got cursed by goddess Kamakhya for watching her dance. Interestingly, the Cooch Behar royal family still believes in the curse and not everyone associated with it visits Kamakhya[112] or even Guwahati directly by air or rail as the path to the city goes right under Nilachal Hill where the shrine is located. Instead, they prefer to fly down to Dibrugarh and enter Guwahati from the other side. Interestingly, a locality in Guwahati today is named after this Afghan general.

Chilarai was released after three years by the sultan as he feared an invasion by Akbar and wanted to have the Koches as ally. This

---

110 Ibid., p. 81.

111 Ibid., p. 86. See footnote 25 for the scholarly disagreement over whether Kamakhya was at all sacked by Kalapahar.

112 Sumir Karmakar, 'The curse of the goddess', *The Telegraph*, Guwahati, 25 June 2017. Available at https://www.telegraphindia.com/india/the-curse-of-the-goddess/cid/1501117.

is what King Nara Narayan had done too when he had released all Ahom hostages in the hope that the Ahom king would be his ally in his impending conflict with the Bengal Sultanate. But just as a similar move by the Koches didn't work with the Ahoms[113], this one too didn't work with the Koches. King Nara Narayan, worried about Ahom aggression and conscious about the designs of aggrandisement of the Afghans, decided to woo the Mughals.

In 1574, when Akbar defeated Daud Khan Kararani, a faction of the Afghans called the Mankalis of Ghoraghat, sought refuge in Koch Behar. King Nara Narayan refused.[114] In 1578, King Nara Narayan sent a proper diplomatic mission to the court of Akbar. Apart from "choice goods" (read gifts) that included 54 elephants,[115] the Koch king also sent a note in which he praised the Mughal emperor.[116]

This wasn't total submission to the Mughals, but an acknowledgement by King Nara Narayan that the Mughal Empire was now the dominant power of the land whose fountainhead should be kept in good humour. The Koch king wouldn't do anything detrimental to Mughal interests. Therefore, when a section of the Mughal nobility in Bengal mutinied against Akbar in 1579, Nara Narayan sent his fleet to help the imperial forces quell the revolt in 1583.[117]

But in 1581, the Koch king decided to partition his kingdom after his nephew Raghu Dev, son of his brother Chilarai, rebelled.[118] Thus, the eastern part of the kingdom came to be known as Kamrup (or Koch Hajo) that included large parts of lower and middle Assam, while the western part remained Koch Behar. Kamrup came to be ruled by Raghu Dev and later his son, Parikshit. While Raghu Dev more or less kept peace with his uncle, he couldn't do so with his nephew, Lakshmi Narayan, who succeeded his father, Nara Narayan, as the king of Koch Behar.

---

113 H.K. Barpujari, *The Comprehensive History of Assam, Vol. II,* pp. 81–2.

114 Ibid., p. 93.

115 Abu'l Fazl, *Akbarnama, Vol. III,* p. 349.

116 Ibid., p. 1067.

117 Ibid., p. 621. *The Comprehensive History of Assam, Vol. II,* puts it in context in p. 94.

118 For details of this episode, see *The Comprehensive History of Assam, Vol. II,* pp. 94–6.

Raghu Dev fought and lost to his nephew and decided to forge an alliance with Isa Khan, the Afghan *zamindar* of Bhati who refused to bow down before the Mughals. This Koch-Afghan alliance gave Lakshmi Narayan the creeps. So, he approached Raja Man Singh, then the Mughal viceroy of Bengal, for an offensive-defensive alliance. To solidify this alliance, the Koch king married off his sister Prabhavati to Raja Man Singh and accepted Mughal suzerainty. This relationship between Koch Behar and the Kachwahas of Amber continued even in the 20th century when a princess of the princely state of Kooch Behar (by then called Cooch Behar) married Raja Man Singh's descendant and namesake, Sawai Man Singh II, and became Maharani Gayatri Devi of Jaipur.

At the political level, this family rivalry among the Koches would pave the way for direct Mughal intervention in Assam during the reign of Emperor Jahangir. That's a tale for some other time, but Akbar's Bengal victory came on the heels of another hard-fought win over the kingdom of Mewar. After Rana Udai Singh, it was being ruled by his son, Rana Pratap Singh.

Pratap wasn't his father's choice to succeed him. Rana Udai Singh willed his successor to be his favourite son Jagmal. After his death, Jagmal did ascend the throne but didn't remain there for long—the nobles who didn't approve of the late king's choice deposed the new king and put his brother Pratap on the throne. It was 1572, the year Akbar stormed Gujarat.

Akbar wanted Mewar to be his ally or feudatory. It isn't mentioned anywhere but the coming to the Mewar throne of a new ruler must have given Akbar some hope of being able to nudge him to serve under the imperial standards. So, he made a peace overture while returning to Agra from Gujarat in 1573. He sent Man Singh, by now declared as *farzand* or son of the emperor and one of his favourite generals, to the Rana's capital of Udaipur via Dungarpur. He sent a *khilat* or a royal robe of honour for the Rana.[119]

Rana Kika, as Muslim sources call Pratap, came out to receive the imperial mission with full honour. He also accepted the *khilat* and put it on. He then invited Man Singh to his palace as guest and

---

119 Abu'l Fazl, *Akbarnama, Vol. III*, p. 57.

entertained him there. Man Singh, it seems, also had the brief to bring Rana Pratap to Akbar's court. The Rana, says Abu'l Fazl, promised to go to the imperial capital, but dilly-dallied and gave the excuse that his well-wishers didn't want him to go.[120] This part has been interpreted by Beveridge and Elliot differently. While Beveridge says this is what Abu'l Fazl wrote,[121] Elliot is of the opinion that the Rana was contemplating on a treacherous course of action against Man Singh but abandoned the thought after his well-wishers advised against it.[122]

Colonel James Tod, however, gives a very different version of this meeting in his *Annals and Antiquities of Rajasthan*. He says that Man Singh came to the Rana without an invite, and the Rana, out of courtesy, hosted a feast in his honour on the banks of the Udaipur lake (Pichola, one would assume). There, the Rana absented himself, leaving his son Amar Singh to entertain the Amber prince. When Man Singh asked why the Rana wasn't there, Amar Singh said his father had a headache. At this, Man Singh realised that it was a mere ploy to avoid eating with him, so he pointedly asked the Rana the reason for that cold treatment. To that the Rana replied that he couldn't break bread with a Rajput 'who gave his sister to a Turk, and who probably ate with him'.[123]

Man Singh took offence and vowed to crush the Rana's pride in battle. To add insult to injury, someone among the hosts also taunted Man Singh by asking him to bring his *phupha* (husband of father's sister, in this case Akbar) along next time.

As historian Rima Hooja rightly notes, this was a 19th-century retelling of the event which differed drastically from contemporary Mughal and Mewar sources.[124] What she doesn't say, however, is that this retelling happened because in the 19th century, Hindu princely states in Rajputana and elsewhere either tried to disown their past association with the Mughals or over-glorified their resistance to the

120 Ibid.

121 Ibid. See footnote.

122 H. M. Elliot, *The History of India As Told By Its Own Historians, Vol. VI*, p. 43.

123 James Tod, *Annals and Antiquities of Rajasthan, Vol. I*, p. 392.

124 Rima Hooja, *Maharana Pratap: The Invincible Warrior* (New Delhi: Juggernaut Books, 2018), p. 90.

House of Timur. Over time, this exercise resulted in the propping up of even phony characters to show the Mughals in poor light and cover their own shame of having been feudatories of the Mughals. A case in point is the story of Kiran Devi of Bikaner, which this author has discussed in Chapter 3 of this book.

Tod's account also gives away the social prejudices of the time wherein he says that the ground where the spread was laid was broken up and purified with water from the Ganges, and the Rana's men bathed and changed their clothes as they had been polluted by Man Singh's mere presence. Strangely enough, such prejudices are rife in the Indian society even today. In 2018, Kannada film actor Prakash Raj, a known critic of the BJP and Narendra Modi and someone who openly says he isn't a Hindu but a Lingayat, had delivered a talk at a seminar in Sirsi, Karnataka. Later, BJP workers 'purified' the venue with *gau mutra* or cow urine and *tulsi* as they alleged that the speakers were anti-Hindu and beefeaters.[125]

Three years after Man Singh's peace mission, Akbar's patience ran dry. He decided to opt for a military solution. He sent Man Singh at the head of an imperial army to force Rana Pratap into submission. On April 3, 1576, the army left Ajmer where the emperor was camped. The army had several top-ranking generals like the Sayyids of Barha, Ghazi Khan Badakhshi, Asaf Khan, Mihtar Khan, Mujahid Beg, Madho Singh, Rai Lonkarn and Man Singh's own uncle, Jagannath Singh. Accompanying this force was also Maulana Abdul Qadir Badaoni, the author of *Muntakhab ut-Tawarikh*.

Badaoni's account of the impending clash between Mewar and the Mughals is quite interesting. He provides troop numbers that Abu'l Fazl doesn't, and his is the first-hand account of the battle, which Abu'l Fazl's is not. However, Badaoni's bigoted description is often selectively quoted to give an impression that Mughals were anti-Hindu, and that they were fighting Rana Pratap to ensure that Hindus killed other Hindus and benefited Muslims. But a full reading

125 Times News Network, 'BJP workers "purify" hall where Prakash Raj spoke', *The Times of India*, Karwar, 17 January 2018. Available at https://timesofindia.indiatimes.com/city/bengaluru/bjp-workers-purify-hall-where-prakash-raj-spoke/articleshow/62532994.cms.

of Badaoni's account shows that while being bigoted, Badaoni did have faith in Man Singh and didn't detest him. In any case, his bigoted view was not the Mughal state's view.

Badaoni writes that he sought the intervention of one Niqab Khan to obtain permission for Badaoni to go on that campaign. Badaoni was in the empire's religious service and his boss was the no-nonsense Sheikh Abdun Nabi, the *sadr-us-sudur* or head of the ecclesiastical department who was also the chief interpreter of Islamic law. Badaoni says he was dying to fight against infidels (read Hindus). Niqab Khan, though, discouraged him initially. 'If a Hindu had not been the leader of this army, I should myself have been the first to have asked permission to join it,' Badaoni quotes him.

He then gives his version:

> But I represented strongly to the said Khan, that I looked on any true servant of the Emperor as a fit leader for myself, and what did it matter, whether it were Man Singh, or another?

Purity of intention is what one should look at, Badaoni added.[126] Convinced by his reply, Niqab Khan personally went to Akbar and argued in favour of Badaoni. Akbar was initially reluctant, but then he gave in.

Man Singh was given an army of 5,000 men by Akbar, including his personal troops. Pratap could only muster 3,000 men to face the Mughals. On 18 June 1576, the two armies met at the mouth of the pass of Haldighati. Abu'l Fazl says that the Rana didn't march in battle array as he was too confident about the might of his arms, but some of his generals thought on their feet and quickly reorganised the lines.

The Rana's right wing carried out a devastating charge on the Mughal vanguard and its left wing. This, as Badaoni specifies, was the doing of Pratap's Afghan general, Hakim Khan Sur. The Mughal left was led by Rai Lonkarn. His troops were pushed to the right by the Rana's charge. Jagannath Singh who was also on the left fought off the enemy bravely but was surrounded and would have been

---

126 Badaoni, *Muntakhab ut-Tawarikh, Vol. II*, p. 233.

annihilated if the *altamash* and Man Singh himself hadn't come to his uncle's rescue.

With the Rajputs on the Mughal side forming a confused mass in the centre, Badaoni asked Asaf Khan how one could distinguish between the Rajputs fighting for the Mughals and those fighting for the Rana. He replied, 'They will experience the whiz of the arrows, be what may. On whichever side there (sic) may be killed, it will be a gain to Islam.'[127]

The Hindu right in India often uses this reference to whip up anti-Muslim and anti-Akbar rhetoric. But it needs to be understood in the proper context. Badaoni was a bigot, and he wasn't the only one in the Mughal court who was so. And yet, perhaps, he was a bit less spiteful towards non-Muslims than some others. He resented Akbar's seemingly heretic ways of adopting non-Muslim customs and religious practices. And he disliked Muslims who treated Hindus with respect or as equals. There's a revealing line in his *Tawarikh* where he narrates an episode involving the Sufi saint Sheikh Muhammad Ghaus[128] in Agra. Badaoni writes:

> While the compiler of this *Muntakhab* was at Agra occupied in acquiring the usual branches of knowledge, the Shaikh came in the dress of a Faqir, with great display and unutterable dignity, and his fame filled the universe. I wished to pay my respects to him. But when I found that he rose up to do honour to Hindus, I felt obliged to forego the pleasure.[129]

This was Badaoni's bias. And yet, he was all praise for Man Singh's valour during the battle as well as of Rana Pratap's troops. Badaoni writes at one place[130]:

---

127 Ibid., p. 237.

128 He is buried in a magnificent tomb in Gwalior that was built by Akbar. In the same complex is also buried Miyan Tansen and his son Bilas Khan.

129 Badaoni, *Muntakhab, Vol. II*, p. 62.

130 Badaoni, *Muntakhab, Vol. II*, p. 238.

> And Rajah Ram Shah of Gwalior (grandson of the famous Rajah Man[131]), who always kept in front of the Rana, performed such prodigies of valour against the Rajputs of Man Singh as baffle description.

At another, he writes,

> And Man Singh, springing into the place of the elephant driver, exhibited such intrepidity as surpasses all imagination…and that day, through the generalship of Man Singh the meaning of this line by Mulla Shiri (a scholar and contemporary of Badaoni who translated Hindu works from Sanskrit to Persian for Akbar) became known: 'A Hindu wields the sword of Islam.'[132]

As the battle raged, the Mughal right wing was also mauled by the Rana's left wing. Not just men, but even animals had a fierce contest. The Rana's elephant corps did particularly well initially. One Mewari elephant named Lona engaged a Mughal elephant named Gajmukta. The contest was tremendous, which also caused panic in the ranks. The Mughal elephant was wounded and was about to run away when the mahout of Lona was hit by a musket ball and had to turn away. But the most fearsome elephant that the Rana had was one Ram Prasad. It mowed down many Mughal soldiers before two Mughal elephants named Gajraj and Ran Madar engaged it. Ram Prasad had almost prevailed in the contest when its mahout got fatally hit by an arrow. It was then easily captured by the Mughals.

The Rana himself led fierce charges upon the enemy and even duelled with Man Singh. Abu'l Fazl doesn't say in detail how they fought; he just says they 'did valiant deeds'. But the imagination of folklorists goes wild here, even suggesting that Rana's horse Chetak mounted two of its forelegs on the trunk of Man Singh's elephant allowing its master to throw a javelin at his enemy, but which narrowly missed the target. An artwork capturing this stands at the Haldighati museum near Udaipur in Rajasthan. In another lore, Man Singh becomes Prince Salim.

---

131 Raja Man Singh Tomar of Gwalior. The palace that he built at Gwalior Fort in the 15th century—the Man Mandir Palace—still stands.

132 Ibid., pp. 238–39.

Nevertheless, three hours into the battle, the Mewar army was a spent force. Its troopers started to pass out due to the intense afternoon heat. Mughal mounted archers with their wheeling tactics and musketeers now started to take a toll on the Mewaris. Hemmed in from all sides, the Rana's army became a confused mass with no hope of victory. The Rana himself was wounded. Seeing that the situation was hopeless, the Rana withdrew from the battlefield.

To cover the Rana's retreat with glory and to create sympathy for him, nationalists have forever paid glowing tributes to him and his wounded horse Chetak that performed extraordinary leaps to put his master out of harm's way but died in the process. But such stories also hide something that was very different about this Rajput king: he didn't suffer from that fatalistic resignation to fate that many other Rajputs suffered, and which turned every defeat into a disaster. Pratap is an honourable exception. He didn't perform *saka* or let his women perform *jauhar*. He had the sagacity to withdraw from a losing battle in order to fight another day.

Pratap's escape from the battlefield of Haldighati that day ensured that he could carry on his struggle against the Mughals longer, thus becoming a legend. He bucked the trend. Of course, my more nationalist readers don't have to agree with me on this, but they might agree with what Sunny Deol as Major Kuldeep Singh Chandpuri says in the 1997 film *Border*: '*Mar kar kisine jang nahin jeeti hai* (Nobody wins battles by dying).'

Pratap had to run from one place to another with Mughals in pursuit of him. Eventually, he had to withdraw to the defiles and forests of his kingdom and suffer untold hardships. But he didn't bow down. When the Mughals eventually withdrew, Pratap came out of the woods and recaptured parts of his kingdom. The conflict wasn't resolved in his and Akbar's lifetime. It would be his son Amar Singh and Akbar's son Jahangir who would make peace after the latter offered honourable terms.

But the Battle of Haldighati was re-fought in 2017 under the aegis of the BJP-led Rajasthan government, aided by a troll army on social media. It was unilaterally decided that people had been taught wrong history for over 400 years and it was Rana Pratap who had won at

Haldighati, defeating the Mughals. Absurd and juvenile arguments were put forward for such an analysis by the then education minister Vasudev Devnani[133] as well as other right-wing worthies.

Soon after, high school textbooks were revised to reflect this new-found enlightenment. By the end of 2018, however, the new Congress government announced that it would change the textbooks to remove anomalies inserted by the previous regime, although it is yet to specify which are those anomalies that it has in mind. One would certainly hope that the Haldighati myth is taken out and replaced with the fact that Akbar's forces won the day on 18 June 1576.

By the end of 1576, Akbar was the master of the land from Gujarat to Bengal with the whole of Rajputana and Central India under his control. He, therefore, turned his attention towards spiritual conquests. And it was here that he attained immortal success and fame, so much so that India still remembers him.

---

133 Sharat Kumar, 'Rajasthan rewrites history: Maharana Pratap, not Akbar, won Battle of Haldighati', *India Today*, Jaipur, 25 July 2017. Available at https://www.indiatoday.in/india/story/maharana-pratap-not-akbar-won-battle-of-haldighati-rajasthan-history-book-1026240-2017-07-25.

Chapter 7

Conquering India's Heart and Mind, and Uniting with Its Spirit

'Whatever imagination their intellect invents
God laughs at the intellect of people of that creed.'[1]

When Akbar returned to Fatehpur Sikri in 1575 from the conquest of Bengal, he carried with him a favourable impression of something that the late Sultan Sulaiman Kararani of Bengal used to do. That, coupled with his own inner churning, were manifested in a building that housed the first nursery of what is today called secularism in India. It was the *Ibadat Khana*.

Badaoni tells us how the emperor's soul was stirred by a spirit of inquiry for years and how he tried to find spiritual and intellectual solace in the teachings of the holy men, learned men, religious scholars and Sufi masters.

> For many years previously, the Emperor had gained in succession remarkable and decisive victories. The empire had grown in extent from day to day; everything turned out well, and no opponent was left

1 Abdul Qadir Badaoni, *Muntakhab-Ut-Tawarikh, Vol. II*, tr. W. H. Lowe (Calcutta: The Asiatic Society, 1884).

> in the whole world. His Majesty had thus leisure to come into nearer contact with ascetics and the disciples of his reverence (the late) Muin (Muinuddin Chishti or Garib Nawaz of Ajmer) and passed much of his time in discussing the Word of God and the word of the Prophet. Questions of Sufism, scientific discussions, enquiries into Philosophy and Law, were the order of the day. His Majesty spent whole nights in praising God: he continually occupied himself in pronouncing *Ya huwa,* and *Ya hadi* in which he was well-versed. His heart was full of reverence for Him, who is the true giver, and from a feeling of thankfulness for his past successes he would sit many a morning alone in prayer and meditation on a large flat stone of an old building which lay near the palace in a lonely spot, with his head bent over his chest, gathering the bliss of the early hours of dawn.[2]

Historian and–Professor Ali Nadeem Rezavi says that special assemblies or *mahzar* where religious discussions were held were known in pre-Mughal India.

> But they appear to have been confined to controversial topics within the predominant Hanafi school of thought. Themes like the legality of the mystic practice of *sama* were taken up in these special assemblies for discussion before declaring them as illegal. Such debates were the instruments of the orthodoxy to consolidate their sway over the dissenters.[3]

Professor Rezavi then contextualises Badaoni's statement on Akbar's religio-spiritual encounters in his book, *Fathpur Sikri Revisited*:

> We get evidence of religious assemblies (*majlis*) being held during the reign of Akbar as early as 1570. According to Bayazid Bayat, when Mirza Muflis, 'a scholar more distinguished than other *mullas* in the *ilm-i-mantiq* came to India, in an assembly organised by him, the Indian scholars like Makhdum ul Mulk Abdullah Sultanpuri and Shaikh Abdun Nabi posed awkward questions to him and ridiculed him.[4]

---

2 Ibid., p. 203.

3 Syed Ali Nadeem Rezavi, *Fathpur Sikri Revisited* (New Delhi: Oxford University Press, 2013), p. 72.

4 Ibid, p. 73.

Badaoni also mentioned the influence of the late Sultan of Bengal on Akbar's decision to build the *Ibadat Khana*:

> When then he (Akbar) heard that Sulaiman Kararani, governor of Bengal, used every night to offer up the prayers in the company of some 150 persons consisting of renowned Shaikhs and Ulema and used to remain in their society till morning listening to commentaries and exhortations, and then, after offering up the morning prayers, would occupy himself in state-business, and the affairs of the army, and of his subjects: and that he had his appointed time for everything and never broke through his good rule...[5]

A third reason, Badaoni says, was the impending visit of Mirza Sulaiman, the ruler of Balkh and Akbar's cousin, to the Mughal capital. Mirza Sulaiman was 'a prince of Sufi tendencies' who had already become a *Sahib-i-hal* and a *murid*.[6] Perhaps Akbar didn't want to be seen as someone who didn't have the adequate means to satiate the intellectual urges of his cousin while he was in India? Or maybe he didn't want to feel inferior to his cousin being the master of the bigger empire? It is anybody's guess. But the *Ibadat Khana* became a very unique experiment in improving the theological discourse. It was a bid to end conflicts among rival religions by creating a middle ground. To what extent it managed to achieve that objective is subject to debate, but it certainly had an impact on the Mughal state system and distanced it further and further from the church. This separation of the state from the church was a stellar achievement of Akbar's empire.

Badaoni says the building was constructed around what was once the room of Shaikh Abdullah Niyazi Sirhindi, a disciple of Shaikh Salim Chishti who later became a devotee of Lord Shiva.[7] That this whole journey of the *Ibadat Khana* began from the room of a Sufi who became a follower of Shiva makes it a very interesting beginning.

The building was completed in 1576. Initially, the discussions were held every Thursday evening among Muslim theologians. These

---

5 Badaoni, *Muntakhab, Vol. II*, p. 203.

6 Ibid., p. 204.

7 Ibid., p. 204.

sessions would at times run the course of the night. But despite that brilliant start, this practice was abandoned the same year. It resumed in 1578, and this time, scholars from all faiths were invited to participate.[8] Abu'l Fazl gives a list[9] of the faiths that were represented. There were Sunnis, Shias, Brahmins, Jains,[10] Charvakas,[11] Christians,[12] Jews, Sabians,[13] Zoroastrians and others.

This meeting of different minds and ideas pushed the Mughal state further and further away from the church. The process began with the state massively withdrawing its patronage of the orthodoxy.[14] This led Badaoni to even accuse the emperor of turning against his own faith and creed. He mentions the arrival of a Persian Shia scholar named Mullah Muhammad Yazidi at the *Ibadat Khana* where he pooh-poohed the *sahaba* (companions of the Prophet) by telling Akbar strange stories about them. He did all this to turn Akbar into a Shia, Badaoni alleges.[15]

Badoni mentions:

> But he was soon left behind by Bir Bar[16]—that bastard!—and by Shaikh Abu'l Fazl, and Hakim Abu-l-Fath, who successfully turned the Emperor from Islam, and led him to reject inspiration, prophetship, the miracles of the Prophet and of the saints, and even the whole law, so that I could no longer bear their company.[17]

Badaoni's frustration is that of every bigot's when surrounded by liberals and progressives. Anyone who is in India today and active on

8 Rezavi, *Fathpur Sikri Revisited*, p. 75.

9 Abu'l Fazl, *Akbarnama, Vol. III*, p. 365.

10 The terms used for them are *Jatis* (*Yatis*) who were monks and *Siuras* (*seweras*).

11 An ancient school of Indian philosophy that represents *nastikas* or atheists within Hinduism.

12 The term used for them is Nazarene or followers of Jesus of Nazareth.

13 Identified in Islam as *Ahl al-Kitab* or 'people of the book' along with Jews and Christians. They are believed to be followers of John the Baptist and today known as Mandaeans.

14 Rezavi, *Fathpur Sikri Revisited*, p. 76.

15 Badaoni, *Muntakhab*, *Vol. II*, p. 214.

16 Popularly known to us as Birbal, the wisecrack.

17 Badaoni, *Muntakhab*, *Vol. II*, p. 214.

social media will understand this. Ever since the Hindu nationalist government of Narendra Modi came to power, all kinds of bigots have felt emboldened. They detest liberal and progressive voices and try to shut them down with vile abuse. At times, the simple term 'trolling' that is used universally is applied to explain such bigotry.

But overwhelmingly, in India's case, it's really anti-Muslim bigotry that's on display. And just like Badaoni calls Birbal a 'bastard' and also a 'dog' elsewhere, reflecting his hate, we now have the BJP leaders[18] and even Indian government ministers[19] obliquely refer to people and groups they oppose or detest as *haramzade*, the Hindustani word for 'bastard' that Badaoni had also used.

What emerges from Badaoni's writing is that Akbar asked several Ulema to write a commentary on the Quran, 'which led to several dissentions among them'. That means there was debate and disagreement. Even Hindus joined in this debate. Badaoni writes[20]:

> Deb Chand Rajah Manjholah—that fool!—once set the whole Court in laughter by saying that Allah after all had great respect for cows, else the cow would not have been mentioned in the first chapter[21] in the Quran.

The Raja's comment shows the freedom to express opinion on Islam even by a non-Muslim in Akbar's court—a remarkable thing to have in the 16th century. But it also shows a caste Hindu's prejudices vis-à-vis the cow.

The cow is the most political animal in India. The current Hindutva regime has overtly or covertly tried to put a stop to consumption of beef across the country. Every time there is an executive move to

---

18 Indo Asian News Service, 'Fight between "Ramzada" and "Haramzada" in Bengal: BJP's Dilip Ghosh', Kolkata, *NewsX*, 6 April 2017. Available at https://www.newsx.com/national/60565-fight-between-ramzada-and-haramzada-in-bengal-bjps-dilip-ghosh.

19 Express News Service, 'Ramzada vs haramzada: Outrage over Union Minister Sadhvi's remark', New Delhi, *The Indian Express*, 2 December 2014. Available at https://indianexpress.com/article/india/india-others/union-minister-spells-out-choice-in-delhi-ramzada-vs-haramzada.

20 Badaoni, *Muntakhab*, *Vol. II*, p. 215.

21 Actually, it's the second chapter, the *Surah al-Baqara*, which is also the longest *surah* in the Quran.

discourage beef eating, resistance comes from opposition parties as well as intellectuals and other progressives. The liberal view that beef shouldn't be banned is often countered by conservative voices, both Muslim and Hindu, who suggest that even the Prophet didn't eat beef as he believed that cow meat could make one fall sick while its milk could cure and heal.[22] Current finance minister, Nirmala Sitharaman, had even gone to the extent to claim that cow protectionism was the spirit behind the Freedom Movement.[23] This author had rebutted that claim in an article and illustrated how trouble and not freedom had come riding on a cow in India.[24]

But even though Badaoni complains that it were the others who were leading the emperor away from Islam, Akbar himself was questioning and doubting the established notions, the dogmas and the teachings. Badaoni says:

> His Majesty also had the early history of Islam read out to him, and soon began to think less of the *sahaba*. Soon after, the observance of the five prayers, and the fasts (*rozas* of Ramzan), and the belief in everything connected with the Prophet, were put down as vain superstitions, and man's reason, not tradition, was acknowledged as the only basis of religion.[25]

Badaoni's lament was the reason for India's delight. That a 16th-century emperor could put reason ahead of tradition and want religion to be rooted in reason isn't something that one comes across frequently in the pages of history. In fact, today's India with all its material advancements is led by a regime that really promotes

---

22 K. G. Suresh, 'Eating beef not an Islamic ritual', New Delhi, *The Pioneer*, 22 December 2015. Available at https://www.dailypioneer.com/2015/columnists/eating-beef-not-an-islamic-ritual.html.

23 Press Trust of India, 'Cow protectionism was the spirit behind Freedom Movement, says Nirmala Sitharaman', New Delhi, *Huffington Post*, 6 April 2017. Available at https://www.huffingtonpost.in/2017/04/05/cow-protectionism-was-the-spirit-behind-freedom-movement-says-n_a_22027899/.

24 Manimugdha S. Sharma, 'Freedom didn't come riding on a cow, trouble did', New Delhi, *The Times of India*, 10 April 2017. Available at https://timesofindia.indiatimes.com/blogs/parthian-shot/freedom-didnt-come-riding-on-a-cow-trouble-did/.

25 Badaoni, *Muntakhab*, *Vol. II*, p. 215.

unreason and is pretty much dogmatic in its approach to religion. It is a country where the leader, Prime Minister Narendra Modi, peddles quackery in the name of science, making dubious claims about stem cell technology existing in ancient India when the great epics were written. While there cannot be a direct comparison, but still, a 16th-century monarch looking like the better man in stark contrast to a 21st-century democratically elected leader is actually terrible news for the India of today. It just shows that the conversation that Akbar started was not carried forward.

But while talking about Akbar's rationality, it is important to understand that his rationality was very Indian and not European as is generally understood.

Historian and Professor Harbans Mukhia described it perfectly in a personal conversation with me sometime ago:

> The times have certainly changed, but certain continuities have remained. Akbar's rationality, and also of Abu'l Fazl, is very important to understand. Because when you utter the word 'rationality', you generally pit it against religion and religiosity. That's what post-Renaissance Europe had seen: rationality taking over from religion and religiosity. So, that idea of rationality is very European. Akbar is also seen to be rational in that way, but I think Akbar's rationality is deeply rooted in religiosity. It's a different kind of rationality, very indigenous, very Indian. It's the rationality of giving everyone equal rights, non-discriminatory rights.[26]

Professor Mukhia argued that Akbar and Abu'l Fazl's idea of *tauhid* or monotheism was rooted in Kabir's idea of it.

> Kabir re-interpreted *tauhid*. And there's a fundamental shift in thinking that comes with Kabir. Earlier, *tauhid* was being interpreted within the confines of Islam. But Kabir broke out of it and reinterpreted it for Islam and Hinduism. So, his *tauhid* was both exclusive and inclusive of all religions. And from here arises the concept of a universal god, which is fundamental to Akbar's thinking. It was no longer your god and my god, but it became everyone's god. And this understanding that we got

26 Author's personal conversation with the historian on 8 January 2019, after most of the book was ready.

> from Kabir and Akbar has stayed with us until today. So, when we sing *Ishwar Allah tero naam, sabko sanmati de bhagwan*[27] we are referring to Kabir's and Akbar's thinking. Because they were the first to think that Ishwar and Allah are not rivals, they are one.[28]

So, from a modern perspective, how does this look like? 'What can be more modern than giving equal rights to people?' Professor Mukhia said.

Badaoni, of course, didn't see the future, nor did he have the benefit of hindsight, as we do today. He was mostly fretting and fuming over the emperor's heresies. He writes about an incident in court when Akbar sought the opinion of his courtiers about adding 'Allahu Akbar' to the imperial seal and coinage. The darbaris mostly nodded, save one Haji Ibrahim who objected on the grounds that Allahu Akbar was ambiguous and might imply that Akbar is god, which is sacrilege. He suggested an alternative phrase, *La-zikrullahi Akbaru* (to commemorate god is the greatest thing). Akbar was entirely displeased at this. He argued that no man would claim divinity so there was no question of people misunderstanding it and distorting the context.[29]

As I have argued earlier, this was another instance of Akbar basking in the glory of a Quranic phrase that became ambiguous when used in his case due to his name. But at the same time, it would be wrong to assume that Akbar was delusional to think that he was god. As Professor Mukhia's explanation makes it clear, Akbar was a rational man who believed in a universal god. But being a powerful emperor who ruled by divine right, this ambiguity was a very useful ally, a kind of propaganda.

That's not to say that whatever he did was mostly propaganda. His pursuits were genuine and varied. And he wanted peace and amity among his subjects. But Akbar would multiply efforts to rise above the

---

27 A line from the *bhajan* or Ram *dhun, Raghupati Raghav Raja Ram,* that was popularised by Mahatma Gandhi, starting from the Dandi March or Salt Satyagraha of 1930.

28 Author's conversation with the historian.

29 Badaoni, *Muntakhab, Vol. II*, p. 213.

clergy and unite his subjects around his person, and the resistance to his efforts would also multiply.

In 1579, Akbar began a process by which he tried to unite in him the spiritual and temporal spheres. The move was more political than religious or social: Akbar didn't want to be fettered by the ulema in exercising absolute power. Badaoni recognises it when he writes that the emperor 'held it to be an insufferable burden to subordinate to anyone'.[30]

On 26 June that year, at the mosque at Fatehpur Sikri, Akbar climbed on the pulpit to lead the Friday prayers. Badaoni says that Akbar had heard that the Prophet had done it before, and his great ancestors Amir Timur and Mirza Ulugh Beg had also read the *khutba* all by themselves before. So, he had a precedent to follow. The objective really was, as Badaoni rightly understands, to portray himself publicly as the *mujtahid*[31] of the age.

This first religious sermon turned out to be a disaster. Badaoni says:

> His Majesty began to read the *khutba*. But all at once he stammered and trembled, and though assisted by others, he could scarcely read three verses of a poem, which Shaikh Faizi (Abu'l Fazl's elder brother) had composed, but came quickly down from the pulpit, and handed over the duties of Imam to Hafiz Muhammad Amin, the court *khatib*.

So, Amin completed the prayer service. The lines of the *khutba* have been given both by Badaoni and Abu'l Fazl:

> The Lord, who gave to us sovereignty,
> Who gave us a wise heart, and a strong hand,
> Who guided us in equity and justice,
> And drove from our thoughts all save equity,
> His description is higher than the range of thought,
> Exalted is His Majesty, Allahu Akbar![32]

---

30 Ibid., p. 276.

31 A person recognised as an original authority of Islamic law.

32 Badaoni, *Muntakhab, Vol. II*, p. 277.

By September 1579, Akbar had sanction from those in his circle of influence, including the leading ulema, to proclaim what is often called, albeit incorrectly, the 'Infallibility Decree'[33], but what was actually the *mahzar* or *mahzar-nama*. This made Akbar the *Imam-i-Adil* (also *Sultan-i-Adil*) or the final interpreter of Islam and Islamic laws, and also *Amir ul-Mu'minin* or 'commander of the faithful', a title often used for the Caliph of Islam, who was the Ottoman Sultan in Akbar's time. With this step, Akbar was also posing a direct challenge to the Ottoman leadership of the Sunnis while, at the same time, announcing a resounding break from the influence of the Safavid Empire whose deputy (*padishah amir*) had been Babur.[34] This challenge to Ottoman leadership became the reason why the Indian Muslims never bothered about the Ottoman Caliph. This was also the reason why Muslim soldiery of the Indian Army had no qualms about going to war against the Ottoman Empire during the First World War.

But at the time of the proclamation of the decree, it was heresy for the orthodox class. They interpreted it as Akbar wishing to equate himself with the Prophet of Islam. What that led to can be gauged from Abu'l Fazl's words:

> There was a market day for liars and falsifiers. Some of the heated fanatics of the desert of destruction said that the Prince of the Age (Akbar) wished to claim to be the prophet of the incomparable Deity. The proof of this imagination of the strife-mongers was that the Shahinshah was continually introducing noble laws, and making verdant the parterres of realm and religion, and pointing out the discrepancies in the doubtful expressions of the ancients. Bewildered hearts and short-sighted persons indulged in these thoughts, and the spectacle of his reciting the *khutba* contrary to custom and his mounting the pulpit for the guidance of mankind helped the delusion. Many from acceptance of hearsay and

33 For the text of the document, see Blochmann's translation of Abu'l Fazl's *Ain-i-Akbari, Vol. I,* pp. 186–87.

34 F. Buckler, 'A New Interpretation of Akbar's 'Infallibility' Decree of 1579', *Journal of the Royal Asiatic Society of Great Britain and Ireland* 4, 1924, pp. 591–608. Retrieved from http://www.jstor.org/stable/25220577.

> belief in idle words came to believe this. Thus, there was a splendid market for strife-mongering and fabrication.[35]

When Akbar heard these rumours, he supposedly expressed disbelief. Akbar said[36]:

> How could it enter into the narrow thoughts of the ignorant that recent creatures belonging to a dependent existence and of feeble intellect should ascribe to themselves a share in Divinity? And have the leaders of humanity who have by thousands of miracles expounded the prophetic office come into the world, and have cycles elapsed, that an opinion like this should be cherished and increase, and that the dust of unbelief be not yet laid? How could such a notion come into my mind? Why does such an evil thought bewilder the superficial and the worshippers of externals? Inasmuch as censure and reproach give a fresh lustre to hearts which are pure, it would be improper to reprove those black-thoughted ones who cause an increase of light.

Akbar's comment gives credence to what Professor Mukhia said earlier and this author also argued about his faith in a universal god. But Akbar's strong retort, and Abu'l Fazl's continuous use of strong language to rubbish the rumours suggests that the opposition was very serious. Fazl mentions the kind of accusations levelled at the emperor:

> A set of evil-thoughted, shameless ones imagined that the Prince of horizons (Akbar) regarded with disfavour the Muhammadan religion (*din-i-Ahmadi*). The sole evidence which those wrong-headed wicked ones, whose understanding was rusted, had for this was that the wise sovereign out of his tolerant disposition and general benevolence, and extensive overshadowing, received all clauses of mankind with affection. Especially did he search for evidence in religious matters from the sages of every religion and the ascetics of all faiths. Nor did he accept replies of the headstrong and uninquiring. Above all, at this time, Christian philosophers assailed the orthodox of the day in the sublime assemblies (at the *Ibadat Khana*), and learned discussions were carried on. The

35 Abu'l Fazl, *Akbarnama, Vol. III*, pp. 397–98.

36 Ibid., p 398.

> calumniators of the enlightened who by pretences had claimed for themselves a learning that did not exist, made a clamour in the court for sovereignty. They were put to shame in the daily market of justice and the heyday of discrimination, and lowered their heads into the folds of ignorance, but in the privy chambers of darkness they joined their confederates in the cry that they were mourning the loss of Faith (Islam), and that the king of the Age (Akbar) had, out of partiality, not accepted their replies...A set of squint-eyed, wicked people taxed him with Shiism; and so led astray simple-minded Sunnis...The favour shown to Persians, most of whom belonged to that sect (Shia), increased the evil thoughts of the turbulent...An impure faction reproached the caravan-leader of God-knowers (Akbar) with being of the Hindu (Brahmin) religion. The ground for this improper notion was that the prince out of his wide tolerance received Hindu sages into his intimacy, and increased for administrative reasons the rank of Hindus, and for the good of the country showed them kindness.[37]

Fazl identified three broad reasons why the Muslim orthodoxy found Akbar's conduct an attack on Islam:

> First—the sages of different religions assembled at court, and as every religion has some good in it, each received some praise. From a spirit of justice, the badness of any sect could not weave a veil over its merits. Second—the season of 'peace with all' (*sulh-i-kul*) was honoured at the court of the Caliphate (Akbar's court and not Ottoman), and various tribes of mankind of various natures obtained spiritual and material success. Third—the evil nature and crooked ways of the base ones of the age.[38]

What's clear from this is that the main reason why the orthodox groups were unhappy is that Akbar was courting people of different faiths and listening to diverse opinions. There were certainly exceptions, but largely, Muslim rulers in the past wouldn't court people of diverse faiths and try to find essence of good in different faiths other than their own. Akbar was disrupting that norm and that was unsettling for the hardliners. So, their reasoning implied that

37 Ibid., pp. 398–400.

38 Ibid., p. 400.

if Akbar was for other faiths, he must be against his own. And if he was criticising a few things about Islam, he must be out to insult the religion. And because he was criticising certain tenets of Islam, he must, therefore, be a Hindu, a *kafir* or infidel.

We see similar arguments put forward today by hardliners. When tennis star, Sania Mirza, became the first Indian woman to reach the fourth round of a grand slam—the US Open—in 2005, she was attacked by the Islamic hardliners for her sports attire that bared her midriff and legs. She was accused of being a bad role model for Muslim youth for wearing 'un-Islamic' clothing and slapped with a series of *fatwas.*[39]

Things didn't change much even over a decade later when Indian pacer Mohammed Shami was attacked for his wife's 'un-Islamic' attire when he shared a photograph of them online in which she was wearing a sleeveless gown. There was a *fatwa* against him and a battery of bigots trolled him massively on social media.[40]

In 2015, music maestro A. R. Rahman was issued a *fatwa* for scoring music for a film by Iranian director Majid Majidi on the Prophet.[41] In 2013, actor and filmmaker Kamal Hasan had been attacked by Hindu and Muslim hardliners for his film *Vishwaroopam*, which the Hindus disliked for using a Sanskrit name instead of a Tamil one and the Muslims disliked for allegedly showing the community in bad light.[42] In 2017, Hindu fundamentalist outfits announced a ₹ 5-crore bounty on the heads of Bollywood star, Deepika Padukone, and director, Sanjay Leela Bhansali—and Bhansali was also physically

39 Associated Press, 'Mirza responds to Muslim criticism of how she dresses', New Delhi, *ESPN.com*, 17 November 2005. Available at http://www.espn.com/sports/tennis/news/story?id=2227000.

40 India Today Web Desk, 'Twitter rises to defend Mohammed Shami, wife after Muslim fanatics trolled him on Facebook over wife's attire', New Delhi, *India Today*, 26 December 2016. Available at https://www.indiatoday.in/fyi/story/mohammed-shami-wife-dress-facebook-photo-muslim-fanatics-troll-359493-2016-12-26.

41 BBC, 'India's AR Rahman responds to "fatwa" on Muhammad film', 15 September 2015. Available at https://www.bbc.com/news/world-asia-india-34254541.

42 Ibid.

attacked—over the movie *Padmavati*, which was eventually released as *Padmaavat*.[43]

In the politically charged environment in India today, where right-wing bigotry is on full display and critics of the BJP, RSS (Rashtriya Swayamsevak Sangh) and other saffron groups are often portrayed as anti-Hindu and anti-national, Akbar's predicament makes sense. This author has first-hand experience of this as he is often branded an anti-Hindu and accused of being a Muslim masquerading as a Hindu whenever he criticises Hindu nationalism, which is really Hindu communalism, the saffron outfits, Narendra Modi and his government. That is largely because this author is seen, and rightly so, as someone who is against the growing majoritarianism in India and who stands up for Muslims whenever they are attacked, their faith insulted, and their patriotism and loyalty to India is questioned. This seems to be a standard template followed by the foot soldiers of Hindutva to de-legitimise and dehumanise Hindus who speak out against their hateful ideology and speak up for the minorities. This was also the template followed by Akbar's orthodox opponents who accused him of *kufr* or infidelity to his faith, by claiming that he had shunned Islam and accepted Hinduism.

Badaoni, however, mixes up the chronology a bit and merges criticism of the later *Din-i-Illahi* with that of the *mahzar*, as is apparent to any reader (he realises this himself as later on in the text, he apologises to the reader for not observing a 'strictly chronological order'). Renowned historian, Professor Irfan Habib, had told me during a visit to Aligarh Muslim University last year that Akbar had stopped using Muhammad in his name, becoming Jalaluddin Akbar instead of Jalaluddin Muhammad Akbar (though he kept using it off and on). We get a hint of it when Badaoni writes his lament:

> And in these days, when reproach began to spread upon the doctrines of Islam, and all questions relating thereto, and ever so many wretches

---

43 *Deccan Chronicle*, "Padmavati: Rs 5 crores bounty on Deepika, Bhansali's heads, announce outfits", Mumbai, 17 November 2017. Available at https://www.deccanchronicle.com/entertainment/bollywood/171117/padmavati-outfits-announce-rs-5-crores-bounty-on-deepika-bhansalis-heads.html.

> of Hindus and Hinduizing *Musalmans* brought unmitigated reviling against the Prophet, and the villainously irreligious *Ulema* in their works pronounced the Emperor to be without sin, and contenting themselves with mentioning the unity of God, they next wrote down the various titles of the Emperor, and had not the courage to mention the name of the Prophet (God be gracious to him and his family, and give them peace in defiance of the liars!)...[44]

Badaoni is even more specific when he writes:

> Names like Ahmad, Muhammad, Mustafa, etc. became offensive to His Majesty, who thereby wished to please the infidels outside and the (Hindu) princesses inside the harem, till after some time those courtiers, who had such names, changed them, and as such, names as Yar Muhammad, Muhammad Khan, were altered to Rahmat.[45]

It appears from Badaoni's lines that many of his courtiers and imperial officers acquiesced to the emperor's whim. Badaoni calls them 'pigs' who didn't deserve the 'jewel', i.e. the Prophet's name.

Badaoni also laments about the *ulema* signing the *mahzar* and ending all scope of challenging the emperor's word on matters of faith and law.

> No sooner had His Majesty obtained this legal document (*mahzar*), then the road of deciding any religious question was open; the superiority of the intellect of the Imam (Akbar) was established, and opposition was rendered impossible. All orders regarding things which our law allows and disallows were abolished, and the superiority of the intellect of the Imam became law. They called Islam a travesty.[46]

Badaoni also tells us that the emperor even came up with a new *kalma*[47]:

---

44 Badaoni, *Muntakhab*, *Vol. II*, p. 277.

45 Ibid., p. 324.

46 Ibid., p. 280.

47 One of the dogmas of Islam. It goes '*la Illaha illallah, Muhammadun Rasool* Allah', or 'no God whatsoever but Allah, Muhammad is the Prophet of Allah'.

> His Majesty had now determined publicly to use the formula. 'There is no God but God and Akbar is God's representative.' But as this led to commotions, he thought better of it, and restricted the use of the formula to a few people in the harem.[48]

Badaoni was particularly miffed with Shaikh Abdun Nabi, the *sadr-us-sudur*, and Makhdum-ul-Mulk, who were both orthodox in their religious beliefs but who went along with the emperor. So, he heaped a mountain of allegations at their doorstep.

> ...Makhdum-ul-Mulk and Shaikh Abdun Nabi tempted mankind by suggesting the forgery of the Quran, and by going out of the way to show the impossibility of inspiration, and by throwing doubts on the authority of prophets and Imams, and utterly denying the existence of demons and angels, and all mysteries and signs and miracles. Also the integrity of the traditional text of the Quran and its verbal authority, and existence of the soul after the dissolution of the body, and reward and punishment other than by means of transmigration they deemed impossible....[49]

Badaoni then alludes to the revolt among the orthodoxy to this heresy by the emperor but, unlike Abu'l Fazl, blames it on Akbar's move, which he calls a 'general disgrace'.

> ...this matter became the cause of general disgrace, and the seeds of depravity and disturbance began to lift their heads in the empire. Besides this base and low men of the higher and lower classes, having accepted the collar of spiritual obedience upon their necks[50], professed themselves his disciples. They became disciples through the motives of hope and fear, and the word of truth could not proceed out of their mouths.[51]

It's important to note that Badaoni's criticism was the reflection of a general assumption that Akbar was hostile to Islam. Akbar seems to have discouraged the offering of *namaz* and had the support of his

---

48 Badaoni, *Muntakhab, Vol. II*, p. 281.

49 Ibid.

50 The analogy used is that of a dog with a collar that's controlled by its master. So, Badaoni really berates the followers of Akbar's spiritual word as his dogs.

51 Badaoni, *Muntakhab, Vol. II*, p. 277.

most loyal and closest supporters in this. Badaoni writes, 'During those days also, the public prayers, and thc *azaan*, which was chanted five times a day for assembly to prayer in the state hall, were abolished.'[52] Those following the orthodox diktats of Islams were really mocked at by the emperor and his confidants. Akbar, while holding full court, and in the presence of clerics and theologians, mocked and rubbished Quranic traditions and the hadiths. Badaoni cites a particular example that he found revolting, and could infuriate any orthodox believer of Islam even today:

> One night, the Emperor, in (Shah) Fathullah's presence, said to Bir Bar, 'I really wonder how anyone in his senses can believe that a man (in this case, the Prophet), whose body has a certain weight, could in the space of a moment leave his bed, go up to heaven, there have 90,000 conversations with God, and yet on his return find his bed still warm! (Badaoni is referring to the *meraj* tradition).' So also was the splitting of the moon (another Quranic tradition) ridiculed. 'Why,' said His Majesty, lifting up one foot, 'it is really impossible for me to lift up the other. What silly stories men will believe!' and that wretch (Birbal) and some other wretches—whose names be forgotten—said 'Yea, Your Majesty is right,' and chirped in confirmation.[53]

This is often the charge against liberals too in modern times: that they mock and insult those who are religious, and don't think twice before pooh-poohing beliefs and matters of faith that really hurt sentiments. In India, increasingly, members of the Hindu right make this charge that liberals and left-leaning individuals always insult Hinduism. This is often an exaggerated claim, no doubt, but there are some liberals who behave that way, and therefore, there is a grain of truth in this charge.

But Akbar's was much more than mere mocking: he seems to have really made an attempt to close down mosques and prohibit *namaz*. Badaoni writes that 'mosques and prayer rooms were changed into store-rooms and into Hindu guard-rooms'.[54] Some historians say all

52 Ibid., p. 324.

53 Ibid., p. 326.

54 Ibid., p. 332.

this is Badaoni's exaggeration. But Professor Iqtidar Alam Khan says Badaoni's words can't be dismissed. He analyses a *firman* of Prince Salim during his rebellion of 1601. The text reads:

> At the instigation of some mischievous persons, my father has abolished the arrangements of *khatib*, muezzin, and *imam* in the mosques and has prohibited the performance of *namaz* in congregation. He has converted many of the mosques into store-houses and stables....'[55]

Another evidence cited is a story by Abdul Baqi Nahavandi in *Maasir-i-Rahimi*.

> He reports that after Daniyal's appointment to the newly conquered *subah* of Deccan and Khandesh (1601), Akbar had written to him ordering him to destroy the *jama masjid* at Asirgarh 'and raise (in its place) a temple on the pattern of Hindus and (other) infidels of Hindustan.[56]

But Daniyal apparently refused to carry out the order. There is another evidence that Professor Iqtidar Alam cites, which is a 1591 letter by Prince Murad to Akbar, asking what he should do if he finds people in his camp performing prayers like Islamic theologians.

> Akbar's response suggests that a person performing *namaz* was considered deserving 'admonition' (*nasihat*) by his superior so as to 'help' him to come 'to the path of reason (*raah-i-aql*)'. But Murad is also warned that such a person is not to be forced to abandon his rites of worship, as this would amount to violation of *sulh-i-kul*.[57]

Whatever may have been the intensity of Akbar's dislike for orthodox Islam, it didn't stay very long, and 'there were no signs of widespread discontent against his policies among Muslims as well as among a

55 Iqtidar Alam Khan, 'Akbar's personality traits and world outlook: A critical reappraisal', in *Akbar and his India,* edited by Irfan Habib. (New Delhi: Oxford University Press, 1997), pp. 93–4.

56 Ibid.

57 Ibid., p. 95.

majority of orthodox theologians'.[58] But what is remarkable is that Akbar advised his officers to guide people to follow the path of reason but not force them into it. This author is reminded of a 2015 conversation he had with Janak Dave, the director of BAPS Research Institute, the Swaminarayan Akshardham Temple in Delhi, when he had recited a few lines from the *Bhagavad Gita* and interpreted that Lord Krishna had told Arjuna that he had shown the path, but it was really up to him to make the choice.[59]

The *mahzar* triggered a revolt among Mughal officers in Bengal and Bihar. They swore loyalty to Mirza Muhammad Hakim of Kabul, Akbar's half-brother and rival. This led to another round of expeditions into Bengal and Bihar, but Akbar didn't lead these personally, relying instead on his loyal commanders and allies (Koch Behar King Nara Narayan's fleet buttressing the imperial fleet in Bengal has been mentioned in the previous chapter). The revolt was crushed and not with great difficulty. Buckler argues that Akbar now had overwhelming support of the Hindu nobles who were powerful kings themselves.

Akbar's engagement with non-Muslim religious heads and preachers wasn't ephemeral; it lasted till the very end of his life, and after his death, his son continued the relationship that the Mughal state had established with them. Akbar had the greatest reverence for the Jain monks, whom he courted very often, and followed their advice and honoured their requests. The most prominent Jain monks whom Akbar courted were the Svetambara monks Hiravijaya Suri, Vijaya Sen Suri and Bhanu Chandra Upadhyaya. So strong was their influence on Akbar that Jain sources say that they even convinced him to ban slaughter of animals during the 12 days of the Jain Paryushan festival—a fact corroborated by at least two *firmans* dated 1584 and

58 Ibid., p. 96.

59 Manimugdha S. Sharma, 'At Akshardham, capital's own boat trip back to the Vedic Age', New Delhi, *The Times of India*, 11 January 2015. Available at https://timesofindia.indiatimes.com/city/delhi/At-Akshardham-capitals-own-boat-trip-back-to-the-Vedic-Age/articleshow/45838735.cms.

1587—and even convinced the emperor about the need to prohibit cow slaughter.[60]

Various state governments in Independent India at various times have also tried what Akbar did, always giving Akbar's example as a historical precedent. The Supreme Court of India also acknowledged this in a judgment in 2008 while hearing a special leave petition against a meat ban imposed by the Gujarat government and Ahmedabad Municipal Corporation. Calling Akbar the 'architect of modern India', the bench of Justice H. Sema and Justice Markandey Katju observed: 'If the Emperor Akbar could forbid meat eating for six months in a year in Gujarat, is it unreasonable to abstain from meat for nine days in a year in Ahmedabad today?'[61]

More recently, several BJP governments in the states implemented meat bans during Jain festivals after they came to power 2014 onwards. Maharashtra took the lead in 2015 to ban the slaughter of birds and animals and sale of meat during the Paryushan festival following a request by a Jain body.[62] There was a lot of protest against this ban, which was ultimately stayed by the Bombay high court. Rajasthan, Chhattisgarh, Gujarat and Haryana followed suit, drawing heavy criticism from opposition parties and ordinary citizens. The medieval impulse of this ban was quite apparent: what a 16th-century Indian emperor had done was being replicated in a democratic country in the 21st century without consulting the stakeholders. While Akbar's ban is acknowledged by the Jains even today, and reams have been written about it in the mainstream press,[63] making it unlikely that those who

---

60 Pushpa Prasad, 'Akbar and the Jains', in *Akbar and his India* edited by Irfan Habib (New Delhi: Oxford University Press, 1997), pp. 97–108.

61 Supreme Court of India, 'Hinsa Virodhak Sangh vs Mirzapur Moti Kuresh Jamat & Ors on 14 March, 2008'. Verdict courtesy Indian Kanoon. Available at https://indiankanoon.org/doc/560071/?type=print.

62 Richa Pinto, 'No slaughter, sale of meat on four days of Paryushan', Mumbai, *The Times of India*, 8 September 2015. Available at https://timesofindia.indiatimes.com/city/mumbai/No-slaughter-sale-of-meat-on-four-days-of-Paryushan/articleshow/48861286.cms.

63 Ashish Vashi, 'Ahmedabad turned Akbar Veggie', Ahmedabad, *The Times of India*, 23 November 2009. Available at https://timesofindia.indiatimes.com/city/ahmedabad/Ahmedabad-turned-Akbar-veggie/articleshow/5259184.cms.

implemented the ban in Maharashtra and elsewhere didn't know about this legacy, the saffron authorities missed an important detail in Akbar's *firman*: he wanted it banned only in those areas where Jains were concentrated. Despite being a medieval despot, Akbar appears more sensible than the rulers of today.

But Akbar wasn't just issuing mere homilies to keep the Jains happy, he was also implementing certain things in his own life and across the empire. Badaoni gives the details:

> Killing of animals on the first day of the week (Sunday) was strictly prohibited, because this day is sacred to the Sun; also during the first eighteen days of the month of *Farwardin*; the whole of the month of *Aban* (the month in which His Majesty was born); and on several other days to please the Hindus. This order was extended over the whole realm and punishment was inflicted on everyone who acted against the command: and his property was confiscated. During the time of these fasts, the Emperor abstained altogether from meat, as a religious penance, gradually extending the several fasts during a year over six months and even more, with a view to eventually discontinuing the use of meat altogether.[64]

The emperor conferred on Hiravijaya Suri the title of '*Jagad* Guru', and also gave the title of *Khwushfahm* (a man of sharp intellect) to his successor, Vijaya Sen Suri.[65] To Bhanu Chandra, he gave the title *Upadhyaya*. Bhanu Chandra had the maximum influence on the emperor, even accompanying him on a mission to Kashmir. He wrote a commentary in Sanskrit on the thousand names of the sun and taught Akbar their significance. Akbar supposedly chanted the thousand names of the sun with great devotion.[66]

Badaoni also refers to this and offers a neater glimpse of Akbar's sun worshipping ways and observation of Hindu rituals.

> A second order was given (in 1583) that the sun should be worshipped four times a day, in the morning and evening, and at noon and midnight.

---

64 Badaoni, *Muntakhab*, *Vol. II*, p. 331.

65 Pushpa Prasad, 'Akbar and the Jains', pp. 97–108.

66 Ibid.

> His Majesty had also one thousand and one Sanskrit names for the sun collected and read them daily at noon, devoutly turning towards the sun; he then used to get hold of both ears, and turning himself quickly round about, used to strike the lower ends of his ears with his fists. He also adopted several other practices connected with sun worship. He used to wear the Hindu mark on his forehead (a *tilak* or talisman) and ordered the band to play at midnight and at the break of day.[67]

One day when Bhanu Chandra was late for court, and Akbar learnt from him that this was because his residence was far away, he gave a plot of land within the Lahore Fort for the Jains to build a magnificent temple of Jain *tirthankara*, Shantinath, and also lodgings.[68] And when Salim's daughter fell ill, Bhanu Chandra also performed a ceremony at the temple with both the emperor and Prince Salim standing in front of the Jaina idol, listening to the hymn chanted in the honour of Adinatha. At the end of it, Akbar washed his eyes with the holy water and passed it on to his harem,[69] just like a Jain patron would have done. In this author's family, Lakshmi Puja is performed a few days after *Vijaya Dashami* where, among many things, coconut water is offered to the goddess. After the puja gets over, the head of the family washes his or her eyes with the coconut water and passes it on to the rest of the family members. The practice seems to be similar.

In 1590, Akbar issued a long *firman* whereby he ordered his officials to extend full tolerance to the Jains.[70] In 1601, he followed it up with another comprehensive *firman*, reconfirming all the guarantees and privileges granted to the Jains.[71] It is no surprise, therefore, that Akbar was a hero for the Jains. The biography of Bhanu Chandra by his disciple Siddhi Chandra is very kind to Akbar.

> There is not a single art, not a single branch of knowledge, not a single act of boldness and strength which was not attempted by the young Akbar…

---

67 Badaoni, *Muntakhab, Vol. II*, p. 332.

68 Pushpa Prasad, 'Akbar and the Jains', pp. 97–108.

69 Ibid.

70 Ibid.

71 Ibid.

> Thieves and robbers were conspicuous by their absence in his empire. His glory was as white as the moon because he had defeated all his enemies. His religious fervour never made him intolerant as is shown by his degree of regard for all the six systems of learning...[72]

Most interestingly, Akbar is also compared to the 'son of Kaushalya'—Lord Rama—in this account.[73] So, the Rajputs weren't the only ones to refer to Akbar as an avatar of Vishnu and compare him to Lord Rama and Lord Krishna.[74]

Akbar also ordered Hindu holy books and other literature translated into Persian. This was a grand project involving the leading scholars of the time, both Hindu and Muslim. And even the bigoted Badaoni was made part of the two biggest works of translation ever undertaken in the Mughal court—translating the Mahabharata and Ramayana into Persian. Some other translations were the *Atharvaveda*, *Rajatarangini*, *Nala-Damayanti*, *Yogavashishta*, *Harivamsa*, *Lilavati*, *Panchatantra* and the *Simhasana Dvatrimsika*, more popularly known today as *Simhasan Battisi*. But it were really the *Mahabharata* and *Ramayana* that were the grandest translation projects of Akbar.

That one of the translators was Badaoni is actually a comment on Akbar's ability to get work out of people he disagreed with, and to recognise and honour talent by ignoring the surround sound. Despite knowing that Badaoni was a bigot, Akbar reposed faith in his ability to play fair and do justice to the job. Badaoni, though, referred to the *Mahabharata* as a 'stock of useless fables'.

Akbar took a more than personal interest in the translation, involving himself in listening to the commentaries on the text by the Hindu scholars and then explaining all that to the Muslim translators who really translated the *Hindustani* explainers that the Hindu Sanskrit scholars prepared. He was so immersed in it that he perceived deliberate inaccuracies inserted by Badaoni into the translation to reflect his bigoted worldview when the *Razmnama* was read out to him. Akbar went ballistic in rage.

---

72 Ibid.

73 Ibid.

74 See the next chapter for details.

M. Athar Ali mentions:

> On the occasion of Nauroz (20 March 1595), Akbar complained to Abu'l Fazl that Badaoni, whom he had thought to be of mystical bent, was really a 'fanatical theologian' (*faqih-i muta'ssib*). He had let his orthodoxy led him to insert into the portion of the *Razmnama* rendered by him, the concept of the Day of Judgment, which was alien to the Indians who believed in transmigration of souls (*tanasukh*). Badaoni had much to do to explain that he had not deviated from the duty of the translator and that Indians did believe that heaven and hell existed as intermediate stages in transmigrations.[75]

This is what Badaoni alludes to when he says that he had to suffer insults from the emperor during the course of his translation work, and was abused by the emperor as 'unlawful earner/eater of unlawful things' (*haramkhor*) and 'turnip eater' (*shalgamkhor*). This also suggests that Akbar had a colourful vocabulary of expletives, which he liberally drew from whenever his passion was incited (see next chapter for a particular Hindustani abuse that Akbar used and which is still in use today). *Shalgamkhor*, as an abuse, really sounds like something from Captain Haddock's list of cuss words from Tintin comics where 'aardvark', 'jellyfish', and 'blistering barnacles', to name a few, are abuses.

And yet, even after this unpleasant episode after which even Badaoni thought that his time in the court was over and that he should really seek out greener pastures elsewhere, away from the heretic emperor and his court, Akbar asked Badaoni to stay and translate the *Ramayana* into Persian. It could be argued that Akbar was fond of Badaoni and that's why he favoured him despite his bigotry to translate Hindu religious texts. But a practical man like Akbar who wanted his Hindu wives, courtiers and lay people to be happy and content with his rule wouldn't run the risk of upsetting everyone by putting a bigot in charge to translate their holy book unless he had faith in the ability of the man to be true to his job.

---

75 M. Athar Ali. 'Translations of Sanskrit Works at Akbar's Court', *Social Scientist* 20, no. 9/10, 1992, pp. 38–45. Available at JSTOR, www.jstor.org/stable/3517715.

Akbar's atelier illustrated the whole book, thus producing some of the most magnificent Mughal paintings ever. Akbar named the translated work the *Razmnama* or 'The Book of War' and made copies for the princes, sections of the nobility, and his allies. These copies are today located throughout the world in museum and university collections as well as private ones. Akbar's personal copy of this as well as the *Ramayana* have been with the Jaipur royal family since the 18th century. These are in the vaults of the Sawai Man Singh II Museum, also known as the City Palace Museum, in Jaipur, but not available for viewing by scholars or the general public. However, two artworks in the form of giant shields based on the illustrations of this copy of the *Razmnama* are available for public viewing at the Albert Hall Museum in Jaipur. No other Mughal text was produced like the *Razmnama*. It became almost mandatory reading in the Mughal Empire, and even the Mughal princes had to learn it as part of their princely training.[76] It's perhaps befitting in a way that Akbar's own copy of his most magnificent literary project survives in the safe keeping of the family of Man Singh, whom he designated as his *farzand* or son.

Man Singh is also the son Akbar wanted but never had. Though a doting, and in many ways an indulgent father to his kids, Akbar didn't find much happiness from his sons when they became adults. Murad and Daniyal died of alcoholism while their father was still alive, causing much grief to him. In fact, it was Daniyal's death in March 1605 that delivered such a knockout blow to Akbar's heart that he never recovered and died a few months later.

But it was Salim, the eldest and dearest son of Akbar, who gave his father the most terrible pain and emotional scars. Salim rebelled against his father and proclaimed himself emperor, even threatening to go to war against him. Many of the leading nobles of the court such as Khan-i-Azam Mirza Aziz Koka, Raja Man Singh and Abu'l Fazl preferred Salim's son, Mirza Khusro, to succeed Akbar. Salim, to spite his father, got Abu'l Fazl murdered by a Rajput chief named Bir Singh Bundela. Fazl and his elder brother Faizi were the closest to Akbar.

---

76 Audrey Truschke, 'Many Persian Mahabharatas for Akbar' in *Culture of Encounters: Sanskrit at the Mughal Court* (New York: Columbia University Press, 2016), pp. 101–41.

While Akbar's great grandson Aurangzeb was unsparing of his own children who rebelled against him, he forgave Salim and even declared him his heir in his dying moments when he was incapacitated by a sudden bout of diarrhoea. He was his father's son. Humayun couldn't kill his brothers or their children even when they rebelled against him and tried every means to kill him and his children. Akbar didn't have to kill any sibling when he came to the throne, and he could never bring himself to even thinking about killing his own son. In this, he was very different from his contemporary, Sultan Suleiman I of Ottoman Empire, who is known to the western world as Suleiman the Magnificent.

Sultan Suleiman, based on an unconfirmed rumour of rebellion, which was really a plot allegedly hatched by his chief wife Hurrem Sultan and grand vizier Rustam Pasha, had his heir apparent, and eldest and ablest son, Sehzade Mustafa, executed. He did the same to another son, Sehzade Bayezid, who had sought refuge in the Safavid Empire of Shah Tahmasp. Abu'l Fazl speaks derisively of Shah Tahmasp because he took money and other favours from Sultan Suleiman in exchange for allowing Ottoman assassins to seize and execute Sehzade Bayezid and his four sons in Safavid Iran. Fazl writes[77]:

> Many good deeds adorned his (Shah Tahmasp) reign except that he in 1559, sheltered Sultan Bayazid the son of Sultan Sulaiman with his four sons and 12,000 followers, and (then) owing to the instigation of flatterers, who were house-destroyers, stained his hand with the sacred blood of his guests. If the might of the Sultan of Turkey had constrained him to do this, then he should not have taken silver and gold for it.

So, Akbar, who is often called Akbar the Great or Akbar the Magnificent, appears to be more deserving of the epithet than his Ottoman counterpart.

Modern academia today would hesitate to use those epithets for any king or queen. But in popular history, the 'great' epithet is often used for rulers who were empire builders and ruthless warriors. For instance, Alexander of Macedon is called Alexander the Great only

77 Abu'l Fazl, *Akbarnama, Vol. III*, p. 897.

because of his ruthless conquests. Peter the Great of Russia is also called that because of his expansionist policies. Sultan Suleiman is called Magnificent because of his conquests. The Hindutva forces have unilaterally declared Rana Pratap as great because of his battles against Akbar; almost nothing is spoken about Pratap's administration or handling of economy or social reforms whenever he is glorified. Akbar, along with Ashoka, seem to be among a handful of kings and queens called great because of their spiritual and social conquests more than their military achievements.

Akbar succeeded where his predecessors and even successors failed: to give equality and dignity to his subjects cutting across faiths. In this, as we have seen in the previous pages of this book, he was aided by the Timurid–Mongol tradition of *Yassa-i Chingizi*, or the code of Genghis Khan, where the ruler had 'to consider all sects as one and not to distinguish one from another'.[78] And since Akbar didn't go through the formal education process of the time, which involved theological lessons, he had a relatively unencumbered mind that was open to receiving different ideas. The amazing flowering of inter-faith discourses and the resultant seeds of tolerance sown in India's soil by the Bhakti and Sufi movements gave Akbar fertile ground to sow the crop of *sulh-i-kul* and reap a rich harvest. The *Nirguna Bhakti* tradition of the worship of the divine as a formless entity and its intellectual criticism of the dogmatic ways of Hinduism and Islam particularly influenced Akbar. But ideological training can only provide a theoretical framework; practical implementation of ideas always has a more lasting influence. Akbar's matrimonial relations with Hindus exposed him in a far more intimate way to India's most dominant faith than any religious discourse possibly could. So, wearing a *tilak* or performing *homa* sacrifice or playing Holi and Diwali, all these things became part of Akbar's life, which any other Muslim king before him had not experienced to that degree.

It is true that there were Sultans in Bengal and in the Deccan who were eclectic monarchs and who even went to the extent of adopting Hindu mannerisms. But since north India traditionally produced

78 Iqtidar Alam Khan, 'Akbar's personality', p. 81.

the most powerful and influential monarchs, so whenever Akbar did something, being the master of Hindustan or north India, the ramifications were far wider. To give a modern analogy, the chief minister of West Bengal sharing something on Twitter or re-tweeting something s/he approves of will get a large audience. But the Prime Minister of India tweeting something gets far wider attention. When many conscientious citizens complain about the Prime Minister following abusive Twitter profiles, this is the reasoning they follow: that the Prime Minister shows the way to the country.

This is what Akbar did. He, being the fountainhead of the most dominant power in the Indian subcontinent, chose a path and showed the country the way. This helped the Mughals win the heart and mind of India and unite with her soul. People who came after him didn't abandon the path shown by him entirely until the 20th century when Muslims thought they could no longer repose faith in *sulh-i-kul* and decided to part ways. Pakistan became a reality and a symbol of defeat of Akbar's system, as it abandoned the separation of state and faith and united both. India, on the other hand, continued to tread on the path shown by Akbar.

Today, however, there has been a climbdown from that established position in India. Fanned largely by a communal ideology that wants to see India become a mirror image of Pakistan but of a saffron hue, this climbdown threatens to take the country hurtling down on the road that it left behind in 1947.

It needs to be seen what sort of a legacy today's saffron shahenshah of India leaves behind for posterity. But surely, he's challenging the legacy left behind by that emperor whom the world calls Akbar the Great.

Chapter 8

Sketch of Akbar on Media's Canvas

Tera ho kya bayan, tu shaan-e-Hindustan
Hindustan teri jaan, tu jaan-e-Hindustan![1]

Despite having ruled India for 300 years, leaving behind a tall and robust sociocultural legacy, the representation of the Mughals in mass media has been less than satisfactory. In the 70 years since Independence, there have been only two noteworthy period films with Akbar as protagonist—K Asif's *Mughal-e-Azam* (1960) and Ashutosh Gowariker's *Jodhaa Akbar* (2008). And depending on what generation you belong to, the name Akbar would either throw up the image of Prithviraj Kapoor or Hrithik Roshan.

Jodhaa Akbar was a largely fictionalised take on Akbar and the legendary Jodha Bai, his queen consort. This was a unique movie for a reason. Perhaps for the first time, the filmmaker approached very eminent historians for help. They said what historians world over largely agree—that Akbar had no wife named Jodha Bai. Yet this had no impact on the filmmaker's plans. Or, let's just say that facts didn't come in the way of a good Bollywood story.

---

1 Lyrics from the song '*Azeem O Shaan Shahenshah*' from the 2008 film *Jodhaa Akbar*.

There were inaccuracies galore right from the beginning. The opening narration by Amitabh Bachchan, which condensed the history of Babur and Humayun down to a few seconds, declared that the Mughals had come to India in 1450—a good 75 years before they had actually arrived and a good 50 years after their great ancestor, Amir Timur or Tamerlane, had seized Delhi.

There was another problem too—the narration said the 'loot and plunder' of India started from 1011 AD, an obvious reference to the plundering raids of Mahmud of Ghazni. This was perfectly in sync with the assumption in India today of military invasions of South Asia being the handiwork of Islamic warriors alone. Every Indian child grows up hearing tales of the 17 invasions of Mahmud of Ghazni. In Assam, this tale assumes a new form and becomes 17 Mughal invasions of Assam. In this discourse, Achaemenid invasions or the conquest of Alexander of Macedon, which predate Islam, rarely register.

The easiest way to explain this would be to blame it on general amnesia in India about history. And amnesia isn't a preserve of Indians; world over, we see such examples. For instance, in Britain, there is little or no awareness about 73 foreign invasions that happened on British soil since 1066.[2] But the Indian amnesia has more to do with the majoritarian bias against medieval Muslim rulers, which is of colonial vintage, than anything else.

But it seems this wasn't always so. Abu'l Fazl shows great understanding of India of his time and before him in his monumental work, *Akbarnama*, of which *Ain-i-Akbari* is a part. The third volume of *Ain-i-Akbari* has an entire chapter (number 10) dedicated to people who came to India from outside. Fazl's guides in this seem to be the *Shahnameh*[3] and the *Zend Avesta*, for many of those individuals mentioned belong to the Pishdadian dynasty, believed to be the first dynasty to rule over Persia, and whose stories are part of the Persian epic and the Zoroastrian holy book.

2 British author Ian Hernon lists 73 invasions that happened since 1066 in a country believed to be a fortress country in his 2013 book, *Fortress Britain: All the Invasions and Incursions Since 1066* (United Kingdom: The History Press, 2013).

3 It's an epic poem commissioned by the Samanid dynasty of Persia and authored by Firdausi, and it covers the mythical and historical past of Persia till the coming of Islam.

Yet Fazl also writes about Alexander of Macedon, Prophet Mani, and Sassanid kings like Bahram before coming to the first Islamic conqueror, Muhammad bin-Qasim. Fazl meticulously then goes on to list the names of Mahmud of Ghazni; Muhammad of Ghor; various Delhi sultans like Qutubuddin Aibak and Iltutmish; Mongol generals like Saldi, Qutlugh Khwaja and Targhi[4]; Amir Timur; and finally ends it with the first two Mughal emperors—Babur and Humayun. What's interesting here is that Fazl includes the first two emperors as foreigners who entered India, but not Akbar—an attestation of the Indian origin of this emperor. This important point was lost on Vincent Smith,[5] and we see it getting lost on the nouveau Indian critics of Akbar who declare him a foreigner. Many of them appear on TV news panels—which double up as pulpits to preach nationalism to people—and insist that Akbar shouldn't be remembered in India.

Jodhaa Akbar tried to favourably weigh in on Akbar's Indian identity too. A particular scene had Akbar appreciating Jodha's straightforward behaviour and courage and declaring that he too is a son of Rajputana's soil. This was one of the high points of the film. But the film as such was a heavily fictionalised take on some real events to tell a compelling love story between a Hindu woman and a Muslim man.

Jodha was shown as the daughter of King Bharmal (or Biharimal) of Amber (or Amer) and the lone wife of Akbar. In reality, the princess of Amber, who may have been named Hira Kunwar or Harkha Bai, was the fourth wife of Akbar, the first three being Ruqaiyya Sultan Begum, a princess known only as 'Abdullah Khan's daughter, and Salima Sultan Begum. In Mughal records, she was known by her formal title, Wali Nyimat Maryam uz-Zamani (Mary of the age) Begum Sahiba.

We know that Akbar was the closest to his first wife. That was because Ruqaiyya was his childhood companion and first cousin. Ruqaiyya was also Akbar's equal in both rank and stature as she didn't become a Mughal woman by marriage but by birth. We know

4 Abu'l Fazl also gives the name of Sultan Alauddin Khilji as having defeated these Mongol invaders.

5 Refer to Chapter 1 for what Vincent Smith wrote and my criticism of it.

she wielded significant influence in the imperial harem and also in court. In modern fiction, Indu Sundaresan's *The Twentieth Wife*[6], talks about harem intrigues involving Ruqaiyya Begum, Jagat Gosain (officially called Taj Bibi Bilqis[7] Makani) and Mehrunnisa, the future Noor Jahan.

At places, *Jodhaa Akbar* relied heavily on Abu'l Fazl's *Akbarnama*. For instance, the depiction of the treatment of Hemu after the Second Battle of Panipat on 5 November 1556. Urged by his regent Bairam Khan to execute the captured man, the teenaged Akbar takes pity on him and refuses to do so, saying that Hemu is badly wounded and barely alive. Bairam Khan then asks the soldiers guarding Akbar to form a human screen around him as he strikes at Hemu with his sword and severs the head. Akbar is then proclaimed a *ghazi* or 'slayer of infidels'.

Badaoni, who always has juicy titbits to offer, narrates the incident similarly but with a difference: Bairam Khan strikes at Hemu's head first, but it's Shaikh Gadai who actually follows it up with another cut that results in the severing of the head. Firishta, who declares early that he heard the versions from Abu'l Fazl, says that Akbar drew his sword and touched the head of Hemu with it, thereby entitling himself to the title of *ghazi* while Bairam Khan severed Hemu's head in a single blow.

There are many possibilities going by the different versions available. It's possible that the boy king tried to do the act himself but failed to strike a fatal blow, requiring the helping hand of Bairam Khan to cover up what would have been a royal embarrassment. The touching of the head with the sword was perhaps a symbolic act too like that of the practice of knighting someone in medieval Europe, though without a parallel in Indian and Timurid cultures. It's also possible that Akbar's refusal was an afterthought by Abu'l Fazl to project a more benign image of the emperor. But one cannot fault the filmmaker for this, for he still used the most popular version of the event handed down to posterity by Akbar's official biographer.

---

6 Indu Sundaresan, *The Twentieth Wife* (New York: Washington Square Press, 2002).

7 Bilqis is the Quranic name for the Biblical Queen of Sheba, known for her beauty, wit and riches and who had famously tested King Solomon's wisdom.

Indeed, Gowariker received no compliments for getting some lesser known historical details right from any of the film reviewers. For instance, as shown in the movie, Bharmal did announce his successor to be his own son Bhagwan Dass and not his nephew Sujamal, who had expected to succeed his uncle. Sujamal's father Puranmal was the Amber king, but upon his death in 1534, Sujamal wasn't allowed to succeed him. Instead, a brother of Puranmal named Bhim Singh became king. He ruled for three years and was succeeded by his son Ratan Singh, who ruled for 11 years until his murder by a step-brother named Askaran. This king ruled for only 16 days and was removed by the nobles, who then put Bharmal on the throne. That was in 1548. When it became clear that he wasn't succeeding his uncle, Sujamal went over to the Mughal subedar of Mewat and Ajmer, Mirza Sharfuddin Husain, and sought his help. In the film, the *subedar* says he would help but Sujamal would have to help him when he attacks the imperial capital. In reality, Sharfuddin had no such plans and actually attacked Amber to help Sujamal.

Abu'l Fazl says Sharfuddin already had a design on Amber. He writes in the *Akbarnama*:

> At this time Sūjā the son of Pūran Mal, the Rajah's elder brother, out of wickedness and because he wanted the chiefship for himself came and paid his respects to the Mīrzā and raised troubles. The Mīrzā led an army against Rajah Bihārī Mal and as the times were unfavourable and the Rajah had not a large force he came to terms.

To guarantee peace, Raja Bharmal, apart from indemnity, had to send three royal hostages to the Mirza—his own son Jagannath, his brother Askaran's son Raj Singh, and brother Jagmal's son Kangar. In 1562, Fazl says, Sharfuddin was collecting more troops to 'extirpate the family'.

All of this is not shown in the movie, but it still gets it right when it shows Raja Bharmal deciding to accept the suzerainty of Akbar and give his daughter's hand in marriage to the emperor. Bharmal's predicament was narrated to Akbar by his senior noble Chagatai Khan, who then convinced the emperor to give Bharmal an audience.

The meeting happened at Sanganer, as rightly shown in the movie, in January 1562. Akbar is shown fighting an elephant in *musth* at that time, and Bharmal and the Rajputs almost get overawed by the reckless courage of Akbar. In reality, this incident had happened in Delhi in December 1556, when Bharmal had been rewarded for his 'excellent loyalty'[8]. And the real incident was even more dramatic than what was shown in the film, as people had fled when the elephant got agitated with Akbar on top of it, but the Rajputs didn't move an inch, impressing Akbar. This was an important detail that shouldn't have been missed, for this was the moment, perhaps, when Akbar figured out the military potential of the Kachwahas[9] even though he must have generally known that the Rajputs were great fighters. The Kachwahas were not the most powerful clan in Rajputana; the Rathores of Marwar were. Marwar also was a bigger kingdom with a much bigger military. But Amber was a prosperous state. And it held the keys to Rajputana. That may have also been a consideration for Akbar.

Nevertheless, Akbar was very sympathetic to Raja Bharmal and accepted his marriage proposal too. He then went ahead to Ajmer where he was joined by Mirza Sharfuddin. Akbar ordered the Mirza to release the Rajput princes and not trouble the Amber kingdom. Abu'l Fazl says the Mirza gave vague assurances and tried to delay it through subterfuge. The emperor gave the Mirza time to come good on his promise, but by no means did he trust his viceroy. This can be gauged from what the emperor said when the royal entourage arrived at Deosa (probably Dausa in today's Rajasthan) and most of the locals fled. Fazl quotes Akbar in the *Akbarnama*:

> We have no other intention than to do good to all mankind. What can be the reason of the flight of those people? Apparently, these rustics of the valley of desolation have drawn an inference from the oppression they have undergone from Sharfuddin Ḥusain and so have run away.

---

8 See Chapter 3.

9 Akbar supposedly said 'we will rear you' (*nihaal khwaahim kard* in Persian) to Bharmal at the end of it, suggesting that he would have Bharmal as an ally later. Abu'l Fazl narrates this incident in *Akbarnama, Vol. II*, p. 70.

Through repeated and quick follow-ups, Akbar ensured that the Mirza delivered the three Amber princes to their family in the imperial presence. And the Kachwahas became the first ruling house in Rajputana to enter Mughal service. It was also perhaps a more natural alliance as it was Sujamal's father Puranmal, who had as Amber king fought for Humayun against Tatar Khan Lodi at the Battle of Mandrayal in 1534 and had fallen in battle fighting under the *sher-o-khurshid* banner.

The delighted and grateful House of Amber married off their princess to the most powerful man in the subcontinent. The marriage was solemnised at the imperial camp at Sambhar, about 80 miles from Amber, and the emperor marched back to Agra with a new wife and her brothers and nephews in tow. Achhe din arrived for the Mughals and the Rajputs, more for the Rajputs. From then on, they would be the main players in the plot, not the extras like in a movie.

All of this was not part of the *Jodhaa Akbar* plot, and the filmmaker cannot be blamed for that as a movie cannot be expected to illustrate all that is documented in history. But then, a movie should not distort history either. And this movie had plenty of them.

Maham Anaga was shown as a vile, scheming woman, green to the point of becoming a goblin in envy of Jodha. When Adham Khan assassinates Shamsuddin Ataga Khan, and Akbar gets him thrown to his death from the ramparts of the fort, a repentant Akbar begs for the elderly woman's forgiveness. This happened in real life too, with Maham Anaga forgiving the emperor. But in the movie, she sows seeds of discord between Akbar and Jodha, resulting in Akbar sending his wife back to Amber. When Akbar eventually learns about the truth, he exiles Maham Anaga to Mecca and vows never to see her face again. In reality, Maham Anaga, already weak from illness when she heard the news of her son's execution, died 40 days after it due to heartbreak. Akbar despatched the body to Delhi so that she could be interred along with her son, and himself accompanied the body till the outskirts of Agra as a mark of deference to the loyal servant of the House of Timur. Both mother and son sleep peacefully in the tomb located in Mehrauli (in Delhi) even today.

There was something else that this particular scene distorted—the way this murder happened and the way the emperor reacted to it. The movie showed Ataga Khan and Todar Mal examining the accounts of the empire and Ataga Khan realising that the account books of Malwa don't add up. Malwa had Adham Khan as *subahdar* or viceroy and Ataga Khan figured out that Adham Khan was indulging in massive corruption. At that point, Adham Khan walked in and threatened Ataga Khan of dire consequences if he didn't hush up the matter. There is a brief altercation between the two and Adham Khan takes out his sword and cuts Ataga Khan down.

The actual incident occurred far more differently and Abu'l Fazl gives the most detailed account of it. He says on 12 Ramzan, 969 AH or 16 May 1562, a Saturday, the emperor had retired for an afternoon nap, but the business of the court was still on. Ataga Khan was sitting there along with Muni'm Khan, the *Khan-i-Khanan* after Bairam Khan, Shihabuddin Ahmad Khan, and others. It was business as usual. And then Adham Khan entered, in a 'riotous manner' and accompanied by others "more riotous than himself". The assembled members rose up to pay him their respects, but Adham Khan went straight to Ataga Khan with his hand on the dagger.

After the Malwa misadventure of Adham Khan,[10] Akbar had wanted to get rid of both Maham Anaga and Adham Khan from the administration and exercise sovereign control over his government. Historians of yore have called the two-year phase after the death of Bairam Khan when Maham Anaga and her son Adham Khan called the shots as 'petticoat government'. Akbar resented this phase. In 1561, aged 19, he tried to restore the balance by appointing Ataga Khan as Vakil us Sultanate.

But this change was resented by Adham Khan, Muni'm Khan and other nobles, and probably even Maham Anaga. Badaoni says Muni'm Khan and Shihabuddin Ahmad Khan, who was a relative of Maham Anaga, instigated[11] Adham Khan to eliminate Ataga Khan. And so Adham Khan arrived with his gang of ruffians. 'Then he angrily signed to his

10 See Chapter 3.

11 Abdul Qadir Badaoni, *Muntakhab ut-Tawarikh, Vol. II*, tr. W. H. Lowe (Calcutta: The Asiatic Society, 1884), p. 49.

servant Khusham Uzbek and the other desperadoes who had come with their loins girt up for strife saying: 'Why do you stand still?"' Fazl writes.[12]

Khusham then took out a dagger and stabbed Ataga Khan in the chest. Shocked by this unprovoked attack, Ataga Khan tried to run towards the door of the hall. But another associate of Adham Khan named Khuda Bardi struck him twice with his sword and that was the end of Ataga Khan.

There was panic and alarm in the palace as Adham Khan went straight to the harem with a naked sword in hand. Akbar was sleeping but 'his fortune was awake', says Fazl.[13] Everyone around, it seems, was too stunned to react to this crime. Fazl questions why Adham Khan was not killed by anyone despite the nature of the crime and his going towards the harem. But when he tried to enter the palace by taking a flight of stairs, a eunuch named Niamat had the good sense of shutting the door. In *Jodhaa Akbar*, Niamat is shown as the chief eunuch who is more like a jester of the zenana but figures nowhere in this crucial scene.

Akbar woke up hearing all the commotion and asked what the matter was. None of the palace women knew what had happened. So, Akbar looked out of the palace wall and was informed by one Rafiq about Adham Khan's deed. The movie showed the palace women informing Akbar about it.

Akbar was horrified to hear it and reacted in disbelief. He asked again, and this time, Rafiq drew his attention towards the body of Ataga Khan that was lying in the courtyard. When Akbar saw the body of the man he looked up to as father after his own father's death, and whose wife, Jiji Anaga, suckled him as a child, he got enraged. He rushed out of the palace, but a servant didn't let him go unarmed and handed him a sword. However, he didn't come out by the main exit but by another way; Adham Khan was standing at the main exit.

When Akbar turned a corner, he saw Adham Khan and blurted out one expletive after another. The movie shows Akbar calling Adham Khan *zaleel* (lowly), *kameenzade* (son of a vulgar woman), *ehsaan-faramosh* (ungrateful), and a *ghaleez shaks* (dirty man). Quite a mouthful! But this cine Akbar was still mouthing the most

---

12 *Akbarnama, Vol II*, p. 269.

13 Ibid., p. 270.

acceptable words of indignation while speaking utterly chaste Urdu. The real Akbar was earthier, and much more Indian than we think he was.

Abu'l Fazl says Akbar called Adham Khan *bachcha-i-laada* or 'son of a bitch'. But it is Bayazid Biyat who gives the most interesting version of this. Bayazid was supposedly present on the occasion and wrote the scene as he saw it. If we believe him, then Akbar came out wearing just a lungi, spoke in Hindustani and not Persian or Turkic, and called Adham Khan a *gandu*[14] or catamite, an expletive pretty much in existence in northern and western India today and routinely heard in Agra where Akbar was at the time of incident. Bayazid wrote this in Persian— '*Hazrat ba-zaban* Hindustani *farmudand ke ae gandu, cara* Atkah *mara kashti* (His Majesty said in Hindustani tongue, "Hey you *gandu*, why did you kill my Ataga?").'

Adham Khan supposedly seized Akbar's hand that carried the scimitar and asked him to calm down and then inquire. He replied that Ataga Khan had been disloyal to him and he only served him the punishment that he deserved. But this didn't calm Akbar down and he seized Adham Khan's hand that was clasped on his with his other hand. Then Adham Khan tried to strike at Akbar with his sword but couldn't because Akbar punched him in the face that threw him off balance. Akbar then asked his guards to seize him, bind him and defenestrate him. This was done twice till he died, and the movie showed this part accurately.

Bayazid's account is much more believable because Akbar was known to use expletives, or *gaali*s as any Indian would understand. Even Fazl says he called Adham a 'son of a bitch'. Most likely, Akbar used both and Fazl only censored the more objectionable of the two. But to the Victorian sensibilities of Mrs. Annette Beveridge, who translated the Humayun Namah of Gulbadan Begum, both phrases were indecent enough to be left out with a comment that since only a few sources talk about it, therefore, one shouldn't believe someone as

---

14 I thank Professor Ali Nadeem Rezavi, the head of Centre of Advanced Study, Department of History, Aligarh Muslim University, for looking it up for me in Bayazid Biyat's work titled *Tazkira-i-Humayun wa Akbar* edited by M. Hidayat Hosain. This book has not been translated into English and the phrase occurs on p. 251.

classy as Akbar could have mouthed such words. About Fazl writing that Akbar called Adham 'son of a bitch', Beveridge implied that Akbar couldn't use it as that was akin to calling his foster brother 'base born' and also insulting Maham Anaga at the same time. Her exact words were these:

> Some writers put into Akbar's mouth, when he addressed Adham, an epithet which would imply baseness in his birth and opprobrium of his mother; but I am advised that from various considerations weight need not be given to the inference of the word, which, moreover, is not used by all the sources. The point is mentioned here because of the contradiction involved in the epithet with the statement of marriage with Nadim *kuka*, and with the terms of respect employed towards the anaga by the Persian writer who uses the degrading epithet.[15]

Beveridge in her characteristic Victorian prudence does not even mention that this 'Persian writer' was none other than Abu'l Fazl, the author of the most definitive account and the official history of Akbar's reign. Did she not want her readers to find out who the author was and what phrase he had written? One can only speculate. But she didn't run an important mind check while coming to that conclusion: this was Akbar's official history commissioned by him, and nothing, almost nothing would have gone into it without his knowledge.

Another account of the reign of Akbar called *Tazkirat ul-Muluk* by Rafiuddin Ibrahim narrates two fascinating incidents about Akbar to illustrate Akbar's unconventional behaviour. One he says happened when a relative of Shah Tahmasp came to Agra and preparations were made to give him a grand reception. Ibrahim says he had then come from Gujarat and had gone to see a pavilion erected for the reception out of curiosity. Professor Iqtidar Alam Khan quotes this extract from Ibrahim's work in his recent book on Akbar[16]:

---

15 *Humayun Namah* by Gulbadan Begum translated by Mrs. A. S. Beveridge, footnote on p. 62.

16 Iqtidar Alam Khan, *India's Polity in the Age of Akbar* (New Delhi: Permanent Black, 2016), p. 143.

> ...all of a sudden there arose a clamour of 'Cheers for the King' (*badshah salamat*). From this circumstance, I concluded that the king had arrived. I looked to my left and my right but could not find anyone with the appearance of a king. As I turned around I saw, standing there, a young man of about twenty years. He supported his head on one of his hands, which rested on the shoulder of a companion. I guessed he was the king. But the men continued to stand around rubbing shoulders with each other. No one [bothered] with observing etiquette—of showing respect [to the king]. I took position at a short distance and observed what was happening. I was greatly surprised and asked (those present): 'Is the custom of showing respect not observed at this court? No one has paid respects to the king.' They replied: 'As compared to other realms the tradition of showing respect and observing etiquette is much more elaborate here. But this king is an exceedingly informal person. He often comes out of his private apartment in ordinary dress and mixes with the people around him, making no distinction between friends and strangers. In this situation, how is it possible [for men] to observe etiquette all the time?'....

In the second incident, Ibrahim says he saw Akbar flying a kite on the terrace of his palace with his head uncovered and wearing only a lungi.[17] So, lungi was Akbar's favourite, it seems. Yet we didn't see even one in *Jodhaa Akbar*. This Akbar was forever dressed in ceremonial robes and always sounded prim and proper.

The closest any Indian political leader of today comes to this unconventional behaviour of Akbar is perhaps Rahul Gandhi. For security personnel of Special Protection Group who guard Rahul Gandhi, his unconventional ways are a nightmare. Indeed, former Union Home Minister Rajnath Singh once publicly complained about Rahul Gandhi violating security protocol a 'hundred times' and freely mixing with people.[18] Rahul Gandhi has ridden bikes; sat down on the ground to eat with poor farmers and Dalit families

---

17 Ibid.

18 PTI, 'Rahul Gandhi violated security protocol a 100 times: Rajnath Singh in Lok Sabha', *The Economic Times*, New Delhi, 8 August 2017. Available at https://economictimes.indiatimes.com/news/politics-and-nation/rahul-gandhi-went-abroad-without-security-rajnath-singh-on-congress-protest/articleshow/59967071.cms..

at their homes[19]; freely mixed with the common man for friendly chit-chats and taking selfies; and has even been kissed by women admirers[20] while attending public functions. And on most of these occasions, Rahul Gandhi has been spotted wearing either casuals or the kurta-pyjamas that he wears in a semi-formal way.

To what extent such mingling by Rahul Gandhi has benefited the Congress party is unknown. But Narendra Modi has also tried to do something similar in a very controlled environment and in a very limited way, but a pliant press has amplified it several times to make it appear as a god-like leader's magnanimity in reaching out to the masses in such a novel way. In reality, Modi's actions have been way less spontaneous and limited in their scope than Rahul Gandhi's. For instance, Modi hasn't gone on bike rides, or eaten a meal from a Dalit man's kitchen, or let anyone come so close to him. On every Independence Day since 2014, Modi has 'baffled' his security detail by going to the children's enclosures to meet them. Every year, the press has celebrated it as a 'break from protocol' by the prime minister. This cycle of being surprised and celebrating it as a novel way has continued for four years now.[21]

But if we see the kind of leader that Narendra Modi has aspired to be like, then the image is closer to that of Delhi Sultan Ghiyasuddin Balban and Mughal Emperor Aurangzeb. Balban believed in the divine right of kingship and tried every means to project himself as a cut above the rest. He was the first Indian king to adopt the Persian concept of 'zill Allah' and made himself appear as a god-like figure.

---

19 Sharat Pradhan, 'Rahul Gandhi's "puri sabzi" dinner in a Dalit village', *Rediff.com*, 18 May 2008. Available at https://www.rediff.com/news/2008/may/18rahul.htm.

20 See Agencies, 'A surprise kiss for Rahul Gandhi on his tour of Assam', *NDTV*, Jorhat, Assam, 27 February 2014. Available at https://www.ndtv.com/india-news/a-surprise-kiss-for-rahul-gandhi-on-his-tour-of-assam-552134.

21 See PTI, 'PM breaks protocol, exits car to meet school children at Red Fort', *Rediff.com*, 15 August 2014. Available at https://www.rediff.com/news/report/pm-modi-breaks-protocol-exits-car-to-meet-school-children-at-red-fort/20140815.htm; PTI, 'PM Narendra Modi breaks security protocol to meet his young admirers', DNA, 15 August 2017. Available at https://www.dnaindia.com/india/report-children-jostle-to-meet-greet-pm-modi-at-red-fort-2530626.

He controlled the *chahalgani* or the powerful clique of forty nobles, pretty much like Modi controls the BJP today.

Aurangzeb, on the other hand, was a darling of the austere and the orthodox. His austere ways are appreciated even by the modern Hindu Right. That Aurangzeb observed Islamic rituals very strictly and kept himself away from wine and such other perceived vices made him the heartthrob of the ulema, the conservative Muslims and the fanatics. Narendra Modi's austere ways that are much advertised, such as observing *navratra* fasts while meeting President Barack Obama and having only lemon juice for dinner were endorsed and celebrated by the orthodox and fanatical Hindus. And despite wearing a monogrammed pinstripe suit costing ₹ 10 lakh, his calling himself a *faqir* (mendicant) is unquestioningly accepted by his followers.

But it fascinates me that the real Akbar behaved like a commoner, dressed like a commoner and even talked like a commoner, using expletives unreservedly. This candid Akbar has somehow frightened historians and continues to frighten modern filmmakers who otherwise have no qualms about making movies where principal characters freely mouth abuses.

Somehow, it never occurs to us lay people that invective, abuse, expletives have not been the sole preserve of our modern world; our ancestors in the distant past have had their own lists of expletives to draw from. That's because even though languages have undergone changes, human emotions have remained the same.

K. Asif's *Mughal-e-Azam* is still pretty much the gold standard for any period film in India. Nobody has ever since tried to recreate the over-elaborate court culture and the grandeur of the Mughals. But this is also the most historically inaccurate film on the Mughals till date. If Jodha Bai was one legend that Gowariker picked, Anarkali was another that K. Asif picked. If we pit them head to head, then *Jodhaa Akbar* wins hands down in accuracy.

Anarkali was depicted as a *nautch* girl[22] who rose in rank due to royal favour, only to fall out of grace later for committing the most quintessential Indian sin—falling in love. And that too with the heir-apparent to the imperial throne. The great Akbar, the paragon of virtue and tolerance, turned into an autocratic and class conscious Indian father who wouldn't soil the exalted name of his dynasty by letting a *nautch* girl become the empress of India.

This led the son to rebel against his father in the name of love, and the father to vow to annihilate his son for the sake of family honour. The son got defeated and the father spared his life at the insistence of Anarkali who promised to disappear for good if Prince Salim was allowed to live. The narrator then appreciated the virtue of Akbar who showed his big heart by letting Anarkali live and still saved the honour of his dynasty. Two things triumphed: defeat in love, and arrogance of power. Both very un-Akbar-like and un-Mughal-like. But this was the perfect recipe for an Indian superhit movie. It had patriarchy, love denial, class prejudices, all brought to the big screen by a top star cast, two exceptionally beautiful women (Madhubala as Anarkali and Nigar Sultana as Bahar), and plenty of great songs and breathtaking shots for their time.

Actually, *Mughal-e-Azam* had little to do with Akbar or the Mughals and more to do with a prejudice-ridden Indian society of

---

22 *Nautch* is an Anglicised version of '*naach*', Hindustani for 'dance'. A *nautch* girl would be a '*naachne-waali*' in Hindustani. These were typically professional dancing women who either performed as part of troupes at public and private gatherings or made solo performances for patrons, either at the performers' own place or at the patrons' place. Though now used interchangeably, a *nautch* girl and a *tawaif* were different, the latter being well-connected courtesans with the rich and the elite of society as clients and who themselves were placed in the upper echelon of society. As the power of the Mughal court and the smaller courts at Avadh and elsewhere waned with the rise of British power, the *nautch* girls lost patronage and disappeared into prostitution. Victorian morality played its part in this, and the British eventually treated nautch girls and *tawaifs* with disdain. This is brought out very well in a particular scene from Shyam Benegal's 1979 film *Junoon* where the character or Ruth Labadoor, played by Nafisa Ali, wears an Indian dress and jewellery and gleefully asks her mother's opinion about her look. The mother, played by Jennifer Kapoor, scornfully remarks, 'Like a nautch girl!'.

the 1950s and 1960s, grappling with western values, ideas, methods and clothing while trying very hard to insulate itself from moral-wrecking western mores like women choosing for themselves, both life partners and career paths. So, even though it was a period film, *Mughal-e-Azam*, if you look closely, was a surprisingly modern film with a very modern reality of young lovers having to part ways due to irreconcilable parents.

Akbar was not like that. The Mughals were not like that. They had a history of slave girls and *nautch* girls becoming royal consorts. Lal Kunwar, a *nautch* girl, became Empress Imtiaz Mahal by marrying Emperor Jahandar Shah. Udham Bai, another *nautch* girl, became Empress Qudsia Begum after marrying Emperor Muhammad Shah Rangila. Hirabai Zainabadi, a *nautch* girl, became Aurangzeb's favourite concubine and got the name Zainabadi Mahal.

Even before the Mughals came, all the Muslim sultanates in the north and the Deccan were equal opportunities employers of talent. A slave in the Islamic understanding of it could rise to become the master. And slaves were often raised by their masters as their own children, giving them education, military training, grooming and teaching them every other skill required to rise high in society. The first Muslim dynasty to rule Delhi, the Mamluk Sultanate, was also called the 'Slave dynasty' for precisely this reason. Qutubuddin Aibak was a slave of Shihabuddin Ghori. Sultan Ghiyasuddin Balban was a slave of Sultan Iltutmish.

Discrimination on the basis of colour was less in these regimes, but the Deccani kingdoms fared much better in this regard. Sultan Raziya, for instance, was fond of an Abyssinian slave general, Malik Jamaluddin Yaqut, whom she made the master of the sultanate's cavalry. In the Deccan, two Abyssinian slaves rose to occupy prime positions in the Ahmednagar, Bijapur and Golconda sultanates. One of them, Ikhlas Khan, was a valiant warrior and commander of men; the other, Malik Ambar, became the prime minister of Bijapur as a contemporary of Akbar and thwarted Mughal attempts to conquer the Deccan. It was Malik Ambar who had famously taught his Maratha troops to combat the well-organised Mughals through guerrilla tactics, which later became famous as *ganimi kava*.

So, of course, it was possible to rise high in the Mughal hierarchy even if you were a slave, though the Deccani kingdoms had a better record at this than the Mughals. Even in the case of Hindus occupying premier posts, the Deccani sultans proved far more egalitarian than the Mughals.[23]

In the military, the Mughals had a special category of troops called *chelas* or followers. These were primarily Hindu converts who had been taken prisoners during war when they were still boys. The various nobles and commanders raised them and trained them for soldiering and various other roles. These were the most loyal retinue of a nobleman, someone he could depend on through thick and thin. The term *chela* has continued in popular lexicon and still means a follower, though at times it is used in a negative way too.

Mughal-e-Azam, in fact, just like *Jodhaa Akbar*, wove fiction around fact. It also had Jodha Bai as Akbar's only wife, and it gave a positive spin to the real rebellion of Salim against his father, which wasn't driven by love but by lust for power.

So, in all respects, barring perhaps the costumes, the war scenes and the sets, *Mughal-e-Azam* was far removed from the Mughals. Yet it managed to present an endearing image of the Mughals, which brought the 20th-century Indians closer to the 16th-century ruler: an image that has lived on in the public consciousness despite calls from various sections to dismiss them as foreign oppressors. The new Indian state, still nursing wounds of Partition, wanted to stress on its secular ethos to end rifts and smoothen faultlines that still existed in the society. With the Pakistan bogie ever present, there was a sense of necessity all around to project a picture of communal harmony and peaceful coexistence in the past to achieve the same in the present.[24]

---

23 Iqtidar Alam Khan, *India's Polity in the Age of Akbar* (New Delhi: Permanent Black, 2016).

24 Loyalty tests on Indian Muslims were quite common in the decades following Partition. S. Irfan Habib gives details of it in his book. The contemporary Indian press also decried the practice and published laments as editorials. It was so serious that when the Indian government invited 'Frontier Gandhi' Khan Abdul Gaffar Khan to address a joint session of the Parliament, he harped on this issue too.

Two other mediums did their bit to make the Mughals and Akbar more endearing—theatre and comics.

Theatre, really, was the first medium, even before cinema, to have made the Mughals popular. It was a 1922 play named *Anarkali* that had inspired both K. Asif's *Mughal-e-Azam* and the 1953 film *Anarkali*. This play was authored by Imtiaz Ali Taj in Lahore, who was just 22 when he authored this play written in the *Chagatai* tradition. Yet these two were only later and more popular adaptations of the play. The first two movies made on it were the 1928 silent films *Loves of a Mughal Prince Anarkali* made by Prafulla and Charu Roy, and *Anarkali* by Ardeshir Irani. Irani's movie was almost shot and released overnight in direct competition to the Roys'.[25]

Taj was quite up to date for the age he was living in. When Ardeshir Irani released *Alam Ara,* the first Indian talkie in 1931, Taj rewrote his play keeping in mind the new innovation in film technology. He always intended this to be made into a film, though his own efforts to translate his wish into reality didn't succeed as by then, Bombay (now Mumbai) had outpaced Lahore in filmmaking. But the reputation of Lahore as the place to learn photography and filmmaking continued right up to Partition. For instance, the late actor Pran, who redefined the Bollywood villain, and who was originally from Delhi, was learning photography in Lahore when Partition happened.

Nevertheless, Taj's talkie version was picked up by R. S. Choudhury in 1935 and another *Anarkali* was made. This film did well. The next big movie adaptation of the play happened in 1953 with Nandlal Jaswantlal's *Anarkali*. All these Anarkali movies nearly stuck to the plot of the play, which was a tragic romance. Anarkali at the end in all these movies, just like in the play, was walled up alive. But K. Asif's *Mughal-e-Azam*, while largely sticking to the plot, gave a positive ending to it by letting Anarkali live in the shadow of Akbar's magnanimity. This was a way more serious attempt to portray Akbar as a humane king and was much more effective in creating a positive image of him.

---

25 Paul Rajadhyaksha and Paul Willemen, *Encyclopaedia of Indian Cinema* (New Delhi: British Film Institute Publishing and Oxford University Press, 1998), p. 108.

Two Telugu films named *Anarkali* (1955), and *Saleem Akbar Anarkali* (1979) were also successful movies that created a positive image of Akbar by changing the ending of Taj's play. The 1979 film was quite a hit as it was made by N. T. Rama Rao, who also essayed the role of Akbar.

There may have been other plays on Akbar, but these are relatively lesser known as movies weren't made on them. But of late, there have been some plays that are hilarious takes on Akbar's life or make him an overblown caricature. A play called *Ab Akbar Banayega Mughal-e-Azam* shows Akbar in the 21st century who is disturbed by K. Asif's film and returns to earth to make his own version of the film.

Some depictions are also inspired by comics. Akbar-Birbal tales have been a childhood staple for many people of my generation. Today, children's entertainment channels have whole series of such stories that are essentially funny but still offer great life lessons. As one all-time favourite story goes, Akbar threw a challenge that whosoever would spend some time in a freezing pond would be handsomely rewarded. A man took the challenge and actually completed the task. When Akbar asked him how he did it, the winner said he saw a lamp in the distance and tried to imagine warmth despite being skin-deep in the icy cold water. Akbar then dismissed him by saying that he had a source of warmth so he couldn't be rewarded. That he was being unfair was visible to all but him. So Birbal decided to teach him a lesson. He invited Akbar for lunch and cooked *khichdi* by placing the fire-wood on the ground and the pot on a tree branch. When Akbar called it foolish on Birbal's part to cook his food that way, Birbal reminded him that this is how he had reasoned to dismiss the achievement of that contestant.

In every such story, Akbar came across as a foolhardy man who wouldn't see sense until his smart courtier figured out a unique way to tell him he was wrong. This was a wholly wrong interpretation of Akbar, but these cute stories made him appear cute and more accessible. Just like King Hooja in *Tantri the Mantri* series in Tinkle. Or Mr Wilson in *Dennis the Menace*.

But there were more serious takes on Akbar in comics, and some of these were surprisingly balanced in their articulation of Akbar's personality and reign. The *Amar Chitra Katha* issue on Rana Pratap, for instance, portrayed Akbar as a good king even while portraying Pratap as an implacable enemy of the Mughals and a great patriot. This was pretty much in tune with Rajput bardic tales that glorified Rana Pratap and also Akbar.

Rajput sources suggest Akbar was held in high esteem in Rajputana. The epithets *shriji*, *nath* and *chhatrapati* were used for him, and he was portrayed as avatars of Vishnu—Lord Rama and Lord Krishna. Some accounts also called him an avatar of Arjuna. In fact, a 17th-century Mewar bardic poet compared the fight between Akbar and Rana Pratap with that of Karna and Arjuna. Here, Akbar was Karna, the elder brother of Arjuna.[26] It isn't difficult to understand what this implied: that both were actually separated brothers who were only victims of circumstances. This really worked in placing Akbar firmly in the otherwise quite endogamous Rajput clan structure. He was seen as a Rajput and no longer a *mlechha* (foreigner or barbarian).

Also, Akbar's military successes in Rajputana and elsewhere were appreciated by the bards in florid verse that said Akbar's conquests even shook the throne of Indra forcing the gods to form a council where Indra assured them that Akbar wouldn't invade *Indralok*.[27]

These bardic tales showed that to raise someone to a hero's status didn't necessarily require the casting down of another to the pits of ignominy. This same tradition was replicated at least in that *Amar Chitra Katha* adventure of 1970s vintage.

TV, of course, had a mixed understanding of Akbar, being a very different beast than cinema.

In 1989, Akbar made a TV debut in Shyam Benegal's magnum opus, *Bharat Ek Khoj*. Based on Jawaharlal Nehru's *Discovery of India*, this was a powerful portrayal of India's history from the point of view of the inclusive Indian nationalism of Freedom Movement vintage. Two episodes were devoted to Akbar. Bollywood actor Kulbhushan Kharbanda, who played Raja Bharmal in *Jodhaa Akbar* two decades later, essayed the role of Akbar in Shyam Benegal's production.

---

26 B. L. Bhadani, 'The Profile of Akbar in Contemporary Rajasthani Literature', *Social Scientist* 20, no. 9/10 (1992), pp. 46–53.

27 Ibid.

This Akbar was less majestic as Kharbanda brought in that neighbourhood uncle kind of familiarity to the character and spoke a more earthy language than the chaste and heavily Persianised Urdu of the Akbar played by Prithviraj Kapoor. But Kharbanda's Akbar was more believable as this Akbar had regular fits of anger, was completely disappointed by the incompetence of his sons, shattered by the cruel murder of his closest friend Abu'l Fazl by his own son Salim, suffered from impotent rage at having to pardon the criminal as it was his own son and only son alive to succeed him, and a man who eventually chastised his son by personally slapping him hard several times and locking him up in the *ghusalkhana*[28] to avenge Fazl.

This Akbar was more historically accurate than all the other Akbars combined, the lone dark spot being Jodha Bai who was still his wife in this serial. But he had a problem—he lived for only two episodes. And it was not enough to leave an imprint on public memory.

The next Akbar came to Indian TV nearly 25 years later, in 2013. That year, there wasn't one but two serials that had Akbar as a principal figure. But while in one Akbar was the protagonist, in the other he was the antagonist.

The first one was *Jodhaa Akbar*, a small screen version of Gowariker's epic but with many more characters and a weird plot. Actually, it only had the name common with Gowariker's saga; rest of it was pure fantasy involving characters from history. This was touted as the most expensive TV production in India and had 566 episodes spanning two years.

The Akbar in this serial was immature, almost juvenile, easily fooled by his intriguing begums and other courtiers, and often took the side of a devious stranger while disbelieving an intimate family member. This saga was about daily intrigues in the life of the emperor, he mistrusting his wife and doing something utterly foolish, but eventually realising his folly and expressing gratitude to his wife Jodha for being such an enlightened and sacrificial wife.

Jodha was portrayed as the quintessential good Hindu Indian wife who put her husband and family before herself and acted as the family

---

28 There isn't a precise equivalent of it today. Though we could safely say it was a bathroom.

shield. The senior wife, Ruqaiyya, was portrayed as a gullible, jealous woman who was vain at one moment and generous at another. In fact, a temporary character called Benazir[29], a Poison Ivy-like woman who was actually an assassin, took Ruqaiyya hostage and humiliated her for being foolish and not being wise enough like Jodha who saw through her game.[30] She mocked Akbar too for being less of a man who didn't deserve the sacrifice made by the noble-hearted Jodha.

The audience loved this series, and when it went off air, a public petition was filed to bring it back on air. But what it essentially did was that it portrayed the Muslim emperor, his Muslim wife and other Muslims in the court as a tad inferior people as opposed to Jodha. And it also cast another wrong notion in stone, just like the eponymous film in 2008: that Akbar was called just Jalaluddin Muhammad originally and Akbar was a title given to him by his affectionate subjects. Yet despite these defects, this Zee TV serial did overall show the Mughals in favourable light. Its contemporary on Sony TV portrayed a radically different picture of Akbar in *Bharat Ka Veer Putra Maharana Pratap*.

This series also ran for over two years starting from 2013 and had 539 episodes. It was not a serial about Akbar but a supposed biopic on Mewar King Rana Pratap Singh Sisodia. But right from the first episode, it became a show about a Hindu king fighting for his honour against Muslim enemies.

The boy prince was shown outclassing an Afghan invasion force sent by Sher Shah Suri, commanded by someone who was a cruel, barbaric and a psychotic killer. This showdown set the stage for the

29 Played by Bollywood actor Meghna Naidu, this character was a '*vish kanya*' or a woman raised through mithridatism to become a hired assassin in adulthood. The belief is that cohabiting with such a woman could be lethal for a man. Kautilya's *Arthasastra* makes reference to it and various other Sanskrit and Hindi works of fiction also talk about *vish kanyas*. Mithridatism comes from Mithridates VI of Pontus, who was one of the greatest enemies of Rome, and who tried to make himself immune to poison by ingesting poison in measured doses. His father had been poisoned to death by his mother and he feared a similar fate. In India, Gujarat Sultan Mahmud Begarha is believed to have tried something similar. Legend says Begarha could badly injure someone with his mere spit.

30 Episode 166 of Season 1.

things to come. Akbar made his debut as a young, villainous prince and a sworn enemy of Pratap. The show also distinguished itself in showing a childhood love triangle between Pratap, his future wife Ajabde Puwar, and Marwar princess Phool Kanwar. Akbar entered this triangle as a young villain who had his lusty eyes fixed on Phool Kanwar. The boy emperor also expressed his love for the Marwar princess, was spurned, and beaten to pulp by the young Pratap, who came to the Hindu princess' rescue as a knight in shining armour.

This was only the beginning, of course, and there would be many more confrontations. Patriot Pratap would mouth racial abuses for Akbar, always referring to him as '*woh Turk-Mughal* (that Turk Mughal)'.

Akbar, on the other hand, distinguished himself in finding ways to foment trouble in Mewar and Pratap's life. He would send seductresses-cum-assassins, invasion forces, encourage people in Pratap's camp to become turncoats—basically every trick from a cartoon villain's playbook was tried.

With age, this Akbar only grew more sinister. He trampled anyone and everyone who came in his way but failed to do any damage to Pratap. He got his mentor, Bairam Khan, killed because he was secretly having an affair with his wife, Salima Sultan Begum. In fact, Salima was a co-plotter. This Akbar also mouthed communal lines openly, even in the presence of Man Singh. But barring Akbar, everyone else around him who was a non-Hindu was portrayed either as a buffoon or as a grotesque creature straight out of an Arthur Miller graphic novel.

As opposed to this was the portrayal of the Rajputs as better looking and better behaved people loaded with the best of virtues like honesty and probity. They were shown as courageous people who won their wars through bravery and *dharma*—their code of chivalry. No matter how hard they tried, the Mughals could make no headway against them. Occasionally when they won, it was through guile and treachery—in tune with the prejudiced retelling of history in Hindutva circles where courage and bravery are the sole preserves of the Hindus while the Muslims always had a trick or two up their sleeves to back-stab and overwhelm the trusting Hindus.

This show was spectacularly unfair in the treatment of Muslim characters. And it strangely reflected the prevailing political narrative after the BJP came to power. As it is no secret that daily soaps have their scripts written only a few days before shooting, this serial's script also incorporated the perceived socio-political demands. For instance, when cow protection or *gau raksha* became an issue with the regime actively promoting ban on cattle slaughter and vigilante mobs sniffing around refrigerators of minorities, the serial in one of the episodes randomly inserted a scene that showed a priest coming to Prince Pratap to remind him of his Kshatriya dharma to protect 'mother cow'. Pratap, then under house arrest on the orders of his father, violated his father's orders and ventured out to protect cows from being stolen (for slaughter).

The multi-layered history of Rajputana and Rajputs, an overwhelming majority of whom sided with the Mughals, was perhaps too complex for this serial to analyse. Through dialogues, facial expressions and special background music, the Rajputs who sided with the Mughals were depicted either as dupes of the Mughals or traitors to the faith and country. The great Rajput warrior and Mughal *mansabdar*, Mirza Raja Man Singh, was portrayed as a devious man gayly plotting against fellow Hindus. In the black-and-white and rather virulent version of nationalism that increasingly occupied centre stage in the country following the coming of the BJP to power, nuance had to be cast aside as it was too heavy a baggage to carry. And *Bharat Ka Veer Putra Maharana Pratap* miserably failed in this.

A nuanced view would have meant acknowledgement of the fact that from the 13th century onwards, Rajput rulers and chieftains had started marrying off their daughters to the Sultans of Delhi so there was nothing shocking or criminal about a Muslim emperor marrying a Rajput woman or even expressing the wish to marry one, as shown in the scene between Akbar and Phool Kanwar.

These marriage alliances helped Rajput rulers to sort out their own territorial insecurities as well as resist challenges from rival clans. States like Amber ended up having more territory with Mughal help. But states that refused to join the empire had an inversion of fortune. Mewar, for instance, lost a lot of territory, resources and influence due to its losing wars with the Mughals as compared to its rivals, Marwar and Amber.

Barbara Ramusack writes in her book *The Indian Princes and Their States*:

> In the 10th and 11th centuries, the Kachhawaha clan migrated into an area known as Dhoondar, south of Delhi and north of Mewar. Dulha Rai, a Kachhawaha leader, supposedly granted estates to indigenous Minas in return for their allegiance, and their symbiotic relationship was acknowledged in two practices: first, a Mina placed the *tilak*[31], an auspicious mark, on an incoming Jaipur ruler during the installation durbar or ceremony, and the second, the Minas were the hereditary guards of the Jaipur treasury.

This notion of power sharing existed before the coming of Islamic rulers and showed a relatively open mind of the Kachwaha Rajputs to allow the Minas, who were considered backward castes, to perform a ritual that was a Brahminical preserve everywhere else in India. This flexibility of the Kachwahas made them establish matrimonial relations with the Mughals too, five centuries later.

Mewar, on the other hand, took an entirely different path. While fighting Alauddin Khilji, the Chittor garrison performed *jauhar* and *saka* and was annihilated in 1304. They did it again in 1534 fighting Bahadur Shah of Gujarat, and again in 1568 fighting the Mughals. Now, Mewar was ruled by the Guhilots in the 14th century and Sisodiyas in the 16th century. Yet both dynasties chose to transform their defeats into unmitigated disasters.

Mewar's resistance finally ended with the defeat of Rana Pratap at Haldighati by Mughal forces led by Mirza Raja Man Singh, a fellow Rajput. Ramusack says:

> These two Rajput rulers illustrated the consequences of two Rajput responses to an expanding imperial system. Amber's acceptance of a client relationship with a Mughal patron yielded an increase in territory, *jagirdari* rights to collect land revenue around his capital, and bardic

31 The Jaipur royal family still follows this tradition.

> condemnation, while Mewar's refusal brought loss of territory but poetic glory.

But it isn't that Rajput marriages were happening only with the Mughals. The Sharqis of Jaunpur who were fighting the Mughals were also being courted by Rajputs of Avadh for matrimonial alliances.[32]

With such a multi-layered history of Hindu–Muslim matrimony, it's surprising that the serial on Rana Pratap chose to vilify Akbar for wanting to marry Phool Kanwar. Incidentally, the issue India was debating around that time was 'love Jihad', a conspiracy imagined by Hindu communal groups that involves Muslim youth posing as Hindus to make Hindu women fall in love with them and elope with them. The Hindu communalists allege this is done to convert those Hindu women into Islam after marriage.

The serial had very few redeeming features, except for the good-looking main star cast. But it defied a widely held axiom that good actors can take a bad script only so far. It ran for over two years with an average star cast without any thrilling acting to boot.

Another feeble attempt was made in 2017 to make a TV biopic on Akbar. Called *Akbar: Rakht Se Takht Ka Safar* was a damp squib that started with the narration in the first episode itself mixing up the names of Jahangir and Humayun, calling the latter Nuruddin Muhammad Humayun when it was Nasiruddin. It was far removed from the history and chronology of Akbar's reign, instead showcasing imaginary happenings and fantasies. It wasn't a terribly popular serial, also because it ran on Big Magic (Zee Magic), a channel that was restricted to certain satellite TV networks and not as popular as the bigger general entertainment channels like Sony or Zee or Star Plus.

But there was another serial called *Siyasat* on EPIC channel, which was based on Indu Sundaresan's *The Twentieth Wife*. This focused on politics inside and outside Akbar's harem in his later years with a rebellious Jahangir increasingly asserting himself while telling the story of how Noor Jahan attained her pre-eminent position in the Mughal

---

32 Ramya Sreenivasan, 'Alauddin Khalji Remembered: Conquest, Gender and Community in Medieval Rajput Narratives', *Studies in History* 18, no. 2, 2002, pp. 275–96.

world. The focus was not so much on Akbar himself. But for the first time, the series focused on other lesser known historical characters like Abu'l Fazl, Mirza Aziz Koka, and Khan-i-Khanan Abdur Rahim Khan. The politics of succession involving the camps of Khusrau and Jahangir were fascinating to watch, even though it was imagination grounded in fact.

The same channel aired another serial called *Time Machine*, which was about a ragtag bunch of people using a time machine to go to the past to steal artefacts. One of the episodes took them to Akbar's India during which they tried to steal Abu'l Fazl's diary. They even rescued Fazl from assassination once during which he told them how he covered-up for the emperor, even protecting his misdeeds and giving them a positive colour. But he also expressed that he was fed up hiding the truth about Akbar. Through fiction, a revisionist take on Akbar was put out that actually matched the various half-truths and outright lies projected by various Hindu communal websites or websites that are apologists of Hindutva and the BJP.

That brings me to the conclusion that India's official broadcaster Doordarshan in the 1980s and 1990s did far more service to the cause of history than any private channel of today. The only largely authentic TV production on Akbar was Akbar Khan's *Akbar the Great*. This serial was aired in the early 1990s, but did not have a successful run, being pulled off air after a while. It didn't have a great star cast, production quality wasn't anything to write home about, and acting hovered between below average and average. Also, it was eclipsed by the glitz and glamour of *The Sword of Tipu Sultan* that preceded it, and *The Great Maratha* that came after it. The latter two, though historically not the most accurate, were made like movies for the small screen by Akbar Khan's elder brother, Sanjay Khan. These had great acting, great cinematography, great action sequences and music. *Akbar the Great* suffered in all these parameters. But it still had something special about it—it was the first TV show on the life of Akbar!

The series, by and large, stuck to Abu'l Fazl's version of the events in Akbar's life. Even when it drew from other sources, like Jauhar's *Tazkirat ul-Waqiat*, it left out the embarrassing bits, or the spicy ones.

For instance, while depicting the haughty conduct of Shah Tahmasp and his insulting attitude towards Humayun, the serial turned it around on its head and showed Humayun in more favourable light. He was shown as having stunned the Persian emperor with his honesty, brevity and wit. Humayun was also shown as having mouthed a rather emotional rhetoric about there being no difference between Sunnis and Shias. Moved, Shah Tahmasp was shown wearing Humayun's robe—a poetic licence at best and outright falsehood at worst.

But then, where in the world is that filmmaker who follows the rulebook to the T, never twists a historical plot, never takes creative liberties and never spices up a script? If there is one such filmmaker, his audience must be entirely museum and archival staff and university professors.

Yet nobody has a case when a universally accepted tolerant emperor is shown as a cruel bigot and bloodthirsty fiend. That's not revisionism, which has some sanctity even in the academia; that's called distortion. And this new image of Akbar hasn't just been promoted by serials like the one on Rana Pratap; Indian TV news channels have played a major part in this too.

One thing that changed after Narendra Modi became the Prime Minister in 2014 was news as we understood it. The Indian TV news media, which pretended to be a bold institution talking truth to power during the UPA regime, quickly changed into a coy bride in May 2014, hesitant to even lift her veil to see if she married a man or an ass.

But it wasn't too long before the watchdog of democracy turned into a lapdog of the regime, barking and growling at anyone even mildly critical of the new occupants of the house. At that very moment, they broke the covenant with the people. Different people reacted differently to it. Some endorsed it, cheering the change and egging on those journalists to break newer grounds; some rejected it, turning to foreign news channels instead.

Any neutral observer can say that the rot in the TV media has only got deeper in the last five years. The phrase 'his master's voice' once reminded one of the cute HMV logo with the dog peeking into a gramophone. Today, it is a nasty phrase that only reminds one of the propagandist news anchors who distort the news with their views to taint the opposition and find redeeming features of the government even when it is in a cesspit of its own incompetence.

With a bunch of baloney every evening, these journalists—some would say pamphleteers—have been playing the ridiculous nation game acting as self-appointed agent provocateurs of the state, making zombies out of gullible folks who religiously watch them.

The manufactured controversies over a celebrity's death or another's suspected pregnancy should open some eyes about how the whole nation is being hoodwinked into believing that those are the only issues that matter, not the Judge Loya death case or the Syrian genocide.

An argument could be made that it is because of these gaslighting acts by the press that a large section of the viewers/readers are no longer willing to believe in the mainstream media and are looking towards social media for news. That's why the social media rumour mill, now pejoratively referred to as 'WhatsApp University', has turned out graduates on such an industrial scale.

It's these 'graduates' who have been spreading hate about the Mughals and Akbar. Anyone who makes even the faintest of noise about the need to remember the Mughals is responded to with a savage din of retribution.

Not that these voices never existed. They did, on the fringes. But now, these voices have attained critical mass and have become the mainstream. At one level, it is actually a very interesting phenomenon. It shows democratisation of space at the grassroots level. Social media has actually provided a voice to the most marginalised of individuals at the remotest parts of the country. And it has provided a level playing field. Someone sitting somewhere in a remote village of Nagaland can now air his grievance on Twitter and also tag the Prime Minister's account to it. On the flip side, it gives that individual the power to even attack or 'troll' the Prime Minister for something he doesn't approve of.

The cheaply available mobile phone has acted as a great weapon in the hands of those left behind in the race of modernity and opportunity, fighting daily oppression of various kinds. At another time, it was the Kalashnikov rifle that had given the Afghan mujahideen the power to take on the might of a global superpower, the Soviet Union. The firepower that the rifle provided gave the Afghans for the first time a level playing field against the superior training and equipment of the Red Army soldier.

However, even though the invader had to bite the dust and withdraw, the Kalashnikov didn't emerge as a great enabler eventually. It turned against the Afghan people and what followed is recent history that most of us have seen it unfold. What the cellphone would do to the Indian people is still in the realm of the future. But already, it has shown its destructive power in the hands of rumour-mongers and political agents. Fake news has become a weapon to target people of different faiths and opinions.

Since 2015, however, rumour-mongering through instant messaging applications has led to the lynching of scores of innocent people.[33] The template of each such crime has been similar: a rumour is spread via WhatsApp, a mob gets together fast, the victim is cornered and thrashed to death, and the whole act is recorded on cellphone cameras, with people even taking selfies with the dying victim. Most of the victims have been hapless Muslims, and the most common rumour that led to those heinous crimes was that the victim had either killed a cow or had beef.

It's a strange and unfortunate slide of a nation that was until five years ago speculating when Chandrayaan, India's planned mission to the Moon, would lift off but is now now speculating what meat is stored in the refrigerator of a Muslim family. A nation that was keen to compete with China to become the biggest Asian economy is today debating that Hindus are under threat, and 'Mother Cow' is under threat, and Pakistan is India's biggest enemy. It is as if a Kraken of hate, bigotry and violence has been unleashed on this country. Or, perhaps this is an ugly manifestation of latent communal feelings in the people that have now mutated and grown uncontrollably, just like viruses grow and spread when the conditions are right. Perhaps a more accurate comparison would be with that alien life form in the 1990s movie *Evolution* that grew to a monstrous size every time it came in

---

33 In 2015, a Muslim man named Mohammed Akhlaq was lynched by a Hindu mob in Bisada village, Greater Noida, on suspicion that he had eaten beef. Photos of a slaughtered cow from some other place were circulated via WhatsApp to mobilise the mob.

contact with fire. Hate is also like that. It ignites violence and then grows manifold in the blaze of fury. It shuts the mind to reason.

In this backdrop, it is important once again to revisit the intellectual debate that Akbar had started, but which, unfortunately, was never followed up properly. At his *Ibadat Khana*, which was the first nursery of secularism in India, Akbar exposed himself and his courtiers and inner circle of friends to all kinds of ideas gleaned from different faiths. Ideas that were illuminating at times and disappointing at other times; ideas that energised the mind and soul at times and enervated them at other times. In this contradiction, Akbar found a way to end strife and heal wounds.

Father Pierre du Jarric, a French missionary writing about the Jesuit visits to Akbar's court and their arguments at the *Ibadat Khana*, made a remark on Akbar that was way off the mark and very accurate at the same time. Jarric wrote:

> But although such acts as these seemed to show that the King held the Christian faith in high esteem, there were, nevertheless, many things which stood in the way of his embracing it. The first was his unwillingness to accept the doctrines of Trinity and the Incarnation without being able to comprehend them; so that he was kept in a state of perpetual irresolution, not knowing where to fix his faith. 'For the Gentiles[34],' he said, 'regard their law as good; and so likewise do the Saracens and the Christians. To which then shall we give our adherence?'[35]

Jarric then analysed the reason behind Akbar's 'irresolution':

> Thus we see in this Prince the common fault of the atheist, who refuses to make reason subservient to faith, and, accepting nothing as true which his feeble mind is unable to fathom, is content to submit to his own imperfect judgement matters transcending the highest limits of human understanding.[36]

34 Gentile or Gentoo is an old English word for Hindu.

35 Father Pierre du Jarric, *Akbar and the Jesuits: An Account of the Jesuit Missions to the Court of Akbar*, p. 15.

36 Ibid.

Jarric also managed to apportion the largest part of the blame on Akbar's numerous wives. He wrote:

> ...the greatest hindrance to his conversion to our faith was the multitude of wives which the Mahometan law permitted him to keep. There were in his seraglio as many as a hundred women; and it was doubtful if he would ever be willing to renounce all of these but one, and to live with that one in lawful wedlock, as the Christian law demands.[37]

Jarric was way off the mark when he assumed Akbar had a feeble mind and that he was irresolute. He wrote this in a condescending manner to show that Akbar didn't understand what was being offered to him—the superior Christian faith—and so rejected it. But he was quite right in saying that Akbar wasn't willing to 'make reason subservient to faith'. Akbar had rejected dogma, and he would rather find his own way instead of following the beaten track. So, when his mother, whom he revered publicly and privately, asked him to tie a Bible around the neck of a dog and let it loose in the markets of Agra as revenge for the Portuguese doing the same with a Koran seized from a Mughal ship in Ormuz, Akbar refused.

He supposedly said:

> That if it were ill in the Portugals to do so to Alcoran, it became not a king requite ill with ill, for that the contempt of any religion was the contempt of God, and he wouldn't be revenged upon an innocent Book.[38]

Much later in 1831, the British editors of the *Asiatic Journal and Monthly Miscellany* contrasted Akbar's attitude to that of Joseph Fouche, a French revolutionary republican who had brutally suppressed an insurrection at Lyons in 1793–94, and who had persecuted the Church in a bid to de-Christianise the country. 'This act, which a Mahomedan thought profane, was performed by the notorious Fouche, who, in 1793, at Lyons, caused the Bible to be

---

37 Ibid.

38 Ruby Lal, *Domesticity and Power in the Early Mughal World*, p. 204.

dragged through the mire at the tail of an ass.'[39] In this, Fouche was the ideological predecessor of Lenin who had cracked down on the Church and carried out a rapacious loot of its riches to fill up the coffers of the new Soviet state, but who had only alluded to Marx's comment on religion being the 'opiate of the masses' as an intellectual cover for this persecution.

But as Jarric had said, Akbar perhaps had also shown signs of becoming an atheist as the years rolled by.

From being called Jalaluddin Muhammad Akbar for most part of his life, Akbar quietly dropped Muhammad from his name later in life and became just Jalaluddin Akbar. Later, his son and successor Jahangir also dropped Muhammad from his name and called himself just Nuruddin Jahangir. In fact, foreign travellers also spread a rumour abroad that Jahangir was never circumcised (the *Akbarnama*, though, gives the date and details of the circumcision of all the three sons of Akbar).

Rafiuddin Ibrahim Shirazi in his *Tazkirat ul-Muluk* said Akbar forever held a grudge against the Prophet Muhammad[40] for declaring himself to be the last Prophet of Islam and thereby denying Akbar a chance to declare himself a Prophet. This could be a fanciful attribution, but definitely not devoid of some merit. For the unencumbered mind of Akbar, anything was possible. That's why perhaps Jawaharlal Nehru had said as a reaction to Jarric's comment on Akbar being an atheist that if this were the case, then every Indian should be like Akbar.[41]

It is a tragedy that this intellectual work that Akbar had started was abandoned by his successors. It is also a tragedy that these fascinating aspects of his life have never been brought out on the silver screen, TV and even comics. No wonder then that politicians and even young guns spew venom about Akbar. It is human nature to detest what we don't understand, but the systematic hate campaign around the Mughals has taken it to another level.

---

39 *The Asiatic Journal and Monthly Miscellany for British and Foreign India, China and Australasia* 6, 1831, p. 266.

40 Iqtidar Alam Khan, *India's Polity in the Age of Akbar*, p. 141.

41 Professor Irfan Habib told me this during a personal interaction with him at his department in 2018.

How all of this would reshape the memory of Akbar, only time would tell. But there's no denying the fact that it would have to be through a war of ideas, at the end of which the world might know whose idea of Akbar would stand. This battle could swing both ways. But it only portends one thing: history would be the casualty. This also means that Akbar would remain in the popular imagination, either clothed in the robe of tolerance or in the mail of bigotry. But he would remain in his birthday suit in the pristine corridors of academia, under the firm, peering gaze of professors and scholars. This Akbar would continue to delight truth seekers.

Amid all this, on 14 May 2018, risk management professional in the banking sector and Mumbai resident Ramachandran Venkatesh left a comment on my Facebook wall in which he echoed what Bombay resident Adi K. Munshi[42] had said in 1941, without knowing what Munshi had articulated. '(We) need a visionary leader like Emperor Akbar to drive unity in diversity and converge diverse political and cultural interests at the top,' Venkatesh wrote.

This gave me the feeling that exciting times are ahead, no matter on which side of the debate one stands. And whether it was 1941 or 2018, Akbar is still relevant and he is still missed by Indians. What does that say about us Indians? That we are a medieval people, creating conditions in the country akin to those that prevailed in Akbar's lifetime, always using past hurt to justify present hate, and therefore needing a medieval monarch to show us the way.

What does that say about Akbar? That he was a medieval king who, with a progressive bent of mind, dared to look ahead to find that common ground for all his people to stand together. That he was a medieval king who is today tempting us to look back into the past to see our future through his eyes.

42 See introduction chapter.

Bibliography

Primary sources

Aftabchi, Jauhar. *Tazkirat Ul-Waqiat*, translated by Major Charles Stewart as *The Tezkereh Al Vakiat, or Private Memoirs of the Mogul Emperor Humayun*. London: Oriental Translation Fund for Great Britain and Ireland, 1833.

Ahmad, Nizamuddin. *The Tabakat-i-Akbari of Khwaja Nizamuddin Ahmad, Vols II–III*, translated by B. De. Calcutta: The Asiatic Society, 1936–39.

Babur, Zahiruddin Muhammad. *Tuzuk-i-Baburi,* translated by Annette S. Beveridge as *The Babur-nama in English.* London: Luzac & Co, 1922; also translated by Wheeler M. Thackston as *The Baburnama: Memoirs of Babur, Prince and Emperor.* New York: Oxford University Press, 1996.

Badaoni, Abdul Qadir. *Muntakhab-Ut-Tawarikh, Vol. II*, translated by W. H. Lowe. Calcutta: The Asiatic Society, 1884.

Bayley, E. C. *The History of India As Told By Its Own Historians: The Local Muhammadan Dynasties. Gujarat, based on a translation of Mirat-i-Sikandari of Sikandar ibn Muhammad Manjhu.* London: W. H. Allen and Co, 1886.

Begum, Gulbadan. *Humayun Nama*, translated by Annette S. Beveridge. London: Royal Asiatic Society, 1902.

Bernier, François. *Travels in the Mogul Empire, A.D. 1656–1668*, translated by Archibald Constable and Vincent Arthur Smith on the basis of Irving Brocks Version and Annotated by Archibald Constable (1891), II ed. London: H. Milford, Oxford University Press, 1914.

Dughlat, Mirza Muhammad Haidar. *The Tarikh-i-Rashidi*, translated by E. Denison Ross, edited by N. Elias as *A History of the Moghuls of Central Asia*. London: Sampson Low, Marston and Company, 1895.

Elliot, H. M., *The History of India As Told By Its Own Historians, Vols V–VI*. London: Trubner & Co, 1873–75.

Fazl, Abu'l. *The Ain-i-Akbari, Vols. I–III*, translated by H. Blochmann (I) and Colonel H. S. Jarrett (II, III). Calcutta: The Asiatic Society, 1868–94, reprinted in 2010.

———. *The Akbarnama of Abu'l Fazl, Vols I–III*, translated by H. Beveridge. Calcutta: The Asiatic Society, 1907–39, reprinted in 2010.

Firishta, Muhammad Qasim. *Tarikh-i-Firishta*, translated by John Briggs as *History of the Rise of Mahomedan Power in India till the year 1612, Vol. II*. London: Longman, Rees, Orme, Brown and Green, 1829.

Jahangir, Nuruddin Muhammad. *Tuzuk-i-Jahangiri*, translated by Alexander Rogers, edited by H. Beveridge as *Memoirs of Jahangir*. London: Royal Asiatic Society, 1909.

Jarric, Father Pierre Du. *Akbar and the Jesuits: An Account of the Jesuit Missions to the Court of Akbar*. London: WM. Brendon and Son, 1926, reprinted in 2005 by Routledge Curzon.

Khan, Ali Muhammad. *Mirat-i-Ahmadi*, translated by M. F. Lokhandwala. Baroda: Oriental Institute, 1965.

Khwandamir. *Qanun-i-Humayuni*, translated by Baini Prashad. Calcutta: The Asiatic Society, 1940.

Manucci, Niccolao. *Storia Do Mogor, Vol. I*, translated by William Irvine. London: John Murray, Albemarle Street, 1907.

Monserrate, Father S. J. *The Commentary of Father Monserrate S.J: On his Journey to the Court of Akbar*, translated by J. S. Hoyland. London: Oxford University Press, 1922.

Neeamat Ullah, Harawi. *History of the Afghans*, translated by Bernhard Dorn. London: Royal Asiatic Society, 1836.

Salim, Ghulam Husain. *Riyaz us-Salatin*, translated by Maulvi Abdus Salam. Calcutta: The Asiatic Society, 1902.

Tavernier, Jean-Baptiste. *Travels in India, Vol. II*, translated by Valentine Ball, edited by William Crooke. London: Oxford University Press, 1925.

Secondary sources: Books and chapters in edited books

Alam, Muzaffar and Sanjay Subrahmanyam. *Writing the Mughal World.* New Delhi: Permanent Black, 2011.

Ali, Daud. *Courtly Culture and Political Life in Early Medieval India.* New Delhi: Cambridge University Press, 2006.

Asher, Catherine B. and Talbot, Cynthia. *India before Europe.* United Kingdom: Cambridge University Press, 2006, reprinted in 2007.

Asher, Catherine B. *The New Cambridge History of India: Architecture of Mughal India.* United Kingdom: Cambridge University Press, 1992.

Augustus, Frederick Count of Noer. *Kaiser Akbar*, translated by Annette S. Beveridge as *The Emperor Akbar: A Contribution towards the History of India in the 16th Century.* London: Thacker, Spinck & Co, 1890.

Barpujari, H. K. *The Comprehensive History of Assam Vol. II.* Guwahati: Publication Board Assam, 2003.

Barua, Pradeep P. *The State at War in South Asia.* Lincoln and London: University of Nebraska Press, 2005.

Cary, Henry. *Herodotus: A New and Literal Version from the Text of Baehr.* New York: Harper & Brothers, Publishers, 1859.

Chand, Tara. *Influence of Islam on Indian Culture.* Allahabad: The Indian Press, 1936.

Chandra, Satish. *History of Medieval India*. New Delhi: Orient Blackswan, 2007.

Citino, Robert M. *Death of the Wehrmacht: The German Campaigns of 1942. Asceticism and its Critics: Historical Accounts and Comparative Perspectives*. New York: Oxford University Press, 2006, 2007.

———. *The German Way of War: From The Thirty Years' War to the Third Reich*. Kansas: University Press of Kansas, 2005.

Coetzee, Daniel and Lee W. Eysturlid. *Philosophers of War: The Evolution of History Greatest Military Thinkers, Volume I: The Ancient to Premodern World, 3000 BCE–1815 CE*. California: Praeger, 2013.

Cort, John E. *Open Boundaries: Jain Communities and Cultures in Indian History*. New York: State University of New York Press, 1998.

Dale, Stephen Frederic. *Babur: Timurid Prince and Mughal Emperor, 1483–1530*. London: Cambridge University Press, 2018.

———. *The Garden of the Eight Paradises: Babur and the Culture of Empire in Central Asia, Afghanistan and India, 1483–1530*. Leiden, Boston: Brill, 2004.

Dashti, Naseer. *The Baloch and Balochistan: A Historical Account from the Beginning to the Fall of the Baloch State*. United States: Trafford Publishing, 2012.

Eaton, Richard M. *The Rise of Islam and the Bengal Frontier, 1204–1760*. Berkeley: University of California Press, 1993.

Edwardes, Stephen M. and Herbert Leonard Offley Garret. *Mughal Rule in India*. New Delhi: Atlantic Publishers And Distributors, 1995.

Eraly, Abraham. *The Mughal World: Life in India's Last Golden Age*. New Delhi: Penguin Books, 2007.

———. *Emperors of the Peacock Throne: The Saga of the Great Mughals*. New Delhi: Penguin Books, 2000.

Ernst, Carl W. *Following Muhammad: Rethinking Islam in the Contemporary World*. Chapel Hill & London: The University of North Carolina Press, 2003.

———. *Eternal Garden: Mysticism, History, and Politics at a South Asian Sufi Center*. New York: The State University of New York Press, 1992.

Fischel, Walter J. *Ibn Khaldun and Tamerlane: Their Historic Meeting in Damascus, 1401 A.D. (803 A.H)*. Los Angeles: University of California Press, 1952.

Freiburger, Oliver. *Asceticism and its Critics: Historical Accounts and Comparative Perspectives. Asceticism and its Critics: Historical Accounts and Comparative Perspectives*. New York: Oxford University Press, 2006.

Garza, Andrew De La. *The Mughal Empire at War: Babur, Akbar and the Indian military revolution, 1500–1605*. New York and London: Routledge, 2016.

Ghosh, Pika. *Temple to Love: Architecture and Devotion in Seventeenth-Century Bengal.* Bloomington: Indiana University Press, 2005.

Glantz, David M. and House, Jonathan M. *When Titans Clashed: How the Red Army Stopped Hitler*. Kansas: University Press of Kansas, 2015.

Gommans, Jos and Dirk Kolf. *Warfare and Weaponry in South Asia, 1000–1800.* New Delhi: Oxford University Press, 2001.

Gommans, Jos. *Mughal Warfare: Indian Frontiers and High Roads to Empire, 1500–1700*. London: Routledge, 2002.

Habib, Irfan S. *Indian Nationalism: The Essential Writings.* New Delhi: Aleph Book Company, 2018.

Habib, Irfan. *Akbar and His India.* New Delhi: Oxford University Press, 1997.

———. *The Agrarian System of Mughal India (1556–1707).* New York: Asia Publishing House, 1963

Hajari, Nisid. *Midnight's Furies: The Deadly Legacy of India's Partition*. London: Amberley Publishing, 2015.

Havell, Ernest Binfield. *Indian Architecture: Its Psychology, Structure, and History from the First Muhammadan Invasion to the Present Day.* London: John Murray, 1913.

Hernon, Ian. *Fortress Britain: All the Invasions and Incursions since 1066*. United Kingdom: The History Press, 2013.

Hooja, Rima. *Maharana Pratap: The Invincible Warrior*. New Delhi: Juggernaut Books, 2018.

Irvine, William. *The Army Of The Indian Moghuls: Its Organisation And Administration*. London: Luzac & Co, 1903.

Kennedy, Pringle. *A History of the Badshahate of Delhi from 1398 AD to 1739*. Calcutta: Thacker, Spink and Co, 1905.

Khan, Iqtidar Alam. *India's Polity in the Age of Akbar*. New Delhi: Permanent Black, 2016.

———. *Gunpowder and Firearms: Warfare in Medieval India*. New Delhi: Oxford University Press, 2004.

Khan, Sayyid Ahmad. *Asar-us-Sanadid*, translated by Rana Safvi. New Delhi: Tulika Books, 2018.

Kistler, John M. *War Elephants*. United States: Praeger Publishers, 2006.

Kothiyal, Tanuja. *Nomadic Narratives: A History of Mobility and Identity in the Great Indian Desert*. New Delhi: Cambridge University Press, 2016.

Kulke, Hermann and Dietmar Rothermund. *A History of India*. Kiel and Heidelberg: Routledge, 2009.

Lacey, James. *Great Strategic Rivalries: From the Classical World to the Cold War*. New York: Oxford University Press, 2016.

Lal, Kishori Saran. *Muslim Slave System in Medieval India*. New Delhi: Aditya Prakashan, 1994.

Lal, Ruby. *Domesticity and Power in the Early Mughal World*. United Kingdom: Cambridge University Press, 2005.

Latif, Syad Muhammad Khan Bahadur. *Agra: Historical & Descriptive with an Account of Akbar and His Court and of the Modern City of Agra*. Calcutta: Calcutta Central Press Company, 1896.

Majumdar, R. C. *The History of Bengal: Hindu Period*. Dacca: The University of Dacca, 1943.

Malleson, Colonel G. B. *Rulers of India: Akbar and the Rise of the Mughal Empire*. Oxford: Clarendon Press, 1896.

Mehta, J. L. *Advanced Study in the History of Medieval India*. New Delhi: Sterling Publishers, 1980.

Monahan, F. J. *The Early History of Bengal*. London: Oxford University Press, 1925.

Moosvi, Shireen. *The Economy of the Mughal Empire c. 1595: A Statistical Study*. New Delhi: Oxford University Press, 1987, reprinted in 2015.

Mukhia, Harbans. *The Mughals of India*. United Kingdom: Blackwell Publishing, 2004.

———. *Historians and Historiography in the Reign of Akbar*. New Delhi: Vikas Publishing House, 1976.

Nehru, Jawaharlal. *The Discovery of India*. Calcutta: The Signet Press, 1946, reprinted in 1985 by Oxford University Press.

Panikkar, K. M. *His Highness the Maharaja of Bikaner: A Biography*. London: Oxford University Press, 1937.

Prasad, Rajiva Nain. *Raja Man Singh of Amber*. Calcutta: World Press, 1966.

Raghavan, T. C. A. *Attendant Lords: Bairam Khan and Abdur Rahim, Courtiers & Poets in Mughal India*. New Delhi: HarperCollins Publishers India, 2017.

Rajadhyaksha, Ashish and Paul Willemen. *Encyclopaedia of Indian Cinema*. New Delhi: British Film Institute Publishing and Oxford University Press, 1998.

Raychaudhuri, Tapan and Habib, Irfan. *The Cambridge Economic History of India, Volume I: c. 1200–1750*. Cambridge University Press, 1982, reprinted in 1987.

Rezavi, Syed Ali Nadeem. *Fathpur Sikri Revisited*. New Delhi: Oxford University Press, 2013.

Richards, John F. *The New Cambridge History of India: The Mughal Empire*. Cambridge: Cambridge University Press, 1993.

Rizvi, Syed Athar Abbas. *A History of Sufism in India: Early Sufism and its History in India to 1600 AD*. New Delhi: Munshiram Manoharlal Publishers Pvt Ltd, 1978.

Roy, Kaushik. *Military Transition in Early Modern Asia, 1400–1750: Cavalry, Guns, Government and Ships*. London: Bloomsbury, 2014.

———. *War, Culture and Society in Early Modern South Asia, 1740–1849.* United Kingdom: Routledge, 2011.

Safvi, Rana. *Forgotten Cities of Delhi*. New Delhi: HarperCollins Publishers India, 2018.

Sangar, Satya Prakash. *Crime and Punishment in Mughal India.* New Delhi: Sterling Publishers, 1967.

Sarkar, Jadunath. *A History of Jaipur, c. 1503–1938.* New Delhi: Orient Longman Limited, 1984, reprinted in 1994.

———. *Military History of India*. Calcutta: Orient Longmans, 1960.

Schimmel, Annemarie and Stuart Cary Welch. *Anvari's Divan: A Pocket Book For Akbar, A Divan of Auhaduddin Anvari, copied for the Mughal emperor Jalaluddin Akbar (r. 1556–1605) at Lahore in A. H. 996/A.D. 1588.* New York: The Metropolitan Museum of Art, 1983.

Sengupta, Nikhil K. *Land of Two Rivers: A History of Bengal from the Mahabharata to Mujib*. New Delhi: Penguin Books, 2012.

Singh, Lieutenant General Harbakhsh. *In the Line of Duty: A Soldier Remembers*. New Delhi: Lancer Publishers, 2013.

Sinha, Mrinalini. *Colonial masculinity: The 'Manly Englishman' and The 'Effeminate Bengali' In the Late Nineteenth Century*. New York: Manchester University Press, 1995.

Smith, Vincent Arthur. *Akbar the Great Mogul.* London: Oxford University Press, 1917.

Stein, Burton. *A History of India.* United Kingdom: Blackwell Publishers Ltd, 2010.

Streets, Heather. *Martial Races: The Military, Race and Masculinity in British Imperial Culture, 1857–1914*. United Kingdom: Manchester University Press, 2004.

Streusand, Douglas E. *Islamic Gunpowder Empires: Ottomans, Safavids, and Mughals*. United States: Westview Press, 2011.

Tod, James. *Annals and Antiquities of Rajasthan, Vols I–III*. New Delhi: Low Price Publications, 2000.

Truschke, Audrey. *Culture of Encounters: Sanskrit at the Mughal Court*. New York: Columbia University Press, 2016.

Wink, Andre. *Makers of the Muslim World: Akbar*. Oxford: Oneworld Publications, 2009.

Yadav, Rupali. *Crime, Criminality and Crime Control in Mughal India, 1526–1707*. Aligarh: Aligarh Muslim University, 2010.

Mason, Philip. *A Matter of Honour: An Account of the Indian Army, its Officers and Men*. Dehradun: Natraj Publishers, 2004.

Journal works and research papers

Ali, M. Athar. "Translations of Sanskrit Works at Akbar's Court", *Social Scientist* 20, no. 9/10 (1992), pp. 38–45.

Bano, Shadab. "Eunuchs in Mughal Household and Court", *Proceedings of the Indian History Congress* 69 (2008), pp. 417–27.

Bhadani, B. L., "The Profile of Akbar in Contemporary Rajasthani Literature", *Social Scientist* 20, no. 9/10 (1992), pp. 46–53.

Buckler, F. "A New Interpretation of Akbar's 'Infallibility' Decree of 1579", *Journal of the Royal Asiatic Society of Great Britain and Ireland* 4 (1924), pp. 591–608.

Chattopadhyay, Pranab K. "Documentation of Cannons of Eastern India", *Indian Journal of History of Science* 47, no.1 (2012), pp. 157–68.

Garbe, Richard. "Akbar, Emperor of India: A picture of life and customs from the sixteenth century", *The Monist* 19, no. 2 (1909), pp. 161–01.

Kumar, Sudhir. "Nation-in-Narration: Lala Lajpat Rai and the Communal Question", *Studies in Humanities and Social Sciences* 7, no. 1 (2000), pp. 139–53.

Leisten, Thomas. "Mashhad Al-Nasr: Monuments of War and Victory in Medieval Islamic Art", in *Muqarnas Volume XIII: An Annual on the Visual Culture of the Islamic World*, edited by Gülru Necipoglu. Leiden: E.J. Brill, 1996, pp. 7–26.

Nooraddin, Hoshiar. "'Al-fina', in between spaces as an urban design concept: making public and private spaces along streets in Islamic cities of the Middle East", in *URBAN DESIGN International*, United Kingdom: Palgrave Macmillan, 1998, pp. 65–77.

Pullen, Richard L. Jr. EdD, RN, "Using leeches to treat wounds", *Nursing 2010* 40, no. 3 (2010), p. 62.

Rai, Lala Lajpat. "Reviewed work: Akbar the Great Mogul by Vincent Smith", in *Political Science Quarterly* 33, no. 4 (1918), pp. 570–3.

Sramek, Joseph. 'Face Him like a Briton: Tiger Hunting, Imperialism, and British Masculinity in Colonial India, 1800–1875", *Victorian Studies* 48, no. 4 (2006), pp. 659–80.

Sreenivasan, Ramya, "Alauddin Khalji Remembered: Conquest, Gender and Community in Medieval Rajput Narratives", *Studies in History* 18, no. 2 (2002), pp. 275–96.

Stevens, Paul and Rahul Sapra. "Akbar's Dream: Moghul Toleration and English/British Orientalism", *Modern Philology* 104, no. 3 (2007), pp. 379–411.

Talbot, Cynthia. "Justifying Defeat: A Rajput Perspective on the Age of Akbar", *Journal of the Economic and Social History of the Orient* 55, no. 2/3, pp. 329–68.

The Asiatic Journal and Monthly Miscellany for British and Foreign India, China and Australasia 6 (1831).

Zilli, Ishtiaq Ahmad. "Fathnama-i-Chitor, March 1568 An annotated Translation", *Proceedings of the Indian History Congress* 33 (1971), pp. 350–61.

Online resources

Encyclopaedia Britannica Online at https://www.britannica.com/.

Encyclopaedia Iranica Online at http://www.iranicaonline.org/.

The National Geographic at www.nationalgeographic.com.

Prominent news outlets

Indian

The Times of India at www.timesofindia.com.

Hindustan Times at www.hindustantimes.com.

The Indian Express at www.indianexpress.com.

The Hindu at www.thehindu.com.

The Telegraph at www.telegraphindia.com.

Deccan Herald at www.deccanherald.com.

Deccan Chronicle at www.deccanchronicle.com.

Daily News & Analysis at www.dnaindian.com.

The Quint at www.thequint.com.

Scroll at www.scroll.in.

The Wire at www.thewire.in.

NDTV at www.ndtv.com.

International

The Washington Post at www.washingtonpost.com.

The New York Times at www.nytimes.com.

The Guardian at www.theguardian.com.

Huffington Post at www.huffpost.com.

Gulf News at www.gulfnews.com.

The National at www.thenational.ae.

Khaleej Times at www.khaleejtimes.com.

Al Jazeera at www.aljazeera.com.

BBC at www.bbc.com.

CNN at www.cnn.com.

Dawn at www.dawn.com.

The Friday Times at www.thefridaytimes.com.

Press reports

Agencies. "A surprise kiss for Rahul Gandhi on his tour of Assam", *NDTV*, 27 February 2014. Available at https://www.ndtv.com/india-news/a-surprise-kiss-for-rahul-gandhi-on-his-tour-of-assam-552134.

Ashraf, Ajaz. "Irfan Habib: The Indian variant of secularism opens the door to majority communalism", *Scroll.in*, 14 August 2015. Available at https://scroll.in/article/748241/irfan-habib-the-indian-variant-of-secularism-opens-the-door-to-majority-communalism.

Associated Press. "Mirza responds to Muslim criticism of how she dresses", New Delhi: *ESPN*, 17 November 2005. Available at http://www.espn.com/sports/tennis/news/story?id=2227000.

Bakhtiyar, Idrees. "Subcontinental Plagiarism", Pakistan: *Dawn*, 12 February 2019. Available at https://www.dawn.com/news/742051.

BBC. "India's AR Rahman responds to 'fatwa' on Muhammad film", 15 September 2015. Available at https://www.bbc.com/news/world-asia-india-34254541.

Chatterjee, Rituparna. "I Get Angry At Criminals Posing As 'Gau Rakshaks', Says Prime Minister Narendra Modi", *Huffington Post*, 6 August 2016. Available at https://www.huffingtonpost.in/2016/08/06/i-get-angry-at-criminals-posing-as-gau-rakshaks-says-prime-mi_a_21446243/.

Deccan Chronicle. "Padmavati: Rs 5 crores bounty on Deepika, Bhansali's heads, announce outfits", Mumbai: *Deccan Chronicle*, 17 November 2017. Available at https://www.deccanchronicle.com/entertainment/bollywood/171117/padmavati-outfits-announce-rs-5-crores-bounty-on-deepika-bhansalis-heads.html.

Express News Service. "Ramzada vs haramzada: Outrage over Union Minister Sadhvi's remark", New Delhi: *The Indian Express*, 2 December 2014, Available at https://indianexpress.com/article/india/india-others/union-minister-spells-out-choice-in-delhi-ramzada-vs-haramzada.

Express Web Desk. "Hashimpura case: 16 PAC men sentenced to life imprisonment for murder of 38 Muslims", New Delhi: *The Indian Express*, 1 November 2018. Available at https://indianexpress.com/article/india/hashimpura-case-delhi-high-court-verdict-16-life-imprisonment-5426836/.

Ghose, Debobrat. "1,200 years of servitude: PM Modi offers food for thought", New Delhi: *Firstpost*, 13 June 2014. Available at https://www.firstpost.com/politics/1200-years-of-servitude-pm-modi-offers-food-for-thought-1567805.html.

Gupta, Saibal. "Bengal tops in sedition arrest", Kolkata: *The Times of India*, 18 September 2016. Available at https://timesofindia.indiatimes.com/city/kolkata/Bengal-tops-in-sedition-arrests/articleshow/54386342.cms.

Gupta, Suchandana. "Former eunuch MLA curses Congress to stay out of power for another 15 years", Bhopal: *The Times of India*, 21 July 2018. Available at https://timesofindia.indiatimes.com/india/former-eunuch-mla-curses-congress-to-stay-out-of-power-for-another-15-yrs/articleshow/65085430.cms.

HT Correspondent. "There is a hate campaign against me: Mamata Banerjee takes a dig at BJP", Kolkata: *Hindustan Times*, 19 April 2017. Available at https://www.hindustantimes.com/india-news/there-is-a-hate-campaign-against-me-mamata-banerjee-writes-on-facebook/story-sUgRitc9LIkhPBmcBRUwEK.html.

IANS. "Oops! It is Spain-Morocco road shown as floodlit Indian border", New Delhi: *Business Standard*, 14 June 2017. Available at http://www.business-standard.com/article/current-affairs/oops-it-is-spain-morocco-road-shown-as-floodlit-indian-border-117061401102_1.html.

India Today Web Desk. "Twitter rises to defend Mohammed Shami, wife after Muslim fanatics trolled him on Facebook over wife's attire", New Delhi: *India Today*, 26 December 2016. Available at https://www.indiatoday.in/fyi/story/mohammed-shami-wife-dress-facebook-photo-muslim-fanatics-troll-359493-2016-12-26.

Indo Asian News Service. "Fight between 'Ramzada' and 'Haramzada' in Bengal: BJP's Dilip Ghosh", Kolkata: *NewsX*, 6 April 2017. Available at https://www.newsx.com/national/60565-fight-between-ramzada-and-haramzada-in-bengal-bjps-dilip-ghosh.

Karmakar, Sumir. "The curse of the goddess", Guwahati: *The Telegraph*, 25 June 2017. Available at https://www.telegraphindia.com/india/the-curse-of-the-goddess/cid/1501117.

Kumar, Sharat. "Rajasthan rewrites history: Maharana Pratap, not Akbar, won Battle of Haldighati", Jaipur: *India Today*, 25 July 2017. Available at https://www.indiatoday.in/india/story/maharana-pratap-not-akbar-won-battle-of-haldighati-rajasthan-history-book-1026240-2017-07-25.

Mitchell, William. "Tiger Hunting in India 1924", *National Geographic Magazine*, 1924, re-released on 2 August 2014. Available at https://news.nationalgeographic.com/news/2014/08/140803-tiger-hunt-1924-india-maharaja-safari.

Mufti, Ifrah. "Modi's visit to Chandigarh: City schools to remain closed today", Chandigarh: *The Indian Express*, 11 September 2015. Available at http://indianexpress.com/article/cities/chandigarh/city-schools-to-remain-closed-today/.

NH Web Desk. "Ceramic factories in Morbi asked to shut down for workers to attend Modi's rally?" *National Herald*, 29 November 2017. Available at https://www.nationalheraldindia.com/gujarat-assembly-elections-2017/ceramic-factories-in-morbi-asked-to-shut-down-for-workers-to-attend-modis-rally.

Panwar, Pramod. "Bairam Khan's mausoleum in Patan lies in shambles", Palanpur: *The Times of India*, 23 November 2013. Available at https://timesofindia.indiatimes.com/city/

rajkot/Bairam-Khans-mausoleum-in-Patan-lies-in-shambles/articleshow/26278708.cms.

Pinto, Richa. "No slaughter, sale of meat on four days of Paryushan", Mumbai: *The Times of India*, 8 September 2015. Available at https://timesofindia.indiatimes.com/city/mumbai/No-slaughter-sale-of-meat-on-four-days-of-Paryushan/articleshow/48861286.cms.

Pradhan, Sharat. "Rahul Gandhi's puri sabzi dinner in a Dalit village", *Rediff.com*, 18 May 2008. Available at http://www.rediff.com/news/2008/may/18rahul.htm.

Press Trust of India. "Cow protectionism was the spirit behind Freedom Movement, says Nirmala Sitharaman", New Delhi: *Huffington Post*, 6 April 2017. Available at https://www.huffingtonpost.in/2017/04/05/cow-protectionism-was-the-spirit-behind-freedom-movement-says-n_a_22027899/.

———. "Eunuchs want Mughal-era role back", Patna: *The Times of India*, 27 April 2008. Available at https://timesofindia.indiatimes.com/city/patna/Eunuchs-want-Mughal-era-role-back/articleshow/2987565.cms.

———. "PM breaks protocol, exits car to meet school children at Red Fort", *Rediff.com*, 15 August 2014. Available at http://www.rediff.com/news/report/pm-modi-breaks-protocol-exits-car-to-meet-school-children-at-red-fort/20140815.htm.

———. "PM Narendra Modi breaks security protocol to meet his young admirers", *DNA*, 15 August 2017. Available at http://www.dnaindia.com/india/report-children-jostle-to-meet-greet-pm-modi-at-red-fort-2530626.

———. "Rahul Gandhi violated security protocol a 100 times: Rajnath Singh in Lok Sabha", New Delhi: *The Economic Times*, 8 August 2017. Available at https://economictimes.indiatimes.com/news/politics-and-nation/rahul-gandhi-went-abroad-without-security-rajnath-singh-on-congress-protest/articleshow/59967071.cms.

———. "UP BJP MLA calls Mamata Banerjee surpanakha", Ballia: *The Times of India*, 25 April 2018. Available at https://timesofindia.

indiatimes.com/india/up-bjp-mla-calls-mamata-banerjee-surpanakha/articleshow/63912371.cms.

Purkayastha, Shorbori. "BJP Municipality Tweet Passes off Canadian Streets as Delhi", India: *The Quint*, 6 April 2017. Available at https://www.thequint.com/news/india/bjp-municipality-delhi-canada.

Radhakrishnan, Sruthi. "The 2002 Gujarat riots cases and their statuses so far", *The Hindu*, 20 April 2018. Available at https://www.thehindu.com/news/national/the-2002-gujarat-riots-cases-and-their-statuses-so-far/article23617950.ece.

RT. "CNN columnist faces backlash for 'Patriarchy kills people' op-ed", *Russia Today*, 8 May 2018. Available at https://www.rt.com/usa/426069-cnn-columnist-patriarchy-kills/.

Sharma, Aasheesh. "Arun Govil: the first Ram", New Delhi: Brunch, *Hindustan Times*, 18 October 2014. Available at https://www.hindustantimes.com/brunch/arun-govil-the-first-ram/story-iKYVwcBwMKdhiw6mfY3o3O.html.

Sharma, Manimugdha S. "If rulers just, courts exemplary; if unjust, quite dangerous", New Delhi: *The Times of India*, 24 March 2017. Available at https://timesofindia.indiatimes.com/city/delhi/If-rulers-just-courts-exemplary-if-unjust-quitedangerous/articleshow/57800026.cms.

———. "Akbar was truly great, Pratap only a great warrior", New Delhi: *The Times of India*, 24 May 2016. Available at https://timesofindia.indiatimes.com/blogs/parthian-shot/akbar-was-truly-great-pratap-only-a-great-warrior/.

———. "From medieval Delhi to Noida: Hate for 'habshi' is still on", New Delhi: *The Times of India*, 29 March 2017. Available at https://timesofindia.indiatimes.com/city/delhi/from-medieval-delhi-to-noida-how-hate-for-habshi-is-still-on/articleshow/57881297.cms.

———. "Freedom didn't come riding on a cow, trouble did", New Delhi: *The Times of India*, 10 April 2017. Available at https://timesofindia.indiatimes.com/blogs/parthian-shot/freedom-didnt-come-riding-on-a-cow-trouble-did/.

———. "At Akshardham, capital's own boat trip back to the Vedic Age", New Delhi: *The Times of India*, 11 January 2015. Available at https://timesofindia.indiatimes.com/city/delhi/At-Akshardham-capitals-own-boat-trip-back-to-the-Vedic-Age/articleshow/45838735.cms.

Suresh, K. G. "Eating beef not an Islamic ritual", New Delhi: *The Pioneer*, 22 December 2015. Available at https://www.dailypioneer.com/2015/columnists/eating-beef-not-an-islamic-ritual.html.

Times News Network, "#DespiteBeingAWoman PM Modi faces flak for sexist comment", *The Times of India*, 8 June 2015. Available at https://timesofindia.indiatimes.com/india/despitebeingawoman-pm-modi-faces-flak-for-sexist-comment/articleshow/47583088.cms.

———. "1984 anti-Sikh riots case: Delhi HC convicts Sajjan Kumar, sentenced to life imprisonment", New Delhi: *The Times of India*, 17 December 2018. Available at https://timesofindia.indiatimes.com/india/1984-anti-sikh-riots-case-delhi-hc-convicts-sajjan-kumar-sentenced-to-life-imprisonment/articleshow/67123074.cms.

———. "BJP workers 'purify' hall where Prakash Raj spoke", Karwar: *The Times of India*, 17 January 2018. Available at https://timesofindia.indiatimes.com/city/bengaluru/bjp-workers-purify-hall-where-prakash-raj-spoke/articleshow/62532994.cms.

———. "Sends pics, videos to prove students saw PM Modi's chat, schools told", *The Times of India*, 20 February 2018. Available at https://timesofindia.indiatimes.com/india/send-pics-videos-to-prove-students-saw-pm-modis-chat-schools-told/articleshow/62990493.cms

Vargas, Richard Edmond. "Guns alone don't kill people, patriarchy kills people", *CNN*, 1 May 2018. Available at https://edition.cnn.com/2018/05/01/opinions/patriarchy-kills-people-opinion-vargas/index.html.

Vashi, Ashish. "Ahmedabad turned Akbar veggie", Ahmedabad: The *Times of India*, 23 November 2009. Available at https://

timesofindia.indiatimes.com/city/ahmedabad/Ahmedabad-turned-Akbar-veggie/articleshow/5259184.cms.

Vikram, Kumar. "Delhi ruled by Hindus after 800 years, says VHP chief Ashok Singhal", New Delhi: *India Today*, 22 November 2014. Available at https://www.indiatoday.in/india/story/vhp-ashok-shinghal-hindu-ruling-delhi-after-800-years-228175-2014-11-22.

Wootson Jr, Cleve R. "Archaeologists unearth a 500-year-old tower of skulls—and another gruesome Aztec mystery", *The Washington Post*, 4 July 2017. Available at https://www.washingtonpost.com/news/retropolis/wp/2017/07/04/archaeologists-unearth-a-500-year-old-tower-of-skulls-and-another-gruesome-aztec-mystery/?noredirect=on&utm_term=.8fc6d2a5a30d.

Index

B